D1318759

SPIRITUAL
JOURNALS

.

Henri J. M. Nouwen

■

SPIRITUAL JOURNALS

The Genesee Diary

¡Gracias!

The Road to Daybreak

■

A Dayspring Edition

CONTINUUM · NEW YORK

1997
The Continuum Publishing Company
370 Lexington Avenue, New York, NY 10017

This edition copyright © 1997 by The Estate of Henri J. M. Nouwen
The Genesee Diary: Report from a Trappist Monastery
© 1976 by Henri J. M. Nouwen
¡Gracias!: A Latin American Journal © 1983, 1993 by Henri J. M. Nouwen
The Road to Daybreak: A Spiritual Journal © 1988 by Henri J. M. Nouwen

All rights reserved. No part of this book may be reproduced, stored
in a retrieval system, or transmitted in any form or by any means,
electronic, mechanical, photocopying, recording, or otherwise, without
the written permission of The Continuum Publishing Company.

Printed in the United States of America

ISBN 0-8264-1010-3

Library of Congress Catalog Card Number: 96-71389

CONTENTS

■

THE
GENESEE DIARY

Report from a Trappist Monastery

■

*To all contemplative men and women
who by their commitment to unceasing
prayer offer us hope in the midst
of a troubled world.*

ACKNOWLEDGMENTS

∎

MANY FRIENDS have helped me make the decision to publish this diary. I want to express my deep gratitude to Ellie Drury, Louis Dupré, Bob Lifton, Mu-Gak, Eric Olson, Colin Williams, Richard White, Arnold Wolf, and Phil Zaeder for the time and the attention they have given to the writings of which this diary is a selection. Without their encouragement, I would have never been able to follow through with the suggestion that my diary might be of interest to more than a small circle of friends.

I owe a special word of thanks to Dorothy Holman who was the first to make me think about the possibility of publication when she said, "This is the most unselfconscious writing you have done. Maybe you should have it printed exactly because you didn't write it with that purpose in mind." That same unselfconsciousness, however, was the cause of many linguistic and stylistic weaknesses. I am very grateful to Stephen Leahy, Bob Werner, and John Mogabgab for the care with which they corrected the manuscript.

Finally, I want to express my appreciation for the editorial help of Bob Heller and the secretarial assistance of Pat Murray Kelly, Cyndy Halverson, Katie Hicks, and Claire Mattern.

CONTENTS

■

INTRODUCTION

∎

MY DESIRE TO LIVE for seven months in a Trappist Monastery, not as a guest but as a monk, did not develop overnight. It was the outcome of many years of restless searching. While teaching, lecturing, and writing about the importance of solitude, inner freedom, and peace of mind, I kept stumbling over my own compulsions and illusions. What was driving me from one book to another, one place to another, one project to another? What made me think and talk about "the reality of the Unseen" with the seriousness of one who had seen all that is real? What was turning my vocation to be a witness to God's love into a tiring job? These questions kept intruding themselves into my few unfilled moments and challenging me to face my restless self. Maybe I spoke more about God than with him. Maybe my writing about prayer kept me from a prayerful life. Maybe I was more concerned about the praise of men and women than the love of God. Maybe I was slowly becoming a prisoner of people's expectations instead of a man liberated by divine promises. Maybe . . . It was not all that clear, but I realized that I would only know by stepping back and allowing the hard questions to touch me even if they hurt. But stepping back was not so easy. I had succeeded in surrounding myself with so many classes to prepare, lectures to give, articles to finish, people to meet, phone calls to make, and letters to answer, that I had come quite close to believing that I was indispensable.

When I took a closer look at this I realized that I was caught in a web of strange paradoxes. While complaining about too many demands, I felt uneasy when none were made. While speaking about the burden of letter writing, an empty mailbox made me sad. While fretting about tiring lecture tours, I felt disappointed when there were no invitations. While speaking nostalgically about an empty desk, I feared the day on which that would come true. In short: while desiring to be alone, I was frightened of being left alone. The more I became aware of these paradoxes, the more I started to see how much I had indeed fallen in love with my own compulsions and illusions, and how much I needed to step back and wonder, "Is there a quiet stream underneath the fluctuating affirmations and rejections of my little world? Is there a still point where my life is anchored and from which I can reach out with hope and courage and confidence?"

While realizing my growing need to step back, I knew that I could never do it alone. It seems that the crucial decisions and the great experiences of life require a guide. The way to "God alone" is seldom traveled alone. For me there was little, if any, question about the need for guidance. At first it was very unclear what exactly that would mean. But my own travels on the roads of the U.S.A. as well as on the paths of the spiritual search had slowly prepared me for an answer.

About ten years ago, while on a long trip from Miami to Topeka, I stopped at the Trappist Abbey of Gethsemani in Kentucky, in the hope of finding someone with whom I could talk. When the guestmaster learned that I had studied psychology and was at the point of joining the faculty of a psychology department, he said with a happy twinkle in his eyes: "But we Trappists have a psychologist too! I will ask him to visit you." A little later Father John Eudes Bamberger walked into the guest room. Very soon I knew that I had met a rare and very convincing person. John Eudes listened to me with care and interest, but also with a deep conviction and a clear vision; he gave me much time and attention but did not allow me to waste a minute; he left me fully free to express my feelings and thoughts but did not hesitate to present his own; he offered me space to deliberate about choices and to make decisions but did not withhold his opinion that some choices and decisions were better than others; he let me find my own way but did not hide the map that showed the right direction. In our conversation, John Eudes emerged not only as a listener but also as a guide, not only as a counselor but also as a director. It did not take me long to realize that this was the man I had needed so badly.

John Eudes' own history, in which both psychology and theology play a major role, offered so many connections with my own story that I had a vital sense of God's guidance in our encounter. His medical and psychiatric training, his theological education and monastic formation and his far-reaching experiences ranging from his duty in the U.S. Navy to his roles as infirmarian and novice master seemed to reflect many of my own endeavors, aspirations, and fantasies.

This unusual combination of differences and similarities offered the graceful context in which spiritual direction could grow and continue to grow. It is therefore not surprising that during my many subsequent visits to Gethsemani I came to know John Eudes not only as a very insightful but also as a very compassionate spiritual guide.

After a three-year stay in Europe, during which my contact with John Eudes was minimal, I heard that he had been elected Abbot of the Abbey of the Genesee in upstate New York. My first visit there gave me the idea that maybe in the near future I could break away from my work, explore my compulsions and illusions, and live as a temporary monk under the regular guidance of John Eudes. I vividly remember my hesitation in formulating this idea. I was so aware of the unusual nature of my desire to be a temporary Trappist, that I didn't expect much more than a smile saying, "We enter here for a lifetime, not for a sabbatical." But the "no" which I had expected did not come. John Eudes was open to the idea and said, "Although our monastic community does not admit temporary members, I will think about your desire, discuss it with the monks, and see if we can make an exception." A half year later a letter came with the good news that I had been "voted in," and that I could come when I was ready for it. Finally on June 1, 1974, after a lot of desk cleaning, I flew to Rochester, New York, to live as a Trappist monk for seven months, and on Pentecost, June 2, I started to write the notes that found their final form in this diary.

1

June

A STRANGER IN PARADISE

∎

Sunday, 2

THANKS BE TO GOD that I am here! When Walter met me last night at the Rochester Airport and drove me through the darkening Genesee valley to the Trappist Monastery, I had a deep sense of gratitude. I knew it was a good decision to interrupt my life for seven months and join the thirty monks who had impressed me so much when I visited them two years ago.

When we drove up to the buildings the splendid red sky had become sparkling dark. Walter showed me my room in the center of a small corridor where the monks had their cells. It was silent. . . . The abbot, John Eudes, had sent a card with Walter to wish me welcome, and on my desk I found a friendly note from the prior, Father Stephen, telling me that breakfast would be on the table between 3 and 5 A.M. In the dark I found the chapel and prayed.

How much reason to say thanks, how much reason to pray that God will turn my heart to him and set me free by his love. Seven months: The only feeling I have is that it will be too short, too temporary, too experimental. But today is Pentecost, and Christmas is far away.

Back in my "cell" I unpacked my suitcase and was surprised by the collection of books I had decided to take with me: A Spanish Bible, the works of Saint John of the Cross, a history of the United States, a book about common weeds, and the novel, *Zen and the Art of Motorcycle Maintenance*. Maybe this selection is the expression of my unconscious fear that I might get bored in a Trappist monastery.

Monday, 3

I met Brother Elias, a hermit of the Abbey. Brother Christian, the cook with whom I had developed a friendship during an earlier visit, showed me the way through the woods and introduced me to this remarkable man. During the twenty minutes we talked, Elias told me practically everything I needed to hear. He told me how the changes in the often rough climate were good—"goo-o-o-d," he said—because they deepened his longing for God. As the storms made him wish for gentle winds, the clouds for the sun, dryness for rains, so his heart learned to yearn for God and take nothing for granted. "What is so good about this part of the country," he said, "is that it makes you realize that all good things are gifts of God—when the sun is always shining you forget that it is God's gift, and you don't pay attention any more." While he said this, his small round bearded face with happy eyes seemed to become transparent.

His directness and simplicity were beautiful. While speaking about his love for the Lord, he said, "When I get excited about the Lord, my temptation is to go out and tell everyone about him—but that I shouldn't do—I should stay here and pray." Looking me right in the face with his great eyes he added, "Don't worry about how to speak about the Lord. When you allow him to enter into your heart, he will give you words."

I needed to hear this because I still *was* worrying about lack of time for study and reading and about courses after this time was over. Was it really wise to interrupt my work for this simple life? How would it help me to be a better teacher? I knew these were the wrong questions. I knew that theology needed to be born out of prayer, but Brother Elias had to say it again so I would not forget it.

We also talked about Thomas Merton. Elias was able to criticize him in the form of a compliment. "He was a good writer—his books are very good—the little bit of solitude he had, he talked about very well." I knew how right he was. Merton's deep desire for solitude had been in constant tension with his gregarious personality. There were always many people around him, if not physically then through mail and books. And he loved it. But until the last days of his life he kept dreaming about a hermitage where he could be alone with God. During his travels through India he wrote about a possible hermitage in Alaska. The tension between his great desire for solitude and his deep compassion for so many people made Merton the writer he was, and Brother Elias knew it.

Brother Elias showed us his few vegetable plants and explained that he did not need drinking water since there was enough of it in the vegetables he ate. I asked about his discipline. He said, "I rise at 2 A.M., do the exercises of the Canadian Army to build my muscles up, and then I do Yoga." During the night hours he prays and takes care of his different needs—small needs but real ones—clothes, food, and the maintenance of his little hut. Early in the morning he leaves the hermitage and goes to his carpentry shop to make furniture for the new church. In the afternoon he studies and meditates. Around 7 P.M. he goes to bed to be ready for a fresh start the next day.

We looked around his little hermitage. A single room with one corner sectioned off as a little chapel. Two tables with books, a bed hooked up against the wall, and a small mat for his Yoga. He showed it with joy. He asked my blessing, said how happy he was to meet me, and kept waving good-bye while we walked away.

Tuesday, 4

Today was "hermit day," which means that you are free from 6 A.M. to 4:30 P.M. to do what you want. It was a good day for me. I slept most of the morning after a walk through the humid fields. My sleep was deep and heavy, as it has been since I came here. I seem to have many "double dreams." Dreams about dreaming, dreams about waking up, dreams about sleeping in, etc.—I must be very tired, but I seem to be catching up. Nothing unexpected.

The continuous silence is a real healing experience for me. The monks mostly communicate in sign language. Only when the subject gets too complicated for their fingers do they invite each other to the rooms that are reserved for necessary conversation.

It was fun making my own lunch. I burned my thumb while trying to bring some water to a boil. John Eudes, noticing my attempts to remain silent with a hurting hand, told me to stick my finger in the butter which I did. The pain was soon gone.

Wednesday, 5

After Lauds—the communal morning prayer at 5 A.M.—Brother Anthony put me to work in the bakery on the "hot-bread line." With baseball-like gloves, I picked up the hot bread—first brown bread, then white bread, then raisin bread—and put them on racks to be pushed away to the "cooling room." The good-natured Brother Christian did the same, and he always makes things look easier. When I saw the hundreds of loaves move in my direction I panicked. But Brother Christian smiled and took a few of "my loaves" when he noticed that I could not keep up.

Meanwhile, I meditated on the sentence "With sweat on your brow shall you eat your bread" (Gen. 3:19). Bread and sweat had never been closer together in my life.

Had a good talk with John Eudes. I told him how I had enjoyed my stay so far, how much I liked the community, and how the whole experience seemed a luxury. He not only didn't deny it but said that the sole idea of the monastic life was that of creating a life-long vacation! "You can't do that on your own, so we form communities and we experience all of life as a gift of God—that is why praise is so central—praise for God's gifts." I said cautiously that maybe I would feel differently after a few months and that there might be more tensions than I had foreseen, but he said, "No, no—you'll like it more, the longer you are here. The Cistercians always considered the monastery as a little paradise on earth. Read St. Bernard." I frankly had not expected so much affirmation of my good feelings but was the more grateful for it. The rest of the time we talked about books on the spirituality of the desert fathers (Hesychasm). John Eudes will be a good guide for the study of this tradition. He gave very helpful suggestions. We went to the library and selected a few books to start with.

Thursday, 6

This has been a workman's day. I worked at the hot-bread line with Brother James, the postulant, who sits in choir in such a devout way that you think that any moment his head will fall off. A fine man. Son of a dairy farmer in Rochester. During the break between the brown and the white bread, he told me that his father no longer worked the farm but wanted one of his sons to take over. James did it for a while, then entered the Trappists four months ago. Now one of his brothers is giving it a try. He said he had enough brothers to try it out, but nobody seemed ready yet to buy the farm. When, after two hours' work, the good-smelling raisin bread came down on the conveyer belt, James turned around, looked at me and said with a big smile, "When I am all through with this I could eat a whole loaf of it."

This afternoon I worked with Brother Brian, who had left the Oxford community in North Carolina and hoped to stay at the Genesee. We stored a load of timber in the attic of the laundry building. The wood was beautiful finished oak for the floor of the new church.

When I thought I had worked long enough, Anthony asked me to load heavy cement blocks in the pickup truck and unload them at a dumping place in the woods. I made two trips and then stopped. Anthony talked about the job as a small errand. After having made two trips—nearly causing a hernia—I told Anthony that I probably would be ready for the job by Christmas. He smiled.

During the day I often thought about a passage in *Zen and the Art of Motorcycle Maintenance* where Pirsig makes a distinction between ego climbing and selfless climbing. It seems a very important passage for me, worthwhile quoting here. Trying to explain why his eleven-year-old son, Chris, is not enjoying a camping trip to the ridge of a canyon, Pirsig writes: "To the untrained eye ego-climbing and selfless climbing may appear identical. Both kinds of climbers place one foot in front of the other. Both breathe in and out at the same rate. Both stop when tired. Both go forward when rested. But what a difference! The ego-climber is like an instrument that's out of adjustment. He puts his foot down an instant too soon or too late. He's likely to miss a beautiful passage of sunlight through the trees. He goes on when the sloppiness of his step shows he's tired. He rests at odd times. He looks up the trail trying to see what's ahead even when he knows what's ahead because he just looked a second before. He goes too fast or too slow for the conditions and when he talks his talk is forever about somewhere else, something else. He's here but he's not here. He rejects the here, is unhappy with it, wants to be farther up the trail but when he gets there will be just as unhappy because then the *it* will be 'here.' What he is looking for, what he wants, is all around him, but he doesn't want that because it *is* all around him. Every step's an effort both physically and spiritually because he imagines his goal to be external and distant."[1]

Pirsig seems to describe me and my problem. I came to the monastery to learn to live in the presence of God, to taste him here and now, but there is so much "ego-climbing" going on within me. I have so many ideas I want to write about, so many books I want to read, so many skills I want to learn—motorcycle maintenance is now one of them—and so many things I want to say to others now or later, that I do not SEE that God is all around me and that I am always trying to see what is ahead, overlooking him who is so close. From ego climbing to selfless climbing; that seems a good ideal for my retreat. But that is a long way and a high mountain.

Maybe I need to get stuck to learn it. I can't make selfless climbing an ego-trip! At another place in his book Pirsig writes: "Stuckness shouldn't be avoided. It's the psychic predecessor of all real understanding. An egoless acceptance of stuckness is the key to an understanding of all Quality, in mechanical work as in other endeavors."[2] This seems a very important thought. God help me when I get stuck. Until now everything has been so beautiful, so rich, so full of joy. I just want to say, "Thanks."

I'd better get some sleep now. Two o'clock is still a little early for me!

Friday, 7

Christian made a monastic outfit for me. He took me to the tailor shop, and we had some fun deciding how long the smock should be. I wanted it shorter than he, but we settled on the idea of "short and decent."

It feels good to wear a habit. Smock with attached hood, dark gray trousers, and a leather belt. Now I feel more a part of the community. I received quite a few smiles and remarks in sign language. People seemed to feel good about the "instant monk." This morning Christian put a note in my locker: "You appear excellent in the monastic habit and are doing very well fitting into the monastic life in general—best wishes for continued success." That is an encouraging note. Meanwhile, I feel a little bit like an overgrown dwarf from Snow White's court.

I have been reading the reports about the different abbeys. These reports were discussed in the general chapter in Rome last month. They tell about the life in the Trappist Communities around the world, summarize the problems, and give some suggestions. Since I know a few abbeys, I read the reports on them with special attention. While all eradiated a very sympathetic and overall positive tone, criticism was not avoided. Three aspects keep striking me: the crucial role of the abbot (much of the mood in a contemplative house seems to depend on his leadership); the struggle with poverty (some houses have become quite wealthy, and that remains a threat for the spiritual life); the problem of spiritual reading (spending "free time" well is not as easy as it seems, and the spiritual and intellectual formation needed for that is not always available). There seems to be an overall need for spiritual leadership.

During the afternoon I worked with Brother Brian in Salt Creek looking for granite stones for the new church. No easy task to differentiate between sandstones and granite stones since many stones are covered with lime which makes them all look alike at the start. But slowly I got a feel for it with the diagnostic help of the quiet Brian.

The whole afternoon I was struggling with the old question: Why didn't I really enjoy the work, and why did I want to go back to my books to read about the spiritual life? Is selecting stones in the creek bed not the best spiritual life possible? Why do I always want to read *about* the spiritual life and not really live it? Brian was so quiet and content, and I so restless and impatient. I kept saying to myself, "Just relax and enjoy what you are doing." After a while I felt better, found a few funny-looking stones, joked with Brian about finding gold (and closing the bakery!), and went home with a better feeling.

Saturday, 8

This morning, I got my hands into the raisins. Brother Theodore, the "head baker," asked me to wash forty boxes of raisins. They had to be emptied on a sort of grill. Then the blocks of compressed raisins had to be broken up by hand and pushed gently through the grill. Theodore stood on the other end and checked to see if all was just raisins that came out. He obviously wanted to prevent people from having wood, paper, or stones in their bread.

During the last few days I have become good friends with Father John, one of the pioneering monks who came in 1951 from Gethsemani to lay the foundation of this monastery. Father John is a great lover of nature and a real expert on birds. This morning at 10 A.M. he took me out for what he called my "first lesson in birdwatching." It ended up being more of a lesson in bird hearing since we saw few birds but heard many. I was very impressed with the discerning ear of Father John. It must be a great joy to be able to walk through the woods recognizing all the sounds and having a dialogue with nature. I didn't even know the difference between chipmunk talk and bird talk. Well, I've a lot to learn about robins, warblers, orioles, and sparrows. Crows and the red-bellied woodpecker (who doesn't have a red belly but a red cap) were the easiest to recognize. But I also heard the catbird and the peewee. And when we walked home we saw a few chimney swifts playing high in the air. Meanwhile, I was bitten by mosquitoes.

The story of the bakery is worth telling. It all began with Brother Sylvester. Many years ago he started to use his navy experience by baking bread for the monks. He took his old navy recipe and changed it a little. He explained, "Since we were not allowed to eat butter on our bread, I tried to bake a kind of bread on which you don't need it. The guests who came to the monastery made so many good comments that I started to bake a few extra loaves." Well, soon orders started to come and the monks smelled not only bread but also business. Sylvester got his recipe patented. Some machinery was bought and soon "Monk's Bread" became a well-known specialty bread in upstate New York. Now three days a week around 15,000 loaves come off the conveyor belts. Sylvester works on the slicing machine and spends the rest of his working time as porter and shoemaker. At times he puts notes on the board such as this one: "I won't repair shoes any longer when the mud hasn't been taken off before they are brought to me!" Sylvester is a real monk and very humble. He also takes no nonsense.

I'd better start thinking a little more about my attitude toward work. If I have learned anything this week, it is that there is a contemplative way of working that is more important for me than praying, reading, or singing. Most people think that you go to the monastery to pray. Well, I prayed more this week than before but also discovered that I have not learned yet to make work of my hands into a prayer.

Sunday, 9

After Lauds, John Eudes gave a talk about the Holy Trinity. He was clear, succinct, mystical, and—extremely practical. From the many things he said, what impressed me most was the simple idea that the praise of God is the criterion of the Benedictine life. He said, "Even the price of our products and the use of our money should be determined by the praise of God's mysterious presence in our lives." This hit me hard since I had just begun to realize how much my own life was motivated by self-glory: even going to a monastery could be a form of self-indulgence. My problem with work is obviously related to my tendency to look at manual labor as a necessary job to earn a couple of free hours to do my own work. Even when this work seems very spiritual, such as reading about prayer, I often look at it more as an opportunity to make interesting notes for future lectures or books than as a way to praise the Lord. I remember vividly how the Jesuits in high school made me write above almost every page, A.M.D.G. (*Ad Majorem Dei Gloriam*—To the Greater Glory of God), but I am overwhelmed by the realization of how little of that has become true during the twenty-four years since high school.

And still I know that living for the glory of God would make everything different. Even living for each other would then be living for the glory of God. It is God's glory that becomes visible in a loving community. This sounds pious and sweet but when John Eudes said, "We get to know each other so well that we take each other for granted and forget to realize that we are more than our characters," I became aware of the powerful implications of living for the glory of God. When we indeed participate in the life of God we will always discover more of God's mystery in each other. John Eudes described heaven as the ongoing discovery of God's mystery by living in the most intimate presence of God and each other. The Christian life on earth is simply the beginning of this heavenly existence.

Monday, 10

This was a very good day, especially because I was not so preoccupied with "time for myself" and really enjoyed the work. While working on the bread-slicing machine, I said the Jesus Prayer—"Lord Jesus Christ, have mercy on me"—meditated on the question why people wanted to have their bread sliced instead of cutting it themselves, and learned a few technical things from Brother John Baptist about what to do when the bread gets cut the wrong way and a big mess comes out of the machine. I pushed the emergency button twice when the bread proved too high to fit in the plastic bag and started flying around. At least a beginning of insight.

Tuesday, 11

Today is the feast of the Apostle Barnabas. I never realized that the word Barnabas means "Son of Consolation." There was a beautiful hymn and also a reading from John Henry Newman about consolation during Vigils. Barnabas was described as a very gentle and caring man.

Nixon has gone on his trip to the Middle East. All the papers are writing about his attempts to distract attention from his Watergate problems. Nevertheless, impeachment seems to become more and more likely. I keep wondering about how I am responding to this. Shouldn't I pray for him and not just hope for sensational impeachment procedures? In many ways he is telling me about my own attachments and about the dangers of my own power games.

Thursday, 13

This afternoon I worked a few hours alone in the river carrying heavy granite rocks to the bank and making piles. While doing this, I realized how difficult "nepsis"—the control of thoughts—about which I read this morning, really is. My thoughts not only wandered in all directions, but started to brood on many negative feelings, feelings of hostility toward people who had not given me the attention I wanted, feelings of jealousy toward people who received more than I, feelings of self-pity in regard to people who had not written, and many feelings of regret and guilt toward people with whom I had strained relationships. While pulling and pushing with the crowbar, all these feelings kept pulling and pushing in me, and I often looked at the curve of the river, wondering if Brian would come to keep me company and help me to quiet them.

My reading about the spirituality of the desert has made me aware of the importance of "nepsis." Nepsis means mental sobriety, spiritual attention directed to God, watchfulness in keeping the bad thoughts away, and creating free space for prayer. While working with the rocks I repeated a few times the famous words of the old desert fathers: *"fuge, tace, et quiesce"* (live in solitude, silence, and inner peace), but only God knows how far I am, not only from this reality but even from this desire.

Once in a while I cursed when the rock was too heavy to carry or fell out of my arms into the water, making a big splash. I tried to convert my curse into a prayer: "Lord, send your angels to carry these stones," but nothing spectacular happened. I heard some red-winged blackbirds making some ugly noises in the air. My muscles felt strained, my legs tired. When I walked home I realized that it was exactly the lack of spiritual attention that caused the heaviness in my heart. How true it is that sadness is often the result of our attachments to the world.

During dinner the reader, Brother Justin, started a new book, *Or I'll Dress You in Mourning* by Larry Collins and Dominique Lapiere. This is a book about the Spanish bullfighter Manuel Benitez, "El Cordobez," who from a poor Andalusian boy soon became one of the greatest Spanish heroes of today. On the evening of his first bullfight, he said to his sister who opposed his plans, "Don't cry, Angelita. Tonight I'll buy you a house or I'll dress you in mourning." Well, he bought more than a house; he now owns hotels. I looked for a long time at his picture in the book. The enormous tensions of his courageous bullfights have made his face heavy, serious, and very sad. How will his life end? Will the people of Spain allow him to die a non-heroic death? Since the beginning of the bullfights in their present form (which was started by Francisco Romero at the beginning of the eighteenth century), more than four hundred torreros have been killed by bull's horns. I am very curious to hear the whole story. A vicarious way of watching a bullfight. What is it in us that makes us so full of desires to see a man risk his life? One answer is: Lack of nepsis.

Friday, 14

During the Eucharist this morning we sang: "Thus says the Lord: By waiting and calm, you shall be saved. In quiet and trust lies your strength" (Is. 30:15). That could be the program for my restless soul for the coming six months! I am impatient, restless, full of preoccupations, and easily suspicious. Maybe I just need to repeat this sentence very often and let it sink deep into my heart: "By waiting and calm, you shall be saved. In quiet and trust lies your strength." If these words could descend from my head into my heart and become part of my innermost self, I would be a converted man. "Lord Jesus Christ, Son of the Living God, have mercy on me, a sinner."

For four and a half hours I worked with Brother Theodore and Brother Benedict at the raisin washer. Theodore washed, Benedict collected the raisins, and I folded empty boxes. Suddenly Theodore stopped the machine and knocked with his fist against his head. Not knowing sign language, I said, "What's the matter?" "A stone went through," he said. I asked him, "How do you know?" He said, "I heard it." I asked, "How could you hear it between the noise of the machine and the raisins cascading through it?" "I just hear it," he said, and added, "We have to find that stone. If a lady gets it in her bread, she can break her tooth on it and we can be sued!" Pointing to the large bathtublike container full of washed raisins, he said, "We have to push those through again until we find that stone."

I couldn't believe it. Benedict hadn't been able to detect the stone while the raisins came out, but Theodore was so sure that objection was senseless. Millions of raisins went through again, and just when I had given up ever finding that stone—it seemed like looking for a needle in a haystack—something clicked. "There it is," Theodore said. "It jumped against the metal wall of the washer." Benedict looked carefully and moved his hands through the last ounce of raisins. There it was! A small purple-blue stone, just as large as a raisin. Theodore took it and gave it to me with a big smile.

In some strange way this event meant a lot to me. Yesterday I was carrying granite rocks out of the river. Today we were looking for a small stone among millions of raisins. I was impressed, not only by Theodore's alertness, but even more by his determination to find it and take no risks. He really is a careful diagnostician. This little stone could have harmed someone—a lady or a monastery.

And I thought about purity and purification. Even the small stone that looks like all these good-tasting raisins has to be taken out. I can't even notice my own little sins, but it offers me consolation to know that someone will keep a careful watch on me and stop the machine when he hears a stone between the raisins. That really is care.

Saturday, 15

Today I had my second talk with John Eudes. He invited me, and I was happy to have the opportunity to have some time with him. I tried to express my feelings about my first two weeks and to tell him not only that everything was well, but also that real inner silence and solitude were still far from my busy mind. He responded very gently and recommended that I stay in my room more even when I was just reading or studying. Until now I had done all my reading and writing in the library where people come and go. "Just try to be more alone—that will help you to find solitude."

We also talked about work and the morbid creations of the mind during routine actions in the bakery or in Salt Creek. John Eudes said some very helpful things. "First of all, it is certainly very hard not to have such thoughts. Recognize them and let them pass. Secondly, keep doing simple work that can attract your attention. It is good to be interested in different types of rocks, in the songs of the birds, in the varieties of trees, etc., but don't make a project out of it. Just enjoy it and be present to where you are and what you are doing. And finally, try to find your own rhythm. Ask yourself how much you can work without it making you too tired to pray. It will take you a while to find your balance."

Then we talked a bit about the hawks and foxes John Eudes had seen and concluded with some discussions on books. He thought that it was a good idea to read *The Ladder of Divine Ascent* by John Climacus, which he called "the most popular book in Eastern monasteries." He also gave me a copy of his own translation of the *Praktikos* by Evagrius Ponticus, plus a *promanuscripto* copy of the *Apophtegms,* a collection of sayings attributed to the desert fathers.

I worked with Christian in the kitchen peeling potatoes. He has an ugly print of a sugar-sweet Madonna hanging above the stove. It would probably have made me think something less than friendly about Christian if he hadn't put in the frame of the same print a sign that reads in the most pompously decorated letters: BLESS THIS MESS. That only made me like Christian all the more. He has a sense of humor that puts all bad taste between parentheses.

Sunday, 16

Today is the feast of the Eucharist. After the Mass there was a short procession which included a simple ground-breaking ceremony for the new church. John Eudes put the blessed sacrament on a small altar near the front lawn, walked off with a big spade, turned some soil, said a few words about the new temple, and Anthony took a picture "for later generations." That was it.

What I want to talk about, however, is the conference John Eudes gave after Lauds. Because his meditations so obviously arise out of contemplation, John Eudes seems able to reach beyond the point where conservatives and progressives go different ways. He reaches a point so deep in the center of the spiritual life that he puts my suspicious spirit at ease and leads me away from the level where my mind tends to argue, agree, or disagree. I have always had some problems with feasts such as those of the Holy Trinity, the Blessed Sacrament, and the Sacred Heart. They seemed to arise out of a devotional period of the history of the Church in which I have a hard time feeling at home. It always seemed to me that the mystery of the Triune God, of the Divine presence in the Eucharist, and of the love of Christ for people are such central realities of the Christian life that you cannot set a special day aside to celebrate them. Certainly a special Sunday for the Eucharist never appealed to me. It was with this sort of rebellious mind that I went to listen to John Eudes. But what he said really took me away from these types of preoccupations and opened new horizons.

The Lord is at the center of all things and yet in such a quiet, unobtrusive, elusive way. He lives with us, even physically, but not in the same physical way that other elements are present to us. This transcendent physical presence is what characterizes the Eucharist. It is already the other world present in this one. In the celebration of the Eucharist we are given an enclave in our world of space and time. God in Christ is really here, and yet his physical presence is not characterized by the same limitations of space and time that we know.

The Eucharist can be seen only by those who already love the Lord and believe in his active, loving presence to us. But is that not true of every good relationship that we have? Friendship is like that, human love is like that. The bonds that unite us with those we love are invisible bonds. They become visible only indirectly, only by what we do as a result of them. But the bonds themselves are invisible. The presence of friends to one another is very real; this presence is palpably physical, sustaining us in difficult or joyful moments, and yet invisible.

Contemplative life is a human response to the fundamental fact that the central things in life, although spiritually perceptible, remain invisible in large measure and can very easily be overlooked by the inattentive, busy, distracted person that each of us can so readily become. The contemplative looks not so much around things but through them into their center. Through their center he discovers the world of spiritual beauty that is more real, has more density, more mass, more energy, and greater intensity than physical matter. In effect, the beauty of physical matter is a reflection of its inner content. Contemplation is a response to a world that is built in this fashion. That is why the Greek fathers, who were great contemplatives, are known as the dioretic fathers. *Diorao* means to see into, to see through. In celebrating the feast of Corpus Christi, the body of Christ, we celebrate the presence of the risen Christ among us, at the center of our lives, at the center of our very being, at the heart of our community, at the heart of the creation . . .

Monday, 17

When I woke up this morning I discovered that I was still in the habit of worrying about "what shall I do today—how shall I do it—what first, second, and third?" Then I realized that all this was no longer necessary. What I would do today would be decided by Brother Anthony, and the day would pass without worries about the order of things.

I think that most of my fatigue is related not to the type of work I do but to the false tensions I put into it. If I could just live the day quietly, obedient to the order of the day and the small instruction which I always find on a piece of paper stuck in my locker door (5:30–8:15, hot-bread line; 1–3, work with crew on lumber), then my mind would be more vacant for God and freer for the simple things of every moment.

I am beginning to discover the "other world" in which I live. When I run, monks smile; when I work very intensely, they make signs to slow down; and when I worry, I know it is usually useless. Last week I asked John Eudes how he thought that I was doing. He said, "I guess O.K. Nobody has mentioned you yet." That would not be a good sign everywhere! I really must enter that "other side," the quiet, rhythmic, solid side of life, the deep solid stream moving underneath the restless waves of my sea.

Some things are unexplainable. I guess the contemplative life is one of these things. Father Marcellus read a story about Beethoven during dinner. When Beethoven had played a new sonata for a friend, the friend asked him after the last note, "What does it mean?" Beethoven returned to the piano, played the whole sonata again and said, "That is what it means." This type of response seems the only possible response to the question, "What does the contemplative life mean?" Still you can keep writing about it just as people have been doing about Beethoven's works.

Today, David, twenty-three years old, entered the community as an "observer," and a long-haired, long-bearded, friendly young man from Brooklyn joined the family brothers. "I hope for life," he said. That sounded awesome to me.

Tuesday, 18

Sometimes when I think about my stay here with the Trappists, I think of myself as a cowbird. The cowbird is a lazy bird in so far as he does not build his own nest but lays his eggs in the nests of other birds—vireos, warblers, sparrows, and flycatchers. Some "hosts" are not very hospitable and puncture the stranger's eggs and throw them out. But most birds tolerate them. Well, I am not building my nest here but still want to lay my eggs in this Trappist place in the hope that they will tolerate them and give them their incubation time. I am very grateful for this hospitality and become more and more aware of how good people are to me. Yet I am not sure that I don't take this too much for granted, and I wonder what this "cowbird mentality" really means. Maybe there is a fear of real commitment. Maybe I keep acting too much as a parasite. It seems that God does not want me to become a Trappist. At least I discover very few indications in that direction. But it might be time to settle a little more solidly.

In the writings of the desert fathers there is much emphasis on renunciation and detachment. We have to renounce the world, detach ourselves from our possessions, family, friends, own will, and any form of self-content so that all our thoughts and feelings may become free for the Lord. I find this very hard to realize. I keep thinking about distracting things and wonder if I ever will be "empty for God." Yesterday and today the idea occurred to me that instead of *ex*cluding I could *in*clude all my thoughts, ideas, plans, projects, worries, and concerns and make them into prayer. Instead of directing my attention only to God, I might direct my attention to all my attachments and lead them into the all-embracing arms of God. When this idea grew in me, I experienced a new freedom and felt a great open space where I could invite all those I love and pray that God touch them with his love.

Meanwhile, nearly spontaneously, my Jesus Prayer changed from "Lord Jesus Christ, have mercy on me" into "Lord Jesus Christ, have mercy on us" and I felt as if all of creation could become transformed by the endless mercy of the Son of God.

Wednesday, 19

Since my greatest technical expertise until today has been driving a Volkswagen, Brother Anthony's order to drive the dump truck and transport huge loads of sand was quite a challenge. After asking casually for some help—"since I am not used to this type of truck"—I took to the road and worked my way through sandy corners to the great sand pile. If nobody knows how unpractical you are, they take it for granted that what you are doing is just routine. It went well. First, I thought that I had jammed up the second gear (of the six), but I was reassured by one of the brothers that "that strange noise is normal, just move fast to the third gear." Backing up was quite a problem since "mirror reading" is not my specialty. But I got to the right place and found the right levers and made the right moves to make the heavy load go "up and off." It still gives me the sensation of great power to operate those large machines, and I had the strange feeling of a well-spent afternoon. Just moving sand from one place to another— but the difference is between the shovel and the dump truck.

Thursday, 20

Tonight I had a dream about Thomas Merton. I never dreamed about him before, but this dream seems significant. I was with a small group of sisters sitting and talking in a recreation room in expectation of Thomas Merton, who was going to give a lecture. The atmosphere was casual and relaxed. The sisters were dressed in civilian clothes and were having a pleasant conversation.

Suddenly Merton appeared. He walked in with large steps. He was baldheaded and dressed in an all-white habit. Immediately after his appearance he left again, supposedly to get his notes for the talk. Then all the sisters vanished and returned within a few minutes all dressed in immaculate white robes. They sat down on the floor and took a very contemplative position. They did not say a word, looked very pious, and were obviously getting themselves ready to listen to the words of the great spiritual master.

When I left the room to see where Merton had gone, I found him in a small shed dressed in brown trousers, tennis shoes, and a yellow T-shirt with something written on it that I could not read. He was very busy fixing something. I started to help him, not knowing exactly how. I asked a few questions about nails and screws, but although he seemed very friendly, he didn't answer me. Then he started to clean an old yellow bench with sandpaper and repaint it with brown paint. I asked him where he got the sandpaper and the paint, but again he didn't answer while inviting me with a silent gesture to help him.

I was aware that the sisters were waiting for him to give the talk, but in some way it didn't seem to make sense to tell him this. I just started to paint with him. Then I woke up.

The spiritual life does not consist of any special thoughts, ideas, or feelings but is contained in the most simple ordinary experiences of everyday living.

Friday, 21

Moods are worth attention. I am discovering during these first weeks in Genesee that I am subject to very different moods, often changing very quickly. Feelings of a depressive fatigue, of low self-esteem, of boredom, feelings also of anger, irritation, and direct hostility, and feelings of gratitude, joy, and excitement— they all can be there, sometimes even during one day.

I have the feeling that these quickly changing moods show how attached I really am to the many things given to me: a friendly gesture, pleasant work, a word of praise, a good book, etc. Little things can quickly change sadness into joy, disgust into contentment, and anger into understanding or compassion.

Somewhere during these weeks I read that sadness is the result of attachment. Detached people are not the easy victims of good or bad events in their surroundings and can experience a certain sense of equilibrium. I have the feeling that this is an important realization for me. When my manual work does not interest me, I become bored, then quickly irritated and sometimes even angry, telling myself that I am wasting my time. When I read a book that fascinates me, I become so involved that the time runs fast, people seem friendly, my stay here worthwhile, and everything one big happy event.

Of course, both "moods" are manifestations of false attachments and show how far I am from any healthy form of "indifference."

Thinking about all of this, I guess that my main problem still is that I have not really made prayer my priority. Still the only reason I am here—I mean, the only reason I *should* be here—is to learn to pray. But, in fact, much of what I am doing is motivated by many other concerns: getting back in shape, learning some manual skills, knowing more about birds and trees, getting to know interesting people—such as John Eudes—and picking up many ideas and experiences for future teaching. But if prayer were my only concern, all these other laudable things could be received as free gifts. Now, however, I am obsessed by these desires which are false, not in themselves, but by their being in the wrong place in the hierarchy of values. That, I guess, is the cause of my moodiness. For the time being it seems important to be at least aware of it.

Sunday, 23

John Eudes spoke this morning about "ardor." He remarked that although St. Benedict was always praised for his moderation, we should not overlook the ardor that permeates his Rule.

Ardor, fervent love, is especially brought to our attention during these days in which we celebrate the Sacred Heart of Jesus, the Immaculate Heart of Mary, and the feast of John the Baptist. Also Mary of Magdala and Mary of Bethany were both full of ardor in their penance and their love.

What struck me most in this conference was the idea that a fervent love was the basis for discernment. Neither John the Baptist nor St. Benedict was directly involved in the politics of his times. However, both were able to discern better

from the periphery—the edge of the desert or Monte Casino—the real ills of
their times than those who were directly involved in organizing or reorganizing
the social structures. Both might have been considered "provincial" in their days,
but John the Baptist recognized the Lord, and St. Benedict, by his concentration
on his own community, laid the foundations of a new Europe.

All these thoughts seem related to a short discussion I had with John Eudes
yesterday about magazines and periodicals in the monastery. He felt that monks
should be in touch with what goes on in the world, but felt that what he called
"journalistic writing" is in conflict with the contemplative vocation and makes
the mind more dispersed than concentrated. For him that had meant the cancella-
tion of the Abbey's subscription to *Commonweal* and the *New York Review of
Books* and also the avoidance of the *National Catholic Reporter, Time, Newsweek,*
and similar magazines.

I tend to agree with the principle but still feel very uncomfortable by the
consequences drawn from it. In fact, the monastery ends up with quite conservative and even reactionary American clerical magazines. But John Eudes was open
to suggestions. Meanwhile, I was happy to discover many excellent French and
German periodicals.

During all this I became very much aware of the influence of the abbot on the
minds of his monks. To be committed without becoming a fanatic and open-
minded without becoming wishy-washy, is one of the main tasks of a contemporary abbot.

Monday, 24

This afternoon I had a long talk with John Eudes. He was very open, personal,
warm, and made it easy to talk freely. I talked mostly about my anger: my
inclination to become angry and irritated with people, ideas, or events. I had
experienced angry feelings toward the easy decision to cancel subscriptions to
"liberal magazines," toward feast days that had negative connotations, etc., etc.
I realized that my anger created restlessness, brooding, inner disputes, and made
prayer nearly impossible. But the most disturbing anger was the anger at myself
for not responding properly, for not knowing how to express my disagreement,
for external obedience while remaining rebellious from within, and for letting
small and seemingly insignificant events have so much power over my emotional
life. In summary: passive aggressive behavior.

We talked about this on many levels and in many ways. Most important for
me at this point seem the following five suggestions:

First: Allow your angry feelings to come to your awareness and have a careful
look at them. Don't deny or suppress them, but let them teach you.

Second: Do not hesitate to talk about angry feelings even when they are related
to very small or seemingly insignificant issues. When you don't deal with anger
on small issues, how will you ever be ready to deal with it in a real crisis?

Third: Your anger can have good reasons. Talk to me (John Eudes) about it. Maybe I made the wrong decision, maybe I have to change my mind. If I feel that your anger is unrealistic or disproportionate, then we can have a closer look at what made you respond so strongly.

Fourth: Part of the problem might be generalization. A disagreement with a decision, an idea, or event might make you angry at me, the community, the whole country, etc.

Fifth: On a deeper level you might wonder how much of your anger has to do with ego inflation. Anger often reveals how you feel and think about yourself and how important you have made your own ideas and insight. When God becomes again the center and when you can put yourself with all your weaknesses in front of him, you might be able to take some distance and allow your anger to ebb away and pray again.

These are some of the ideas I took with me from our meeting. John Eudes might have said them in this way or not. But in these words they remain with me. They give me enough to do.

We also talked about the history of the Abbey of the Genesee, about being an abbot, about some people we both know, and finally about the idea that solitude becomes really hard when you realize that nobody is thinking about you anymore. Then some place for God might become available in your occupied mind and heart.

It was a very good meeting. Gentle, open, warm, honest, and remarkably pleasant.

Wednesday, 26

While taking the hot loaves from the conveyor belt and trying to say the Jesus Prayer, my thought went to Spain and Angela Benitez, the mother of "El Cordobez," who died in Palma del Rio from hunger and exhaustion on May 7, 1941. From all I have read and heard during these weeks, the few pages about the death of this woman read during dinner settled most deeply in my mind.

This is how her daughter Angelita tells the story: "She kept looking at us, at each one of us standing around her. Manolo was so small then, his head hardly came up over the edge of the bed. He was crying, too, but he didn't know his mother was dying. My mother looked at me and cried. I don't think she suffered then but she was so worn from overwork and exhaustion, there was nothing left inside her. It was all used up. She slid her hand down the bed to where I was. She took my hand. There was no force in her hand anymore, that hand that had worked so hard. I had to hold it or it would fall. After a while she whispered to me, 'Angelita, Angelita, I give you your brothers and sisters. You will have to be their mother now.' A few minutes after that she was dead and all that was left of her was that tired look on her face. She was thirty-six."[3]

While taking the fresh hot loaves from the belt, I kept seeing this woman in front of me. She would have been so happy with the hundreds of crumbs falling on the side and being swept away.

Her face became an accusation. When Angela died, I was nine years old. Manolo, her youngest son, now "El Cordobez," was five years old then. I was living in prosperity in Holland. He was on the edge of starvation a few hundred miles south of where I lived. And today? Do we have to wait until some African or Indian child becomes famous and worthy of a book to really feel and understand the suffering of his mother who is dying today?

Meanwhile, I realized how much I eat every day, much too much, and how hard it is to overcome my passion of gluttony, about which John Climacus and Evagrius wrote so eloquently. "Happy the poor"—I am wealthy, overfed, and well taken care of. The mother of Manuel Benitez was poor, really poor. I am eating bread without any limits. She had to eat grass, and today many are like her.

Do I have to go back to teach the well-dressed, well-sheltered, and well-fed? Are there other choices? What do I do with the money from writing books? "Angela Benitez, you will never be declared a saint, but to you I pray to help me become honest with myself."

Friday, 28

Anger is indeed one of the main obstacles of the spiritual life. Evagrius writes: "The state of prayer can be aptly described as a habitual state of imperturbable calm." The longer I am here, the more I sense how anger bars my way to God. Today I realized how, especially during work which I do not like much, my mind starts feeding upon hostile feelings. I experience negative feelings toward the one who gives the order, imagine that the people around me don't pay attention to my needs, and think that the work I am doing is not really necessary work but only there to give me something to do. The more my mind broods, the farther away from God and neighbor I move.

Being in a monastery like this helps me to see how the anger is really mine. In other situations there are often enough "good reasons" for being angry, for thinking that others are insensitive, egocentric, or harsh, and in those circumstances my mind easily finds anchor points for its hostility. But here! People couldn't be nicer, more gentle, more considerate. They really are very kind, compassionate people. That leaves little room for projection. In fact, none. It is not *he* or *they*, but it is simply *me*. I am the source of my own anger and no one else. I am here because I want to be here, and no one forces me to do anything I do not want to do. If I am angry and morose, I now have a perfect chance to look at its source, its deepest roots.

I always knew it: "Wherever you go, you always take yourself with you," but now I have nothing and no one to blame for my being me except myself. Maybe allowing this realization to exist is one little step on the way to purity of heart. How powerful are St. Paul's words: "Even if you are angry, you must not sin: never let the sun set on your anger or else you will give the devil a foothold. . . . Be friends with one another, and kind, forgiving each other as readily as God forgave you in Christ" (Ep. 4:26, 27, 32).

Tomorrow is the feast of St. Peter and St. Paul. Each a man of fervent temperament, both found their anger converted into an always-forgiving love.

Saturday, 29

Walking through one of the buildings where I hadn't been before, I came across a reproduction of Hazard Durfee's beautiful flute player with the text by Henry David Thoreau: "Why should we be in such desperate haste to succeed and in such desperate enterprises? If a man does not keep pace with his companions, perhaps it is because he hears a different drummer. Let him step to the music which he hears, however measured or far away."[4] It is quite understandable why one of the books on Thomas Merton is called *A Different Drummer*, and the longer I look at the quiet concentrated face of Durfee's flutist, the more I realize that the contemplative life is like hearing a different drummer.

Outside my window the song sparrow is singing loudly. For him it is not yet time to go to bed. It is seven o'clock and still very light. But I had better stop if I want to sing at 2 A.M. while the song sparrow sleeps.

Sunday, 30

This morning, during his weekly conference, John Eudes made a remark about the relationship between solitude and intimacy that touched me deeply. He said, "Without solitude there can be no real people. The more you discover what a person is, and experience what a human relationship requires in order to remain profound, fruitful, and a source of growth and development, the more you discover that you are alone—and that the measure of your solitude is the measure of your capacity for communion. The measure of your awareness of God's transcendent call to each person is the measure of your capacity for intimacy with others. If you do not realize that the persons to whom you are relating are each called to an eternal transcendent relationship that transcends everything else, how can you relate intimately to another at his center from your center?"

2

July

YOU ARE THE

GLORY OF GOD

■

Monday, 1

AT NOON I HAD another session with John Eudes. I took up the subject of
my anger again and explained how often my anger seemed related to experiences
of rejection. I mentioned three situations of the past week: a visitor to the Abbey
whom I know very well, but who didn't even ask me how I was doing; students
whom I had helped to get summer jobs, but who didn't even drop me a note of
thanks; and a few monks who seemed unfriendly to me without indicating any
reasons. In all those cases I didn't just feel a little irritated but felt deeply hurt,
so much so that in moments of prayer my thoughts became involved in angry
ruminations and revengeful scenes. Even my concentration during my reading
got more difficult since practically all my energy went into the experience of the
felt rejection.

John Eudes pointed out my difficulties with "nuanced responses." The problem, he said, is not that your feelings are totally illegitimate. In fact, you might
have a good reason to feel rejected. But the problem is that your response has
no proportion to the nature of the event. In fact, the people you felt rejected by
really don't mean that much to you. But little rejections like these open up a
huge chasm, and you plunge right into it all the way to the bottom. You feel
totally rejected, unloved, left alone, and something like a "blind rage" starts
developing that takes over and pulls you away from concerns and interests that
are much more important to you. The problem is not that you respond with
irritation but that you respond in a very primitive way: without nuances.

We tried to explore the reason for this fact. Somewhere there must be a need
for a total affection, an unconditional love, an ultimate satisfaction. I keep hoping
for a moment of full acceptance, a hope that I attach to very little events. Even
something rather insignificant becomes an occasion for this full and total event,
and a small rejection then easily leads to a devastating despair and a feeling of

38

total failure. John Eudes made it very clear how vulnerable I am with such a need because practically nobody can offer me what I am looking for. Even if someone did offer me this unconditional, total, all-embracing love, I would not be able to accept it since it would force me into an infantile dependency which I, as an adult, cannot tolerate.

Why this need and the related fears? We both agree that right under the threshold of my "bravery," there is a tremendous insecurity and self-doubt that is easily triggered and laid bare by a small event. The great, often disproportionate, hostile sentiments are easily understood as reactions to a perceived threat to the core of my selfhood. We left it at that. It seemed quite a lot for forty-five minutes and certainly enough to think about for a week.

We also talked a little about Spain, Chile, and the Buddhists in South Vietnam.

Today we held a solidarity fast for the Buddhist monks who had refused to be enlisted in the army, had been put in jail, and had planned a hunger strike today. John Eudes and many others had sent protest telegrams. The result was a promise to release the monks. In fact, however, they were dispersed over many different prisons. At this moment nobody knew for certain if the fast was still being planned since the Buddhist monks were now separated from each other. No word had yet come about this from the Buddhist peace delegation in Paris. But we held a fast anyhow, and that certainly helped us to become more aware of the great suffering of other monks in this world.

Tuesday, 2

Today my friend Claude, who teaches political science, sent me some material on the Chilean crisis. The Chicago Commission Report and the Amnesty Report on the situation in Chile are so disturbing, so overwhelming in their description of the present terror, that I could hardly sleep last night. The description of the torture, the execution, and the all-pervasive oppression left me with a deep feeling of despair.

The Amnesty Report, summarized by Rose Styron in the *New York Review of Books,* makes it clear that we are not dealing here with a spasmodic explosion of revenge but with a well-organized system of oppression. Styron writes: "The sophistication and systematic use of methods of repression and revenge is the most depressing aspect of the current regime."[1] A note smuggled out of the Santiago stadium is one of the many witnesses. The author, a young man, writes: "They tied me to a table. They passed cables over my naked body. They wet me and began to apply currents to all parts of my body . . . blows began to my abdomen, ribs, chest, testicles. . . . They were laughing but assured me they were not kidding and threw acid on my toes. They stuck me with needles. . . . They took us back to the camp. There no one slept because of our moans. The prisoners cried with us. They took us another day and it was worse. . . . They did things that cannot be told . . . threats of death if we didn't sign what the interrogator wanted. 'No one knows about you,' he said, and he tortured us. He was making fun of us. We were no longer men. We were shadows. . . . This is our ordeal. Why, my God, why? We trusted in justice" (Estado, Chile, February 1974).[2]

To realize that this goes on while I am sleeping quietly in a monastery is very hard, and there is a tendency to find a "mental solution" that gives sense to the contrast. But nothing else than the naked absurdity of our human condition came to my mind. The horrible thing is: It is nothing new. It happened with the same systematic rigor to the Jews under Hitler. I quote from the Chicago Commission Report: "The campaign of terror developed by the Junta seems to have assumed a systematic and organized character. Repression is more selective than during the first months following the takeover, but it is thorough and well-prepared. Names of prisoners, their location and details of arrest are computerized; it is assumed their lists include potential prisoners as well."[3]

Occasionally during the last weeks I had problems with the harshness of the psalms, but now they have become easier to understand. When I identify myself with the Chilean man who sent the note from the Estado, Chile, it is not hard to say:

> Let the groans of the prisoners come before you;
> let your strong arm reprieve those condemned to die.
> Pay back to our neighbors seven times over
> the taunts with which they taunted you, O Lord (Ps. 78).

> The proud have risen against me;
> ruthless men seek my life:
> to you they pay no heed.

> But you, God of mercy and compassion,
> slow to anger, O Lord,
> abounding in love and truth,
> turn and take pity on me . . .

> Show me a sign of your favour
> that my foes may see to their shame
> that you console me and give me your help (Ps. 85).[4]

I could go on and quote many more psalms because after reading about Chile they become like burning prayers. I wish that those in prison could pray them and so find courage and strength.

When I let all the images of torture stories pass through my mind, I feel lost. What am I really experiencing? Powerlessness? Anger? Compassion? Restlessness? Desires to leave here and *do* something? Lack of faith in a loving God?

Paralysis? It seems that all these feelings are there, all fighting for priority but constantly moving back and forth.

One question, however, seems important: Is it less compassion than just blind anger that dominates my emotions? When the torture scenes go through my head and I wonder what I would do, think, feel, or say in such a situation, I realize that there is a violent anger in me, a desire to see the torturers shamed, a hope for victory over those who do wrong. These feelings are really there and mostly stronger than feelings of compassion for those who suffer and of forgiveness for those who do them wrong.

Maybe it is realistic to recognize these feelings and be thankful that the psalms give me a chance to express them even in the intimacy of prayer. Maybe these feelings have to be led directly to the center of my relationship with my God, who is "slow to anger," and there converted into compassion and forgiveness. Maybe I am not ready yet to suffer for the Kingdom of God. My heart is too impure, my soul too divided, my love too fragile.

Before I fell asleep I wondered why I was here in the monastery. The one thing I am sure of is that I have to be here. There is a real *must*, but I honestly do not know what the purpose of it all is. When I think about Chile, I become very frightened.

This morning Anthony shaved my hair off. Practically all of it. He started hesitantly to trim it a bit, but when I encouraged him to take off as much as he wanted, he went all the way and made my head as unsophisticated as that of all the other monks.

I must confess that I was attached to the little bit of long hair I had left, and when I looked at my shaved head in the mirror, I felt very strange. Somehow it seemed that someone had taken away something from me that I didn't want to let go, but somewhere I also felt that it was a good thing.

Hair cutting has many associations for me: Cardinal Alfrink cutting a little bit of my hair during the tonsure ceremony in Rijsenburg in 1955, Dutch women who collaborated during the war being shaved as punishment, Samson losing his hair and his strength, the rebellious hair of my friend Richard, the gentle long hair of Jim, Nancy, and Frank. But when I threw my hair in the waste basket, I thought that by cutting away individual difference—by becoming "one of us," as Anthony said—I might be more able to focus on the innermost personal uniqueness of my relationship with God and my fellow monks and come in closer touch with my real self.

Wednesday, 3

Today: feast of St. Thomas the Apostle. During a dialogue homily, two of the monks remarked in different ways that although Thomas did not believe in the resurrection of the Lord, he kept faithful to the community of the apostles. In that community the Lord appeared to him and strengthened his faith. I find this a very profound and consoling thought. In times of doubt or unbelief, the community can "carry you along," so to speak; it can even offer on your behalf what you yourself overlook, and can be the context in which you may recognize the Lord again.

John Eudes remarked that Dydimus, the name of Thomas, means "twin," as the Gospel says, and that the fathers had commented that all of us are "two people," a doubting one and a believing one. We need the support and love of our brothers and sisters to prevent our doubting person from becoming dominant and destroying our capacity for belief.

Thursday, 4

A bad day. I felt low, depressed, morose, most of the day. The morning work in the bakery made me very tired. In the afternoon Anthony made me take down with a sledge hammer the part of the gatepost we couldn't finish last week. It was very hot and I just had no energy left. Meanwhile, I felt angry because with better equipment I could do in five minutes what would take me at least a day. I said this to Anthony, but he didn't change his mind and made a flippant remark about the monastic way of doing things. I then said that if monastic means impractical, I was not in favor of the monastic way. Well, a young fellow named Frank helped me a little, and Anthony brought a heavier sledge hammer. But I could hardly lift it.

Then Father Jean-Vianney, who was working close to me on the Trojan tractor shovel, saw me at work and said, "Relax, it is too hot for this—let me try to pull it out with the Trojan." He threw a heavy cable around the concrete post and attached it to the Trojan. He started the motor and pulled the whole post out of the ground as if it were a match. Well, I thanked him very much, cleaned the area, and went home.

My mind remained heavy, preoccupied with Brother Anthony's "monastic way of doing things" and my physical fatigue. I couldn't concentrate during Mass. For a moment I felt it would be better not to concelebrate in this mood, but I decided against it.

Meanwhile, I read that St. Dositheus became a saint "because he had attached himself to obedience and had broken his own will."[5] Quite disconcerting reading in the context of a depressing day. I did not find much consolation in reading this. Somewhere there is an enormous gap to be bridged. I keep thinking, It is not only true that in order to become a saint you have to obey the will of God and detach yourself from your own will—but it is also true that you have to be a saint in order to allow your will to be interpreted by someone else as the will of God.

But this is a very hostile thought and lacks gentleness. I hope that tomorrow will be better.

Friday, 5

My depression lifted a little bit in the evening, mostly as the result of finding a room that was relatively cool, had good lights, and was far away from the noise of the carpenters and the truck drivers.

Saturday, 6

Today I read some valuable pages on spiritual direction in the "Instructions of Dorotheus of Gaza." He says: "Nothing is more harmful than self-direction, nothing more fatal. . . . I never allowed myself to follow my thought without asking advice."[6]

Collected many rocks with Father Stephen, Brian and John, a new observer. Sometimes our ambitions got out of hand and we tried to move unmovable rocks. There is a fine distinction between building a church and building a new tower of Babel. I think that there is a permanent temptation to forget the difference.

Sunday, 7

Today I read a short biography of Charles de Foucauld by Georges Gorree contained in a photographic essay on Foucauld's life.

I read this remarkable story again (after having read it in the seminary) in order to be able to think better about the desert fathers and their words in the context of our contemporary situation. I have to read more about this modern saint to understand fully what his life means to me. He left a wealthy life to become a hermit in the desert. Somewhere he wrote:

> Think————————
> that you must die as a martyr,
> robbed of everything,
> stretched out on the ground,
> naked, unrecognizable,
> covered with blood and wounds,
> violently and painfully killed—
> and desire
> that that may be today.[7]

On December 1, 1916, he was killed by a group of fellagah in Tamanrasset. Today I realized for the first time that Charles de Foucauld lived in two Trappist monasteries (in France and Syria) and, for a while, thought of becoming a Trappist monk.

Monday, 8

The most important part of this day was my meeting with John Eudes. I told him about my depression, my fatigue, my irritability, my frustrations of not having time to read, and my general feeling of exhaustion.

He responded very sympathetically. First of all, he explained that this was to be expected. He said that it took him a year to get used to rising at the early hour, and that manual labor, no meat, and other changes in life-style can, after the first enthusiasm has vanished, cause fatigue, depression, psychosomatic complaints, and questions about your vocation. When the monastic life does not hold anything new any more, when people do not pay any special attention to you any more, when nothing "interesting" is distracting you any more, then the monastic life becomes difficult. Then room opens up for prayer and ascesis.

Speaking about me, John Eudes felt that I should start by accepting my limitations and make small changes in my day for a while. After some discussion, it seemed best that on bakery days I should work only in the bakery and on the other days only during the morning or the afternoon. The extra time I should use for study. John Eudes felt that nothing should be forced, and that the first month of involvement had made me aware of my weaknesses and could now help me to rearrange my life. He also felt that I should not deny my desire to read and study more. "If you had plans to stay, living the ascetical life without much reflection might have been better, but for you it seems important that you have a chance to integrate your experience into your thinking more explicitly."

Then we talked awhile about the phenomenon that in the monastic setting you become so aware of very primitive needs. I told John Eudes that although I did not fast in any special way, I thought much more about food than ever before. He said, "We all want, desire, and need satisfaction, but in a context like this the traditional ways to get satisfaction—talking, attention, distractions, etc.—are not available. So you start responding more primitively; you start thinking about food and sex. You become much more aware of very basic cravings. In a sense, you fall apart, you regress, but it is also there that you become available for spiritual direction and can find a place for prayer and ascetical life. It is all a very sensitive thing. It can also lead to an egocentric preoccupation. You need guidance to prevent that."

It made much sense to me. It made me particularly aware of how much I was in need of guidance but also how grateful I should be to have a guide such as John Eudes at this point in my life.

Tuesday, 9

I saw a hummingbird this morning—a funny-looking little bird with a long bill with which it sucks nectar out of honey flowers. The hummingbird hums straight up, hangs in the air like a helicopter, and zooms away like a jet plane.

I am increasingly impressed by Dorotheus of Gaza. His chapter, "About resentment," could have been written by a very modern phenomenologist and was very good for me to read. It describes in detail how the mind can move from being troubled by a critical remark to being irritated, from irritation to anger, and from anger to vengefulness. Dorotheus quotes Evagrius Ponticus who says:

"He who has conquered anger, has conquered demons. He, on the other hand, who is the victim of this passion, is an absolute stranger to the monastic life."[8] He describes in a vivid way how we can develop a morbid destructive inner attitude toward our neighbor. It might start with a little brooding about an ill-placed remark and grow into a devastating cancer that takes away our peace of mind, is harmful for the other, and leads us away from the road to God.

As the most important way to deal with this passion, Dorotheus points to prayer for him who has hurt us. Quoting Evagrius again: "He who prays for his enemies cannot be revengeful."[9]

The mother of Martin Luther King, Jr., was assassinated during a Sunday service in the Ebenezer Church in Atlanta. The assassin planned to kill her husband. I keep thinking about Martin Luther King, Sr., who has been the preacher in that church for forty years. God is really testing his faith. He lost his two sons and now his wife. You must be a saint to preach the Gospel after that with a pure heart, asking not for revenge but for forgiveness.

Wednesday, 10

Charles de Foucauld, the modern desert father, keeps me spellbound. Although his conversion to God after an obviously irreligious, pleasure-oriented youth, changed him profoundly, there is a remarkable sameness in this stubborn freedom during all the phases of his life. I am amazed how free this man was from peer pressure, how courageous in his disobedience, how persistent in pursuing a goal. With the same extremism that makes him defy military orders by taking his girl friend to Algiers and that makes him explore Morocco as an itinerant Jew, he gives himself to God.

In her book *The Sands of Tamanrasset*, Marion Mill Preminger creates a dialogue between Charles de Foucauld and his spiritual director, Abbé Huvelin, where this extremism becomes visible:

"Father," he said, "I should like to dedicate my life to God." Abbé Huvelin shook his head sadly: "You are not yet prepared, my son. You cannot yet be sure."

"From the moment I believed there was a God, I knew that I could not help living for him alone."

"You must not make such an important decision impulsively. You must think carefully."

"I have been thinking for two years, Father."

"You have been many things in your short life, my son. But when you leave the world to give yourself to God, there is no return."

"I have made up my mind, Monsieur l'Abbé."

Again the priest shook his head, "Prepare," he said. "Travel. Walk the sacred ground where Our Lord has walked. Pray where he has prayed. When you return, we will discuss your future."[10]

The sentence: "When you leave the world to give yourself to God, there is no return" hits me hard. It is an echo not only of Jesus' call to leave everything behind to follow him but also of the many voices of the desert fathers. I am more and more certain that I still have not left the world but keep lingering on the edges. I am plainly and simply scared of the "no return," and fear that the road of total commitment to God is arduous, painful, and very lonely. This reminds me of John Eudes' playful remark in Chapter: "We are not here on a sabbatical— for us, it is for keeps!" Everybody laughed and smiled kindly at me, but I realized that he had touched a central nerve of my spiritual life.

Trappist for life is something fundamentally different from Trappist for seven months. "Trappist for seven months," in fact, is a contradiction in terms. John Eudes said, "When I studied medicine and something happened that I didn't like, I could always say, 'Well, I will be out of this situation in a while.' When I was in the Navy and found the life disagreeable, I could always look forward to the day of my discharge, but when I was in the novitiate of the Trappists, there was not such a way out. This time it was 'for keeps,' and what was hard, unpleasant, or disagreeable had to be accepted and lived with as a way to purity of heart."

It is this type of extremism, of absolutism, of total surrender, of unconditional "yes," of unwavering obedience to God's will, that frightens me and makes me such a wishy-washy soul, wanting to keep a foot in both worlds. But that is how one stumbles.

Thursday, 11

Feast day of St. Benedict. I have been thinking how much I would like to be and remain close to this community of Benedictines. At this moment there is no sign that I should or could be a Trappist. Just as I am convinced that I should be here now, I am convinced that I should leave again. But could this become my community, my family, my "home," my point of orientation?

The Gospel today and John Eudes' sermon were telling the story. We are called to a radical break away from ourselves and a total surrender to God. St. Benedict, who so often is praised for his moderation and has even been called a humanist, is no less radical when he speaks about humility, obedience, and having everything in common.

If I wish to share in this radicalism, I should be willing to be fully obedient to my spiritual director; I should be humble enough to let him point the way; and I should be willing to share with him all my thoughts, feelings, and plans. Otherwise, the whole thing would be just romanticism.

I had many unexpected fantasies about my death today. I thought that this abbey would be the best place to be buried. But then I realized that a few months here hardly give one a title to be buried within the walls. John Eudes said in his sermon that most of the monks of this community had lived the rule of St. Benedict for more than half of their lives.

Friday, 12

When you keep going anxiously to the mailbox in the hope that someone "out there" has thought about you; when you keep wondering if and what your friends are thinking of you; when you keep having hidden desires to be a somewhat exceptional person in this community; when you keep having fantasies about guests mentioning your name; when you keep looking for special attention from the abbot or any one of the monks; when you keep hoping for more interesting work and more stimulating events—then you know that you haven't even started to create a little place for God in your heart.

When nobody writes anymore; when hardly anyone even thinks of you or wonders how you are doing; when you are just one of the brothers doing the same things as they are doing, not better or worse; when you have been forgotten by people—maybe then your heart and mind have become empty enough to give God a real chance to let his presence be known to you.

Saturday, 13

I have always had a strange desire to be different than other people. I probably do not differ in this desire from other people. Thinking about this desire and how it has functioned in my life, I am more and more aware of the way my life-style became part of our contemporary desire for "stardom." I wanted to say, write or do something "different" or "special" that would be noticed and talked about. For a person with a rich fantasy life, this is not too difficult and easily leads to the desired "success." You can teach in such a way that it differs enough from the traditional way to be noticed; you can write sentences, pages, and even books that are considered original and new; you can even preach the Gospel in such a way that people are made to believe that nobody had thought of that before. In all these situations you end up with applause because you did something sensational, because you were "different."

In recent years I have become increasingly aware of the dangerous possibility of making the Word of God sensational. Just as people can watch spellbound a circus artist tumbling through the air in a phosphorized costume, so they can listen to a preacher who uses the Word of God to draw attention to himself. But a sensational preacher stimulates the senses and leaves the spirit untouched. Instead of being the way to God, his "being different" gets in the way.

The monastic experience attacks this type of attention drawing. It asks you to say, write, and do things not differently but the same. It asks you to be obedient to age-long traditions and to form your mind and heart according to often proved and approved principles. In the spiritual literature I have read since I came here, there is a remarkable attempt to be faithful to the Gospel, to the words of the early fathers, to the insights of the spiritual director of the time, and an equally remarkable avoidance of trying to be different, sensational, and original. It seems that all the great spiritual writers are saying, "You cannot be original. If anything you say is worth saying, you will find its origin in the Word of God and his saints." What this place is calling me to be is—the same, and *more* of the same. The same as the monks, the same as the saints, the same as Jesus, the same as the heavenly Father. The rule of St. Benedict—the returning rhythm of the day, the continuous recitation of the 150 psalms and the uniformity of dress, food, and place—slowly makes you aware of a powerful sameness that transcends time and place and unifies you with the one God who is the Father of all people, all places, and all times, and who is the same through ages unending.

The monastic life is indeed very unsensational. I keep catching myself with the desire to do something special, to make a contribution, to add something new, and have to remind myself constantly that the less I am noticed, the less special attention I require, the less I am different, the more I am living the monastic life. Maybe—when you have become fully aware that you have nothing to say that has not already been said—maybe then a monk might be interested in listening to you. The mystery of God's love is that in this sameness we discover our uniqueness. That uniqueness has nothing to do with the "specialties" we have to offer that glitter like the artificial silver balls on a Christmas tree, but has everything to do with our most personal and most intimate relationship with God. When we have given up the desire to be different and experienced ourselves as sinners without any right to special attention, only then is there space to encounter our God who calls us by our own name and invites us into his intimacy.

Jesus, the only son of the Father, emptied himself "and being as we are, he was humbler yet, even to accepting death, death on a cross. But God raised him high and gave him the name which is above all other names" (Ph. 2:7–9). Only through ultimate sameness was Jesus given his unique name. When St. Paul calls us to have the mind of Jesus Christ, he invites us to that same humility through which we can become brothers of the Lord and sons of the heavenly Father.

Today was the feast of St. Henry. All the attention went to Brother Henry. I guess I had hoped for a little extra attention. Not getting it helped me to give a little more "flesh" to my meditation on sameness.

Painting was my afternoon job. The weather was beautiful—sunny and cool. I enjoyed scraping away the peeling paint, sandpapering and repainting the damaged spot, and looking out over the field from the vantage point where I was working. A big wasp kept me company the whole afternoon and did not sting. Brother Pascal said, "Don't make panicky moves. Just be gentle and it won't bother you." He proved to be right.

Sunday, 14

My father, who retired from the University of Nijmegen last year, wrote me: "As a man on pension, you see the world recede. No one needs you any more, so you have to stand on your own feet. Thus the Abbey will be a good preparation for that time which only seemingly is so far away from you."

My father is not a bitter man. The opposite: He is joyful, lively, and full of energy. I even dare to say that he is more so since he has retired. Therefore, his words to me are very meaningful and very real.

I know too well how hard it is to live without being needed, being wanted, being asked, being known, being admired, being praised. Just a few years ago I retired from my teaching job in Holland and lived for a year as a student in a rented room in the city. I had expected to be free at last to study and do many of the things I couldn't do when I was so busy and so much in demand. But what happened? Without a job I was soon forgotten. People I had hoped would come and visit me didn't come; friends I expected to invite me remained silent; fellow priests whom I thought would ask me to assist them in their Sunday liturgy or to preach once in a while didn't need me; and my surroundings had pretty well responded as if I were no longer around. The irony was that I always wanted to be alone to work, but when I was finally left alone, I couldn't work and started to become morose, angry, sour, hateful, bitter, and complaining.

During that year I realized more than ever my vulnerability. That year of "quasi-retirement" showed me that being alone does not necessarily lead to inner peace and solitude of heart but can cause resentment and bitterness.

Now, three years later, I am back in the same situation. Every time I walk to the mailbox only to find it empty, some of the same feelings I had in Holland threaten to return. Even in this protective place with many good people around me, I am afraid of being forgotten, of being left alone. Yet I chose to be alone; I wanted it.

My father is very right when he says that the Abbey is a good preparation for the time when nobody will need me any longer. Here I have the chance to look at my emerging feelings of bitterness and hostility and unmask them as signs of spiritual immaturity. Here I have the chance both to be left alone and slowly to see this as an occasion to meet God, who will be faithful even when no one cares any longer. Here I have the chance to convert my feelings of loneliness into solitude and allow God to enter into the emptiness of my heart. Here I can experience a little bit of the desert and realize that it is not only a dry place where people die from thirst but also the vast empty space where the God of love reveals himself and offers his promise to those who are waiting in faithfulness. When I can open my heart just a little to my God, maybe I will be able to carry him with me into the world and to love my neighbor without becoming dependent on his gratitude or gifts.

Indeed, my retirement is only seemingly far away. Twenty-five years go fast, and who says that many forms of retirement will not be necessary much sooner? If, in a spiritual sense, I could retire now, that is, become independent of the success of my work, then I could probably live much more creatively and be much less vulnerable.

This monastic experience gives me some new understanding of what it means to "grow old gracefully," to live life less as an attempt to conquer new land and hold on to it and more as a grateful response to the gifts of God. In any case, this monastery is a good training place for aging.

Monday, 15

When I went to see John Eudes today my head seemed so filled with questions that I wondered how we could focus a little bit and bring some order into the chaos of concerns.

When I left I had the feeling that many things had indeed come together by focusing on the glory of God. The question, "How to live for the glory of God and not for your own glory?" has become very important to me. During the last weeks I have realized more and more that even my seemingly most spiritual activities can be pervaded with vainglory. There is something special and in some people's eyes "heroic" about going to the Trappists, and I wondered if it is really God I am seeking. Even my most intense attention to the ascetic and mystical writings of the early fathers easily turns into ideas and insights to be used for others' conversion instead of my own. Yes, there is a great temptation to make even God the object of my passion and to search for him not for his glory but for the glory that can be derived from smart manipulation of godly ideas.

John Eudes wasn't very surprised by my worries. He welcomed them as important enough to worry about, to think about, to live through.

How to dispel the passions that make us manipulate instead of worship? Well, the first thing to realize is that you *are* the glory of God. In Genesis you can read: "Yahweh God fashioned man of dust from the soil. Then he breathed into his nostrils a breath of life, and thus man became a living being" (Gen. 2:7). We live because we share God's breath, God's life, God's glory. The question is not so much, "How to live for the glory of God?" but, "How to live who we are, how to make true our deepest self?"

With a smile John Eudes said, "Take this as your koan: 'I am the glory of God.' Make that thought the center of your meditation so that it slowly becomes not only a thought but a living reality. You are the place where God chose to dwell, you are the *topos tou theou* (God's place) and the spiritual life is nothing more or less than to allow that space to exist where God can dwell, to create the space where his glory can manifest itself. In your meditation you can ask yourself, 'Where is the glory of God? If the glory of God is not there where I am, where else can it be?'"

Obviously, all this is more than an insight, an idea, a way of seeing things. That is why it is a subject for meditation and not so much for study. But once you start "realizing" in this very intimate and personal way that you indeed are the glory of God, then everything is different, then your life takes a decisive turn. Then, for instance, your passions which seemed so real, more real than God, show their illusory nature to you and sort of dwindle away.

These thoughts led us to a short conversation about the experience of God. I told John Eudes that for many years, I had the fantasy that one day God just might break through the hard shell of my resistance and reveal himself to me in such an intensive and convincing way that I finally would be able to let my "idols" go and commit myself unconditionally to him. John Eudes, not too surprised by the fantasy, said, "You want God to appear to you in the way your passions desire, but these passions make you blind to his presence now. Focus on the nonpassionate part of yourself and realize God's presence there. Let that part grow in you and make your decisions from there. You will be surprised to see how powers that seem invincible shrivel away."

We talked about many more things, but what I remember best of the final part of our conversation was the idea that I should be happy to be part of the battle, independent of the question of victory. The battle is real, dangerous, and very crucial. You risk all you have; it is like fighting a bull in a bull ring. You will only know what victory is when you have been part of the battle. People who have tasted real victory are always very modest about it because they have seen the other side and know that there is little to brag about. The powers of darkness and the powers of light are too close to each other to offer the occasion for vainglory. That's what a monastery is all about. In the many little things of everyday life we can recognize the battle. It can be as small as a desire for a letter or a craving for a glass of milk. By staying at one place you get to know the battlefield quite well.

Tuesday, 16

I had the following thought: At the moment that I have a strong and real desire to stay here for life, I am ready to leave. Because at the moment that I feel the inner readiness to live my life only for the glory of God, I am ready to live creatively in the world and be open to my neighbors, since then I no longer depend on their affection.

Dorotheus writes: "Don't look for the affection of your neighbor. He who looks for it is troubled when he does not get it. You yourself, however, have to give witness to the love for your neighbor and to offer him rest, and thus you will bring your neighbor to love."[11]

Wednesday, 17

One of the things a monastery like this does for you is give you a new rhythm, a sacred rhythm. While teaching in New Haven I was very much aware of Sunday as a special day, but beyond that all the days seemed the same—only different in their relationship to the school calendar. Here the rhythm is different. Not only Sundays are different, but all the days of the week have their own nuance, determined by the psalms and hymns you sing, the Scripture lessons you hear, and, most of all, by the Eucharist you celebrate. In the beginning I was hardly aware of how I was being pulled slowly into a new lifestyle, a new way of perceiving time and a new way of experiencing God's presence. But now after more than a month of participating in the daily rhythm of this community with a minimum contact with my previous life, I find myself thinking about the Holy Trinity, the life of Christ, about St. John the Baptist, St. Benedict, St. Bonaventure, about an often repeated Gospel passage, a certain psalm, and a catch phrase in a biography of a saint. It seems as if I am being slowly lifted up from the gray, dull, somewhat monotonous, secular time cycle into a very colorful, rich sequence of events in which solemnity and playfulness, joy and grief, seriousness and lightness take each other's place off and on.

It is an important experience for me to celebrate the feast days of the saints again. In the milieu in which I have worked the last three years, there is hardly any room for saints, but here saints are like roommates with whom you can have long conversations. Sometimes I can't keep up with the feasts of saints. One day the whole house seems filled with praise to God because of St. Benedict, but when I just have started to read his life, everyone else is already excited about another saint. Moreover, since the monks celebrate not their birthdays but their saint's days, many feast days have special meaning for individual monks. That gives it all an even more personal touch.

I remember from my high school years with the Jesuits and from my seminary years, how the secular and the sacred cycles always intersected each other. But here there is nothing to intersect with. Here the only cycle is the liturgical cycle, and here the time is indeed redeemed. You see and feel that the monastic day, week and year are meant to be time-bound anticipations of a heavenly existence. Already you are invited to participate in the intimate life of the Holy Trinity, Father, Son, and Spirit, and to be joyful because of those who came so close to God in their historical existence that they have a special place in the heavenly kingdom. So contemplation is indeed a beginning of what is to be fulfilled in the resurrection.

Today was the feast day of my neighbor in choir, Brother Alexis. He looked happy and radiant.

Thursday, 18

I hardly remember what it was, but a small critical remark and a few irritations during my work in the bakery were enough to tumble me head-over-heels into a deep, morose mood. Many hostile feelings were triggered and in a long sequence of morbid associations, I felt worse and worse about myself, my past, my work, and all the people who came to mind. But happily I saw myself tumbling and was amazed how little was needed to lose my peace of mind and to pull my whole world out of perspective. Oh, how vulnerable I am!

The milieu of this place full of prayerful people prevents me from acting out, from getting angry, from bursting open. I can sit down and see how quickly the little empty place of peace in my heart is filled again with rocks and garbage falling down from all sides.

It is hard to pray in such a mood. But still during Terce, the short prayer immediately after work, standing outside in our dirty work clothes, we read: "Is anyone among you in trouble? He should turn to prayer." Indeed prayer is the only real way to clean my heart and to create new space. I am discovering how important that inner space is. When it is there it seems that I can receive many concerns of others in it without becoming depressed. When I sense that inner quiet place, I can pray for many others and feel a very intimate relationship with them. There even seems to be room for the thousands of suffering people in prisons and in the deserts of North Africa. Sometimes I feel as if my heart expands from my parents traveling in Indonesia to my friends in Los Angeles and from the Chilean prisons to the parishes in Brooklyn.

Now I know that it is not I who pray but the spirit of God who prays in me. Indeed, when God's glory dwells in me, there is nothing too far away, nothing too painful, nothing too strange or too familiar that it cannot contain and renew by its touch. Every time I recognize the glory of God in me and give it space to manifest itself to me, all that is human can be brought there and nothing will be the same again. Once in a while I just know it: Of course, God hears my prayer. He himself prays in me and touches the whole world with his love right here and now. At those moments all questions about "the social relevance of prayer, etc." seem dull and very unintelligent, and the silent prayer of the monks one of the few things that keeps some sanity in this world.

But then again, how little it takes to have everything cave in on me and make my heart into a dark place of ignorance! Just today I read: "Faith is a thought of God free from passion."[12] How meaningful that sounds after a passionate day.

Friday, 19
During the four and a half hours of raisin washing this morning, I couldn't concentrate on anything except the desire to see the last raisin go through the machine.

In *U.S. News and World Report,* I read that Edwin Aldrin, the second man on the moon, wrote a book, *Return to Earth,* describing his problems of adjusting to a world in which he finds no more goals to reach. It also says that he is afflicted by moments of deep depression. I would like to understand his depression better. Having visited the moon must have affected his understanding of the earth profoundly.

Saturday, 20
Reflecting on my past three years of work, I realize more and more that it lacked unity. The many things I did during those years seem disjointed, not really relating to each other, not coming from one source. I prayed during certain hours or days but my prayer seemed separated from the lectures I gave, the trips I made, the counseling I did. When I think of the many lecture invitations I declined with the argument that I had no time to prepare, I see now how I looked at every speaking engagement—be it a lecture, a sermon, or a commencement address—

as a new performance that calls for new preparation. As if I had to entertain a demanding audience that could not tolerate any poor performance. No wonder that this attitude leads to fatigue and eventually to exhaustion. Even small daily tasks such as talking with your own students becomes an anxiety-provoking burden.

Now I see that I was all mixed up, that I had fragmented my life into many sections that did not really form a unity. The question is not, "Do I have time to prepare?" but, "Do I live in a state of preparedness?" When God is my only concern, when God is the center of my interest, when all my prayers, my reading, my studying, my speaking, and writing serve only to know God better and to make him known better, then there is no basis for anxiety or stage fright. Then I can live in such a state of preparedness and trust that speaking from the heart is also speaking to the heart. My fears and my resulting fatigue over the last three years might well be diagnosed as a lack of single-mindedness, as a lack of one-eyedness, as a lack of simplicity. Indeed, how divided my heart has been and still is! I want to love God, but also to make a career. I want to be a good Christian, but also have my successes as a teacher, preacher, or speaker. I want to be a saint, but also enjoy the sensations of the sinner. I want to be close to Christ but also popular and liked by many people. No wonder that living becomes a tiring enterprise. The characteristic of a saint is, to borrow Kierkegaard's words, "To will one thing." Well, I will more than one thing, am double-hearted, double-minded, and have a very divided loyalty.

"Set your hearts on his kingdom first . . . and all these other things will be given you as well" (Mt. 6:33). Jesus is very clear about it. You cannot love God and mammon, you cannot be for him and against him, you cannot follow him just a little bit. Everything or nothing.

John Eudes said that his conferences with the monks grew out of his meditations. They were like sharing with others his own prayer. If I could slowly come to that trust in God, that surrender, that childlike openness, many tensions, and worries would fall away, would be unmasked as false, empty, unnecessary worries, not worth the time and energy, and I could live a simple life. My preaching and teaching, my lecturing and counseling could be like different forms of a meditative life. Then I probably would have an open mind, open to perceive many things I didn't notice before, open to hear many people I didn't hear before. Then I wouldn't worry about my name, my career, my success, my popularity and would be open to the voice of God and his people. Then I probably also would know much better what is worth doing and what is not, which lectures to accept and which to refuse, which people to spend time with and which people to keep at a distance. Then I most likely would be less plagued by passions causing me to read the wrong books, hang around the wrong places, and waste my time with the wrong company. Then—no doubt—I would have much more time to pray, to read, to study, and to be always prepared to speak the word of God when the right time has come. Wherever I am, at home, in a hotel, in a train, plane, or airport, I would not feel irritated, restless, and desirous of being somewhere else or doing something else. I would know that here and now is what counts and is important because it is God himself who wants me at this time in this place.

Here in the safe surrounding of the Abbey I can see it all quite clearly. I hope that some of that vision will last when I leave this place and enter again the fragmented and fragmenting world.

One of the monks said to me today, "Monks are like children: very shy and very sensitive. When you ruffle them, they tend to withdraw. They are not like college students who can take some mental pushing and pulling. They are very vulnerable, and if you come on too strong, they might respond by hiding themselves from you."

Sunday, 21

On Sundays there always is a bouquet of flowers in front of the altar. Today it was a bouquet of wheat to announce the wheat harvest which is to start tomorrow. The sight moved me deeply. Not just because of the obvious relationship between the wheat and the mystery of the Eucharist, but also because of our growing knowledge of the lack of wheat in the northern countries of Africa.

A letter from the White Fathers who have their missions in Africa was on the bulletin board. A despairing letter telling about the starvation of millions of people while we in the U.S.A. publish articles about how to reduce weight. During the Roman Empire these same African countries were prosperous, full of wheat and cattle. Now they are a desolate desert growing wider and wider. In Chapter, John Eudes spoke about his visit to Nigeria in May. He told how the farmers kept plowing their dry land simply so that they might not lose their skill but without hope of a harvest. Every year the desert advances from three to twenty miles. Every year fewer miles to cultivate and more miles of dry, fruitless sand.

And we? John Eudes said, "When I returned from Africa, our land looked like paradise—green, rich, fruitful." What is it that makes us able to produce so much and unable to share it with starving people only eighteen flight hours away?

It is a number of complex factors. But whatever the explanations are, they cannot keep us from feeling that we haven't done enough to prevent it. Brother Anthony asked, "Do we know where *our* wheat is going?" The answer was, "Only that it will be eaten by people and not by animals, but by whom it is eaten is beyond our control."

It is necessary to think more about all this and to act wisely. When I think about my work after I leave this monastery, I must ask myself how it relates to this world problem, which unquestionably will be with us for many years to come. For now, it seems that some fasting is the best way to remind myself of the millions who are hungry and to purify my heart and mind for a decision that does not exclude them.

Monday, 22

Today during my meeting with John Eudes I discussed my relationship to Our Lady, the Blessed Mother of God. When I was a child she played a very important role in my religious development. The May and October devotions in my family are a real part of my childhood memories. We built little altars, sang songs, prayed rosaries, and seemed to enjoy it. But after my seminary years, a certain antidevotionalism developed in the circles where I lived, and Mary, the Mother of Jesus, became less and less important in my religious life.

But this week "she returned." Not by any conscious attempt to restore my devotion to Our Lady or by a book or any advice, but without any intrusiveness I found her in the heart of my search for a more contemplative life. If anything helped, it was the Icon of Our Lady of Vladimir in the Abbey chapel. I couldn't keep my eyes off this most gentle painting which, in fact, is a reproduction made by a monk of Gethsemani.

With a somewhat sad, melancholic gaze, Mary looks at you and points with her right hand to the child she holds on her left arm. The child is embracing her in a very affectionate way. The intimacy of the child's embrace is expressed by the little hand that, appearing from under the veil covering Mary's head, gently touches her left cheek. The child looks like a small adult in a monk's habit.

I keep looking at this intimate scene, and peace invades my soul. Mary speaks to me about Jesus. To him she directs me but without fearful warnings, without strong challenges, without a demanding stern look. It is as if she says, "Look, he who is your Lord and Salvation has become small and vulnerable for you. Why don't you come closer and listen to what he has to say?" At the same time it seems that she invites me to share in the intimacy between her and her child.

This week I often experienced resistance toward private prayer. Every time I tried to sit down and pray alone my thoughts wandered to the book I was reading and wanted to continue reading, to my feelings of hunger, to a monk I couldn't figure out, to a hostile feeling or a daydream I couldn't shake off. Usually I ended up reading a few minutes trying to focus my thoughts again. But when I knelt in front of the Icon of Our Lady of Vladimir, it was different. In some way my resistance against meditation subsided, and I simply enjoyed being invited to enter into the intimacy between Jesus and Mary.

John Eudes didn't run away from the psychological implications of all this. He made me see how masculine my emotional life really is, how competition and rivalry are central in my inner life, and how underdeveloped my feminine side had remained. He told me about St. Bernard, who didn't hesitate to call the task of the monk a woman's task (compared with the virile task of the secular priest) and to remind the abbot (the word comes from *abba* = father) of his motherly responsibilities. John Eudes also reminded me that the Hebrew word for God's

Spirit, *Ruach,* is both masculine and feminine, and thus emphasizes that God is male and female. Mary helps me to come in touch again with my receptive, contemplative side and to counterbalance my one-sided aggressive, hostile, domineering, competitive side. "It is not so surprising that you are easily depressed and tired," he said. "Much of your energy is invested in keeping your hostilities and aggressions under control and in working on your appearance of gentleness and kindness."

I hope and pray that through a renewed devotion to Our Lady, the Blessed Mother of God, I can allow my other side to grow to maturity and to become less self-conscious, less suspicious, less angry, and more able to receive God's gift, more able to become a contemplative, more able to let the Glory of God dwell in me as it dwelled so intimately in Mary.

Tuesday, 23

In the contemplative life every conflict, inner or outer, small or large, can be seen as the tip of an iceberg, the expressive part of something deeper and larger. It is worthwhile, even necessary, to explore that which is underneath the surface of our daily actions, thoughts, and feelings.

The most persistent advice of John Eudes in his spiritual direction is to explore the wounds, to pay attention to the feelings, which are often embarrassing and shameful, and follow them to their roots. He keeps telling me not to push away disturbing daydreams or hostile meanderings of the mind but to allow them to exist and explore them with care. Do not panic, do not start running but take a careful look.

It is interesting to mention here Diadochus of Photice's views on the discernment of spirits. He says that we have to keep the surface calm so that we can see deep into the soul. "When the sea is calm, the eyes of the fisherman can penetrate to the point where he can distinguish different movements in the depth of the water, so that hardly any of the creatures who move through the pathways of the sea escape him, but when the sea is agitated by the wind, she hides in her dark restlessness what she shows in the smile of a clear day."[13]

What is the importance of this? Diadochus says that with a clear mind we will be able to distinguish the good from the bad suggestions so that the good ones can be treasured and the bad ones dispelled.

That indeed is the value of being able to follow the movements of the soul. When we do not panic and create waves, we will be able to "think them through" to the end. When the end proves to be a dead end, a blind alley, then we can be free to search for a new way without the false suspicion that the old way might be the better one. When we keep a diagnostic eye on our soul, then we can become familiar with the different, often complex stirrings of our inner life and travel with confidence on the paths that lead to the light.

I was surprised and happy to find a somewhat similar idea in the sermon of Bernard of Clairvaux to the university students in Paris. There he says: ". . . he who hears the word of the Lord: Return ye transgressors to the heart (Is. 46:8) having discovered such great obscenities in his inmost self, like some eager explorer makes every effort to trace them to their sources one by one and to learn how it was that they entered there."[14] Bernard shows how a radical understanding of our evil thoughts leads to a confession of our sinfulness and sets us free to accept God's compassion and mercy: "that weakness which is serviceable is the weakness which seeks the aid of a physician."[15]

These many images and ideas might sound somewhat confusing but two ideas are clear. First: Do not run away from your inner feelings even when they seem fearful. By following them through you will understand them better and be more free to look for new ways when the old ways run into a blank wall. Second: When you explore in depth your unruly and wild emotions you will be confronted with your sinful self. This confrontation should not lead to despair but should set you free to receive the compassion of God without whom no healing is possible.

Today I collected rocks with Brian while the rain poured down on us. When we came home, we looked like two drowned cats, but everyone is grateful for the rain after three dry weeks. It interrupts the wheat harvest, but the wheat will be better for it.

Wednesday, 24

I would like to think a little more about love. This monastery definitely exudes a real atmosphere of love. You can indeed say, the monks love each other. I even dare to say they show a real love to me. I think that this is a very important experience because they not only make me feel love but also help me to understand love better.

My first inclination has been, and in many ways still is, to connect love with something special in me that makes me lovable. When people are kind and friendly toward me, I feel happy because I think that they are attracted to me and like me in a special way. This more or less unconscious attitude got me into trouble here since the monk who is nice and good to me proves to be just as nice and good to everyone else. So it becomes hard to believe that he loves me because of something special that I have and others do not have. I am obviously not more or less attractive than others. This experience was in the beginning a painful one. I tended to react by thinking, "Well, if he is just as friendly to everyone else as he is to me, his friendliness cannot be real. It is just one of those poses, one of those 'frozen smiles.' He is friendly because he is supposed to be friendly. He is just following the rule. His love is only the result of obedience. It is not natural, not spontaneous, not real. Underneath his friendly surface he probably couldn't care less about me as an individual."

But these ruminations were exactly that: ruminations. I knew that I was fooling myself, that there was something very important I was missing. I knew it simply because the story I told myself was not true. The monks who show me love, show love to me not as an abstraction but as a real individual with his own strengths and weaknesses, habits and customs, pleasant and unpleasant sides. The love they show me is very alert, awake, and based on the real me. When I ask something, they listen with attention and try to help me, and when I show a need for support, information, or interest, they offer me as well as they can what I need. So although their love for me is not exclusive, particular, or unique, it is certainly not general, abstract, impersonal, or just an act of obedience to the rule.

It is important for me to realize how limited, imperfect, and weak my understanding of love has been. Not my theoretical understanding but my understanding as it reveals itself in my emotional responses to concrete situations. My idea of love proves to be exclusive: "You only love me truly if you love others less"; possessive: "If you really love me, I want you to pay special attention to me"; and manipulative: "When you love me, you will do extra things for me." Well, this idea of love easily leads to vanity: "You must see something very special in me"; to jealousy: "Why are you now suddenly so interested in someone else and not in me?" and to anger: "I am going to let you know that you have let me down and rejected me."

But love is "always patient and kind; it is never jealous; love is never boastful or conceited; it is never rude or selfish; it does not take offense, and is not resentful" (I Cor. 13:4–5).

It is this understanding of love that I must slowly learn. But how? It seems that the monks know the answer, "You must love the Lord your God with all your heart, with all your soul, with all your mind." This is the greatest and the first commandment. It seems that the life the monks are living is a witness to the importance of keeping the first commandment first so that the second, "which resembles it" can be realized as well: "You must love your neighbor as yourself" (Mt. 22:37–39). I am beginning to experience that an unconditional, total love of God makes a very articulate, alert, and attentive love for the neighbor possible. What I often call "love for neighbor" too often proves to be a tentative, partial, or momentary attraction, which usually is very unstable and does not last long. But when the love of God is indeed my first concern, a deep love for my neighbor can grow.

Two more considerations may clarify this. First of all, I discover *myself* in a new way in the love of God. St. Bernard of Clairvaux describes as the highest degree of love the love of ourselves for God's sake. Thomas Merton commenting on this says: "This is the high point of Bernard's Christian humanism. It shows that the fulfillment of our destiny is not merely to be lost in God, as the traditional figures of speech would have it, like a 'drop of water in a barrel of wine or like iron in the fire' but found in God in all our individual and personal reality, tasting our eternal happiness not only in the fact that we have attained to the possession of his infinite goodness, but above all in the fact that we see his will done in us."[16]

Secondly, it is not only ourselves we discover in our individuality but our fellow human beings as well, because it is God's glory itself that manifests itself in his people in an abundant variety of forms and styles. The uniqueness of our neighbors is not related to those idiosyncratic qualities that only they and nobody else have, but it is related to the fact that God's eternal beauty and love become visible in these unique, irreplaceable, finite human beings. It is exactly in the preciousness of the individual person that the eternal love of God is refracted and becomes the basis of a community of love.

When we have found our own uniqueness in the love of God and have been able to affirm that indeed we are lovable since it is God's love that dwells in us, then we can reach out to others in whom we discover a new and unique manifestation of the same love and enter into an intimate communion with them.

The guestmaster, Father Francis, showed me a letter of gratitude written by the leader of a group of retarded boys who visited the monastery last week. It is a moving letter. Vespers had impressed them the most. One boy, who was used to being elbowed out of church because of his "litany of obscenities," was surprised that this did not happen this time and asked to go back again.

Indeed, I think that often those who are poor at verbal communication sense better the mood and atmosphere of a place or an event than very cerebral, "discussing" types. These retarded boys had sensed the mystery hidden under the meanings of the words.

Friday, 26

Since I have lived in this Abbey of the Genesee, I have written many more letters than I planned to write when I came. My original idea was: no telephone, no letters, neither outgoing nor incoming, no visitors, no contact with guests—but a real retreat "alone with the Alone."

Well, most of my plans are coming through except for my letter writing. Is this good or an initial sign of compromise? Maybe both.

One of the experiences of silence is that many people, good old friends and good old enemies, start seeking attention. Often a thought led to a prayer and a prayer to a letter and a letter to a real feeling of peace and warmth. A few times, after having dropped a small pile of letters in the mailbox, I had a deep sense of joy, of reconciliation, of friendship. When I was able to express gratitude to those who had given me much, sorrow to those whom I had offended, recognition to those I had forgotten, or sympathy to those who are in grief, my heart seemed to grow and a weight fell from me. These letters seemed to restore the part of me wounded by past resentment and take away the obstacles that prevented me from bringing my history into my present prayer.

But there also is another side. Perhaps part of my letter writing shows that I do not want to be forgotten here, that I hope that there still are people "out there" who think of me. Maybe part of my letter writing is my newly found way of seducing people into paying attention to me here in the enclosure of a monastery. I am sure that that is part of it because just as I feel happy when I drop my letters in the mailbox, so do I feel disappointed when I don't receive much in return. Then my heroic remarks about not writing to my friends shrivel into feelings of being forgotten and left alone.

I thought about all of this when I read about the remarkable friendship between Bernard of Clairvaux and William of St. Thierry, both very sensitive people but very different characters. William, Abbot of a Benedictine Monastery, had a great admiration and affection for Bernard. He wrote him many letters, but Bernard did not always respond as fast as William hoped he would. Once after many unanswered letters, William wrote: *"Plus amans, minus diligor."* (I love more than I am loved.) This was enough to provoke Bernard to a long passionate answer: "You can reach me if you but considered what I am, and you can reach me still whenever you wish if you are content to find me as I am and not as you wish me to be." In this and many other sentences Bernard responded to the suggestion that his affection for William was less than William's for him.

Louis Bouyer, discussing this exchange, remarks dryly: ". . . it remains no less clear that what was happening with Bernard was what so often happens with very sensitive and passionate people. So long as he had his friends in mind, he was entirely taken up with the thought of them; but he could very well go for a month without thinking of them."[17]

There is much of William of St. Thierry's need for friendship in me, and sometimes that need shows more a lack of a real sense of self than a realistic enjoyment of good relationships. When I still need letters to convince me of my value, when I still need attention even after having told all my friends that I was going to "retreat" for half a year, then there is a good reason to question if I really want to be "alone with the Alone."

Still, I am deeply convinced that when I allow God to enter into my loneliness, when I allow him to let me know that I am loved far more deeply than I can imagine, only then can I give and receive real friendship and write letters free from seductive motivations. When I can say with Paul, "not I live, but Christ lives in me," then I no longer need to depend on the attention of others to have a sense of self. Because then I realize that my most important identity is the identity I have received as a grace of God and which has made me a participant in the divine life of God himself.

Meanwhile, it remains remarkable how little is said and written about letter writing as an important form of ministry. A good letter can change the day for someone in pain, can chase away feelings of resentment, can create a smile and bring joy to the heart. After all, a good part of the New Testament consists of letters, and some of the most profound insights are written down in letters between people who are attracted to each other by a deep personal affection. Letter writing is a very important art, especially for those who want to bring the good news.

Saturday, 27

A few days ago we finished *Or I'll Dress You in Mourning*, the book about the Spanish bullfighter. The last page describes the meeting between the thirty-two-year-old millionaire matador and Generalissimo Franco. In many ways it is a sad ending. A young man still hardly able to read or write has become just as distastefully wealthy as he was distastefully poor. He has not become a very happy man. He reached a wealth and popularity far beyond his own wildest dreams, but somehow he has not been able as yet to understand the real tragedy of his country. With a naïve pride he let himself be photographed with Franco, the man who imprisoned his father in his labor camps. Now we are reading *The Great Hunger* by Cecil Woodham Smith. It is a detailed history of the Irish potato famine of the 1840s which caused the death of about a million peasants and was one of the major stimuli of the great Irish emigration to the United States. After hearing about poverty and hunger in Spain, now we hear an even more detailed account of the suffering of the Irish peasants during the last century.

Meanwhile, the papers keep us aware of the starvation of the people in North Africa. I don't think that any monk will have any illusions when he does a little bit of fasting. The simple meals here start looking and even tasting like luxurious banquets when you take in these hunger stories together with your food.

One of the characteristics that the psycho-historian Bob Lifton discerns in modern men and women is their historical dislocation. They miss that sense of continuity that is so important for a creative life-style. They find themselves part of a nonhistory in which only the sharp moment of the here and now is valuable.

I was thinking about this when I read an article called, "Quest for Identity: Americans go on a genealogy kick." It says: "Many young people of the 'now generation' of the 1960s who once voiced disinterest in a 'dead' past—are joining the rush to find out: 'What is my past? Who are my forbears? What were they like? What did they do?' . . . Libraries and archives with genealogical holdings report that business is on the increase. At the National Archives in Washington, D.C., written inquiries have climbed from about 3,000 a month in 1954 to about 4,000 per week this year. In addition, nearly 1,000 people each week come in person to search through a million cubic feet of records."[18]

Something seems to be changing and changing fast. The mood at university campuses this year is strikingly different from three years ago. Less activistic, more reflective, less avant-garde, more traditional, less concerned with the "latest," more with the "earliest," less restless, more sedate. Some people speak about a return to the fifties. Maybe so, but it is more than that. For those who have lived through the sixties, the seventies will necessarily be different from the fifties. But we are certainly searching for our roots. I sense it in myself. Here I am first reading John of the Ladder, Evagrius, Dorotheus, Diadochus—men who wrote their works between 350 and 650—and now I am immersed in Bernard of Clairvaux, William of St. Thierry, and Aelred of Rievaulx, three great personalities of the twelfth century.

I feel very close to them. I feel that these "old men" help me immensely in my search for myself and my God. They do much more than remind me that my problems are not new and original. They give me a new sense of self, deeply embedded in the tumultuous history of God's people. I am not very interested in my genealogy, but maybe what I am doing and what many young people are doing in the Washington Archives is not so different after all: We are searching for our roots. For those who have heard little, if anything, about God's entry into history through his son, Jesus Christ, the Washington Archives are a quite understandable place to start looking for an answer to the question, "What is my past and what does that tell me about myself here and now?"

Sunday, 28

What do you do when you are always comparing yourself with other people? What do you do when you always feel that the people you talk to, hear of, or read about are more intelligent, more skillful, more attractive, more gentle, more generous, more practical, or more contemplative than you are? What do you do when you can't get away from measuring yourself against others, always feeling that they are the real people while you are a nobody or even less than that?

It is obvious that these feelings are distorted, out of proportion, the result of projections, and very damaging for a healthy spiritual life, but still they are no less real and can creep up on you before you are aware of it. Before you know it you are comparing other people's age and accomplishments with your own, and before you know it you have entered into a very harmful psychological competition and rivalry.

I talked about this with John Eudes today. He helped me analyze it a little more. We talked about the vicious circle one enters when one has a low self-esteem or self-doubt and then perceives other people in such a way as to strengthen and confirm these feelings. It is the famous self-fulfilling prophecy all over again. I enter into relationships with some apprehension and fear and behave in such a way that whatever the others say or do, I experience them as stronger, better, more valuable persons, and myself as weaker, worse, and not worth talking to. After a while the relationship becomes intolerable, and I find an excuse to walk away feeling worse than when I started it. My general abstract feeling of worthlessness becomes concrete in a specific encounter, and there my false fears increase rather than decrease. So real peer relationships become difficult, if not impossible, and many of my emotions in relation to others reveal themselves as the passive-dependent sort.

What do you do? Analyze more? It is not hard to see the neurotic dynamism. But it is not easy to break through it to a mature life. There is much to say about this and much has been said by psychologists and psychotherapists. But what to say about it from a spiritual perspective?

John Eudes talked about that moment, that point, that spot that lies before the comparison, before the beginning of the vicious circle or the self-fulfilling prophecy. That is the moment, point, or place where meditation can enter in. It is the moment to stop reading, speaking, socializing, and to "waste" your time in meditation. When you find your mind competing again, you might plan an "empty time" of meditation, in this way interrupting the vicious circle of your ruminations and entering into the depth of your own soul. There you can be with him who was before you came, who loved you before you could love, and who has given you your own self before any comparison was possible. In meditation we can come to the affirmation that we are not created by other people but by God, that we are not judged by how we compare with others but how we fulfill the will of God.

This is not as easy as it sounds because it is in meditation itself that we become painfully aware how much we have already been victimized by our own competitive strivings and how much we have already sold our soul to the opinions of others. By not avoiding this realization, however, but by confronting it and by unmasking its illusory quality, we might be able to experience our own basic dependency and so dispel the false dependencies of our daily life.

The more I think about this, the more I realize how central the words of St. John are, words so central also in St. Bernard's thought: "Let us love God because God has loved us first."

Monday, 29

Many contrasting emotions entered my heart today. Between the pages filled with news about the impeachment procedures in Washington, the New York *Times* "Week in Review" mentioned the happy news that the Greek military dictatorship had come to an end after its failure to bring Cyprus under its power, and that the new premier, Caramanlis, had released all political prisoners. I keep thinking about the joy of those men and women who suffered so dreadfully in the Greek prisons and who are now suddenly free. I keep seeing people embracing each other with tears of joy on the streets of Athens. Who could have dreamed a week ago that this was possible? How I hope that this will happen in Chile, Paraguay, and Brazil as well!

But also sad news. The news bulletin of the Fellowship of Reconciliation mentions that four Buddhist monks were shot to death and ten wounded in Kien Thanh in the South Vietnamese district of Kien Giang when police teargassed and fired upon two hundred demonstrating monks. This happened on June 6. No news from the many Buddhists in prison.

All the monks in the Abbey signed a petition to President Nixon asking for immediate and drastic measures to alleviate the hunger in North Africa and to prevent full-scale starvation. The petition, organized by "Bread for the World," asks the President to share our resources with hungry people everywhere, urges an immediate increase in food aid, and stresses the importance of building a world food security system. It also says, "We are willing to eat less to feed the hungry." I am happy that we can at least make our voices heard in this way. Maybe fasting can receive new meaning again, just in a period when Church laws on fasting have practically vanished outside the monastery.

Tuesday, 30

Whether it is good or bad I do not know, but there is no doubt that solitude leads me to think often about my past. The silent rhythm of the monastic life makes me explore my memory. I am amazed how little I remember. What did I do, think and feel between the ages of six and twelve? Little fragments come to mind. A friendly brother in the first grade who told a story about missionaries in Africa, a severe teacher in the sixth grade who one day invited all his students to his home, classmates laughing at me because I was cross-eyed, my first communion, the beginning of the war and my parents crying, the death of my grandmother and her funeral, Indian games and cowboy fights—but except for these flashes of memories, large empty periods. What happened during my teen-age years? How many names of classmates in high school do I remember? Where are they now? I am amazed by the big gaps and long stretches of time that seem void of memorable events. What in heaven's name did I do during those long six years in the seminary. I worked hard, but did I learn much?

Did I really live my life or was it lived for me? Did I really make the decisions that led me to this place at this time, or was I simply carried along by the stream, by sad as well as happy events? I do not want to live it all again, but I would like to remember more, so that my own little history could be a book to reflect on and learn from. I don't believe that my life is a long row of randomly chained incidents and accidents of which I am not much more than a passive victim. No, I think that nothing is accidental but that God molded me through the events of my life and that I am called to recognize his molding hand and praise him in gratitude for the great things he has done to me.

I wonder if I really have listened carefully enough to the God of history, the God of my history, and have recognized him when he called me by my name, broke the bread, or asked me to cast out my nets after a fruitless day? Maybe I have been living much too fast, too restlessly, too feverishly, forgetting to pay attention to what is happening here and now, right under my nose. Just as a whole world of beauty can be discovered in one flower, so the great grace of God can be tasted in one small moment. Just as no great travels are necessary to see the beauty of creation, so no great ecstasies are needed to discover the love of God. But you have to be still and wait so that you can realize that God is not in the earthquake, the storm, or the lightning, but in the gentle breeze with which he touches your back.

The weather today was splendid. Sunny, clear, cool, fresh, and joyful. I went bird watching for a while with John Eudes. We got caught in thorn apple bushes and our shoes got terribly muddy from walking through a freshly plowed field. We saw some nice killdeer in flight.

This afternoon I worked in the creek and found more granite rocks than usual. The purple loosestrife colored the edges of the creek. On our way back, Father

Stephen pointed out to me the beautiful trees called sunburst locust. Within a few weeks they will "burst out" in yellow colors.

Wednesday, 31

Kevin's mother died. Kevin is a carpenter who lives with the Genesee Community. A few weeks ago he flew to Ireland to visit his mother who was fatally ill with diabetes. Last week he returned not knowing how long his mother could live.

The death of Kevin's mother brought back many memories of Donegal, the county where Kevin's family lives. I remember very vividly my hitchhike travels through the dark, melancholy hills of Northern Ireland. I wrote stories about the storytellers of Donegal in the Dutch newspapers and, while Kerry and Killarney left hardly any memories in my mind, Donegal I will never forget.

There was something somber but also profound and even holy about Donegal. The people were like the land. I still see vividly the simple funeral of a Donegal farmer. The priest and a few men carried the humble coffin to the cemetery. After the coffin was put in the grave, the men filled the grave with sand and covered it again with the patches of grass which had been laid aside. Two men stamped with their boots on the sod so that it was hardly possible to know that this was a grave. Then one of the men took two pieces of wood, bound them together in the form of a cross and stuck it in the ground. Everyone made a quick sign of the cross and left silently. No words, no solemnity, no decoration. Nothing of that. But it never has been made so clear to me that someone was dead, not asleep but dead, not passed away but dead, not laid to rest but dead, plain dead. When I saw those two men stamping on the ground in which they had buried their friend, I knew that for these farmers of Donegal there were no funeral-home games to play. But their realism became a transcendent realism by the simple unadorned wooden cross saying that where death is affirmed, hope finds its roots. "Unless a wheat grain falls on the ground and dies, it remains only a single grain; but if it dies, it yields a rich harvest" (Jn. 12:24).

The Mass we celebrated for Kevin's mother was simple and beautiful. Kevin came afterward to shake hands with the celebrant and concelebrants. All the way through the ceremony I saw the simple men of Donegal digging their grave and sticking their cross in the ground. "Margaret, may she dwell in the house of the Lord . . ."

3

August

NIXON AND ST. BERNARD

■

Friday, 2

THE EVENING PRAYERS called Compline (meaning: to make the day complete) form one of the most intimate moments of the monastic day. It is the moment during which all the monks are present, even those who sometimes have to be absent during other prayers, and during which you sense a real togetherness. The prayers are always the same. Therefore, nobody needs a book. Everyone can stand wherever he wants, and therefore no lights are necessary. All is quiet in the house. It is the beginning of what the monks call the great silence which lasts from 6:30 P.M. until 5:30 A.M.

Compline is such an intimate and prayerful moment that some people in the neighborhood come daily to the Abbey to join in this most quiet prayer of the day.

I start realizing that the psalms of Compline slowly become flesh in me; they become part of my night and lead me to a peaceful sleep.

> Ponder on your bed and be still:
> Make justice your sacrifice and trust in the Lord.
> I will lie down in peace and sleep comes at once
> for You alone, Lord, make me dwell in safety (Ps.4).

Trust is written all through the evening prayer:

> He who dwells in the shelter of the Most High
> and abides in the shade of the Almighty
> says to the Lord: "My refuge,
> my stronghold, my God in whom I trust!"

> It is he who will free you from the snare
> of the fowler who seeks to destroy you;
> he will conceal you with his pinions
> and under his wings you fill find refuge (Ps. 90).

Slowly these words enter into the center of my heart. They are more than ideas, images, comparisons: They become a real presence. After a day with much work or with many tensions, you feel that you can let go in safety and realize how good it is to dwell in the shelter of the Most High.

Many times I have thought: If I am ever sent to prison, if I am ever subjected to hunger, pain, torture, or humiliation, I hope and pray that they let me keep the psalms. The psalms will keep my spirit alive, the psalms will allow me to comfort others, the psalms will prove the most powerful, yes, the most revolutionary weapon against the oppressor and torturer. How happy are those who no longer need books but carry the psalms in their heart wherever they are and wherever they go. Maybe I should start learning the psalms by heart so that nobody can take them away from me. Just to be able to say over and over again:

> O men, how long will your hearts be closed, will
> you love what is futile and seek what is false?
>
> It is the Lord who grants favors to those whom he
> loves; the Lord hears me whenever I call him (Ps. 4).

That is a prayer that really can heal many wounds.

Yesterday they started to lay the foundations for the new church. Amazing how fast it all goes. What was a piece of flat ground is now opened up by deep trenches, and already concrete has been poured into the wooden forms. Monks were watching silently as the large machines did their work and young men shouted orders to each other. Building a shelter for the Most High.

This morning I kicked over a big pile of boxes with freshly washed raisins. It was a real mess. But nobody seemed upset. "That has happened before," Brother Theodore said. Then he turned on the machine and washed them again.

Monday, 5

Today I read *Living and Dying* by Robert Jay Lifton and Eric Olson. One theme hit me with new force. Speaking about the survivors of the Hiroshima atomic explosion, they write: "Among the survivors there quickly developed a profound kind of guilt. This guilt was related both to having remained alive while others (including loved ones and neighbors) died and to the inability to offer help to those who needed it. All of this became focused in a question that remained at the center of a life struggle for the survivors: 'Why did I remain alive when he, she, they died?' And this question itself sometimes became transformed into the haunting suspicion that one's own life had been purchased at the cost of the others who died: 'Some had to die; because they died I could live.' This suspicion led to a feeling among survivors that they did not deserve to be alive and that one could justly remain alive only by coming in some way to resemble the dead."[1] The great all-pervasive idea of the book is formulated in the statement: ". . . we are all survivors of this century's holocausts."

Although I had read this before, it struck me with new force because I started to wonder how far my preoccupation with those who suffer and die in prisons all over the world and my growing concern about the millions who starve in North Africa are tainted by this survivors' guilt? "Why them, why not me?" "Why the poor and not the prosperous?" Behind all of that lurks the question: "Is there a way to become part of their pain to justify my own being alive?"

I oiled a few thousand bread pans this morning. Noisy work but not too bad.

Tuesday, 6

Today: the great feast of the Transfiguration. A silent hermit day. After the simple liturgy in the chapter room everyone went his own way into the silence.

I read Merton's article on the Pasternak affair[2] and parts from Pasternak's *I Remember* and *Doctor Zhivago*. I am surprised to find a beautiful story about Psalm 90. It tells how Dr. Zhivago found the text of this psalm on the bodies of two soldiers, one a Red partisan, the other a White Russian volunteer: the first dead, the second wounded. Pasternak writes: "The text was believed to be miraculous and a protection against bullets. It has been worn as a talisman by soldiers in the latest imperialist war. Decades later prisoners were to sew it into their clothes and mutter its words in jail when they were summoned at night for interrogation."[3]

> You will not fear the terror of night
> nor the arrow that flies by day,
> nor the plague that prowls in the darkness
> nor the scourge that lays waste at noon (Ps. 90:5–6).

Russian soldiers prayed it, Red and White, monks pray it, black and white, I pray it—I'd better learn it by heart so that I don't need to sew it in my clothes and so that it can become ingrained in my innermost being.

The House Judiciary Committee voted (all Democrats [twenty-one] and seven Republicans) to recommend to the House of Representatives that President Nixon be impeached. It is the event that will dominate the news during the summer.

Wednesday, 7

During Sext, the short communal prayer before dinner, Brother Alberic came into the church making a gesture that caused about half of the monks to walk out of church as fast as they could. The others, myself included, stayed, not knowing what was going on. We finished our prayers and went to the dining hall to eat. During dinner the others returned and it became clear that the straw in the field had caught fire and that a few men were needed to extinguish it.

I spent the afternoon with Brother Henry at his beehives. This was my first encounter with the bees. Although I was well protected, one bee found its way into one of the legs of my pants. Well, he stung and died as a hero. A remarkable world. Now I am reading up on bees: Murray Hoyt's book, *The World of Bees*. There I found an example of American pragmatism that makes you cry. Based on the biblical expression of Israel as the "land flowing with milk and honey," Professor Mykola H. Haydak wanted to test whether this were the perfect diet combination. After two months on a diet of milk and honey, "his skin became dry, pimples marred his face and whitish round spots appeared on his tongue"— the obvious result of lack of vitamin C. "He added ten ounces of orange juice a day and all these symptoms disappeared." Hoyt remarks after describing the experiment: "So perhaps the 'land flowing with milk and honey' should be changed to 'a land flowing with milk and honey and ten ounces of orange juice.'"[4]

Friday, 9

When Christian writes a note to me or to anyone, he always marks a little cross on top of the page. This morning while I had my head deep in the tub of raisins, he came over to the bakery and handed me one of his notes. There was the little cross and under it: "Nixon resigned."

In the afternoon I drove to Rochester to see the dentist. The doctor had a T.V. set placed high up in a corner of his office so that his patients could watch it while he was watching their bad teeth. At noon they had seen the inauguration of the new President, Gerald Ford, half an hour after the Nixon family had left the White House. The picture of a patient watching the inauguration of the new President of the U.S.A. with open mouth in a dentist's chair stuck in my mind as quite appropriate for the occasion.

Saturday, 10

Worked with John Eudes and Brian in Salt Creek collecting stones. Brian drove the pickup truck right into the creek to load it up with stones. While he was driving the loaded truck out of the water with all four wheels engaged, the truck jumped so badly that half the load rolled out again and the old rusted fender nearly broke off. We reloaded the truck, pulled the thing out of the water, and came safely home in time for a shower before Vespers.

Sunday, 11

After my visit to Rochester, a passage from Merton's *Conjectures of a Guilty Bystander,* which John Eudes quoted in Chapter had a special meaning to me. It speaks about one of Merton's trips to Louisville: "In Louisville, at the corner of Fourth and Walnut, in the center of the shopping district, I was suddenly overwhelmed with the realization that I loved all those people, that they were mine and I theirs, that we could not be alien to one another even though we were total strangers . . . though 'out of the world' [monks] are in the same world as everybody else, the world of the bomb, the world of race hatred, the world of technology, the world of mass media, big business, revolution and all the rest. We take a different attitude to all these things, for we belong to God. Yet so does everybody else belong to God. We just happen to be conscious of it and make a profession out of this consciousness. But does that entitle us to consider ourselves different, or even *better,* than others? The whole idea is preposterous . . .

"I have the immense joy of being *man,* a member of a race in which God himself became incarnate. As if the sorrows and stupidities of the human condition could overwhelm me, now I realize what we all are. And if only everybody could realize this! But it cannot be explained. There is no way of telling people that they are all walking around shining like the sun.

"This changes nothing in the sense and value of my solitude, for it is in fact the function of solitude to make one realize such things with a clarity that would be impossible to anyone completely immersed in the other cares, the other illusions, and all the automatisms of a tightly collective existence. My solitude, however, is not my own, for I see how much it belongs to them—and that I have a responsibility for it in their regard, not just in my own. It is because I am one with them that I owe it to them to be alone, and when I am alone, they are not 'they' but my own self. There are no strangers!"[5]

Rochester is to Genesee what Louisville is to Gethsemani. Merton wrote this after more than fifteen years in the monastery. Still—after only nine weeks in the monastery—I had similar feelings when I was in Rochester. When I walked into a flower shop to buy some white and yellow chrysanthemums for friends in town I felt a deep love for the florist who, with a twinkle in his eye, told me that chrysanthemums were "year-round flowers," not bound to the seasons. I felt open, free and relaxed and really enjoyed the little conversation we had on flowers, presidents, and honesty in politics.

I am becoming more and more aware that solitude indeed makes you more sensitive to the good in people and even enables you to bring it to the foreground. No, "there is no way of telling people that they are all walking around shining like the sun" but God's glory in you can bring out God's glory in the other when you have become more conscious of this shared gift. God speaks to God, Spirit to Spirit, Love to Love. It is all a gift, it is all grace.

Monday, 12

I told John Eudes today that I felt that the past week had been somewhat "bourgeois." My mind had been focused more on the news than on other things, and

I had settled in a somewhat comfortable pattern of living which, as far as its spiritual content is concerned, is not so different from my previous life. I said that I felt the temptation to make the monastic life a comfortable, settled existence without much challenge and that I realized that this, in fact, meant that religion then is just a commodity and no longer a spiritual adventure.

John Eudes laughed a little and said that it showed on the one hand that I had started to feel at home and that is a good thing, but on the other hand that indeed there was "work" to be done. The he said, "But don't worry. It won't last long this way. This is the time in which meditation becomes very important; this is an invitation to enter deeper into prayer. Otherwise, you will start complaining within a few weeks that the monastery is not severe enough, not poor enough, not strict enough, and you, as many others before, will leave and start a life which, in fact, is much less poor and less severe."

Speaking about prayer, I asked John Eudes a question that seemed very basic and a little naïve: "When I pray, to whom do I pray?" "When I say 'Lord,' what do I mean?"

John Eudes responded very differently than I expected. He said, "This is the real question, this is the most important question you can raise; at least this is the question that you can make your most important question." He stressed with great and convincing emphasis that if I really wanted to take that question seriously, I should realize that there would be little room left for other things. "Except," he said smiling, "when the question exhausts you so much that you need to read *Newsweek* for a little relaxation!" "It is far from easy," John Eudes said, "to make that question the center of your meditation. You will discover that it involves every part of yourself because the question, Who is the Lord to whom I pray? leads directly to the question, Who am I who wants to pray to the Lord? And then you will soon wonder, Why is the Lord of justice also the Lord of love; the God of fear also the God of gentle compassion? This leads you to the center of meditation. Is there an answer? Yes and no. You will find out in your meditation. You might some day have a flash of understanding even while the question still remains and pulls you closer to God. But it is not a question that can be simply one of your questions. In a way, it needs to be your only question around which all that you do finds its place. It requires a certain decision to make that question the center of your meditation. If you do so, you will realize that you are embarking on a long road, a very long road."

Tuesday, 13

This morning Father John explained to me that the killdeer is a bird that fools you by simulating injury to pull your attention away from her eggs which she lays openly on a sandy place. Beautiful! Neurosis as weapon! How often I have asked pity for a very unreal problem in order to pull people's attention away from what I didn't want them to see.

Sometimes it seems that every bird has institutionalized one of my defense mechanisms. The cowbird lays her eggs in some other bird's nest to let them do the brooding job; the Baltimore oriole imitates the sounds of more dangerous birds to keep the enemies away, and the red-wing blackbird keeps screaming so loudly overhead that you get tired of her noise and soon leave the area that she considers hers. It does not take long to realize that I do all of that and a lot more to protect myself or to get my own will done.

Thursday, 15

The feast of Our Lady's Assumption is an important feast for monks because under this title Mary is the patroness of all the monks. I didn't understand this well enough when I came here, but the longer I am here, the more I realize that Mary is for the monks the most pure contemplative. Luke describes her as contemplating the mysteries of the redemption. After telling about the visit of the shepherds to the Child, he writes: "As for Mary, she treasured all these things and pondered them in her heart" (Lk. 2:19), and after describing how she found Jesus in the temple among the doctors of law, he adds: "His mother stored up all these things in her heart." She is the contemplative of whom the aged Simeon says that a sword will pierce her soul (Lk. 2:35).

The doctrine of her Assumption affirms the fulfillment of this contemplative life in heaven. There the most redeemed human being, the woman in whom God touched us in the most intimate way, the mother of Jesus and all who believe in him—there she stands in the presence of God, enjoying forever the beatific vision that is the hope of all monks and all Christians.

Brother James entered the novitiate today, after six months of postulancy. He is one of those exceptional people who seem transparent in their openness, simplicity, and prayerfulness. A hard-working, honest, straightforward farmer "incapable of deceit" (Jn. 1:47). When the ceremony was supposed to start, he was the only one who had not arrived yet. The novice master went out looking for him and when he was found and in his seat, the abbot said dryly, "Since we are all here, I guess we can start."

It is an honor to be around a man like James. He teaches me more about single-minded commitment than many books. He read the Magnificat and other texts relating to Mary as "his texts" and when he came to the words: "the Almighty has done great things to me," he looked up from his little piece of paper and straight in his brothers' faces. It was a moving moment. Now he is all white. He walks in his new habit with the same somewhat dragging gait as he did in his old one, but something new has happened to him, and he knows it.

Friday, 16

"If I see three oranges, I have to juggle. And if I see two towers, I have to walk." These remarkable words were spoken by the tightrope-walker, Philippe Petit, in answer to the question of the police as to why he had walked (at 7:50 A.M.) on a rope shot with a crossbow from one tower of the New York World Trade Center to the other. When Philippe had seen the two spires of the Notre Dame in Paris, he had done the same. *"L'Art pour l'Art"* is this highwire artist's philosophy.

I have been thinking today, off and on, about this beautiful man Philippe Petit. His answer to the police is priceless and deserves long meditation. We always want answers to impossible questions. Why do you love her? Any answer to such a question is usually ridiculous. Because she is beautiful? Because she is intelligent? Because she has a funny pimple on her nose? Nothing makes much sense. Why did you become a priest? Because you love God? Because you like to preach? Because you don't like women? Why did you become a monk? Because you like to pray? Because you like silence? Because you like to bake bread without being bothered? There are no answers to those questions.

When they asked Philippe Petit why he wanted to walk on a slender wire strung between the two tallest towers of New York City, everyone thought he did it for money, for publicity, for fame. But he said, "If I see three oranges, I have to juggle. And if I see two towers, I have to walk."

We don't believe the most meaningful answer. We think that this man must be insane. In fact, they took Philippe to a city hospital for psychiatric examination but soon found out that Philippe was as healthy as could be. "Sane and ebullient," says the newspaper.

His is the true answer. Why do you love her? When I saw her, I loved her. Why are you a priest? Because I must be a priest. Why do you pray? Because when I see God, I must pray. There is an inner must, an inner urge, or inner call that answers all those questions which are beyond explanation. Never does anyone who asks a monk why he became a monk receive a satisfying answer. Nor do children give us an explanation when we ask them, "Why do you play ball?" They know that there is no answer except, "When I see a ball, I have to play with it."

The police who arrested Philippe Petit seemed to understand this because they dropped the original charge of trespassing and disorderly conduct in exchange for Philippe's promise to perform his aerial feats for the children in Central Park. That at least brought some real humanity back into the picture. Meanwhile, I keep saying to myself, "If I see three oranges, I have to juggle. And if I see two towers, I have to walk."

Saturday, 17

After a series of dry, sunny days, the rain poured down this morning with much vehemence and noise. It was a special sensation to walk through this low-built, barracklike monastery and see and hear the water on all sides while remaining dry and comfortable. Many people in this country and elsewhere in this world are waiting for it. Here it has been coming at regular intervals and has brought about a very good wheat harvest.

In the afternoon John Eudes, Brian, Robert—a new observer—and I went to the creek to collect more stones. From the flat wagon drawn by the tractor, the land looked very beautiful. A mysterious veil covered the fields just harvested, and the gentle hills of New York State seemed grateful for the moist air and showed themselves in a new beauty. I felt happy and grateful and kept thinking an old thought: I wished that all my friends whom I love so much could see and feel what I can see and feel today. But I know they never will. On this earth the experience of great beauty always remains mysteriously linked with the experience of great loneliness. This reminds me again that there still is a beauty I have not seen yet: the beauty that does not create loneliness but unity.

Theodore found a little piece of metal between the thousands of raisins he pushed through the raisin washing machine. He showed it to me. It looked as sharp as a razor blade. Well, someone eating his raisin bread is saved from a bleeding stomach, thanks to Theodore, who will never hear a grateful word for it. That is the drawback of preventive medicine.

Sunday, 18

Liturgically this was quite a violent Sunday. During Vigils, the communal night prayer at 2:30 A.M., we heard the word of Yahweh through his prophet Joel:

> Proclaim this among the nations,
> "Prepare for war!
> Muster the champions!
> Warriors, advance,
> quick march!
> Hammer your plowshares into swords,
> your sickles into spears,
> let the weakling say, 'I am a fighting man!'"
> (Jl. 4:9–10)

During Mass we first heard how Jeremiah was thrown by his enemies into a cistern. "There was no water in the well, only mud, and into the mud Jeremiah sank" (Jer. 38:6). Then the writer of the letter to the Hebrews says: "Think of the way he [Christ] stood such opposition from sinners and then you will not give up for want of courage" (Heb. 12:4). Finally, we heard the words of Jesus: "Do you suppose that I am here to bring peace on earth? No, I tell you, but rather division" (Lk. 12:51).

This is a side of the Bible I tend to forget. But the Bible is a realistic book and does not avoid any part of human reality. It speaks about the life, thoughts, and history of men and women from the perspective of the God of history. It is good to be reminded of this realism. God is not only where it is peaceful and quiet but also where there is persecution, struggle, division, and conflict. God, indeed, did not promise us a rose garden.

Monday, 19

The news in the New York *Times,* the letters from India posted on the bulletin board and the increasing requests for money, food, and clothes give me more and more the feeling that I belong to the happy few allowed into the Ark of Noah. The comparison does not work too well with all these celibates, but I keep thinking about sitting on the top of a mountain while the world around me is washed away. While we have a very abundant wheat crop, the papers speak about floods in India washing away whole crops and about droughts in North Africa and parts of the U.S.A. creating endless misery there and inflation here. While we have healthy, strong-looking men here, the pictures show emaciated people floating nowhere on self-made rafts. While we have peace and an atmosphere of trust here, in Cyprus, Greece, Chile, Brazil, the Middle East, South Korea, etc. hostilities break out everyday. Still I often feel homesick for the world with its pains and problems.

Sometimes the mentioning of a prayer intention becomes like a news service. Father Marcellus said during Vespers, "Let us pray for the wife of the President of South Korea"—then he realized that nobody except he had read the latest newspaper, and quickly added—"who was assassinated"—then it probably flashed through his mind that nobody could understand why anyone would want to assassinate the wife of the President of South Korea, so he added—"while someone was trying to assassinate the President himself"—then he realized that by now the monks wanted to know the end of the story, so he concluded his intention with the words—"who safely escaped."

That is what happens when you are librarian and read the paper first!

Tuesday, 20

Feast of St. Bernard. The liturgy was filled with gentle, sometimes sweet, compliments to this great saint of the twelfth century. During the night Office, one of his sermons was read. Simplicity, soberness, and austerity were Bernard's ideals. He practiced them too, but his language is wealthy, decorative, ornate, playful, and nearly baroque. His sermons on the Song of Songs belong to the classics of world literature but certainly not because of their sobriety!

Brian celebrated his feast day. I didn't understand. First, I thought that Brian was the name of an Irish Saint. Wrong. There simply is no Saint Brian. Only a famous King Brian. Dom James Fox, who was abbot of Gethsemani when Brian entered there, told him that "Brian" was Gaelic for "Bernard," that he was to be called "Brian," and that his feast day would be that of St. Bernard, August 20. Well, Brian obeyed and that was that. Today the monks prayed especially for their brother Brian.

Wednesday, 21

Yesterday I stumbled over a book, which made me feel that God had put it in my way so that I would pick it up and read it. The book is called *A Passion for Truth*. It is the last book by Abraham Joshua Heschel, which he delivered to his publisher a few weeks before his death.

When I read Heschel, I often have the same feeling of being "at home" as when I read Thomas Merton. Both seem to speak a language that has an easiness and obviousness which I miss with other spiritual writers. They both seem to speak directly to me and very little, if any, "translation" seems necessary.

During the last weeks I have become increasingly aware that my diary shows a strong contrast between notes on the joy of God's presence, the silence and quietude of the monastery, the love of the monks, the beauty of nature, and notes on hunger in Africa and India, torture in Chile, Brazil, Vietnam, wars everywhere, and the general state of misery of the world. It almost seems as if there were two persons in me experiencing life quite differently, praying differently, and listening differently. I started to wonder how they both could live together in peace.

In the introduction to his book *A Passion for Truth*, Heschel explains why he had to write this book. He tells how two figures played a great role in his youth and continuing spiritual life: The Baal Shem Tov and Reb Menahem Mendl of Kotzk, both representing a real part of himself. The Baal Shem Tov, the father of Hassidism, represented his experience of peace, joy, beauty, while Menahem Mendl represented anxiety, restless search, austere denial of self. Heschel writes: ". . . I realized that in being guided by both the Baal Shem Tov and the Kotzker [Menahem Mendl], I had allowed two forces to carry on a struggle within me. . . . In a very strange way, I found my soul at home with the Baal Shem but driven by the Kotzker. Was it good to live with one's heart torn between the joy of Mezbizh [the Baal Shem Tov] and the anxiety of Kotzk?. . . I had no choice; my heart was in Mezbizh, my mind in Kotzk. I was taught about the inexhaustible mines of meaning by the Baal Shem; from the Kotzker I learned to detect immense mountains of absurdity standing in the way. . . . The one reminded me that there could be a Heaven on earth, the other shocked me into discovering Hell in the alleged Heavenly places in our world. . . . The Baal Shem dwelled in my life like a lamp, while the Kotzker struck like lightning. To be sure, lightning is more authentic. Yet one can trust a lamp, put confidence in it; one can live in peace with a lamp. The Baal Shem gave me wings; the Kotzker encircled me with chains. I never had the courage to break the chains and entered into joys with my shortcomings in mind. I owe intoxication to the Baal Shem, to the Kotzker the blessings of humiliation."[6]

It says it all. So powerful and clear. Just to see these tensions expressed by Heschel gives me a great sense of being accepted.

I saw two monks having a lively discussion in sign language. Their rapid hand and arm movements made it quite a scene to see. Just when I was wondering what they were talking about, I recognized the signs saying, "Let's go into that room there so we can talk about it." Sign language obviously has its limits.

Thursday, 22

Brother Alexis, the bookkeeper, induced me to buy a stapler with ball-point pen and ruler under one plastic cover, all for $.96! I didn't really need any of it, but he made me feel that without it something would go wrong in my life. Brother Alexis is a great salesman, and since I am the only real buyer in this place, he practices his skills on me.

He has a sharp eye for "good buys" and saves all the ads announcing special sales with reduced prices. Then when the time is ripe, he has someone run to the stores to buy enormous quantities of it, probably leaving the store owner under the impression that his article is very popular and that he made a mistake by reducing the price. But in a place like this anything gets used some day, some week, some year, by someone. The Trappist order certainly won't collapse from a lack of Scotch tape and ball-point pens. Brother Alexis has hundreds of feet of the one and an endless amount of the other.

I have a stapler now and it works as long as you don't expect miracles of it. When you want to staple more than five pages together at once, it will probably develop a fatal illness and collapse with a squeak. But what greedy man wants to staple more than five pages together?

Friday, 23

I got trapped today by the new Encyclopedia Britannica. This is the fifteenth edition of the E.B.—the 1974 edition. It had just arrived in the library and a note on the bulletin board had invited us to take a look at this newcomer. I just wanted to have a quick look and ended up staying two hours playing with the thirty volumes. It is indeed a sort of game.

I looked up "Christ" in the Micropaedia. It said: "See Jesus of Nazareth." God became a name among other names. In this context, Jesuits come earlier than Jesus of Nazareth!

Saturday, 24

While pressing what seemed to me about two hundred bed sheets, my fellow worker told me about his decision to enter the monastery.

Coming from an Oriental family with very close family ties, his desire to go to a Christian monastery not only was not supported but was criticized and never understood. "I never could explain it to them," he said with a certain sadness. "When I told them that I would never come home again, not even on the day of my parents' funeral, they just couldn't accept it." It must have been a great struggle. His deep family loyalty made him feel like his parents and brothers, but at the same time, the monastery kept calling him, nearly against his own desire. "I delayed for five years," he said. "When I prayed, I said, 'Tomorrow, Lord, tomorrow, not today, not yet.'" Finally he went.

When his father died, he did not go home and every year when his mother came to the monastery, she came to take him with her. Now seventy-five years old, she has accepted the fact that her son will not return to the family. She accepts it but still doesn't understand. There is only one consolation for her. When she dies, her son will come to the funeral. A change in rules has made this possible. The Orientals feel that whoever the Christian God is, he cannot be a good God if he does not want children to bury their parents. Today it seems that the Trappists feel the same.

Sunday, 25

If there is any good way to get rid of the desire to become famous, it is by reading the book *Return to Earth* by the astronaut Buzz Aldrin. The book arrived two days ago and I find it very telling. The book doesn't speak much about the moon trip, but talks mostly about the life of the Aldrin family after the trip was over. I remember watching Aldrin on T.V. in Chile as he set foot on the moon. Some Chileans in the poor section of town were afraid that something terrible would happen when the astronauts stepped on the moon. They considered it a sacrilegious act. Well, something terrible happened—not what some Chileans expected, but the growing unhappiness of the man who touched the moon. I have to read more.

Monday, 26

Talked with John Eudes about obedience. I said, "I don't think I ever could become a monk because of my problem with obedience. If you or anyone else told me to go collect stones every day while I was deeply convinced that I should write, read, study, or whatever, I would not be able to take it and would become so restless and hostile that I would leave sooner or later."

He said, "The reasons you give not only would make you a poor monk but also a poor diocesan priest. Your problem is not that specific for monks. If you cannot be detached from all you do and like to do, you cannot live a full spiritual life."

So we talked about obedience. It was helpful because John Eudes made me see that the problem of obedience is a problem of intimacy. "Obedience becomes hard when you have to be vulnerable to the other who has authority. You can play the obedience game in such a way that you never disobey any rule while keeping from your guide and director, your abbot or superior those things about which you do not want to hear a 'no.' You need a lot of trust to give yourself fully to someone else, certainly to someone to whom you owe obedience. Many people adapt very quickly but are not really obedient. They simply don't want to make waves and instead go along with the trend. That is not obedience. That is just adaptation."

If I were able to trust more, to open myself more easily, to be more vulnerable, then obedience would not be so hard. I would be able to disagree without fear of rejection, to protest without resentment, to express different viewpoints without self-righteousness, and to say after all arguments: "If I am still asked to do something I do not like to do, perhaps I must be open to the idea of God's preparing me for something greater and more important than I can imagine."

With that attitude, life in obedience indeed can be quite exciting since you never really know what is next. But I have a long way to go to develop that attitude in my innermost self.

Wednesday, 28

My dreams are getting wilder and wilder. Last night I dreamed that I was sitting on a bench covered by a soft mattress that was attached to the outside railing of the Golden Gate Bridge in San Francisco. The bench moved gently from one side of the bay to the other, giving me a fantastic view of the water underneath with ocean liners and sailboats and of the clear sky above me with little sheeplike clouds. Slowly I moved toward the city which was beautifully white with impressive clean buildings and high skyscrapers.

My friends, Don and Claude, welcomed me when I arrived at the city and took me to a big hotel where we went to the bar and had a most pleasant conversation with the bartender. In fact, he liked us so much that he showed us the parts of the hotel reserved for those with special club membership. He had the keys of all the doors and showed us the different luxurious meeting rooms. As we walked around, I saw a group of well-dressed men leaving for another location with wall-to-wall carpeting and lounge chairs.

When the bartender led us back to the lounge of the hotel, I noticed a group of Trappist priests in their white habits and black scapulars. They told me that they were going to say mass for the different key clubs. I was very angry with this religious support of elitist segregation and discrimination but did not protest and just left with Don and Claude.

Quite a revealing dream, I thought. While during the day I try to be in the world without being of it, during the night I am fully of it without really being in it.

Thursday, 29

At times, writing becomes a real event. During the last few days I have been worrying about how to write on the prayer of the heart. I reread different books on the prayer tradition of the desert fathers and went over the excerpts I had made earlier, but I still felt uneasy, not really ready to write. Today I simply decided to start and see what would happen. After the second sentence, it seemed as if my pen pulled me into a totally different direction than I had expected, and while I wrote one page after another, I realized that my concentration on the desert fathers had kept me from thinking and writing about more important things which fit much better into the totality of the book I am trying to write.

It was a remarkable sensation to see ideas and words flowing so easily, as if they had always been there but had not been allowed expression.

Meanwhile, I become more and more aware that for me writing is a very powerful way of concentrating and of clarifying for myself many thoughts and feelings. Once I put my pen on paper and write for an hour or two, a real sense of peace and harmony comes to me. Consequently, I feel much more willing and able to do little routine jobs. After a day without any writing and filled with only reading and manual work, I often have a general feeling of mental constipation and go to bed with the sense that I did not do what I should have done that day.

It is good to become aware of all this. This seems to help me to understand quite a few of my bad moods in New Haven during the past few years.

Friday, 30

This was one of those days that pass with many distractions and few real events. I washed raisins for more than four hours without even finishing the whole job, received a lot of mail that needed immediate attention, talked for a few hours with one of the guests who asked for some help in his life. Finally, I read that depressing weekly, *U.S. News and World Report*, which is obviously written for businessmen and not for monks.

In fact, this was a "typical" day when I think about my life before I came here. Busy, active, talkative, but very superficial and without much concentration on anything. It seems good to avoid more of such "typical days."

Saturday, 31

Writing about prayer is often very painful since it makes you so aware of how far away you are from the ideal you write about. People who read your ideas tend to think that your writings reflect your life. The only advantage of that is that your readers become your counselors and guides. They invite you and challenge you to live up to your own thoughts and insights.

This week all I am reading and writing about is prayer. I am so busy with it and often so excited about it that I have no time left to pray, and when I pray, I feel more drawn to my ideas on prayer than to praying.

While it is true that in order to pray you have to empty your heart and mind for God, you also have to empty your heart and mind of your feelings and ideas on prayer. Otherwise, prayer gets in the way of praying.

I have a strong feeling that my intellectual formation is just as much a hindrance as a help to prayer. It is hard not to desire good insights during prayer and not to fall into a long inner discussion with myself. Every time some kind of insight comes to me, I find myself wondering how I can use it in a lecture, a sermon, or an article, and very soon I am far away from God and all wrapped up in my own preoccupations. Maybe this is what makes the Jesus Prayer so good for me. Simply saying, "Lord Jesus Christ, have mercy on me" a hundred times, a thousand times, ten thousand times, as the Russian peasant did, might slowly clean my mind and give God a little chance.

4

September

PRAY FOR THE WORLD

∎

Sunday, 1

TODAY STARTS my fourth month here. The idea that there are only four months left makes me apprehensive. Where will I be when Christmas comes around? But why ask such questions? "There is no need to worry," says St. Paul, "but if there is anything you need, pray for it, asking God for it with prayer and thanksgiving, and that peace of God, which is so much greater than we can understand, will guard your hearts and your thoughts in Christ Jesus" (Ph. 4:6–7). That must be enough for me.

Yesterday I received a letter asking for an article on the Holy Spirit. I answered that it seems better not to accept the invitation so that I might keep as faithful as possible to my retreat plans. But this morning, during my meditation, I found myself wondering what I could have written, and I got very involved in all kinds of "exciting" ideas on the Holy Spirit. When I woke up from my mental wandering, I said to myself, "Don't let yourself get distracted by thoughts about the Holy Spirit, but pray!" Then I had to laugh at the realization that the Holy Spirit got in his own way. How complicated can you get! But filling your mind with ideas about an article on the Holy Spirit is quite different from emptying your mind so that the Holy Spirit can pray in you. It is a difference as great as that between speaking about God and speaking with him. It seems to me that all asceticism starts with the recognition of this difference and becomes a real task when you want to *live* its implications. It is hard but not depressing, difficult but challenging as well.

Father Stephen celebrated his fiftieth birthday today. An intention during Vespers offered the information. I had never realized that he was older than I. Monks look young and Father Stephen even youthful. But like all of us, he too is aging.

His great zeal in collecting stones fills me with a growing admiration for him. He really makes a vocation out of that job. When he goes out with his men to collect stones he means business. To be "a rolling stone" at this age is quite an accomplishment!

Monday, 2

In meditation today I read: ". . . prayer must be sought with no scant effort: then God, seeing our travail, will give us what we seek. True prayer will not be achieved by human efforts: it is a gift of God. Seek and you will find."[1] ". . . one must remember that success in any aspect of the spiritual life is the fruit of the grace of God. Spiritual life comes entirely from his most holy Spirit. We have our own spirit but it is void of power. It begins to gain strength only when the grace of God flows into it."[2]

I wonder if depression in the spiritual life does not mean that we have forgotten that prayer is grace. The deep realization that all the fruits of the spiritual life are gifts of God should make us smile, and liberate us from any deadly seriousness. We can close our eyes as tightly as we can and clasp our hands as firmly as possible, but God speaks only when he wants to speak. When we realize this our pressing, pushing, and pulling become quite amusing. Sometimes we act like a child that closes his eyes and thinks that he can make the world go away.

After having done everything to make some space for God, it is still God who comes on his own initiative. But we have a promise upon which to base our hope: The promise of his love. So our life can rightly be a waiting in expectation, but waiting patiently and with a smile. Then, indeed, we shall be really surprised and full of joy and gratitude when he comes.

Today I received a message saying that next Monday morning I have to appear at the Immigration and Naturalization office in Connecticut to obtain permanent residence in the U.S.A. That will take me away from here for a day and home for a night.

Wednesday, 4

After three months of manual work, I am realizing that I do not really enjoy it. When the novelty of it is gone, it becomes very boring. Packing bread, taking hot bread from the conveyor belt, washing raisins, pressing sheets, or collecting stones are all good jobs for one or two afternoons, but after three months my main question during work becomes: "When is this over?" The only thing that can take some of the dullness away is a good-natured co-worker.

I told all this to John Eudes because I felt it was important to wonder how I could make my work more a part of my prayer and not just an occasion to fret. John Eudes could well understand my feelings. To my amazement he said that many, in fact most, monks, especially the older ones, really enjoyed their work and did not feel as I do. I had been wondering about that. John Eudes showed me that this type of work gives me a good occasion to feel deeply my unrelatedness. In other situations I have intellectual defenses and strong repressions which prevent me from really feeling fully my unrelatedness. When I study, write, or lecture, I can make things interesting by manipulating them in certain ways. But in the bakery or in the creek, it is practically impossible to make things interesting. Then I am faced with "just a job to do" and nothing else and then I discover my deep alienation. If I really felt related to my world, really a part of it, I would not complain about dullness and boredom.

Uninteresting work confronts a monk with his unrelatedness, and it is in this confrontation that prayer can develop. If the experience of unrelatedness does not lead to prayer, it may lead a monk out of the monastery. In prayer I can enter into contact with the God who created me and all things out of love. In prayer I can find a new sense of belonging since it is there that I am most related.

Manual work indeed unmasks my illusions. It shows how I am constantly looking for interesting, exciting, distracting activities to keep my mind busy and away from the confrontation with my nakedness, powerlessness, mortality, and weakness. Dull work at least opens up my basic defenselessness and makes me more vulnerable. I hope and pray that this new vulnerability will not make me fearful or angry, but instead, open to the gifts of God's grace.

Thursday, 5

To become a permanent resident of the U.S.A., I have to prove that I am not a communist and that I have no syphilis. For the first, I have to be interviewed; for the second, my blood has to be analyzed.

This afternoon I was in Batavia, the nearest town of any importance, for the blood test. Everyone was pleasant, friendly, and very co-operative. Tomorrow I have to return for the results at the county building where my blood is being given the Wassermann test. It was a refreshing ride. I picked up two teen-age hitchhikers on their way home from football practice. "School starts tomorrow," they said. It is strange to hear people talk about going back to school while for me it is still four months away. I can't remember one semester since I was six years old when I was not in school as student or teacher. This will be my first real schooltime when school will mean *schola:* "free time."

Saturday, 7

In the afternoon, I had to drive the backhoe. I learned how to raise and lower the large bucket and how to scoop with it. When I drove the big machine back to the garage, I did not realize that its boom was too high to pass under the garage door which had not been raised all the way up. Suddenly I heard a loud cracking noise and when I turned around, I saw that I had given the lower part of the garage door much more than a bruise.

Brother Michael saw it all happening. As always, he kept smiling and said that this reminded him of the text of Revelations: "The tail of the dragon swept the stars from the heavens." With a twinkle in his eye he added, "Events like this always help me to remember the Bible better." With that consolation I went home and forgot about it quickly.

Tomorrow back to Connecticut to become a permanent resident in the U.S.A.

Monday, 9

At four o'clock I was back "home" in the Abbey. Friendly greetings met me from all sides. John Eudes came by and said, "Welcome home" and Brother Anthony wrote, "Good to have you back." I had been gone for twenty-six hours! It felt good to be missed, even for a few hours.

I am totally exhausted. Have a headache, toothache, I'm hungry, sleepy, and in a general state of disorder. But sleep and food will probably cure me soon. It is good to be back, and I am very happy to have more than three months left to be here.

Wednesday, 11

The short trip to New Haven has given me a very distinct feeling of starting the second half of my stay. Returning to the monastery truly felt like returning home. I realize how comfortable I feel here. I know the monks—and not only by name—I know the style of life, I know my way around, not only the house but also around the rules. The monks seem to feel at ease with me and consider me part of their life. All that sounds fine, but it is a real temptation, too. Somewhere I realize that the cozy feelings are not necessarily good for my spiritual life and that it will take a new conscious effort to keep my eyes on God and avoid settling comfortably in this house. I can collect around me many interesting and entertaining little activities, and slowly fill up all the empty space that the monastery offers me for being alone with God. Writing about prayer can become an excuse for not praying, responding to the different interests of the monks can become a reason for not really being alone. It will require special effort in the coming months to realize the fact that this is not my permanent home and never will be, even if I should stay for life.

In Abraham Heschel's *A Passion for Truth* I read today the words of the Kotzker (Rabbi Menahem Mendl of Kotzk): "He who thinks that he has finished *is* finished."[3] How true. Those who think that they have arrived, have lost their way. Those who think they have reached their goal, have missed it. Those who think they are saints, are demons. An important part of the spiritual life is to keep longing, waiting, hoping, expecting. In the long run, some voluntary penance becomes necessary to help us remember that we are not yet fulfilled. A good criticism, a frustrating day, an empty stomach, or tired eyes might help to re-awaken our expectation and deepen our prayer: Come, Lord Jesus, come.

Thursday, 12

Silence. Indeed, silence is very important for me. During the last week, with a trip to New Haven full of discussions and verbal exchanges, with many seemingly necessary telephone conversations, and with quite a few talks with the monks, silence became less and less a part of my life. With the diminishing silence, a sense of inner contamination developed. In the beginning, I didn't know why I felt somewhat dirty, dusty, impure, but it dawned on me that the lack of silence might have been the main cause.

I am becoming aware that with words ambiguous feelings enter into my life. It almost seems as if it is impossible to speak and not sin. Even in the most elevated discussion, something enters that seems to pollute the atmosphere. In some strange way, speaking makes me less alert, less open, and more self-centered. After my discussion with students in New Haven last Sunday, I not only felt tired and strained, but I felt as if I had touched something that should not be touched, as if I had distorted something simply by talking about it, as if I had tried to grasp a dew drop. Afterward I felt restless and could not sleep.

St. James really does not exaggerate when he writes: "Among all the parts of the body, the tongue is a whole wicked world in itself; it infects the whole body; catching fire itself from hell, it sets fire to the whole wheel of creation. Wild animals and birds, reptiles and fish can all be tamed by man, and often are; but nobody can tame the tongue . . ." (Jm. 3:6–7).

St. Benedict is very clear about the importance of silence. He feels that silence is better than speaking about good things. He seems to imply that it is practically impossible to speak about good things without being touched by the evil ones too, just as it is virtually impossible to eat meat without killing. He writes: ". . . on account of the seriousness of silence, let permission to speak seldom be given even to perfect disciples, though it be for good and holy and edifying talk, for it is written: 'In much speaking thou shalt not avoid sin' (Prov. 10:19); and elsewhere: 'Death and life are in the power of the tongue' (Prov. 18:21). For it is becoming to the master to speak and to teach: to the disciple to be silent and to listen."[4] Silence needs to become a real part of my life when I return to school. "In much speaking thou shalt not avoid sin." Many people ask me to speak, but nobody as yet has invited me for silence. Still, I realize that the more I speak, the more I will need silence to remain faithful to what I say. People expect too much from speaking, too little from silence. . . .

Friday, 13

Talked with John Eudes. My main concern is related to my awareness that three and a half months from now I will be gone from here. I wonder about the influence of this retreat on my future life. One desire is clear: to have a continuing contact with this community and its abbot. While I feel a great admiration, respect, and gratitude toward my fellow priests in Holland, they are too far away to fulfill my more intimate spiritual needs.

John Eudes considered my desire understandable, realistic, and meaningful and suggested that in the coming months I develop some ideas about my future life-style. What struck me most was his opinion that once I had made concrete decisions about prayer, availability, hours of rising and going to bed, and lived accordingly, my friends and students would support me and help me live this way. I would soon discover that those who are attracted to that life-style would want to join in it. In other words: A clear, visible, and well-defined life-style would give me a way of relating better to people and offer a criterion for my judgments in developing more or less intimate relationships.

John Eudes mentioned two possible points of concentration: the "Liturgy of the Hours" and meditation, and two possible times: early in the morning and before going to bed. He felt that recurring days of retreat would be really fruitful only when there was a daily discipline. Without a continuing rhythm of prayer, occasional or regular days of retreat would lose their connection with the rest of life.

We also discussed the importance of a better integration between prayer and work. Lecturing, preaching, writing, studying, and counseling, all these would be nurtured and deepened by a regular prayer life. John Eudes told me that Merton only wrote during "work hours" but had no problems finding ideas and subjects since it all seemed to flow easily from his prayer. He had two monks who worked for him as secretaries. One day they complained that together they could hardly keep up with Merton's daily output. But Merton himself did not feel he was forcing himself. What he wrote came easily and was part of his contemplative life. This is a "telling" story, and it holds important suggestions for me.

It seems crucial that I make clear-cut, concrete decisions and stick to them for a prolonged period. Then I should evaluate the experience with my director, make changes, try it again for a certain time, evaluate again, etc., until I have found a more or less permanent life-style, always open to changes but with a great deal of continuity. Both flexibility and continuity seem to be important aspects for a spiritual life-style in an active profession.

Theodore found a button among the raisins this morning. When he showed me the button, I thought of a poor Chicano who had been picking grapes in the hot sun of California and lost his button while carrying a full box to the truck. Today his button showed up in the raisin washing machine of a Trappist monastery. How good it would have been to be able to return the button with a big box of raisin bread for him and his family. But as always: The poor are and remain anonymous.

Saturday, 14

Monks go to a monastery to find God. But monks who live in a monastery as if they had found God are not real monks. I came here to come "closer" to God, but if I ever were to make myself believe that I am any closer to God than anyone else, I would just be fooling myself. God should be sought, but we cannot find God. We can only be found by him.

Two passages from Elie Wiesel's *Souls on Fire* about the Kotzker offer a powerful illustration of these paradoxes. In the first passage I read: "A disciple tells the Kotzker his woes: 'I come from Rizhn. There everything is simple, everything is clear. I prayed and I knew I was praying; I studied and I knew I was studying. Here in Kotzk everything is mixed up, confused; I suffer from it, Rebbe. Terribly. I am lost. Please help me so I can pray and study as before. Please help me to stop suffering.' The Rebbe peers at his tearful disciple and asks: 'And who ever told you that God is interested in your studies and your prayers? And what if he preferred your tears and your suffering?'"[5]

In the second passage it says: "'Certain experiences may be transmitted by language, others—more profound—by silence; and then there are those that cannot be transmitted, not even by silence.' [The Kotzker.] Never mind. Who says that experiences are made to be shared? They must be lived. That's all. And who says that truth is made to be revealed? It must be sought. That's all. Assuming it is concealed in melancholy, is that any reason to seek elsewhere?"[6]

These passages have a Kierkegaardian quality. I can quite well understand that Heschel was struck by the parallel between the Kotzker and Kierkegaard. But there also is a mood that I find reflected in the early desert fathers. God cannot be understood; he cannot be grasped by the human mind. The truth escapes our human capacities. The only way to come close to it is by a constant emphasis on the limitations of our human capacities to "have" or "hold" the truth. We can neither explain God nor his presence in history. As soon as we identify God with any specific event or situation, we play God and distort the truth. We only can be faithful in our affirmation that God has not deserted us but calls us in the middle of all the unexplainable absurdities of life. It is very important to be deeply aware of this. There is a great and subtle temptation to suggest to myself or others where God is working and where not, when he is present and when not, but nobody, no Christian, no priest, no monk, has any "special" knowledge about God. God cannot be limited by any human concept or prediction. He is greater than our mind and heart and perfectly free to reveal himself where and when he wants.

Sunday, 15

After Lauds this morning, Tony Walsh, a Canadian who for many years was the director of St. Benedict Joseph Labre House in Montreal, spoke to the community. A very impressive man. He must be in his sixties, thin with very deep facial characteristics, simply—if not poorly—dressed, intelligent, witty, compassionate, warm, and catholic in the best sense of the word. He said, "The Gospel needs to keep its shocking effect. You can never claim to have fully understood the Gospel. It always should keep you on edge and never satisfied."

I was happy to meet this remarkable man. He suggested to me that one of the greatest temptations is to make the Gospel complex and so weaken its message.

Monday, 16

"When God prays, how would he pray?" Abba Arkia [Rab], a celebrated sage who died in 247, suggested the following: "May it be my will that my mercy may surpass my anger, that my mercy may prevail over my other attributes, so that I may deal with my children in the attribute of mercy and on their behalf stop short of the limit of stern justice."[7] We have always struggled to understand how God can be just as well as merciful. Indeed, the mystery of God is that he can be both to the highest degree. But *we* cannot. God's mercy does not make him less just. His justice does not make him less merciful. But *we* have to struggle to prevent mercy from becoming lack of justice, and justice lack of mercy. The pardon of former President Nixon by his successor, President Ford, is therefore quite understandably perceived by many as an act of grave injustice.

Tuesday, 17

This morning I put this question to John Eudes: "How can I really develop a deep prayer life when I am back again at my busy work? I have the tendency to finish small and large jobs as soon as possible, and as long as I remain surrounded by unfinished tasks, my prayer is nearly impossible since I use the time for prayer to wonder about the many things I still have to do. It always seems that there is something more urgent and more important than prayer."

John Eudes' answer was clear and simple; "The only solution is a prayer schedule that you will never break without consulting your spiritual director. Set a time that is reasonable, and once it is set, stick to it at all costs. Make it your most important task. Let everyone know that this is the only thing you will not change and pray at that time. One hour in the morning before work and a half hour before you go to bed might be a good start. Set the exact time and hold on to it. Leave a party when that time approaches. Simply make it an impossibility to do any type of work, even if it seems urgent, important, and crucial. When you remain faithful, you slowly discover that it is useless to think about your many problems since they won't be dealt with in that time anyhow. Then you start saying to yourself during these free hours, 'Since I have nothing to do now, I might just as well pray!' So praying becomes as important as eating and sleeping, and the time set free for it becomes a very liberating time to which you become attached in the good sense.

"In the beginning," John Eudes said, "your thoughts will wander, but after a while you will discover that it becomes easier to stay quietly in the presence of the Lord. If your head seems filled with worries and concerns, you might like to start with some psalms or a Scripture reading that can help you to concentrate and then you will be better prepared for silent meditation. When you are faithful in this, you will slowly experience yourself in a deeper way. Because in this useless hour in which you do nothing 'important' or 'urgent,' you have to come to terms with your basic powerlessness, you have to feel your fundamental inability to solve your or other people's problems or to change the world. When you do not avoid that experience but live through it, you will find out that your many projects, plans, and obligations become less urgent, crucial, and important and lose their power over you. They will leave you free during your time with God and take their appropriate place in your life.

It seems very convincing to me, even obvious. The only task left is this: simply doing it in obedience.

Wednesday, 18

It has become quite clear to me that my good plans for later will only be real if I start living accordingly now. Although I spent many hours in church, I had not yet set a special time for meditation. So I decided to make the time from 10:45 to 11:15 free for meditation. I had to interrupt other things to do it and realized how important it is to have this appointment with myself. Just sitting silently in church without anything to do while my mind is full of plans, ideas, and concerns is in itself an experience.

This morning I found it simply funny. I could see my thoughts running wild and getting nowhere. Indeed I heard myself say, "Since I am here for this half hour anyhow, I might just as well pray." I sensed the slow withdrawal of my nervousness, and the time went very fast.

One of the experiences of prayer is that it seems that nothing happens. But when you stay with it and look back over a long period of prayer, you suddenly realize that something has happened. What is most close, most intimate, most present, often cannot be experienced directly but only with a certain distance. When I think that I am only distracted, just wasting my time, something is happening too immediate for knowing, understanding, and experiencing. Only in retrospect do I realize that something very important has taken place. Isn't this true of all really important events in life? When I am together with someone I love very much, we seldom talk about our relationship. The relationship, in fact, is too central to be a subject of talk. But later, after we have separated and write letters, we realize how much it all meant to us, and we even write about it.

This is very real to me. When I think about prayer, I can talk about it with moving words and write about it with conviction, but in both situations I am not really praying but reflecting on it with a certain distance. But when I pray, my prayer often seems very confused, dull, uninspiring, and distracted. God is close but often too close to experience. God is closer to me than I am to myself and, therefore, no subject for feelings or thoughts.

I wonder if in this sense I am not participating in what the apostles experienced. When Jesus was with them, they could not fully realize or understand what was happening. Only after he had left did they sense, feel, and understand how close he really had been to them. Their experience after the resurrection became the basis for their expectation.

Thursday, 19

Today I had the strong feeling that things are basically quite simple. If I could love God with all my heart, all my soul, and all my mind, I would feel a great inner freedom, great enough to embrace all that exists, great enough also to prevent little events from making me lose heart. During a few hours I felt that the presence of God was so obvious and my love for him so central that all the complexities of existence seemed to unite in one point and become very simple and clear. When my heart is undivided, my mind only concerned about God, my soul full of his love, everything comes together into one perspective and nothing remains excluded. I felt the great difference between single-mindedness and narrow-mindedness. For the first time I sensed a real single-mindedness; my mind seemed to expand and to be able to receive endlessly more than when I feel divided and confused. When all attention is on him who is my Creator, my Redeemer, and my Sanctifier, I can see all human life—joyful as well as painful— and all of creation united in his love. Then I even wonder why I was so tormented and anxious, so guilt-ridden and restless, so hurried and impatient. All these pains seemed false pains, resulting from not seeing, not hearing, and not understanding. The real pain is the pain that I find in God, who allowed all of earth's suffering to enter into his divine intimacy. The experience of God's presence is not void of pain. But the pain is so deep that you do not want to miss it since it is in this pain that the joy of God's presence can be tasted. This seems close to nonsense except in the sense that it is beyond sense and, therefore, hard to capture within the limits of human understanding. The experience of God's unifying presence is an experience in which the distinction between joy and pain seems to be transcended and in which the beginning of a new life is intimated.

Friday, 20

Abraham Heschel reveals an aspect of spirituality in his discussion of the Kotzker that seems practically absent in Christian life and certainly has never been stressed in my life. It is the aspect of protest against God. He writes: "The refusal to accept the harshness of God's ways in the name of his love was an authentic form of prayer. Indeed, the ancient Prophets of Israel were not in the habit of consenting to God's harsh judgment and did not simply nod, saying, 'Thy will be done.' They often challenged him, as if to say, 'Thy will be changed.' They had often countered and even annulled divine decrees."[8] . . . "A man who lived by honesty could not be expected to suppress his anxiety when tormented by profound perplexity. He had to speak out audaciously. Man should never capitulate, even to the Lord."[9] . . . "There are some forms of suffering that a man must accept with love and bear in silence. There are other agonies to which he must say no."[10]

This attitude shows, in fact, how close the Jew, who can protest against God, feels to God. When I can only relate to God in terms of submission, I am much more distant from him than when I can question his decrees. Most remarkable, therefore, is that this intimacy with God leads to a feeling that has never been part of my thinking but might be very important: Compassion *for* God.

Heschel tells the beautiful story of the Polish Jew who stopped praying "because of what happened in Auschwitz." Later, however, he started to pray again. When asked, "What made you change you mind?" he answered, "It suddenly dawned upon me to think how lonely God must be; look with whom he is left. I felt sorry for him."[11]

This attitude brings God and his people very close to each other, so that God is known by his people as the one who suffers with them.

Heschel writes: "The cardinal issue, Why does the God of justice and compassion permit evil to persist? is bound up with the problem of how man should aid God so that his justice and compassion prevail."[12] The most powerful sentence of Heschel is: "Faith is the beginning of compassion, of compassion for God. It is when bursting with God's sighs that we are touched by the awareness that *beyond all absurdity* there is meaning, truth, and love."[13] This is an experience of deep mysticism in which active protest and passive surrender are both present, and man struggles with God as Jacob wrestled with the angel.

Monday, 23

Often I said to people, "I will pray for you" but how often did I really enter into the full reality of what that means? I now see how indeed I can enter deeply into the other and pray to God from his center. When I really bring my friends and the many I pray for into my innermost being and feel their pains, their struggles, their cries in my own soul, then I leave myself, so to speak, and become them, then I have compassion. Compassion lies at the heart of our prayer for our fellow human beings. When I pray for the world, I become the world; when I pray for the endless needs of the millions, my soul expands and wants to embrace them all and bring them into the presence of God. But in the midst of that experience I realize that compassion is not mine but God's gift to me. I cannot embrace the world, but God can. I cannot pray, but God can pray in me. When God became as we are, that is, when God allowed all of us to enter into his intimate life, it became possible for us to share in his infinite compassion.

In praying for others, I lose myself and become the other, only to be found by the divine love which holds the whole of humanity in a compassionate embrace.

Tuesday, 24

Yesterday I shared with John Eudes some of my thoughts about prayer for others. He not only confirmed my thoughts but also led me further by saying that compassion belongs to the center of the contemplative life. When we become the other and so enter into the presence of God, then we are true contemplatives.

True contemplatives, then, are *not* the ones who withdrew from the world to save their own soul, but the ones who enter into the center of the world and pray to God from there.

Wednesday, 25

Today I imagined my inner self as a place crowded with pins and needles. How could I receive anyone in my prayer when there is no real place for them to be free and relaxed? When I am still so full of preoccupations, jealousies, angry feelings, anyone who enters will get hurt. I had a very vivid realization that I must create some free space in my innermost self so that I may indeed invite others to enter and be healed. To pray for others means to offer others a hospitable place where I can really listen to their needs and pains. Compassion, therefore, calls for a self-scrutiny that can lead to inner gentleness.

If I could have a gentle "interiority"—a heart of flesh and not of stone, a room with some spots on which one might walk barefooted—then God and my fellow humans could meet each other there. Then the center of my heart can become the place where God can hear the prayer for my neighbors and embrace them with his love.

Thursday, 26

This morning—or this night—Brother Cyprian started to mix the dough one hour too soon. Most people tend to oversleep and start an hour too late, but Brother Cyprian suddenly discovered that instead of starting at 1 A.M., he had started at midnight. And since fermentation does not adapt itself to human errors, everything had to start an hour earlier. The bread went into the oven an hour earlier, came out an hour earlier, was sliced an hour earlier, and packed an hour earlier, and—because of a new rise in price—it also was labeled an hour earlier. So I was ready an hour earlier. But I felt a little off schedule and very tired during the afternoon.

Since I could not concentrate on my reading, I took a walk southward from the bakery and found Brother Alberic loading two railroad grain cars with wheat. Alberic had talked the railroad people into repairing an old railroad track that goes through the property. This made it possible to bring the cars very close to the Abbey to be loaded with grain. There was enough grain for at least four cars. It was an impressive view to see the golden grain pulled up in an auger and poured into the brand new, shiny, silver train hoppers. I climbed on the roof and peered in the large space. Thousands of bushels poured in. It is good to know that the Abbey has committed itself to use the money earned from grain for the hungry and poor in India, the Philippines, Nigeria, Peru, and other countries.

Saturday, 28

John Eudes' little three-year-old nephew was making joyful noises during Compline and was the first to run up to his uncle to be sprinkled with holy water.

The monks let him go first and smiled when he got more water on his head than he had expected.

Sunday, 29

During his conference in Chapter this morning, John Eudes said, "Unless our prayer is permanent, our heart is not yet pure." That struck me as very meaningful. John Eudes stressed that not only liturgy but also spiritual reading and manual work are prayer.

St. Benedict sees as the three main aspects of the monastic life: *Opus Dei* (liturgy), *Lectio Divina* (spiritual reading), and *Labor Manuum* (manual work). All three form essential aspects of prayer. When manual work no longer leads us closer to God, we are no longer fully realizing our vocation to pray without ceasing.

How can manual work be prayer? It is prayer when we not only work with our hands but also with our hearts, that is, when our work brings us into closer relationship with God's creation and the human task of working on God's earth.

Spiritual reading also should be done from the heart. It should bring us into more intimate contact with God who reveals himself to us in Scripture, in the lives of the saints and in the reflections of the theologians.

When manual work and spiritual reading are no longer prayer but only a way to earn money or be intellectually stimulated, we lose purity of heart; we become divided and are no longer single-eyed and single-minded.

It is obvious that the simplicity that all this presupposes is not easy to attain. I find that my life constantly threatens to become complex and divisive. A life of prayer is basically a very simple life. This simplicity, however, is the result of asceticism and effort; it is not a spontaneous simplicity. It could be called a "second naïveté." The great saints are characterized by this "second naïveté" which is "willing one thing" (Kierkegaard) or "selling everything to buy the treasure you have found" (Mt. 13).

This morning I worked five hours in the bakery. First two and a half hours packing, then two and a half hours sticking price tags on the bags. It was very tiring and gave me a bad headache since I broke my glasses and could hardly see anything beyond a few feet. In any case, inflation feels real to me. Even my head feels inflated.

5

October

STRANGERS AND FRIENDS

∎

Wednesday, 2

LAST WEEK THE DISTRIBUTOR on whom the monastery is dependent suddenly raised the price of a loaf of Monk's Bread from $.55 to $.59. The monks had just received 500,000 plastic bread bags on which the old price was printed. The result is that for at least the next three months every bag has to be tagged with a label on top of the old price saying: "$.59." This morning I labeled a few thousand loaves which came out of the bagging machine. After a few hours of this dull job I felt numb as well as irritated. The thought that this sudden price rise would keep me labeling for at least a month did not especially help to restore my peace of mind. When I finally was replaced and walked away, hot from sweat and anger, I discovered that on the end of the same line on which I had been working, two monks were tagging other labels on the same bags saying: "Special Sale: $.53"! All upset, I said to Brother Benedict, "Why not just put on the special sale labels since that makes it two cents cheaper than the old price?" But Benedict, obviously understanding capitalism better than I, said quickly, "A reduction of two cents is not attractive to the buyer. The way it is now, we have a reduction of six cents. When people see that difference, they are more inclined to buy."

Meanwhile, hundreds of working hours were spent in raising and lowering the price on the same bag. Certainly a strange type of monks' work!

Finally, I wrote to Edwin Aldrin. It took a long time before I received his book *Return to Earth*, and it took also a long time before I had read it and was able to let it sink in. Aldrin's story of his trip to the moon with Neil Armstrong and Michael Collins is extremely revealing, not because of what it says about this great victory of modern technology, but because of what it says about the personal, more intimate experiences of the astronauts. The enormous competition and rivalry to be in line for this first moon walk, and the uncanny experiences afterward—traveling over the world and shaking hands with presidents, kings, and queens, as the man "who walked on the moon"—all against the background of a middle-class American family life, creates quite a story.

Aldrin's is a very honest book. Never have I seen such common human experiences described in the context of such an exceptional voyage. He writes about his depressions, his fears of speaking in public, his disorientation, his sexual problems, his psychiatric treatment, his conflicts with his wife, and, finally, his attempt to deepen his commitment to his family and to live a civilian life.

Few people are able to write successful books about their everyday family life. Yet Aldrin's story is of interest because it is set against the backdrop of his heroic journey into space. And so we learn more about the strange emptiness of the life of a modern family than about the moon.

I still have not been able to fully articulate what fascinates me so much in this book. In some way it seems to touch the essence of the crisis of our modern civilization. Maybe it is the strange absence of the spiritual, the numinous, the transcendent that is so alienating in this book. Although Aldrin, an Episcopalian, takes the Holy Communion in the spacecraft his response to the whole enterprise seems strangely aspiritual. This becomes especially clear in the events after the trip. Aldrin has very little to draw from when the tensions are building up. He went to the moon. Now he has to go to the inner heart of life to prevent the moon from destroying him.

Thursday, 3

Tomorrow: the feast day of St. Francis of Assisi, a day that needs my special attention since I will need a lot of guidance to find an answer to the question, "What place does poverty really have in my life?" From a statistical point of view, I belong to the few very wealthy people of this world. I earn more money than I need. I have enough to eat, good clothes, a pleasant place to stay, and I am surrounded by family and friends who are willing to help when I have any problems.

Still, without a certain attempt to live a life of poverty I can never call myself a sincere Christian. Giving away all I have does not seem to be very realistic. First of all, I do not have many possessions, and giving away my money would simply mean becoming dependent on others, who have enough to worry about.

One form of poverty I have thought about is to adopt my monastic habit as a permanent form of dress, in this way eliminating the constant need for buying new clothes. Thus, I would also have the advantage of being easily recognizable by others as a man who desires to live a religious life and to keep himself from forms of living not appropriate to that desire. I talked it over with John Eudes during two meetings. At first, it seemed a good idea, but now it has become clear that in my work milieu, it simply would be an oddity and what seems a sign of poverty might just become an ostentatious way of being different. Now

I feel as strongly about not having a monastic habit as I formerly did about having one. After John Eudes expressed his opinion that adopting this form of clothing was inappropriate the whole idea fell away from me and I could hardly believe that for a while it had taken such a central role in my thoughts about my future life-style.

Three aspects of poverty remain attractive to me: first, living a simple and sober life; second, not trying to be different from my colleagues in externals; and third, spending a good amount of time working with the poor and giving as much money as possible to people who are working to alleviate poverty. I hope that St. Francis will help me to discover how to make this concrete.

G. K. Chesterton writes in his book, *St. Francis of Assisi*, that St. Francis' argument for poverty was "that the dedicated man might go anywhere among any kind of men, even the worst kind of men, so long as there was nothing by which they could hold him. If he had any ties or needs like ordinary men, he would become like ordinary men."[1]

The idea that poverty makes a person free is of special interest in the context of the Senate hearings on Nelson Rockefeller, who wants to be confirmed as Vice-President. His wealth is there the main concern.

Friday, 4

Chesterton gives a beautiful insight into the conversion of Francis by describing him as the "tumbler for God" who stands on his head for the pleasure of God. By seeing the world upside down "with all the trees and towers hanging head downwards," Francis discovers its dependent nature. The word *dependence* means *hanging*. By seeing his world, his city, upside down, Francis saw the same world and the same city but in a different way. "Instead of being merely proud of his strong city because it could not be moved, he would be thankful to God Almighty that it had not been dropped."[2]

This conversion, this turn around, this new view made it possible for Francis to make praise and thanksgiving his central attitude in a world that he had redis-covered in its most profound dependence on God.

Here, indeed, we reach that mysterious point where asceticism and joy touch each other. Francis, who was a very severe ascetic, is, nevertheless, known as the most joyful of saints. His joy about all that is created was born out of his full realization of its dependence on God. In fasting and poverty, he reminded himself and others of God's lordship. In his songs of praise and thanksgiving, he revealed the beauty of all that is obedient to its Creator.

Sunday, 6

Chesterton on Francis' compassion: "To him a man stays always a man and does not disappear in a dense crowd any more than in a desert. He honored all men; that is, he not only loved but respected them all. What gave him extraordinary personal power was this: that from the Pope to the beggar, from the sultan of

Syria in his pavilion to the ragged robbers crawling out of the wood, there was never a man who looked into those brown burning eyes without being certain that Francis Bernardone was really interested in *him*, in his own inner individual life from the cradle to the grave; that he himself was being valued and taken seriously and not merely added to the spoil of some social policy or the names of some clerical document. . . . He treated the whole mob of men as a mob of kings."[3]

Tuesday, 8

This afternoon I washed quite a few rocks. The rock collecting phase seems to be over. The rock washing phase—scrubbing lime off the granite rocks—is now in full swing. Meanwhile, the church is starting to take shape. The main pillars are poured and the form of the church is becoming visible. It looks as if it is going to be a very intimate circle of monks and guests. My guess is that it is going to be a very meditative, quiet place that easily will invite prayer.

Friday, 11

Just before dinner Jay appeared. It was a great and happy surprise to see him. He had intended to come for a few days next week, but his plan to drive became impossible when his car was stolen, and so he took a plane to Rochester and hitchhiked to the Abbey. He will stay for a week and I hope that it will be a good stay for him. Jay is the first of my students to come to the Abbey. I discover in myself the desire to make him feel, see, and experience all I have done in the last four months, but realize that God touches each one in a different way. I hope at least that there will be enough quietude and silence for him to hear God's voice.

Sunday, 13

This morning John Eudes spoke in Chapter about autumn as a time of plenitude, a time of fulfillment in which the richness of nature becomes abundantly visible, but also a time in which nature points beyond itself by the fragility of its passing beauty. He started by reading Psalm 64, which speaks about the beauty of nature. He couldn't have chosen a better day to speak about this psalm. When I walked out I was overwhelmed by the beauty of the landscape unfolding itself before my eyes. Looking out over the Genesee valley, I was dazzled by the bright colors of the trees. The yellow of the hickory trees, the different shades of red from the maples and oaks, the green of the willows—together they formed a fantastic spectacle. The sky was full of mysterious cloud formations, and just as I walked down to the guesthouse, the sun's rays burst through the clouds and covered the land with their light, making the corn fields look like a golden tapestry.

The beauty of the fall is unbelievable in this part of the country. I can only say with the psalmist: "The hills are girded with joy, they shout for joy, yes, they sing."

Two weeks from now the colorful leaves will have whirled to the ground and the trees will be bare, announcing the coming of winter and snow. It will be only a few months before all the hills will be white and the green of the winter wheat covered with a thick blanket of frozen snow. But then we can remember the rich powers hidden underneath which will show themselves again to those who have the patience to wait.

Monday, 14

Thinking back on how I came to the ideas I have written down on paper, I realize how much they were the result of a constant interaction with people. I write against the background of my own history and experiences and others respond to me from their different histories and experiences, and it is in the interaction of stories that the ideas take their shape.

Someone might read what I wrote and discover something there that I myself did not see, but which might be just as valid as my original thought. It seems important to allow this to happen. If I were to try to prevent people from drawing "wrong" implications from my thoughts, I might fall into the temptation of thinking that I know what all the implications are. Maybe I should be happy that I do not know them. In this way, many people with quite different stories can move between the lines of my hesitant ideas, opinions, and viewpoints and there create their own. After all, people will never follow anyone's ideas except their own; I mean, those which have developed within their inner self.

Tuesday, 15

Jay and I visited Brother Elias this morning. It was a happy event. At 7:15 A.M. we walked together through the woods to the hermitage. Nature was still waking up. The clouds were heavy and the paths were covered with the colored leaves pulled from the branches by the heavy rain.

Elias welcomed us full of joy and with a sort of divine excitement. After a short, silent prayer in front of his chapel altar, we talked. Elias' eyes so eradiated the experience he talked about that Jay and I felt ourselves to be in the presence of a holy man. "The Lord is so good, so good to me," he said repeatedly and then he spoke about the sun and the clouds, the rain and the winds, the wheat and the weeds, the heat and the cold, all as great gifts of the Lord given to bring Elias into a closer, more intimate contact with him.

There were laughter and smiles, tenderness and conviction, down-to-earth observations and ecstatic utterances all flowing quite naturally from him but definitely revealing another world to us.

"Isn't the rain beautiful?" he said. "Why do we keep resisting rain? Why do we only want the sun when we should be willing to be soaked by the rain? The Lord wants to soak us with his grace and love. Isn't it marvelous when we can feel the Lord in so many ways and get to know him better and better! He lets us experience his presence even now in all that surrounds us. Imagine how it must be when we can see him face to face!"

Jay looked at Elias, all smiles and joy. He felt that Elias not only spoke about the Lord but spoke the Lord. Every time Elias used the word "Lord," his whole body leaped with joy, and he was beaming with heavenly satisfaction. We spoke about many things: about Lebanon, where Elias' parents came from; about its hermit, Sharbel, whose beatification took place at the end of the Second Vatican Council; about Yoga, fasting, meditation, Scripture reading, books on saints, and many other things. But it all seemed like just one subject: how good the Lord is.

When Jay and I walked back to the monastery, we both felt grateful for having met this holy man. It even seemed that he had helped us come closer to each other.

Thursday, 17

This afternoon I drove Jay to the airport. He was happy about the week. The meeting with Elias had filled him with joy, and he felt it a great privilege to have met a man whose heart was so wide and deep that it could contain the beauty of people and nature.

At the airport we talked for a while, and it seemed as if a bitter spirit invaded me and compelled me to complain about the lack of response in people to whom I had offered gifts. I even went so far as to make it personal and told Jay how much I had regretted that he had not responded at all when I sent him an expensive book about which I was very excited. Jay pointed out that I obviously could not give without wanting something in return. He offered Elias as an ideal to strive for and said that my need for a response showed a basic insecurity. I became defensive in return and our discussion became trite.

How I wish that this had not happened. When I drove back to the monastery, I felt so depressed that I developed a headache and couldn't think about anything other than my own narrow-mindedness and lack of generosity. Why did I create such a petty atmosphere at the end of such a good week?

The only thing I can say now is that this incident revealed mercilessly my vulnerability and showed me clearly how little it took to make me fall into very immature behavior. It even proved hard not to be defensive in my thoughts afterward. I hope that I can simply say that I am sorry and allow the wound to be healed by God, who showed me how little I had understood.

Thursday, 24

Busy day. At 4:15 A.M. I started working on the hot-bread line. The wheat bread came out of the oven so fast I couldn't get it on the racks and into the cooling room fast enough. Happily, John Baptist helped me out and prevented the bread from flying around. Meanwhile, I burned my arm on a hot pan. Stupid.

Theodore, busy with "feeding the oven," today celebrates the twenty-fifth anniversary of his entrance into the monastery.

This afternoon I worked in the creek collecting more stones for the church. The masons want large, heavy, granite rocks which they can still place as long as the roof is not yet completed. After that, the low-reaching roof will prevent the boom of the backhoe from setting the heavy rocks down on the right spot. We got about six huge rocks in the bucket of the Trojan. The heavy machine did well in the creek and Father Stephen maneuvered the "beast" carefully around the curves and between obstacles. We were proud of the "catch," and Joe, the head mason, showed great satisfaction but also made it clear that we had to wash the lime off before they could be used.

The altar, one large limestone block, was moved to its place today. Before the beams for the roof go up, the altar had to be placed. Too heavy and too large to be brought in later through the door. All went well with the large crane.

With all that heavy equipment and material the danger of accidents remains real. Yesterday a beam fell on Brother Quentin's left hand. Three of his fingers were badly damaged. They "sewed him up" in the nearby Health Center and gave him pain killers. I was amazed to see him back and around as if nothing had happened.

Saturday, 26

Last night, this morning, and this afternoon I was part of a retreat of twenty-five students from the Newman Center of Geneseo State College. It is the first time since May that I have given conferences or meditations. I used a large wagon wheel to make the point that the closer we come to God—the hub of our life—the closer we come to each other, even when we travel along very different paths (spokes). The wheel stayed in the center of the room during the retreat.

The mood was warm, receptive, friendly, and gentle, and I felt part of things. But I also was totally exhausted when I went to bed last night at 11 P.M. More than ever, I feel how much energy is required to speak. How hard it is to speak from heart to heart about God and prayer. I now realize how careful I have to be in accepting invitations to speak. If words have to grow out of silence, I will need much silence to prevent my words from becoming flat and superficial.

The remarks by the students about prayer were beautiful and full of meaning. Only they themselves did not know it. When I went home last night, I thought, "What do I have to say to these men and women who are so earnest in their search for God and live such good lives?" But then I realized that the only thing I have to do is to say loudly what they already know in their hearts so that they can recognize it as really theirs and affirm it in gratitude.

Sunday, 27

John Eudes spoke in Chapter this morning about the monastic vocation. The occasion was the celebration of the twenty-fifth year of monastic life of Father Bede, Father Francis, and Brother Theodore and the twenty-fifth year of profession of Brother John Baptist. Their dates were different but this day was set apart to celebrate them all.

One thought in John Eudes' conference touched me very much. He said that to respond to God's love was a great act of faith. He compared it to people who have felt very lonely and isolated, very rejected and unloved during many years of their life and who suddenly meet someone who cares. For such people it is very hard to believe that his or her care is authentic and honest. It requires a great act of faith to accept the love that is offered to us and to live, not with suspicion and distrust, but with the inner conviction that we are worth being loved.

This is the great adventure of the monk: to really believe that God loves you, to really give yourself to God in trust, even while you are aware of your sinfulness, weaknesses, and miseries.

I suddenly saw much better than before that one of the greatest temptations of a monk is to doubt God's love. Those who enter a contemplative monastery with the intention of staying there for life must be very much aware of their own brokenness and need for redemption. If the monastic life should lead them to a morbid introspection of their own sinfulness, it would lead them away from God for whom they came to the monastery. Therefore, the growing realization of one's sins and weaknesses must open the contemplative to a growing awareness of God's love and care.

During the Eucharist John Eudes spoke about the parable of the penitent publican. He made the observation that monks are not necessarily better or holier people than others. Instead, he said, they might very well be weaker and more vulnerable and come to the monastery to find the support of a community to enable them to be faithful in their search for God and to keep responding to his continuing love.

I was deeply moved by these thoughts. They had an unusual clarity and lucidity for me, and I felt very grateful that I was part of this community. I also realized that my coming here might well be seen more as a sign of my weakness than my strength.

During dinner we listened to the Fifth Symphony of Tchaikovsky. The music overwhelmed me by its powerful melodic streams and gave me a deep sense of joy.

Monday, 28

Last night my close friends Claude and Don arrived from Notre Dame. This morning I saw them at Lauds, and after my work with the hot pans, I showed them the bakery. They seemed tickled by my bakery suit and the unusual context in which they saw me. We had so much to share that we decided to wait with all our stories until 1975. They had traveled for the whole summer through Latin America, had had many new experiences in their teaching at Notre Dame University and many new plans for the future. And I had my five months of monastic experiences to talk about. So instead of using this three-day stay as an occasion to catch up with each other's story, we tried to make it into a real retreat experience.

It is very good to see my friends again and to make them part of my life, even though it is only for a few days. Our regular retreats together would become less deep if my experience here could not become to some degree their experience also.

Tomorrow morning we will spend some time with John Eudes so that he, too, may become part of our constantly growing friendship.

Tuesday, 29

The meeting of John Eudes with Don, Claude, and me was very meaningful. We started by asking John Eudes about the political influence of monasticism, referring especially to St. Bernard's great political impact, and moved from there to a discussion of the meaning of monasticism.

John Eudes made it very clear that monasticism may have political, sociological, psychological, and economic implications, but that anyone who enters a monastery with these in mind would leave it soon. He described his own vocation as a response to his world, but a response in which God and God alone became his goal.

John Eudes described how the monastic life has three aspects: the *praktikos*, the ascetic practice; the *theoria physica*, a deeper understanding of the inner relationship of things; and the *theologia*, the mystical experience of God. By self-denial, such as fasting, obedience, and stability, the monk learns to understand the forces of the world better and to look beyond them to God. John Eudes also explained the full sense of the classic saying that the Christian life consists of "fasting, almsgiving, and prayer." When fasting means self-denial, almsgiving means charity, and prayer the search for union with God, then indeed this short expression summarizes the life of the Christian.

John Eudes stressed that great politicians always are much more than tacticians. When you cannot look beyond tactics, you lose perspective, distance, and the vision to which you can relate your actions. That is why for Plato a politician had to be a philosopher.

Claude remarked that John Eudes was turning things upside down for him. While he in his studies was trying to add a religious dimension to politics, he noticed that John Eudes was stressing the importance of relativizing politics by pointing beyond it. Obviously, John Eudes and Claude were not in contradiction with each other, but the contrast in emphasis was apparent.

John Eudes did not deny the political implications of monasticism, just as nobody would deny the political implications of marriage. Even as a man and a woman do not marry because of the political character of the marriage institution, so no monk enters a monastery to be politically relevant. His single-minded interest is God and God alone.

I was very happy that Don and Claude had a chance to meet John Eudes and that, in this way, he became much more for them than someone I often talk about.

Wednesday, 30

This was a very tiring day. Working in the bakery, answering mail, talking with an old friend from Bolivia, spending time with Claude and Don.

It is good to realize how empty and fatigued I feel. Why? I don't really know. Probably because I am trying to keep the monastic atmosphere and unconsciously protest against all these interruptions. At one level, I feel I should not have so much mail and become so involved in people's lives; on another level, I feel I should. So there is the conflict. Instead of simply accepting the good interruption and enjoying it fully, I am holding back, saying to myself, "I really shouldn't be talking so much. I should be praying."

But still, all was very good and pleasant. The talks were far from "just chatting." They were exchanges on a deep personal level.

Thursday, 31

Before Don and Claude left, we had a meditation together. At Don's suggestion we reflected on Romans 12:3–21. After our days together, St. Paul's words had a new and very convincing power for us. We had spoken about personal renewal, about renewal of the religious community of which we are part, and about being in but not of the world.

St. Paul seemed to speak about all of this in the text we chose: "Do not conform outwardly to the standards of this world, but let God transform you inwardly by a complete change of your mind. . . . Love must be completely sincere. Hate what is evil, hold on to what is good. Love one another warmly as brothers in Christ and be eager to show respect for one another. Work hard, and do not be lazy. Serve the Lord with a heart full of devotion. Let your hope keep you joyful, be patient in your troubles, and pray at all times. Share your belongings with your needy brothers, and open your home to strangers" (Rm. 12:2, 9–12).[4]

The words which seemed to summarize everything are: "Do not conform outwardly to the standards of this world but let God transform you inwardly by a complete change of your mind" (Rm. 12:2).[5] We used the Phillips translation, which says: "Don't let the world around you *squeeze* you into its own mould."[6] We became aware during these days of how much we had allowed the world to squeeze us in and, therefore, had not created enough freedom to let God enter into our innermost self and transform our hearts and minds.

It was a good meditation that brought us very close to each other and made us depart from each other with new confidence.

6

November

MANY SAINTS BUT ONE LORD

■

Friday, 1

FEAST OF ALL SAINTS. The readings, mostly from the Apocalypse, gave a glorious picture of the New Jerusalem. A city with splendid gates, full of beauty and majesty. We heard about the throne of God and the twenty-four thrones of the elders dressed in white robes with golden crowns on their heads. "Flashes of lightning were coming from the throne, and the sound of peals of thunder, and in front of the throne there were seven flaming lamps burning, the seven Spirits of God" (Rev. 4:5).

The whole day was full of glorious visions, glorious sounds and glorious spectacles, and it became clear that in this way we were presented with an image of the world to come.

During the day, however, I also read "The Week in Review" of the New York *Times* and was overwhelmed by the misery of this world. More and more it seems that dark clouds are gathering above our world: Asia, Africa, Latin America, Europe, the United States—all over the globe it seems that people are worrying about the dark forces that lead to hunger, war, violence, poverty, captivity and wonder if there is anyone who has the vision and the power that can offer hope for a better future.

I was deeply struck by these contrasting panoramas. How do they relate to each other? Where do they intersect and connect? The Church does not seem to be able to give much of a foretaste of the heavenly glory.

It seems that the vision of All Saints' Day remains "up in the sky," and that even sincere attempts to make it come closer by concrete changes in our present dark world are not very successful. All this made All Saints' Day a somewhat ambiguous feast.

Sunday, 3

"The monastery is the center of the world." This drastic statement by John Eudes in Chapter this morning reminded me of exactly that same statement made by

Thomas Merton when he came to the Abbey of Gethsemani for the first time. The monastery is not just a place to keep the world out but a place where God can dwell. The liturgy, the silence, the rhythm of the day, the week, and the year, and the whole monastic life-style with the harmony of prayer, spiritual reading, and manual labor, are meant to create space for God. The ideal of the monk is to live in the presence of God, to pray, read, work, eat, and sleep in the company of his divine Lord. Monastic life is the continuing contemplation of the mysteries of God, not just during the periods of silent meditation but during all parts of the day.

In so far as the monastery is the place where the presence of God in the world is most explicitly manifest and brought to consciousness, it is indeed the center of the world. This can be said in humility and with purity of heart because the monk, more than anyone else, realizes that God dwells only where man steps back to give him room.

The many guests who come here all seem to sense this and feel more unified after their visit, even when it is a short one. Some even go home with the feeling of "having seen the Lord" and feel a new strength to face the struggle of every-day living.

Wednesday, 6

At 10 A.M. I had my weekly meeting with John Eudes. I asked him about my fatigue which keeps plaguing me every time I become involved with people. Especially after the retreat for the Geneseo College students, it was a real problem.

John Eudes said that I should accept this condition by taking the necessary extra sleep, but he also made it clear that it was definitely a psychosomatic situation. I put too much energy into any encounter, as if I have to prove each time anew that I am worth being with. "You put your whole identity at stake—and every time you start from scratch," John Eudes suggested. "Prayer and meditation are important here because in them you can find your deepest identity, and that keeps you from putting your whole self on the line every time you work with other people." He also told me that it is a proven fact that those who meditate regularly need less sleep. They are more at one with themselves and don't use others in their identity struggle.

We had talked about these things before, but today they had a new relevance for me.

Friday, 8

For the past few weeks we have had a Friday night lecture by a visiting seminary professor. He has been speaking about the doctrine of the Trinity and especially about the Holy Spirit. For me these lectures are a special experience.

What fascinates me about them is that they give me such a powerful sense of *déjà vu.* When I listen to them I feel as if I am back in the theological seminary. All the feelings I had then seem to return: I like the lectures, I am intrigued, I don't want to miss any—but at the same time I feel dissatisfied on a level I did not understand in the past but is now closer to my consciousness. After my ordination I was asked to continue to study theology. I asked the bishop to change that request and to let me study psychology instead. Somewhere I then felt that theology had left a whole area of my life experience untouched. I hoped that psychology would fill the need. It did so, although only very indirectly.

Listening to the lectures reawakened in me all my seminary feelings. I kept saying to myself, "How interesting, how fascinating, how insightful"—and at the same time I said to myself, "So what? What do all these words about God the Father, the Son, and the Spirit have to do with me here and now?" As soon as I step outside the circle of his terminology, which is very familiar to me, the whole level of discourse seems extremely alienating.

How do you speak about the Holy Spirit in such a way that it is clear and has something to do with my concrete life experience? I had that question in 1954, and now I find myself raising it again. But now I understand the question a little better.

Saturday, 9

The whole afternoon I tried to hammer large nails into a large beam. At a distance it always seemed so easy, but my nails had the strange habit of bending just before the head touched the wood. Standing on a platform, I tried very hard to get the "right swing." Michael explained kindly to me that I should not push the nail in the wood with the hammer but use "wrist power." I have the idea but not yet the technique. Of every four nails, one made it to the end. The others I clipped off with a big pair of scissors and then drove the rest into the wood, hoping that future generations would not see them.

But it was a pleasant afternoon. Quentin and Michael showed endless patience and broad smiles, and Ross, my fellow worker, consoled me with stories about his own hard beginnings. But he surely did better than I. Meanwhile, I found it all a welcome change from the rock collecting routine. If I get a few more chances at it, I might better my average for successful nails.

Meanwhile, the church is starting to take shape and you can feel a happy anticipation of the day when it will be ready for the monks to make it the center of their lives. In the liturgy today we celebrated the dedication of the Basilica of St. John Lateran in Rome. I am sure that more thoughts went out toward the new church here than toward the old basilica in Rome.

Monday, 11

This was a very flat day. Three hours on the hot-bread line, two hours answering mail, and three hours trying to make a reading list for next semester's courses.

In between I had a "debate" with John Eudes about Hitchcock's book *The Recovery of the Sacred*, which is read during dinner. I told him that I found it a "gossipy" book, pulling things out of context without a real sense for history, and basically narrow-minded, prejudiced, ultra-conservative, and at times, offensive. John Eudes said that I overreacted, that the book only wanted to make the point that there had been a lot of irresponsible liturgical experimentation, a point worth making, and he stated that he enjoyed hearing it. He also said that he had been waiting for my negative reaction, a remark which made me angry.

Well—we went around and around and got nowhere. I disagreed with John Eudes' idea that I overreacted, and he disagreed with my idea that he was biased in his sympathies. So not much of anything happened. We closed with some good laughs, and—in a certain sense—I did not feel badly about having expressed these feelings, but I decided that it was probably better not to use his time or mine for this sort of argument. It is tiring and, considering the short time of my stay, not very helpful for anyone—for John Eudes, the monks, or myself.

I now feel somewhat dizzy and sloppy. Better get some sleep.

Tuesday, 12

To live a spiritual life is to live in the presence of God. This very straightforward truth was brought home to me forcefully by Brother Lawrence, a French Carmelite brother who lived in the seventeenth century. The book *The Practice of the Presence of God* contains four conversations with Brother Lawrence and fifteen letters by him.

He writes: "It is not necessary for being with God to be always at church. We may make an oratory of our heart wherein to retire from time to time to converse with him in meekness, humility, and love. Everyone is capable of such familiar conversation with God, some more, some less. He knows what we can do. Let us begin, then. Perhaps he expects but one generous resolution on our part. Have courage."[1]

"I know that for the right practice of it [the presence of God] the heart must be empty of all other things, because God will possess the heart *alone;* and as he cannot possess it alone without emptying it of all besides, so neither can he act *there,* and do it in what pleases, unless it be left vacant to him."[2]

Brother Lawrence's message, in all its simplicity, is very profound. For him who has become close to God, all is one. Only God counts, and in God all people and all things are embraced with love. To live in the presence of God, however, is to live with purity of heart, with simple-mindedness and with total acceptance of his will. That, indeed, demands a choice, a decision, and great courage. It is a sign of true holiness.

Wednesday, 13

"God indeed hears our prayers." This joyful thought and feeling has dominated the entire day, after an unexpected phone call from California.

In 1971 my dear friend from Los Angeles, Richard, had an accident that caused a growing back pain. While visiting me in Holland his pain grew to such a degree that he had to be hospitalized. When finally he returned to Los Angeles, the pain had hardly decreased. From then on his life seemed a long battle of coping with the pain that made him more and more an invalid. He underwent surgery, went to chiropractors, had acupuncture, saw a very competent neurologist on the East Coast, tried psychotherapy, sat in whirlpools, lay flat for weeks, tried to act as if nothing were wrong—and took an endless amount of drugs. Just two weeks ago he had written: "No good news—only shit—the pain gets worse and I am getting more and more depressed."

About a month ago I told Brother James about Richard and said, "Please pray for my friend. He needs your prayers badly. It is not just his back. There is much more that needs healing." James prayed. He even prayed aloud for "the man who needs our prayers" during Vespers one evening.

After Richard's last despairing letter, I wrote back: "I pray for you—I really pray—and I am sure you will be better soon. I am even somewhat angry that you are not better yet." I usually don't write things like that to Richard since words like: God, Church, priest, prayer, Jesus, all tend to evoke anger, irritation, and hostility in him. But this time I simply did so.

This morning John Eudes put a note under my door asking me to call Richard. "It is urgent," the note said, "but nothing bad." I called at 10 A.M. Richard's voice was full of joy as he said, "For five days I have not taken a pill. I have never felt so good."

Then he told me what had happened to him. One of the older students in his seminar on Latin American history had told him, "I will cure you." Richard had laughed but went to her home where she told Richard to shout, wrestle, jump and do all sorts of things which you would not normally ask of a man with a bad back. After an hour, much of the pain was gone. Although there were still many discomforts, Richard felt like another person. He had been shouting the last few days so much that his voice seemed different. Hoarse, of course. He also had been jumping and doing a lot of "acting out" and he felt great. From his description, it seemed that his therapist is a very responsible woman who knows what she is doing and has been able to sense the core of Richard's problem. After several therapy sessions Richard was so excited about the success that he wanted to tell me the story by phone. Suddenly he was full of new plans: finishing his dissertation, going to Paraguay, etc., etc. Although I was very glad, I kept telling him not to give up if a setback should come.

After dinner I told James. He beamed all over with joy. I said, "Please don't stop. Keep praying for him. It is just beginning." He said, "You so seldom know if God hears your prayers, and I feel so good that he listened to my request." Then I saw him walk away and kneel in the chapel. Meanwhile, I pray with him that this time Richard will be able to start a new life in all respects.

Thursday, 14

With great interest I read Evelyn Underhill's *The Mystics of the Church*. In this book Underhill discusses in a very lively and incisive way the main mystical figures in the Western Church. It is one of the most convincing arguments for the Christian belief that the love of God lived in its fullest sense leads to a most selfless dedication to the neighbor. Underhill shows how, after living through the most ecstatic experiences, the mystics are frequently capable of unbelievable activity. Paul is the prime example, but Augustine, Teresa of Avila, Catherine of Siena, and many others show the same capacity. Mysticism is the opposite of withdrawal from the world. Intimate union with God leads to the most creative involvement in the contemporary world. It seems that ecstasies and visions are slowly replaced by a "steady inward certainty of union with God and by a new strength and endurance."[3] Although frequently experiencing "sudden waves of fervent feelings" in this often very active period, the mystic is "none the less calm and sober in his practical dealings with men."[4]

Friday, 15

The Jesus Prayer has been very important to me ever since I came here. During the first weeks of my stay in the Abbey, I read many articles and books about Hesychasm in which the Jesus Prayer plays such a central role.

In recent days, I have come to realize how strong the devotion to the name of Jesus also is in the Western Church. I knew about this devotion, but more in the sense of a romantic piety than in the sense of a real road to deep prayer.

St. Bernard of Clairvaux plays a central role in the devotion to the name of Jesus. In his fifteenth sermon on the Song of Songs he writes: "When I name Jesus, I set before me a man who is meek and humble of heart, kind, prudent, chaste, merciful, flawlessly upright and holy in the eyes of all; and this same man is the all-powerful God whose way of life heals me, whose support is my strength. All these re-echo for me at the hearing of Jesus' name."[5]

So the name of Jesus indeed becomes the summary and expression of all prayer. This is very beautifully expressed in "The Rosey Sequence" (*Jesu dulcis memoria*), a poem formerly ascribed to St. Bernard but now presumed to be by an unknown English Cistercian.[6] The first stanza says:

> The memory of Jesus is sweet
> giving true joys to the heart;
> but sweeter than honey and all things
> is His sweet presence.

Here I found again how the memory of Jesus makes him present and how his presence makes me remember him. In the prayer of the name of Jesus, the memory and presence of God become one and the same and lead us into intimate union with him.

Monday, 18

What do you do when you are a monk and everyone around you is in the playful habit of cursing when something doesn't go as expected? This is no theoretical question since this is the case at the church building site where monks work closely together with good-natured and good-cursing workers.

I wondered how *I* would react. Probably I would not say anything but slowly get angry until I finally exploded and said, "Don't you know you are not supposed to curse!" Then we would all be angry, the air would be tense, and charity hard to find.

Well—Anthony told me *his* response. After having heard the name of Jesus used "in vain" (without effect—fruitless), he thought, "Should I say something about it?" He said to himself, "Why not?" Then the next time someone dropped a beam or bent a nail and used the name of the Lord again "without effect," he put his arm around him and said, "Hey, you know—this is a monastery—and we love that man here." The man looked up at him, smiled, and said, "To tell you the truth—I do too." And they both had a good laugh.

Having read so much about the Jesus Prayer and the power of the name of Jesus, this beautiful story has special meaning to me. Indeed, we should not use the name of the Lord in vain but only to bear fruit.

Tuesday, 19

I was struck by the following words in Henry Suso's *Little Book of Eternal Wisdom.* Jesus speaks: "Sometimes a clear eye is as quickly blinded by white flour as by gray ashes. Could the presence of any human being be more harmless than my presence among my beloved disciples? There were no unnecessary words, no unrestrained gestures, no conversations which begin with spiritual topics and end in useless babbling. True earnestness and complete, absolute truth dominated all our intercourse. Yet, my bodily presence had to be withdrawn in order to prepare the disciples to receive the Spirit. How great an obstacle, therefore, can human presence be. Before men are led into themselves by one person, they are drawn outward by thousands; before they are once taught with doctrine, they are many times confused by bad example."[7]

The world in which we live today and about whose suffering we know so much seems more than ever a world from which Christ has withdrawn himself. How can I believe that in this world we are constantly being prepared to receive the Spirit? Still, I think that this is exactly the message of hope. God has not withdrawn himself. He sent his Son to share our human condition and the Son sent us his Spirit to lead us into the intimacy of his divine life. It is in the midst of the chaotic suffering of humanity that the Holy Spirit, the Spirit of Love, makes himself visible. But can we recognize his presence?

Wednesday, 20

In my meeting with John Eudes today I asked him about total commitment to Christ. During the past few weeks I have often had a sudden insight into what that might mean. I have had a glimpse of the reality of being unconditionally committed to Christ, of a total surrender to him. In the glimpse I also saw how divided I still am, how hesitantly I commit myself, with what reluctance I surrender. I realized how totally new my life would be if I made Christ my only concern and at the same time how really "old" my life still is. I often say to myself, "I am very interested in Christ but also in many other things." That shows how uncommitted I am, how far from the experience out of which Henry Suso writes.

This probably explains also my fear of physical and mental pain. Reading about the torture to which so many people are subjected, I often wonder how long I could uphold my conviction under mental or physical pressure. I always end up with the realization of my weakness, lack of faith, and lack of unyielding commitment.

John Eudes pointed out to me that all these questions and concerns are part of the same problem. As long as I am plagued by doubts about my self-worth, I keep looking for gratification from people around me and yield quickly to any type of pain, mental or physical. But when I can slowly detach myself from this need for human affirmation and discover that it is in the relationship with the Lord that I find my true self, an unconditional surrender to him becomes not only possible but even the only desire, and pain inflicted by people will not touch me in the center. When my "self" is anchored not in people but in God, I will have a much greater resistance against pain.

We talked for a moment about torture and brainwashing, and John Eudes told me that in his psychiatric practice he had met a man who, as prisoner of war, underwent much torture but never gave an inch. He was a very simple, down-to-earth man with little political or ideological sophistication. But no pressure was able to force him to any kind of confession. John Eudes explained this by pointing to the man's sense of identity. No self-doubt, no insecurities, no false guilt feelings that could be exploited by his enemies.

How to come to this simplicity, this inner sense of self, this conviction of self-worth? "Meditate," John Eudes said, "and explore the small daily events in which you can see your insecurity at work. By meditation you can create distance, and what you can keep at a distance, you can shake off."

This led our discussion to a more profound question. If I allowed no one but the Lord to determine my identity, would I know the Lord? Or is it a fact that even in my meditation I relate to the Lord as I relate to people—that is—by manipulation and projection. Just as I can behave in my contacts with people in such a way as to provoke an affirmative response, so I can relate to the Lord on my own terms, thereby trying to make him like me. But then I am still more concerned with myself than with the Lord. Slowly I have to learn to meditate not on my terms but on his. Maybe I don't even know at all who the Lord is; maybe I have never allowed him to enter into my center and give me my real self, my identity. But when I discover the Lord on his terms, I will be able to let go of my own worries and concerns and surrender to him without any fear of the pains and sufferings this might lead to.

I see, I see—but when is God going to break through all my defenses so that I can see not just with my mind but with my heart as well?

I have been moving lumber from the garage to the church. In June I helped put all the lumber into the garage; now I am helping to move it out. I had the feeling of coming full circle. It made me aware that I was not just working on the completion of the roof of the church but also on the completion of my stay here. Five weeks from now I will be in Holland and I will have to ask myself what these seven months have meant to me. I am still in it, but I see the end and the slow moving away to new experiences. During these months a church was built, a new space for God. Is this going to be true for me, too?

Friday, 22

André Malraux remarks in his *Anti-Memoirs* that one day we will realize that we are distinguished as much from each other by the forms our memories take as by our characters. I am wondering what form my memory is taking. It seems that this depends a great deal on myself. I have little to say about events, good or bad, creative or destructive, but much about the way I remember them—that is, the way I start giving them form in the story of my life. I am starting to see how important this is in my day-to-day living. I often say to myself; "How will I remember this day, this disappointment, this conflict, this misunderstanding, this sense of accomplishment, joy, and satisfaction? How will they function in my ongoing task of self-interpretation?"

Saturday, 23

The influence of Thomas Merton seems to have grown ever since he died in December 1968. Many people are writing masters' theses on him as well as doctoral dissertations. Books and articles on Merton keep appearing. Since I have been here, at least three books have appeared.[8]

One of the things that strikes me is that Merton is like the Bible: he can be used for almost any purpose. The conservative and the progressive, the liberal and the radical, those who fight for changes and those who complain about them, political activists and apolitical utopians, they all quote Merton to express their ideas and convictions. He is considered to be the man who inspired Dan Berrigan, Jim Forest, and Jim Douglas, but he also is used as "safe" spiritual reading in the refectories of many religious houses. Monks say that you cannot understand Merton when you do not see him primarily as a contemplative, while many non-monks prefer to see him as a social critic, a man living on the periphery of the monastery and deeply involved in the struggle for peace and justice. Christian admirers tend to stress Merton's orthodoxy, but many non-Christians who are looking to the Far East for new spiritual strength also claim him as their model and supporter. And although Merton, during his last days in Asia, wrote in the most unambiguous terms that he was and always would remain a Christian monk, some even want to believe that he planned to become a Buddhist.

What to think about this? Who is right and who is wrong? Merton never tried to be systematic and never worried about being consistent. He articulated skillfully and artfully the different stages of his own thoughts and experiences and moved on to new discoveries without worrying about what people made of his old ones. Now he is dead. He can no longer answer the question, "What did you really mean?" He probably would only have been irritated by such a question. But his death has made him an even stronger catalyst than he was during his life. He indeed made his own life available to others to help them find their own—and not his—way. In this sense, he was and still is a true minister, creating the free space where others can enter and discover God's voice in their lives.

Sunday, 24

Today: the feast of Christ the King. No easy feast day for me since I always have associated this feast with a certain triumphalism in the Church and with a militant spirituality, both of which were so much part of my pre-Vatican II Jesuit formation. It also is the day in which I am always confronted with the problem of authority in the Church because it makes me realize how many people in the Church like to play king in Jesus' name. Finally, it is the day in which I have to deal with my own unresolved struggle with obedience and submission, a struggle of which I have again become very conscious in a monastery such as this where the abbot is such a clear-cut authority figure.

St. Benedict says in the Prologue of his Rule: "My word, then, directs itself to you who have rejected the impulses of your own will and have taken up the powerful and splendid weapons of obedience in order to serve in the army of the Lord Christ, the true King."[9]

These words leave no room for ambiguity. Christ is King and therefore his will and not mine should be the ultimate criterion of my actions. Enough to start feeling very uncomfortable. But today in the liturgy as well as during my meditation, I started to see and feel that Christ became our King by obedience and humility. His crown is a crown of thorns, his throne is a cross. The soldiers knelt before him saying: "'Hail, king of the Jews!' And they spat on him and took the reed and struck him on the head with it" (Mt. 27:30). While he hung on the cross, they said: "'If you are the King of the Jews, save yourself.' Above him there was an inscription: 'This is the king of the Jews'" (Lk. 23:36–38).

The great mystery of this feast is that we are asked to be obedient to him who was obedient unto the death on the cross, that we are asked to renounce our will for him who prayed to his Father: "Let your will be done, not mine" (Lk. 22:43), that we are challenged to suffer humiliation for him who was humiliated for our sake. Christ became King by emptying himself and becoming like us.

We are asked to be obedient to him to whom no human suffering is alien. How often do I say, think, or feel toward someone, "Who do you think you are to tell me what to do, to think, or how to behave?" When I say that to Jesus, he answers, "I am the Son of God who did not cling to my divine state but assumed the condition of a slave for you." (See Ph. 2:6–8.) The authority of Christ is an authority based on humility and obedience and received by experiencing the human condition in a deeper, broader, and wider way than any person ever did or ever will do.

This must make me realize that the kingdom of Jesus is "not of this world" (Jn. 18:36). It is not based on power but on humility, not the result of a revolt but given in response to obedience. It is in this kingdom that Jesus could receive the man who prayed on his cross: "Remember me when you come into your kingdom." "Today," the answer was, "you will be with me in paradise" (Lk. 23:43).

It is for this kingdom that St. Benedict wants to prepare his monks and, therefore, he presents them with obedience and humility as the way. It is the way which the King himself went.

The hard reality is that in our world humility and obedience are never totally separated from power and manipulation: We are challenged to see the will of God in people who are sinful like ourselves and always subject to using their authority more for the worldly kingdom, even when called Church, than for the kingdom of Christ. But Jesus allowed the will of his Father to be done through Pilate, Herod, mocking soldiers, and a gaping crowd that did not understand. How little is asked of me. I am asked only to obey people who share my love for Christ and have often had a greater share in his suffering than I have.

But let me at least realize today that if I ever am asked to accept or exercise authority over others, it should be an authority based on a sharing in the suffering of those whom I ask to obey.

Monday, 25

More and more the hunger in the world is entering our consciousness. I have heard and read about it for years, but now it is the dominating issue. Without any doubt it is the question, the concern, the problem, and the challenge of the '70s. In the beginning of the '60s, civil rights occupied the center of our attention; at the end of the '60s the Vietnam War was the central issue. Now it is hunger, starvation, famine, death. It is an issue that is so enormous and so overwhelming that it is nearly impossible to grasp in all its implications. Millions of people are faced with death; every day thousands of people die from lack of food. It makes it all the more frustrating to think about this in a monastery where three days a week about 15,000 loaves of bread come out of the oven and where the wheat and corn harvest was better than in many previous years.

Thursday, 28

Thanksgiving Day is a most American day. It also seems to me the day which the people of this nation know how to celebrate best. It is a family day, a day of hospitality, a day of gratitude. It is the day that—unlike Father's Day, Mother's Day, and Christmas Day—has escaped commercialization. It is the day that makes me desire to be with a family here. It is the only day that makes me a little melancholic because in a Trappist monastery Thanksgiving cannot be celebrated in the traditional way. It is significant that the wine which was given to the monastery for Thanksgiving was used instead for the feast of Christ the King. Except for cranberry sauce—without turkey!—dinner had little to do with Thanksgiving. I keep wondering why monks don't seem to be interested in national feast days. I had expected Thanksgiving to be celebrated as a great feast, especially since it is the feast in which deep national and deep religious sentiments merge. But although Anthony had made a beautiful display of harvest grain and fruit under the altar, although Father Marcellus had us listen to Beethoven's Sixth Symphony during dinner, and although the Mass was the Mass of Thanksgiving, you could sense that the monks were not really celebrating as on Pentecost, on Assumption Day, or All Saints' Day. Maybe they resent the fact that the Pilgrims were not Catholics! Maybe, indeed, Thanksgiving is more a Protestant feast in history and character. Maybe it is just hard to celebrate Thanksgiving without your family.

Thanksgiving, however, is first of all a North American feast. This nation is affluent and has more than it needs. The realization that what we have is a free gift can deepen our desire to share this gift with others who cry out for help. When we bless the fruits of the harvest, let us at least realize that blessed fruits need to be shared. Otherwise, the blessing turns into a curse.

Saturday, 30

Vespers this evening opened the Advent season. A large green wreath with four candles, symbolizing the four Sundays before Christmas, was hung in the center of the choir. This simple decoration in the otherwise so sober chapel touched me deeply. Four weeks of expectation have begun. Expecting the day Christmas, expecting my final day in the Abbey, expecting my visit to Holland, and expecting my return to New Haven. It is good, very good, to have these weeks of expectations and to deepen my realization that all these small expectations help me come to a deeper awareness of the great day on which the Lord will return to fulfill his promises.

The expectation of Advent is anchored in the event of God's incarnation. The more I come in touch with what happened in the past, the more I come in touch with what is to come. The Gospel not only reminds me of what took place but also of what will take place. In the contemplation of Christ's first coming, I can discover the signs of his second coming. By looking back in meditation, I can look forward in expectation. By reflection, I can project; by conserving the memory of Christ's birth, I can progress to the fulfillment of his kingdom. I am struck by the fact that the prophets speaking about the future of Israel always kept reminding their people of God's great works in the past. They could look forward with confidence because they could look backward with awe to Yahweh's great deeds.

All this seems extremely important in a time in which our sense of history is so weak. Still it was the memory of the aspirations of the Founding Fathers, crystallized in the United States Constitution, which strengthened this country during the Watergate trauma and made it possible to regain some sense of national self-respect. Without anchors in its early promises and aspirations a nation is in danger of drifting and losing direction. And not only a nation, but the Church as well. It seems that progress is always connected with a refreshing of our collective memory. Practically all reforms in the Church and the Orders of the Church have been marked by a new appreciation of the intentions of the early Church and a renewed study of the past, not to repeat it but to find there the inspiration for real renewal. George Santayana once said: "Those who forget the past are doomed to repeat it."

I pray that Advent will offer me the opportunity to deepen my memory of God's great deeds in time and will set me free to look forward with courage to the fulfillment of time by him who came and is still to come.

7

December

WAITING QUIETLY AND JOYFULLY

■

Sunday, 1

THIS FIRST Sunday of Advent was a beautiful day and the liturgy made me constantly aware of the great expectation. I find myself singing a most beautiful Latin versicle which keeps welling up from my innermost being: "*Rorate coeli desuper et nubes pluant justum*" (You heavens send down your dew and let the clouds rain down the Just One); and the beautiful response: "*Aperiatur terra et germinet Salvatorem*" (Let the earth be opened and bring forth the Saviour). The strong supplicating melody keeps ringing through my head, and I see the divine dew covering the earth. God's grace is indeed like a gentle morning dew and a soft rain that gives new life to barren soil. Images of gentleness. My call is indeed to become more and more sensitive to the morning dew and to open my soul to the rain so that my innermost self can bring forth the Saviour.

Monday, 2

A heavy snowfall changed the scene today. There was a strong wind that made work outside practically impossible. The roof of the new church is still not finished and with this snow it is too difficult to work on such high, slippery places. Everybody hopes for another sunny week before the winter dominates the scene, but nobody can tell how great the chances are that this will happen. John Eudes returned late this evening from a retreat he gave in California. His plane had to land in Syracuse instead of Rochester, and it took him a long time to make it to the Abbey.

Tuesday, 3

"The grass withers, the flower fades, but the word of our God remains for ever" (Is. 40:8). The Word of God is powerful indeed. Not only the Jesus Prayer but many words from the Scriptures can reshape the inner self. When I take the words that strike me during a service into the day and slowly repeat them while reading or working, more or less chewing on them, they create new life. Sometimes when I wake up during the night I am still saying them, and they become like wings carrying me above the moods and turbulences of the days and the weeks.

In Isaiah I read: "Young men may grow tired and weary, youths may stumble, but those who hope in Yahweh renew their strength, they put out wings like eagles. They run and do not grow weary, walk and never tire" (40:30–31). The words of God are indeed like eagles' wings. Maybe I can deepen my hope in God by giving more time and attention to his words.

Once in a while I see a monk reading from a small pocket book of the psalms while doing something else (stirring soup, for instance). I know that he is trying to memorize the psalms. I recently read a letter written by a Trappistine sister in which she wrote that she knew more than half of the 150 psalms by heart. What a gift to be able to pray those words at any time and at any place. I can understand better now how they can give us eagles' wings and renew constantly our strength.

The words about God's coming not only remind us that God will appear, but also that he will slowly transform our whole being into expectation. Then we will no longer have expectations but be expectation, then all we are has become "waiting."

Wednesday, 4

Trudy Dixon, who edited *Zen Mind, Beginner's Mind*, writes concerning the special relationship between the Zen teacher and his student: "A roshi is a person who has actualized that perfect freedom which is the potentiality for all human beings. He exists in the fulness of his whole being. The flow of his consciousness is not the fixed repetitive patterns of our usual self-centered consciousness but rather arises spontaneously and naturally from the actual circumstances of the present. The results of this in terms of the quality of his life are extraordinary—buoyancy, vigor, straightforwardness, simplicity, humility, serenity, joyousness, uncanny perspicacity and unfathomable compassion. His whole being testifies to what it means to live in the reality of the present. Without anything said or done just the impact of meeting a personality so developed can be enough to change another's whole way of life. But in the end it is not the extraordinariness of the teacher which perplexes, intrigues and deepens the student, it is the teacher's utter ordinariness. Because he is just himself, he is a mirror for his students. When we are with him, we feel our own strengths and shortcomings without any sense of praise or criticism from him. In his presence we see our original face and the extraordinariness we see is only our true nature. When we learn to let our own nature free, the boundaries between master and student disappear in a deep flow of being and joy in the unfolding of Buddha mind."[1]

This beautiful description of the teacher-student relationship helps me very much to understand what the apostles must have experienced when they met Jesus and lived with him.

Thursday, 5

Today in Holland everyone is exchanging presents. St. Nicholas evening—the most playful, folkloric celebration of Holland. Full of surprises. The children are in the center, but nobody is excluded from attention. I miss it tonight. Many Dutchmen who are not in Holland will miss it also or will create their own St. Nicholas evening with other Dutchmen whom they gather together.

I am reading about a very non-Dutch idea: "In the beginner's mind there is no thought 'I have attained something.' All self-centered thoughts limit our vast mind. When we have no thought of achievement, no thought of self, we are true beginners. Then we can really learn something. The beginner's mind is the mind of compassion. When our mind is compassionate, it is boundless."[2]

I like these words. Also very important for Advent. Open, free, flexible, receptive. That is the attitude that makes us ready. I realize that in Zen you are not expecting anything or anyone. Still, it seems that all the things Shunryu Suzuki tells his students are important for Christians to hear and realize. Isn't a beginner's mind, a mind without the thought, "I have attained something," a mind opened for grace? Isn't that the mind of children who marvel at all they see? Isn't that the mind not filled with worries for tomorrow but alert and awake in the present moment?

Reading Shunryu Suzuki is like hearing far-away sounds which resonate in your innermost soul. They are far, they are close, they are strange, they are familiar, they are Buddhist sounds, they are Christian sounds. They are like the strange Magi from the East who were among the first to find the child.

Suzuki says: "After some years we will die. If we just think it is the end of our life, this will be the wrong understanding. But, on the other hand, if we think that we do not die, this is also wrong. We die, and we do not die. This is the right understanding."[3]

That is a sound coming from afar that resounds in my deepest self. It makes me recognize the words of the Man of Nazareth again, who left and yet remains, who died and yet lives, who came and is still to come.

Friday, 6

Sylvester told me today that he had received a postcard from Bob, one of my students who had spent a few days at the Abbey. He was beaming with joy and gratitude. This makes me realize how small signs of friendliness can create much joy and small disturbances between people much sadness while the "great events" of the day often do not touch us so deeply. An unexpected note from a friend or the passing remark from a neighbor can make or break my day emotionally, while inflation and recession, war and oppression do not touch my emotions directly. A distant catastrophe has less effect than a nearby mishap, and an inter-personal tiff raises more hackles than a world-wide calamity. The burning down of the monastery would be less "dangerous" than rivalry within its unharmed walls.

But how little do we use this knowledge? What is easier than writing a thank-you note, than sending a card "just to say hello," or to give a call "just to see how things have been." But how seldom do I do this. Still, I realize that every time someone says, "I liked your talk" or "I appreciated your remark" or "Your note really helped" or "You really seem to feel at home here"—I feel my inner life being lifted up and the day seems brighter, the grass greener, and the snow whiter than before. Indeed, the great mystery is that a small, often quite immaterial gesture can change my heart so much. The way to the heart always seems to be a quiet, gentle way. After Thanksgiving, I received a note from someone I do not know telling me how much she felt part of my life because of my writings. It seems that these are the most precious moments of life.

Sylvester's joyful eyes told me a story which I hope I'll never forget.

Saturday, 7

This year the Immaculate Conception of Mary the mother of God is celebrated one day before the official feast day. In this feast it seems that all the quiet beauty of Advent suddenly bursts forth into exuberance and exultation. In Mary we see all the beauty of Advent concentrated. She is the one in whom the waiting of Israel is most fully and most purely manifested; she is the last of the remnant of Israel for whom God shows his mercy and fulfills his promises; she is the faithful one who believed that the promise made to her by the Lord would be fulfilled; she is the lowly handmaid, the obedient servant, the quiet contemplative. She indeed is the most prepared to receive the Lord.

It seems that there is no better time to celebrate this feast than during these Advent days. It is the celebration of the beauty of her who is ready to receive the Lord. It is like admiring the palace where the King will enter, the room to which the bridegroom will come, the garden where the great encounter will take place.

I think of the painting on the ceiling of the Sistine Chapel where God stretches out his hand to Adam to call him to life. How beautifully humanity is created. Now God again is stretching out his arm to her who waits for his touch by which humanity is re-created even more beautifully. The celebration of this feast is the anticipation of the great event of Christmas. It makes me feel like a child on the evening before a wedding, full of joy and anticipation. I have already seen the bridal gown. I have already smelled the flowers. I have already heard the wedding song. There is no longer any doubt. Tomorrow it will surely happen; everything is ready to be fulfilled.

This feast day gives Advent its true character. It is indeed primarily a season of joy. It is not, like Lent, primarily a time of penance. No, there is too much anticipation for that. All-overriding is the experience of joy.

Sunday, 8

John Eudes said in Chapter that we should desire not only the first coming of Christ in his lowly human gentleness but also his second coming as the judge of our lives. I sensed that the desire for Christ's judgment is a real aspect of holiness and realized how little that desire was mine.

In his Advent sermon, Guerric of Igny understands that it is not easy to desire with fervor this second coming. Therefore, he says that if we cannot prepare ourselves for the day of judgment by desire, let us at least prepare ourselves by fear. Now I see better how part of Christian maturation is the slow but persistent deepening of fear to the point where it becomes desire. The fear of God is not in contrast with his mercy. Therefore, words such as fear and desire, justice and mercy have to be relearned and reunderstood when we use them in our intimate relationship with the Lord.

Monday, 9

The New York *Times* "Book Reviews" for December 1 gave a fascinating recap of the new books that appeared during 1974. Not only the articles but also— even more so—the advertisements gave a good impression of what keeps the minds of writers and readers occupied.

Among the hundreds of books announced, described, recommended, and criticized, very few are religious in nature. As a lonely dove among the many hawks, I saw the advertisement of *The Way of the Pilgrim* by Seabury Press. It says: "Now available in a beautiful slip-cased clothbound edition $7.50." I was thinking about the irony of this poor wanderer in Christ, whose only concern was to pray without ceasing, entering in this expensive dress into the competitive world of American publishers. But, except for the Russian pilgrim, most authors and their subjects represent different concerns. My impression is that most of the new books are looking backward rather than forward and are more about "those good old days" than about good new days. No doubt, a resurgent romanticism roams the land. Many books bring to mind forgotten treasures of former generations, help find the world's few leftover quiet spots, or reveal the simple life-styles of the past. Even their titles—*The Way Life Was, Farmboy, Times to Remember, The Last of the Nuba*—all suggest that there were better times and that there are better places than our time and place.

Seeing so many books displayed and discussed does not discourage me from writing. On the contrary, I feel a growing desire to enter into this world and to speak a word of hope. During periods of political or economic crisis, people tend to become more introverted and pensive. Sometimes books encourage a sort of collective daydreaming and create a world in which to escape. But they also can offer consolation and new strength. Hopefully, the readers of these books will gain a refreshed memory that will lead to new aspirations and new motivations to face reality now and to work in unity for a new world.

Tuesday, 10

On December 10, 1941, Thomas Merton entered Gethsemani. On December 10, 1968, he died in Bangkok. We prayed for him during Mass this morning.

I have been trying to make these last weeks in the Abbey weeks of special recollection. Sort of a retreat within a retreat. I did not want the last weeks to become weeks of packing mental suitcases but instead weeks of entering more deeply into the monastic experience. Advent helps very much. I have felt a great peace and inner quietude since Advent started. I am sufficiently used to the life and the people here to feel at home. I have not too much manual work to do, and what I do is routine work in the bakery or with the rocks. I have no strong desire to read great books or gather new materials and ideas. So I am quite free to give much attention to prayer, Scripture reading, and just a quiet way of living. At times, I feel a little guilty that I do not work more since everyone is so busy with the new church, but I realize that these guilt feelings are false and that I should not act upon them. At times, I want to delve into new books, but I realize that this is not the important thing to do and I let the idea pass as a temptation. I try to be quiet, to let the sense of expectation for the coming of the Lord grow in my heart and to simply enjoy being here and now.

Calmness, repose, even-mindedness, restful joy, gentleness: these are the feelings that describe best my present life. No great hostilities or disappointments, no great anxieties about leaving or fears about returning home. Nothing of that. No apprehensions, not even about the socio-economic or political future. I read the paper today and although last week proved in no way better than the weeks before, I did not feel deeply disturbed or restless. Most of the afternoon I carried slippery, snow-covered rocks into the church to be used for the inner walls. At times I thought that I recognized a rock I had picked up from the creek in June. I enjoyed it and felt friendly toward people and stones. I talked when I wanted and was silent when I wanted. It really didn't seem to matter very much. I feel very much at ease and still, and neither noise nor words nor actions seem to disturb this stillness. It is a grace-filled time and God is close.

Wednesday, 11

I had a very helpful session with John Eudes. When I told him that I felt deeply quiet, less restless, more prayerful, less compulsive, and freer, he said that if I had come to stay, this would have been the time to receive the habit of a novice. He was happily surprised that I could confirm the general experience that after six months the postulant is sufficiently at home to enter the novitiate.

I explained to John Eudes that I felt somewhat free from my compulsions. Normally, when I receive many letters I complain that I am too busy, and when I receive none I complain about lack of attention; when I work a lot I complain about lack of time to study and pray, when I work little I feel guilty for not making a contribution. In this sense I very much confirmed the vision of the French chaplain who, after fifteen years of hearing confessions, had learned two things: "People are not very happy and we never grow up."[4] But during the past few weeks I have felt an inner distance which has allowed me to *see* my compulsions and therefore to lose them, and I have experienced some new inner freedom.

John Eudes showed me how much my compulsive behavior could be seen as part of a way of being in which everything is experienced in terms of an "ought." I ought to be here, I ought to think such and such, etc. This way of being has many levels and touches many aspects of the personality. But when I am able to start seeing some of its symptoms from a certain distance and recognize them as symptoms of the "ought" compulsion, then I can slowly go all the way down to its roots and choose another way of relating to the world.

As John Eudes pointed out, the "ought modality" is closely tied up with the identity struggle. As long as I am constantly concerned about what I "ought" to say, think, do, or feel, I am still the victim of my surroundings and am not liberated. I am compelled to act in certain ways to live up to my self-created image. But when I can accept my identity from Cod and allow him to be the center of my life, I am liberated from compulsion and can move without restraints.

Saturday, 14

Last night Father van Torre from St. Bernard's Seminary in Rochester spoke to the monks. In his talk he used an illustration that I had heard before but that struck me suddenly as very revealing and convincing. When someone is very excited about the stained glass windows that Marc Chagall made for the synagogue of the Hadassah-Hebrew University Medical Center in Jerusalem, the only way to convince friends of their beauty is by bringing them into the synagogue.

This idea stayed with me the whole day because it convinced me more than ever of the importance of teaching spirituality from the inside. Next semester I will be fully occupied again with teaching. My task is not to make beautiful windows but to lead students into the synagogue where they can see the splendid colors when the sunlight shines through them. As long as students say that they are interested in spirituality but prefer to remain on the outside, no argument, enthusiastic description, or rich vocabulary will make them see what I see. Only by entering with me into the experience with which spirituality deals will any real learning take place. That does not mean that critical distance is not available and that subjectivity becomes the only criterion. On the contrary. Even from the inside we can step back and remain critical. Not everything we see from the inside is necessarily beautiful, worthwhile, or good. In fact, we are better able to make distinctions between bad and good, ugly and beautiful, appropriate and unfit from the inside than from the outside.

Does that mean that the only way to talk about prayer is by praying together? I don't think so. You don't have to be a Jew in order to be able to enjoy or appreciate the windows of Chagall, although as a Jew you will have a deeper understanding of their beauty than will someone to whom the Jewish religious tradition is unknown. But you have to enter into the world of the Jew, the synagogue, to enjoy its stained glass windows at all. In order to understand the meaning of prayer you have to be willing to enter into the world of praying men and women and discover the power and beauty of prayer from within. All this leads to the important question: How to introduce strangers into the world of prayer without forcing them into a kind of behavior that makes them feel uncomfortable?

Sometimes I am so excited about my new experiences here at the Abbey that I can hardly believe it when someone else does not share this excitement. But then, I have forgotten that I am shouting from the inside and that my shoulder-shrugging friends are looking at the same thing from the outside and wonder why I "exaggerate" all the time.

There is no doubt in my mind that it is worth my time and energy to lead my friends first to the inside of the building before I start trying to convince them of the beauty of the stained glass windows. Otherwise, I shall make a fool of myself by impatience and lack of ordinary educational insight.

Sunday, 15

Today is "Gaudete" Sunday, the Sunday to rejoice. For the entrance song of the Eucharist we sang the words of St. Paul: "Rejoice, again I say rejoice. The Lord is very near."

In Chapter John Eudes gave a beautiful meditation about this anticipatory joy. We are joyful already now because we know that the Lord will come. Our expectation leads to joy and our joy to a desire to give to others. Real joy always wants to share. It belongs to the nature of joy to communicate itself to others and to invite others to take part in the gifts we have received.

Advent is indeed a time of joyful waiting and joyful giving. John Eudes observed how much this mood is also part of our whole society. The period before Christmas has that remarkable quality of joy that seems to touch not only Christians but all who live in our society. When you, as a Westerner, live in another society, such as the Japanese society, where Advent and Christmas do not exist as universal events, you realize the lack of this joyful anticipation most painfully.

But Advent is not only a period of joy. It is also a time when those who are lonely feel lonelier than during other periods of the year. During this time many people try to commit suicide or are hospitalized with severe depression. Those who have hope feel much joy and desire to give. Those who have no hope feel more depressed than ever and are often thrown back on their lonely selves in despair.

Surrounded by a loving, supportive community, Advent and Christmas seem pure joy. But let me not forget my lonely moments because it does not take much to make that loneliness reappear. If I am able to remember loneliness during joy, I might be able in the future to remember joy during loneliness and so be stronger to face it and help others face it. In 1970 I felt so lonely that I could not give;

now I feel so joyful that giving seems easy. I hope that the day will come when the memory of my present joy will give me the strength to keep giving even when loneliness gnaws at my heart. When Jesus was loneliest, he gave most. That realization should help to deepen my commitment to service and let my desire to give become independent of my actual experience of joy. Only a deepening of my life in Christ will make that possible.

Monday, 16

During my meeting with John Eudes today, I asked him if he had any ideas, observations, suggestions, or recommendations in regard to my stay here or my future life. In practically all our sessions over the last seven months I had set the tone and determined the subject of the conversation. Now I wondered if he perhaps had seen anything that I had missed or felt anything that needed to be expressed.

John Eudes felt that during the seven months we had talked about the most important things, and he did not feel that I had missed anything of special importance. But he felt it was crucial for me to find concrete ways to prevent myself from drowning in activities and concerns on my return home. We had often discussed my tendency to become overinvolved, to be carried away by sudden enthusiasm, to accept too many invitations, and to invest too much energy without considering whether or not it was worth it. If I want to maintain a steady prayer life and keep a certain purity of heart in the midst of all my actions, I need to set limits and find ways to say "no" more often.

I tried to formulate how I had come to see my own vocation more clearly during this retreat. Two things seem central: I am a priest and I am called to study and teach in the field of Christian Spirituality. Since I was six years old I have wanted to be a priest, a desire that never wavered except for the few moments when I was overly impressed by the uniform of a sea captain. Ever since my studies for the priesthood I have felt especially attracted to what was then called, "Ascetical and Mystical Theology," and all my other studies in psychology, sociology, and similar fields never seemed fruitful for me unless they led me to a deeper understanding of the questions of the spiritual life.

I have always moved from the psychological to the theological level and from clinical considerations to spiritual concerns. A sequence of courses—personality theory, clinical psychology, psychology of religion, pastoral psychology, ministry and spirituality, the history of Christian Spirituality, prayer and the spiritual life—seems to illustrate the movement of which I have always been part.

Where should my emphasis be now? It seems that my retreat has affirmed and deepened an already existing trend. What is becoming clear is the need to enter into both realities—the priesthood as a function and a life-style and the spiritual life as a field of special concentration—more deeply, more fully, more extensively, and in a more scholarly way. "Less speaking, more praying, more studying, and more writing" seems to summarize best the direction to take.

John Eudes strongly affirmed my self-evaluation. He felt that the direction I had pointed out seemed to be the way to go. He remarked that thus it would be much easier for me to maintain a spiritual discipline and refrain from spreading myself too thin. He also affirmed strongly the idea of combining more scholarly work in the field of spirituality with more long-term writing plans. He felt strongly that I should be more concerned with writing than with speaking, more with studying than with counseling, more with praying than with social life.

All of this makes me aware that I have entered into my last full week at the Abbey and that the "termination process" has indeed begun.

Tuesday, 17

Richard wrote a letter saying: " . . . it is now over a month without codeine! Actually the pain is diminishing steadily. Yesterday I spent four hours driving. I have almost reached the point where I don't think of it anymore. The headaches are still a problem, but I am working on them. Have also been writing these past days. Looks like I am getting it together at that end, too."

This letter makes me leap for joy. After my intensive prayer in which I could nearly feel his painful back, after asking James for special prayers, and after recommending Richard to the prayers of the whole community, this letter sounded like music to me. I realize now how I really never doubted for a moment that God would hear our prayers and heal Richard very soon and completely, and also how grateful and joyful I was when he indeed responded so richly. "Not being surprised" and "being totally surprised" seems to have become one and the same emotion.

Richard has been very much in my thoughts and prayers since I received his letter. I have asked James and the whole community to continue in their prayers. I know how hard it is to allow healing to take place in our whole person—body, mind, and soul. But I also know that this is Richard's "hour," and that he has the strength to let go of his pains and open himself to others and the Other who reach out to him. Just knowing all this adds special joy to these final days here.

I moved rocks for three hours this afternoon and enjoyed it. The weather was mild and the mud not too bad.

Thursday, 19

During the last week of Advent it seems as if the liturgy can no longer hide the excitement about the coming of the Lord and bursts forth in anticipatory joy. During Vespers the "O" antiphons express unrestrained exhilaration. "O Wisdom that proceeds from the mouth of the Most High, O Adonai and leader of the House of Israel, O Root of Jesse who stands as the ensign of the peoples, O Key of David and Scepter of the House of Israel, O Orient, Splendor of eternal light, O King of nations, the One for whom they long, O Emmanuel, the Expectation and Savior of the nations—come to us, O Lord, Our God." Every evening between December 17 and 24 a new "O" is sung and, slowly, waiting and welcoming, expecting and seeing, hoping and receiving, future and present merge into one song of praise to the Lord who has visited his people.

What strikes me is that waiting is a period of learning. The longer we wait the more we hear about him for whom we are waiting. As the Advent weeks progress, we hear more and more about the beauty and splendor of the One who is to come. The Gospel passages read during Mass all talk about the events before Jesus' birth and the people ready to receive him. In the other readings Isaiah heaps prophecy on prophecy to strengthen and deepen our hope, and the songs, lessons, commentaries, and antiphons all compete in their attempt to set the stage for the Lord who is to come.

There is a stark beauty about it all. But is this not a preparation that can only lead to an anticlimax? I don't think so. Advent does not lead to nervous tension stemming from expectation of something spectacular about to happen. On the contrary, it leads to a growing inner stillness and joy allowing me to realize that he for whom I am waiting has already arrived and speaks to me in the silence of my heart. Just as a mother feels the child grow in her and is not surprised on the day of the birth but joyfully receives the one she learned to know during her waiting, so Jesus can be born in my life slowly and steadily and be received as the one I learned to know while waiting.

This last week is indeed a happy one.

Brian was hurt during work and will be in bed for quite a while. The bucket of the Trojan, loaded with stones, was lowered on the big toe of his right foot. The toe was smashed and the nail lost. Now he thrones in bed with a huge toe sticking out from under the sheets. The doctor told him: one week in bed and two weeks on crutches. Brian called it a "nuisance." With this understatement he put things in perspective. The pain is practically gone and he can read, write letters, and receive visitors. During the first day he had no lack of attention. During Lauds Brother Pat prayed for "Brian, who broke his toe."

Saturday, 21

Extra loaves and extra rocks. This morning 10,000 extra loaves were baked in the hope of conquering new "shelf space" in Cleveland. The distributor feels that the Abbey should expand the distribution of Monk's Bread because with the increase of prices, sales will drop off if limited to a small area. To give it a try all machines were turning their wheels today.

This afternoon we went back to the creek to pick up some heavy stones. The creek which was so quiet and sedate in June now looked like a small torrent. I had a hole in my right boot and the icy water found its way quickly to my shoe and foot. After changing boots with Brother Patrick who sat high and dry on the Trojan, I could help John Eudes better to push the rocks out of the water into the bucket.

At three o'clock I cleaned my room. Huge clouds of dust affirmed the fact that I had forgotten to clean it for three weeks. I got into a cleaning mood, threw every article of clothing that I could do without into the laundry, took a shower, combed my hair which had grown long enough again to be combed, put on a clean habit, and showed up in Vespers all shining. Four candles on the wreath were burning. First Vespers of the last Sunday in Advent.

Sunday, 22

This morning during Chapter John Eudes invited me to share with the community some of my impressions about my stay. He had told me a week ahead that he would do so, and I was happy to share with 'my brothers' my feelings of gratitude and joy.

Nevertheless, it is not easy to express in a few minutes experiences and emotions that are deep and often very broad. I ended up saying something about the Lord, something about the world, something about the brethren, and something about the saints. Let me try to write down the main content.

When I was a young child, my mother taught me the simple prayer: "All for you, dear Jesus." A simple prayer indeed but hard to realize. I discovered that, in fact, my life was more like the prayer: "Let us share things, Jesus, some for you and some for me." The commitment to serve the Lord and him alone is hard to fulfill. Still, that is the mark of sanctity. My life has always been sort of a compromise. "Sure, I am a priest, but if they don't like me as a priest, then I can still show them that I am also a psychologist, and they might like me for that." This attitude is like having hobbies on the side which offer gratification when the main task does not satisfy. The last seven months have revealed to me how demanding the love of the Lord is. I will never be happy unless I am totally, unconditionally committed to him. To be single-minded, to "will one thing," that is my goal and desire. Then also I can let go of the many pains and confusions that are the result of a divided mind. By allowing the Lord to be in the center, life becomes simpler, more unified, and more focused.

My stay at the monastery, however, has not only brought me closer to Christ, it has brought me closer to the world as well. In fact, distance from the world has made me feel more compassionate toward it. In my work in New Haven I am often so busy with immediate needs asking for an immediate response that my world narrows down to my daily worries, and I lose perspective on the larger problems. Here in the monastery I could look more easily beyond the boundaries of the place, the state, the country, and the continent, become more intimately aware of the pain and suffering of the whole world and respond to them by prayer, correspondence, gifts, or writing. I also felt that in this retreat my friends and family came closer to me. I experienced especially that a growing intimacy with God creates an always widening space for others in prayer. I had a real sense of the power of prayer for others and experienced what it means to place your suffering friends in God's presence right in the center of your heart.

But without the support of the community of brethren all this would have been practically impossible. My stay gave me a real new sense of community. When I experienced that I was accepted in the community, that my mistakes were hardly criticized and my good deeds rarely praised, that I did not have to fight for continuing acceptance, and that I was loved on a level deeper than that of successes and failures, I could come into a much deeper contact with myself and with God. God is the hub of the wheel of life. The closer we come to God the closer we come to each other. The basis of community is not primarily our ideas, feelings, and emotions about each other but our common search for God. When we keep our minds and hearts directed toward God, we will come more fully "together." During my stay in the Abbey I saw and experienced how many men with very different backgrounds and characters can live together in peace. They can do so not because of mutual attraction toward each other, but because of the common attraction toward God, their Lord and Father.

Besides communion with the brethren, I also discovered communion with the saints. In the past, the saints had very much moved to the background of my consciousness. During the last few months, they re-entered my awareness as powerful guides on the way to God. I read the lives of many saints and great spiritual men and women, and it seems that they have become real members of my spiritual family, always present to offer suggestions, ideas, advice, consolation, courage, and strength. It is very hard to keep your heart and mind directed toward God when there are no examples to help you in your struggle. Without saints you easily settle for less-inspiring people and quickly follow the ways of others who for a while seem exciting but who are not able to offer lasting support. I am happy to have been able to restore my relationship with many great saintly men and women in history who, by their lives and works, can be real counselors to me.

The words and questions after my short talk were very warm and sympathetic. John Eudes expressed his feeling that I had become a real member of the community even without vows or formal ties and hoped that the relationship that had developed over the past months would continue to grow in the future. That makes me feel joyful.

Tuesday, 24

In every respect a day of farewell. Many of the monks called me aside to say "good-bye" and to wish me well. Anthony made some photographs of me. First he showed up at 3 A.M. in the refectory with his camera to "catch me" while eating breakfast. When I appeared at 4:15 A.M. in the bakery to work with John Eudes on the hot pans, Brother Anthony had his large lamp waiting for me there. He made some interesting shots—a few with Brother Theodore at the oven, a few with John Eudes at the cooling racks, and a few at the hot pans. He also took some photographs during Mass and finished his series of "monastic situations" with some more shots in the chapel and the library.

Meanwhile, the whole day was one of preparation. Benedict was busy cleaning the chapel. James and Joseph had their hands full with two Christmas trees. Gregory walked around with a great Star of David filled with light bulbs. Anthony tried to find the most artistic way to set up the Christmas scene under the altar. I just ran up and down with boxes, books, and clothes to get everything packed and ready before Vespers.

Everyone was in a playful mood, less serious than usual and more childlike. At 6:15 we sang Compline with a Christmas song at the start and now everything is quiet, very quiet for a few hours. I will try to sleep a little in the hope of being fully fresh and alert to sing Christmas Vigils and welcome God into this our suffering world so desperately in need of the Saviour. May his light shine in our darkness and may I be ready to receive it with joy and thanksgiving.

Wednesday, 25

How shall I describe this Holy Night? How shall I give expression to the multitude of feelings and ideas that come together in this most joyful celebration? This night is the fulfillment of four weeks of expectation; it is the remembrance of the most intimate mystery of life, the birth of God in an agonizing world; it is the planting of the seeds of compassion, freedom and peace in a harsh, unfree, and hateful society; it is hope in a new earth to come. It is all that and much, much more. For me it is also the end of a most blessed and graceful retreat and the beginning of a new life. A step out of silence into the many sounds of the world, out of the cloister into the unkept garden without hedges or boundaries. In many ways I feel as though I have received a small, vulnerable child in my arms and have been asked to carry him with me out of the intimacy of the monastery into a world waiting for light to come.

This day is the day in which I will experience not only the beauty of the night with songs of peace but also the wide ocean stretching out between two continents. This day the smallness and vulnerability of the child and the vastness of our earth will both enter my soul. I know that without the child, I have no reason to live but also that without a growing awareness of the suffering of humanity, I will not fulfill the call that the child has given me.

The monks smile and embrace me, the night is soft and quiet, the gentle sounds of the bells during the midnight "Gloria" still echo in my soul. All is still and quiet now. The branches of the trees outside are decorated with fresh white snow and the winds have withdrawn to let us enjoy for a moment the unbelievable beauty of the night of peace, the Holy Night.

What can I say on a night like this? It is all very small and very large, very close and very distant, very tangible and very elusive. I keep thinking about the Christmas scene that Anthony arranged under the altar. This probably is the most meaningful "crib" I have ever seen. Three small wood-carved figures made in India: a poor woman, a poor man, and a small child between them. The carving is simple, nearly primitive. No eyes, no ears, no mouths, just the contours of the faces. The figures are smaller than a human hand—nearly too small to attract attention at all. But then—a beam of light shines on the three figures and projects large shadows on the wall of the sanctuary. That says it all. The light thrown on the smallness of Mary, Joseph, and the Child projects them as large, hopeful shadows against the walls of our life and our world. While looking at the intimate scene we already see the first outlines of the majesty and glory they represent. While witnessing the most human of human events, I see the majesty of God appearing on the horizon of my existence. While being moved by the gentleness of these three people, I am already awed by the immense greatness of God's love appearing in my world. Without the radiant beam of light shining into the darkness there is little to be seen. I might just pass by these three simple people and continue to walk in darkness. But everything changes with the light.

During these seven months the light has made me see not only the three small figures but also their huge shadows far away. This light makes all things new and reveals the greatness hidden in the small event of this Holy Night. I pray that I will have the strength to keep the light alive in my heart so that I can see and point to the promising shadows appearing on the walls of our world.

Now the only thing I can say on this Christmas morning, at the end of the event that started on Pentecost, is, "Thanks be to God that I have been here."

Conclusion

∎

MORE THAN HALF A YEAR has passed since I wrote the last entry in my Genesee diary. Rereading the many pages that I wrote during those seven months not only brought back to life many beautiful memories, but also confronted me with the present state of my heart and mind. Perhaps the greatest and most hidden illusion of all had been that after seven months of Trappist life I would be a different person, more integrated, more spiritual, more virtuous, more compassionate, more gentle, more joyful, and more understanding. Somehow I had expected that my restlessness would turn into quietude, my tensions into a peaceful life-style, and my many ambiguities and ambivalences into a single-minded commitment to God.

None of these successes, results, or achievements have come about. If I were to ask about my seven months at the Abbey, "Did it work, did I solve my problems?" the simple answer would be, "It did not work, it did not solve my problems." And I know that a year, two years, or even a lifetime as a Trappist monk would not have "worked" either. Because a monastery is not built to solve problems but to praise the Lord in the midst of them. I had known this all along, but still I had to return to my old busy life and be confronted with my own restless self to believe it. Those who welcomed me back expected to see a different, a better man. And I had not wanted to disappoint them. But I should have known better. Using the monastery to develop a "successful" saintliness only makes me like the possessed man of whom Jesus says that "when an unclean spirit goes out of him it wanders through waterless country looking for a place to rest, and cannot find one. Then it says, 'I will return to the home I came from.' But on arrival, finding it unoccupied, swept and tidied, it then goes off and collects seven other spirits more evil than itself, and they go in and set up house there, so that the man ends up being worse than he was before" (Mt. 12:43–45). These words of Jesus have often entered my mind when old and new demons entered my soul. I hardly had an opportunity to think that seven months as a Trappist monk had cleansed my heart enough to be pure for the year to come. It took only a few weeks of being back to realize that I was having some troublesome visitors again. Without exaggeration I can say that some of my most humbling experiences took place after my return. But they had to take place to convince me once again that I cannot be my own exorcist, and to remind me that, if anything significant takes place in my life, it is not the result of my own "spiritual" calisthenics, but only the manifestation of God's unconditional grace. God himself certainly is the last one to be impressed by seven months of monastic life, and he did not wait long to let me know it.

Why did I go at all? Because there was an inner "must" to which I received a positive response. Why did I stay? Because I knew I was at the right place and nobody told me otherwise. Why was I there? I don't know fully yet. Probably I will not know fully before the end of the cycle of my life. Still, I can say that I have a most precious memory which keeps unfolding itself in all that I do or plan to do. I no longer can live without being reminded of the glimpse of God's graciousness that I saw in my solitude, of the ray of light that broke through my darkness, of the gentle voice that spoke in my silence, and of the soft breeze that touched me in my stillest hour. This memory, however, does more than bring to mind rich experiences of the past. It also continues to offer new perspectives on present events and guides in decisions for the years to come. In the midst of my ongoing compulsions, illusions, and unrealities, this memory will always be there to dispel false dreams and point in right directions. When Peter, James, and John saw the Lord in his splendor on Mount Tabor, they were heavy with sleep, but the memory of this event proved a source of hope in the midst of their later hardships. Maybe there can be only one Tabor-experience in my life. But the new strength gained from that experience might be enough to support me in the valley, in the garden of Gethsemani, and in the long dark night of life. The seven months at the Genesee Abbey might indeed have been enough to remind me constantly that now I see only "a dim reflection in a mirror," but one day I will see "face to face" (I Cor. 13:12).

NOTES

Chapter 1: June

1. Robert M. Pirsig, *Zen and the Art of Motorcycle Maintenance* (New York: Wm. Morrow, 1974), Chap. 17, pp. 211–12.
2. Ibid., Chap. 24, p. 286.
3. Larry Collins and Dominique Lapiere, *Or I'll Dress You in Mourning* (New York: Simon and Schuster, 1968), p. 104.

4. Henry D. Thoreau, *Walden, and Other Writings,* The Modern Library (New York: Random House, 1950), p. 290.

Chapter 2: *July*

1. *New York Review of Books,* May 30, 1974, p. 42.
2. Ibid.
3. Ibid., p. 38.
4. All psalms are quoted from *A New Translation from the Hebrew Arranged for Singing to the Psalmody of Joseph Gelineau* (New York: Paulist Press, 1968).
5. Dorothée de Gaza, *Oeuvres Spirituelles* in Sources Chrétiennes, No. 92 (Paris: Editions du Cerf, 1963), Par. 13, p. 145.
6. Ibid., Par. 66, p. 259.
7. Georges Gorree, *Charles de Foucauld* (Lyon: Editions du Chalet, 1957), Introduction.
8. De Gaza, op. cit., Par. 1, p. 307.
9. Ibid., Par. 94, p. 319.
10. *The Sands of Tamanrasset* (New York: Hawthorn, 1961), pp. 95–96.
11. De Gaza, op. cit., No. 5, p. 527.
12. Ibid., Par. 1, p. 307.
13. Diadoque de Photicé, *Oeuvres Spirituelles* in Sources Chrétiennes, No. 5 bis (Paris: Editions du Cerf, 1955). pp. 97–98.
14. See St. Bernard, "On Conversion," trans. and notes by Watkin Williams (London, 1938), p. 12 (Anchin Manuscript).
15. Ibid., p. 14.
16. *The Last of the Fathers* (New York: Harcourt, Brace, 1954), p. 52.
17. *The Cistercian Heritage,* trans. Elizabeth Livingstone (Westminster, Md.: Newman Press, 1958), pp. 72—74.
18. *U. S. News and World Report,* July 29, 1974, p. 41.

Chapter 3: *August*

1. Robert Jay Lifton and Eric Olson, *Living and Dying* (New York and Washington: Praeger, 1974), p. 116.
2. Thomas Merton, *Disputed Questions* (New York: Farrar, Straus & Cudahy, 1960), pp. 3–67.
3. Pasternak, *Doctor Zhivago* (New York: Pantheon, 1958), p. 335.
4. Murray Hoyt, *The World of Bees* (New York: Coward McCann, 1965), pp. 25–26.
5. *Conjectures of a Guilty Bystander* (New York: Doubleday, 1966), pp. 140–42.
6. Abraham Joshua Heschel, *A Passion for Truth* (New York: Farrar, Straus & Giroux, 1973), pp. xiv–xv.

Chapter 4: *September*

1. Theophan the Recluse in Igoumen Chariton, *The Art of Prayer,* ed. by T. Ware (London: Faber and Faber, 1966), p. 125.
2. Ibid., p. 131.
3. Heschel, op. cit., p. 87.
4. *The Rule of St. Benedict,* intro. and new trans. by Basilius Steidle, Eng. trans. Urban Schnitzhofer (Canon City, Colo.: Holy Cross Abbey, 1967), p. 112.
5. Elie Wiesel, *Souls on Fire,* Portraits and legends of Hasidic Masters (New York: Random House, 1972), p. 235.
6. Ibid., p. 240.
7. Heschel, op. cit., p. 131.
8. Ibid., p. 265.

9. Ibid., p. 269.
10. Ibid., p. 271.
11. Ibid., p. 303.
12. Ibid., p. 298.
13. Ibid., p. 201.

Chapter 5: October

1. Gilbert K. Chesterton, *St. Francis of Assisi* (New York: Doubleday Image Books, 1957), p. 101.
2. Ibid., pp. 74–75.
3. Ibid., pp. 96–97.
4. *Good News for Modern Man*; The New Testament in Today's English (New York: American Bible Society, 1966), p. 361.
5. Ibid.
6. J. B. Phillips, *The New Testament in Modern English* (London and Glasgow: Collins), p. 172.

Chapter 6: November

1. Brother Lawrence, *The Practice of the Presence of God* (Mount Vernon, N.Y.: Peter Pauper Press, 1973), p. 48.
2. Ibid., p. 43.
3. Evelyn Underhill, *The Mystics of the Church* (New York: Schocken Books, 1964), p. 43.
4. Ibid., p. 44.
5. *Bernard of Clairvaux*, On the Song of Songs I, Cistercian Fathers Series, Number Four (Spencer, Mass.: Cistercian Publications, 1971), p. 111.
6. *Penguin Book of Latin Verse*, intro. and ed. Frederick Brittain (Baltimore, Md.: 1962), p. xxxi.
7. *The Exemplar: Life and Writings of Blessed Henry Suso, O.P.*, Volume Two, intro. and notes N. Heller, Eng. trans. M. Ann Edwards, O.P. (Dubuque, Iowa, Priory Press, 1962), pp. 26–27.
8. Frederic Joseph Kelly, S.J., *Man Before God: Thomas Merton on Social Responsibility* (New York: Doubleday, 1974), Dennis Q. McInerny, *Thomas Merton: The Man & His Work*, Cistercian Studies Series, No. 27 (Washington: Consortium, 1974); Bro. Patrick Hart (ed.), *Thomas Merton—Monk: A Monastic Tribute* (New York: Sheed, 1974).
9. *Rule of St. Benedict*, op. cit., p. 57. Alterations in the translation are mine.

Chapter 7: December

1. Shunryu Suzuki, *Zen Mind, Beginner's Mind*, ed. Trudy Dixon (New York and Tokyo: Weatherill, 1970), p. 18.
2. Ibid., p. 22.
3. Ibid., on "Posture," p. 25.
4. From an interview with William Sloane Collin, *Yale Alumni Magazine*, December 1974, p. 17.

¡GRACIAS!

A Latin American Journal

■

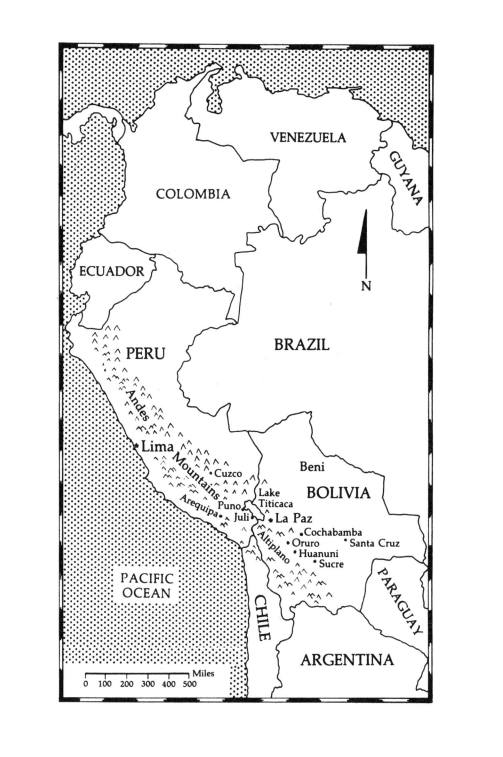

*To all who bear witness to the presence of
the suffering Christ in Latin America*

CONTENTS

∎

Acknowledgments

■

THIS JOURNAL would never have been written without the generous hospitality and skillful assistance of many friends in Latin America. Therefore my gratitude extends first to my many hosts. Pete Byrne, the Superior of the Maryknoll fathers in Peru, was the first to greet me when I came to Latin America. His faithful friendship became the context for many enriching experiences. In the months to follow, many other members of the Maryknoll community offered me a warm welcome, especially Alex Walsh, Bill McCarthy, Pete Ruggere, Tom Burns, and Charles Murray. They made me feel at home in the Maryknoll Center house in Lima and let me become part of their ministry in Ciudad de Dios. I am especially grateful to Pablo and Sophia Oscco-Moreno for letting me live with their family during my time in the parish.

My stay at the language institute in Bolivia would not have been such a good experience without the great care and attention that I received from the director, Gerry McCrane. Even if I had not learned much Spanish, just coming to know him as a friend would have made the trip worthwhile. I am also deeply grateful to Nancy and Rodolfo Quiroga, who made me a true member of their family during my two months in their home in Cochabamba. I fondly remember their kindness and great patience in correcting my mistakes in Spanish.

Two dear friends, Fran Kersjes in Bolivia and Anne Marie Tamariz in Peru, deserve a special word of thanks. They typed and retyped the text as it was first written, making it possible for me to send it to friends who wanted to know how things were going. It was a joy to work with them.

This journal would never have been published without the dedicated help of friends in the United States. I owe a deep gratitude to Bobby Massie, who spent many hours, days, and weeks editing the manuscript, suggesting cuts and changes, and helping me to separate the wheat from the chaff. His personal interest and his many words of encouragement have been essential for the progress of this project. Phil Zaeder and Peggy Schreiner generously offered their time and talents when the text needed a final critical reading. For their countless literary suggestions I am very grateful. I also want to say thanks to Richard Alan White, Robert Durback, and Fred Bratman for their insightful criticisms. Mabel Treadwell, June Hagan, and Carol Plantinga did much of the hard administrative and secretarial work during the last stages of this journal. Their generous help in sending the text to different readers and in typing and retyping it was indispensable. I cannot say "thanks" to them often enough.

John Shopp, my editor at Harper & Row, has been a great support all along the way. His personal interest in this journal and his great availability in discussing even minute details have been a real source of encouragement to me.

Finally, I want to say thanks to Joseph Núñez. He gave this journal its title and, by so doing, helped me see its main theme more clearly than ever before. When he said, "Why don't you call it *Gracias*—isn't that what you heard and said most of all?" I knew that he had made me aware of the main experience of my journey to Latin America.

Thus I can say to all who are mentioned in this journal, to all who helped it to be written and published, and to all who stand around it without being mentioned by name: *Gracias a Dios, gracias a ustedes, muchísimas gracias.*

INTRODUCTION

In Search of a Vocation

■

THIS JOURNAL is the personal report of my six-month sojourn in Bolivia and
Peru. I wrote it in an attempt to capture the countless impressions, feelings, and
ideas that filled my mind and heart day after day. It speaks about new places and
people, about new insights and perspectives, and about new joys and anxieties.
But the question that runs through all its pages and binds the many varied fragments together is: "Does God call me to live and work in Latin America in the
years to come?" This vocational question has guided me in the selection of issues
to comment upon, it has directed me in my observations, and it has deeply
influenced my responses to what I have seen and heard. This journal, therefore,
is neither a travel diary, nor an analysis of Latin American conditions, nor a
critical study of political and religious movements. Even though I often mention
interesting sights, describe distressing living conditions, and comment on the
impact of political and religious currents, I do not claim more expertise than the
expertise that comes from an honest search for a new vocation. This journal
records a six-month journey toward discernment. In the midst of all the travels,
language studies, conversations, and encounters, I tried to discern God's voice;
and in the midst of the great variety of my inner responses, I tried to find the
way to be obedient to that voice.

The question: "Does God call me to Latin America?" was not a new question
for me. From the day I left Holland to teach pastoral theology at Yale Divinity
School, I had been wondering about the connection between the northern and
the southern parts of the American continent. Somehow I felt that teaching future
ministers in the United States about God's mysterious work with people could
not be done unless the word "people" included the millions of Spanish- and
Portuguese-speaking human beings whose destiny is intimately linked with that
of their English-speaking brothers and sisters. Somehow, I knew that God's voice
could not be heard unless it would include the voices of the men, women, and

children of Latin America. With this "knowledge," I made short visits to Mexico, Chile, and Paraguay, and took some language training in Bolivia. Although these excursions led only to piecemeal involvements and limited commitments, they deepened my conviction about the spiritual unity of the American continent.

Finally, after ten years, I felt free enough to confront directly the question that had haunted me for so long. I left the Divinity School, moved in temporarily with my Trappist friends at the Abbey of the Genesee in upstate New York, and started to prepare myself for a more systematic discernment of a possible vocation in Latin America. Meanwhile, the Maryknoll fathers in Peru had invited me to make Peru the center of my activities. They suggested, however, that I first go to Bolivia for some additional language training. Thus, in October 1981, I flew to Peru to get to know my Maryknoll hosts and from there to Cochabamba, Bolivia, for a three-month course designed to improve my Spanish. In January 1982, I returned to Peru for three months of orientation "in the field." It is these six months, from October 1981 to March 1982, that this journal records. In it, I tried to impose some order on the myriad experiences that were part of this journey. But, most of all, I have tried to find an answer to the question: "Does God call me to live and work in Latin America in the years to come?"

I am very glad that I can share this search for a new vocation with others, because I know that all who love God strive constantly to hear his voice more clearly. I therefore hope that telling my story will offer encouragement to others to tell theirs.

1

October

THE LORD OF THE MIRACLES

■

Sunday, October 18
Lima, Peru

THANKS BE TO GOD for bringing me here. The closer I came to the day of departure, the more convinced I was that going to Latin America was indeed the thing to do. Off and on the thought occurred to me that I was not ready for this change. I felt too tired, too preoccupied with personal struggles, too restless, too busy, too unprepared. But as the day of departure drew closer, I felt a growing sense of call. What had seemed little more than an adventure now presented itself as a vocation.

I left the Abbey of the Genesee in upstate New York on Sunday, October 11, for a one-week visit to Yale Divinity School in New Haven, where I had taught for ten years. It proved to be an important week, in which all the contacts, discussions, prayers, and celebrations helped me to listen more carefully to God's call, to let go of what was past, and to look forward to a totally new ministry. It seems paradoxical, but the expressions of friendship at Yale of former students and colleagues, and the deep personal conversations, gave me a profound sense of mission. I realized that I was not going just because it seemed like a good idea, but because those who love me most sent me on my way with affection, support, and prayers. The more I realized that I was truly loved, the more I felt the inner freedom to go in peace and to let all inner debate about motivation subside.

The Eucharistic celebration on Friday afternoon meant more to me than I can express in words. I had a strong sense of community, and an awareness that this community will stay with me wherever I go. The Lord himself brought us together and has made it clear to us that we are One in him and that this unity will allow us to be free, courageous, and full of hope. Whatever my experience in Latin America will bring to me, it will be part of a body formed in love and it will reverberate in all its members. The Body and Blood of our Lord Jesus Christ are indeed food for eternal life, a life that liberates us to live without fear and to travel without apprehension.

John Vesey drove me to the airport. He had come from Brooklyn to spend the last day in New Haven with me to help me pack. Our friendship started in Bolivia in the summer of 1972, when I was there for language training, and we have stayed in touch ever since. Having just returned from a seven-year ministry in Paraguay, he expressed his enthusiasm for my decision to return to Bolivia for more training and to join the Maryknoll fathers in Peru. His strong sense of God's guidance in our lives and his deep awareness of the beauty of the Divine in the midst of this dark world convinced me more than ever that it was good to go.

Monday, October 19

On the airplane to Lima, I spoke with the woman next to me. She told me that she was returning home with her mother, who had undergone three operations in the United States. "Is your mother better now?" I asked. "Oh yes, she is totally cured," she said with fervent conviction, "and the whole family is waiting at the airport to welcome her home." After a few minutes of silence, she wanted to know my reasons for going to Peru. When I told her that I was a priest planning to work with the Maryknoll missioners, her face changed dramatically. She leaned over to me, grabbed my hand, and whispered in an agonized way: "Oh Father, mother has cancer and there is little hope for her."

The first thing I learned about Peruvians was that they have an unlimited trust in priests. Even though the Church certainly has not earned such unconditional respect during the last centuries, the people of Peru give their confidence to their priests without hesitation. This impression was strongly affirmed on Sunday morning, when I found myself in the huge crowd on the Plaza de Armas, welcoming the procession of *el Señor de los milagros* (the Lord of the Miracles). As soon as the bystanders realized that I was a priest, they let go of their inhibitions, handed me their children to lift above the crowds, and told me about their joys and sorrows.

Peru: from the moment I entered it, I felt a deep love for this country. I do not know why. I did not feel this when I went to Chile or Bolivia in the past. But looking at the busy streets of Lima, the dark open faces and the lively gestures, I felt embraced by a loving people in a way I had not known before. Walking through the busy streets, looking at the men, women, and children in their penitential dress—purple habits with white cords—and sensing the gentle spirit of forgiveness, I had the strange emotion of homecoming. "This is where I belong. This is where I must be. This is where I will be for a very long time. This is home." Everything seemed easy. Thousands of people, but no pressing crowds; countless voices, but no shouts or cries; a multitude of faces, but no anger or frustration. I had never experienced this before. The obvious explanation is that I saw Peru for the first time on the feast day of the Lord of the Miracles, a day celebrated with a procession characterized by repentance and quiet prayer. But for me it was a day of comfort and consolation, a day on which the decision to come to this country was affirmed.

I felt as though the crowds of Lima were embracing me and showering me with the affection I had missed during the past months. It seemed as if the whispering crowds, the gentle movements of the bearers of the picture of the Lord of the Miracles, and the uninhibited smiles of the children all said to me: "Do not be afraid, the Lord loves all of us . . . you too."

Yes, I saw the Lord! How strange was that first day in Lima. In the central square, with its many balconies, thousands of people had gathered. On one balcony, president Fernando Belaúnde Terry stood waiting to pay homage to the Christ being carried into his presence. On another, the mayor was ready to hand the key of the city to the Lord of the Miracles; and on a third balcony, the church dignitaries stood to bless the image of the Crucified. Who was bowing to whom? Who was using whom? Who was trying to win votes, admiration, or sympathy? Who knows? But the people applauded the One whom they trusted and left the president, the mayor, and the bishops to their own speculations. New bouquets of flowers were continually brought to the platform on which the Image of Christ slowly moved through the crowds. When I lifted up a little Peruvian girl and showed her the Lord of the Miracles, I felt that the Lord and the little girl were both telling me the same story: presidents, mayors, and bishops come and go, but our God continues to enter our lives and to invite children to climb on the shoulders of adults and recognize him.

On the evening of this first day in Peru, I had the sensation that I had been here for a long time and that all that I had heard and seen had a deep and old familiarity. Everything whispered, "Welcome home, my friend."

Tuesday, October 20

It took only a few hours to be immersed in the real questions. Monsignor Alberto Koenigsknecht introduced me to them without knowing he was doing so. Alberto, a Maryknoller, is the prelate of the diocese of Juli in the Altiplano. He is staying at the Maryknoll Center house in Lima to organize a day of prayer to protest the attacks against the Christian community in his prelature. On August 15, the Institute for Rural Education was ransacked. On September 19, dynamite exploded in the entrance of Alberto's home and a note was found with a death threat.

Alberto was careful in his explanation. "We do not know who did it and why it was done, but it certainly was well planned." In August 1979, a pastoral week was held in the diocese of Juli. This meeting showed a strong and unwavering commitment to the poor and the oppressed. The final text says: "We decide to commit ourselves to the poor, that is, to those who form the oppressed class, those who depend on their work but do not have the means to live a dignified life, since they are exploited by others who deny them their rights." These are very strong words when spoken or written in and about Peru, and it certainly is possible that the recent attacks and death threat are among the responses.

Alberto spoke to the underminister of justice, but received little support. An investigation was promised, but nothing happened. And now it is the Church's turn to respond. In a few weeks, on November fifteenth, Christians of Peru will be called to Juli to express solidarity with the poor and to give a clear sign that attacks and death threats are not going to change the chosen direction. Alberto realized that he was taking a risk, but he felt that he had to do it. Gustavo Gutiérrez, the father of liberation theology, and his staff were consulted. It had become evident that a clear sign was needed to show the strength of the Church's commitment.

I sense that all of this might be just the beginning of a long road of suffering. Similar things have happened in El Salvador, similar things are happening in Guatemala, and the small rumblings in Peru seem to belong to that same awakening of the people of God in Latin America.

Wednesday, October 21

Pete Byrne, the superior of the Maryknoll fathers in Peru, drove me to the Ciudad de Dios (the City of God). "This is the parish where you will live and work when you come back from language school," he said with excitement. "You will love it. Now it all looks strange and unfamiliar to you, but it won't take long for you to feel part of the people here. They will love you and you will love them." Pete drove his car through the crowds gathering around the marketplace and took me to the Pamplona Alta section, where Maryknoll missioners Pete Ruggere, Tom Burns, and Larry Rich are living.

I was struck not only by the obvious poverty of the people, but also by their dignity. They care for what they own, and they manage to keep little gardens in the midst of this dry, sandy, and dusty place. Thousands of people live here—125,000—but there is space between houses as well as between people. The area is poor, very poor, but not depressing. It is full of visible problems, but not without hope.

Later in the day an elderly laywoman dressed as a nun—Maria is her name—told me about the beginning of the Ciudad de Dios. Ciudad de Dios was the result of a popular invasion on Christmas Eve 1954. Maria remembered that day with a sense of pride. She belonged to the founding fathers and mothers. On that Christmas night, thousands of people illegally occupied the barren land and immediately started to develop it. The government had no choice but to comply and eventually help, and now there is the City of God with countless brick houses, a large church, a school, and several medical posts.

The invasion of Ciudad de Dios was one of the first in a long series of similar invasions. Poverty and lack of land forced a constant migration from the countryside to the city. The Indian migrants first lived with relatives and friends; but when they became too numerous and desperate for a space and a livelihood, they organized themselves and seized the barren desert land surrounding the city. Today Lima has a large belt of "young towns," many of which are the result of these illegal land seizures.

Pamplona Alta, which belongs to the same parish, developed a few years after Ciudad de Dios was founded. From the many little shacks visible on the bare hills beyond Pamplona Alta, it is clear that invasions—although on a much smaller scale—are still taking place today.

Pete Ruggere welcomed me to the house where I would stay in January. It consists of brick walls, a cement floor, and a roof put together with pieces of wood, plastic, and straw. "It gets wet here when it rains," Pete observed, "but it seldom rains." We visited the neighbors: a husband, wife, and eleven children, all living in two rooms. There were lots of smiles, laughter, and affection, but I noticed exhaustion on the face of the mother. She carried a two-month-old baby in her arms while pointing to the one-and-a-half-year-old girl on the bed. I tried to get a smile from her, but found little response. Pete told me she was just diagnosed as having Down syndrome.

I spent the day visiting Maureen, a Dominican nurse, walking around the area, attending a mass during which the sick were anointed, talking to Sister Vivian, a Maryknoll doctor, and just wondering what it would be like to live here.

During the evening, I picked up some of Gustavo Gutiérrez's early writings. My visit to Ciudad de Dios makes his words sound very real. This, indeed, is a theology born out of solidarity with the people. The people speak about God and his Presence in ways I must slowly come to understand. It will take time, much time, but a willingness to learn is one thing I can bring here.

Before leaving for Bolivia, I would like to make some notes about Maryknoll and its role in Latin America. The first objective of the Maryknoll Society, as expressed by the General Chapter in 1979, is: "To recognize and elaborate a mission of spirituality which integrates community, prayer, a simple life-style, apostolic work, and commitment to the poor." I like the word "recognize." A true spirituality cannot be constructed, built, or put together; it has to be recognized in the daily life of people who search together to do God's will in the world.

I am impressed by the documents written about Peru by the Maryknollers. Their socioeconomic, political, and religious analyses are well-documented, clearly explained, and skillfully integrated into their self-understanding as missioners. A few simple facts are worth remembering. The present population of Peru is about 17 million (54% mestizo [mixed Indian and white], 33% Indian, 13% white). The main perspective of the Maryknoll missioners in Peru is summarized well in the following quote:

> The vast majority of Peruvians are classified as poor or "lower class" workers, campesinos or unemployed. This class is distinguished by race: it is composed of Indians, blacks and mestizos. It is dominated by the "upper

class" and it is considered inferior. The Peruvian "middle-class" is composed of professionals who are generally either white or mestizos and though economically and politically it is gaining strength, it is numerically small and no rival to the power of the "upper class." The "upper class" is white and though minute it controls the wealth and the political power of the country.

One fourth of one percent of the population receives more than 33% of all income in the country. The predominant social dynamic in Peru is the structural oppression and domination of the "lower class" and the emerging resistance of the poor to this domination (*Peru Regional Directory*, 1980, p. 3).

This is the context of the work of the Maryknoll Society, and the background against which its commitment to the poor needs to be understood. There are about forty-eight people directly connected with the work of the Maryknoll fathers in Peru (priests, associate priests, brothers, and lay missioners). Their activities are varied: parish work, religious training and formation, counseling, teaching, small group work, publishing, research, and so forth. They work in the Juli Prelature, in Arequipa, Huacho, and Lima. Maryknoll came to Peru in 1943, and has focused in different ways on the development of the local church. "To create self-directing, self-sustaining, and self-propagating Christian Communities captures the thrust of Maryknoll work in Peru from the beginning but the manner and emphasis have changed over the years."

The change in "manner and emphasis" of the missionary activities of Maryknoll over the years is of crucial importance. One Maryknoll priest, Ralph Davila, remarked during dinner: "It is the change from selling pearls to hunting for the treasure." Indeed, not too long ago, the main task was seen as selling the pearls of good news to the poor and ignorant people. Now a radically new perspective dominates the Maryknoll activities: to search with the poor for the treasure hidden in the ground on which they stand. It is this shift from spiritual colonialism to solidarity in servanthood that explains the style of life, the way of speech, the kind of literature, and the overall mood that I have become part of during the last few days.

I really feel that I am welcome here, not just as a guest who can learn a lot from Maryknoll, but also as someone from whom some contribution is expected. At this moment I cannot think of myself as someone who has anything to offer— I feel like someone surrounded by experts—but I am willing to live with the supposition that he who truly receives also gives. It is encouraging to feel part of a true community of apostolic love and fervor so soon. I now am ready to go to Bolivia for language training, because I now know that I will be welcome here when I return.

Thursday, October 22
Cochabamba, Bolivia

Today I flew from Lima to La Paz and from La Paz to Cochabamba. It was a magnificent flight over Lake Titicaca and over the wild and desolate mountain ranges of Bolivia. In the plane I talked with Henry Perry, a surgeon from Duke University, who hopes to set up elaborate health services in Achacachi, and with a young woman from San Francisco, who is dedicated to studying the intricate weaving techniques of the Indians in Ecuador, Peru, and Bolivia.

Warm summer weather engulfed me when I stepped off the plane, and the taxi ride to the Instituto de Idiomas, the language school, showed me clearly that Cochabamba is, indeed, the garden city of Bolivia. The great wealth of flowers reminded me that it is spring here, and that it will be midsummer when December comes.

Gerald McCrane, the director of the institute, welcomed me warmly and invited me to look with some of the students of the institute at a videotape of a CBS report on El Salvador. And thus, staying in one of the most lovely towns of Latin America, I am reminded that violence, oppression, persecution, torture, and indescribable human misery are all around. The film showed the civil war in El Salvador in gruesome detail. The Bolivians who watched it with us remarked that similar things were happening here.

Latin America: impressive wealth and degrading poverty, splendid flowers and dusty broken roads, loving people and cruel torturers, smiling children and soldiers who kill. It is here that we have to hunt for God's treasure.

I pray that my stay in Bolivia will teach me much more than Spanish.

Friday, October 23

Today was a day of getting used to my new environment. This seems easy: friendly people, beautiful gardens, and a smoothly run school. But when I reflect on what is going on underneath this comfortable exterior, I realize that I probably will never get used to my new world.

Chris Hedges, a Harvard Divinity School student, told me about the drug traffic in Bolivia. A Maryknoller visiting the institute explained to me how the military pushes Bolivia into bankruptcy, creates terror all through the country, and imprisons, kills, and tortures at random.

At lunch I met the Archbishop of La Paz, Monsignor Manrique. A short man with dark, Indian features, he impresses me as a simple and humble person. As the many stories indicate, he is one of the few people who dare to resist the regime. His faith gives him the moral power to speak out forcefully against the oppression of his people. In 1978, twelve hundred people staged a three-week-long hunger strike to reinforce their demands for an amnesty for all political prisoners and exiles. The government of General Banzer was forced to capitulate, but only after Manrique threatened to close all the churches of the diocese. He once said to the military: "You play tigers in La Paz in front of unarmed citizens, but you are cowards on the borders when you are facing the Chileans. You haven't won one war yet." Archbishop Manrique is undoubtedly one of the most courageous Christian leaders in Latin America, deeply loved by the miners and workers of Bolivia for his consistent demands for justice. I asked him if there were any priests in prison. He said: "At this moment, no. The human rights committee of the UN is coming to Bolivia today, and that helps."

Bolivia desperately wants recognition from the United States as a way to prevent total economic chaos. The Reagan administration requires an end to the drug traffic as a condition for recognition. The military, however, is so heavily involved in this illegal business, which brings in more money than all the mining industries put together, that any significant action can hardly be expected. So now there are some sporadic antidrug actions in the Beni (Bolivian lowlands). The victims—as always—are not the big cocaine traffickers, but some innocent *campesinos*. Meanwhile, the United States government seems to be placated with these gestures, and the newspapers expect a speedy recognition from Reagan.

I guess it is better not to get used to my new environment too soon.

Saturday, October 24

Although it is only a week ago that I came to Latin America, I have been here for a long time. The many new things I saw and heard during the last seven days must have intensified my mental activity. At the same time, I have had more time for myself than I have had for a long time—more time to pray, more time to read, more time to talk to people, more time to relax and just look around.

Today was a day in which prayer was uppermost on my mind. Last night the Franciscan priest, Justus Wirth, said in his reflection on the Gospel that the new commitment to the poor and the new emphasis on prayer were both signs of the action of the Holy Spirit in our time. When he said this, I suddenly realized that, indeed, prayer and work with the poor belong together and that the need to pray had grown in me ever since I have been confronted with the oppression and exploitation of the poor in Peru and Bolivia.

The several times I awoke last night, I found myself saying: "Lord, give me a true desire to pray"; and today I found it easier than before just to sit in the presence of God and listen quietly. I am grateful for this experience, and I am slowly becoming aware that something new is happening in me.

One image has been with me ever since I saw Pamplona Alta in Lima. It is the image of living as a hermit in the midst of the poor. That image must have been vague and subconscious, since I never wrote or spoke about it. But when a visiting priest from the St. Louis, Missouri, diocese said to me: "I am living in a poor section of La Paz as a hermit among the people," I immediately understood him. Yes—indeed, just to pray for, with, and among the poor spoke to me as a true missionary vocation. Wouldn't that be an authentic way of entering into solidarity with those who have nothing to lose?

True prayer always includes becoming poor. When we pray we stand naked and vulnerable in front of Our Lord and show him our true condition. If one were to do this not just for oneself, but in the name of the thousands of surrounding poor people, wouldn't that be "mission" in the true sense of being sent into the world as Jesus himself was sent into the world? To lift up your hands to the Lord and show him the hungry children who play on the dusty streets, the tired women who carry their babies on their backs to the marketplace, the men who try to forget their misery by drinking too much beer on the weekends, the jobless teenagers and the homeless squatters, together with their laughter, friendly gestures, and gentle words—wouldn't that be true service? If God really exists, if he truly cares, if he never leaves his people alone, who is there to remind him of his promises? Who is there to cry out: "How long will you frown on your people's plea? . . . Turn again, we implore, look down from heaven and see. Visit this vine and protect it, the vine your right hand has planted. . . . Let your face shine on us, and we shall be saved" (Ps. 80)? I feel that in a world rushing to the abyss, the need for calling God to the task, for challenging him to make his love felt among the poor, is more urgent than ever.

There were many wars, conflicts, and much poverty and misery in the thirteenth century, but we do not remember the political struggles and the socioeconomic events of that century. We remember one man who lived in the midst of it and prayed, prayed, and prayed until his hands and feet were pierced with the wounds of Christ himself. Who will be the St. Francis of our age? Many are asking themselves this question again. Who will lift up the world of today to God and plead for his mercy? Why does God still allow this world to continue? Because of Ronald Reagan, Begin, Brezhnev, Thatcher, Marcos, Belaúnde, or Torrelio? Or perhaps because of the few hermits hidden in the forests of Russia, on the roofs of New York City, and in the *favelas* of Brazil, Peru, and Bolivia? When the Lord looks down on us, what does he see? He sees his son Jesus in the faces of the few who continue to cry out in the valley of tears. For Jesus' sake he will save us from total destruction.

Prayer is the ongoing cry of the incarnate Lord to the loving God. It is eternity in the midst of mortality, it is life among death, hope in the midst of despair, true promise surrounded by lies. Prayer brings love alive among us. So let us pray unceasingly.

Sunday, October 25

Donald Stoker, an English priest, said to me last night: "Did you notice the night sounds here? When you go to bed you hear the bullfrogs croak. When you wake up at two in the night you hear the dogs bark. When you wake up at four you hear the cocks crow, and when you get up at six you hear the birds sing." Indeed, there are no silent nights in Bolivia. And during the day the voices of playing children join the birds in their chatter. All these sounds come together to form a single unceasing prayer to the Creator, a prayer not of thoughts and words but of sounds and life. How sad it is that thinking often makes prayers cease.

Monday, October 26

Chris Hedges gave me an article to read called, "Up to Our Steeple in Politics." It is written by Will D. Campbell and James Holloway and published in *Christianity and Crisis* on March 3, 1969. In it, the authors explore the issue of exactly how far the Church can become involved in politics without being corrupted by it, how far one can go into the world of Caesar before one loses sight of God.

The questions Campbell and Holloway raise are as important for the Latin American upheavals as they were for the civil rights movement in the United States, about which they were writing. Will we ever know whether we are living witnesses to the light or serving the prince of darkness? That is the question for the four priests who participated in the revolution in Nicaragua and are now members of the new Sandinista cabinet. That, too, is the question for Christians active in agrarian reform, in the development of cooperatives for the *campesinos*, and in programs for better health and better housing.

The Christian is called to live in the world without being of it. But how do we know whether we are just in it, or also of it? My feeling is that every Christian who is serious about his or her vocation has to face this question at some point.

How, then, are we to find the right answer for ourselves? Here we are called to discern carefully the movements of God's Spirit in our lives. Discernment remains our lifelong task. I can see no other way for discernment than a life in the Spirit, a life of unceasing prayer and contemplation, a life of deep communion with the Spirit of God. Such a life will slowly develop in us an inner sensitivity, enabling us to distinguish between the law of the flesh and the law of the spirit. We certainly will make constant errors and seldom have the purity of heart required to make the right decisions. We may never know whether we are giving to Caesar what belongs to God. But when we continuously try to live in the Spirit, we at least shall be willing to confess our weakness and ask for forgiveness every time we find ourselves again in the service of Baal.

Tuesday, October 27

This is my second day of language training, frustrating and exhilarating at the same time. It is frustrating, since I make the same mistakes I made nine years ago and continue to have the feeling that I should be much more advanced after the many weeks and months I have worked on Spanish in the past. There are frequent moments during which I say to myself: "I will never master this language." But the same experience is also refreshing. I can be a student again. I can spend many hours doing simple exercises that often appear as little puzzles, and I can be with other people who go through the same frustrations as I do. The teachers are dedicated and are always in a good mood and willing to help inside and outside of classes. The institute is equipped with the best possible facilities and everything is well organized. I can hardly think of a better place to learn a new language.

During the sixties, I spent two weeks in Madrid and a month in Cuernavaca with the conviction that Spanish was essential for my future work. But I never practiced it outside the formal training periods. Then I came here in the summer of 1972 and gave it another try. Again my acquired knowledge slipped away and now—nine years later—I feel that again I am beginning from scratch.

As I reflect on this fragmented approach to mastering Spanish, I can only say that I never gave up the deep conviction that I must learn it somehow, sometime. I never have been able fully to explain this conviction to myself or to anyone else. But the urge always was there and still is there; my desire to know Spanish and to know it well is as strong as ever. Why? I don't know. I hope that I will know before I die. There must be a meaning to such a strange passion!

I just read Paul Blustein's article about the Maryknollers in Peru. It gave me a strong sense of *déjà vu*. Blustein speaks about his encounter with Pete Ruggere and about his visit to Pete's neighbors:

> On a urine-soaked bed near the entrance lies an infant girl who, Father Ruggere says, suffers from malnutrition and almost certainly won't live beyond her fifth birthday. When the priest swoops the baby into his arms, gurgling endearments in Spanish, the child neither laughs nor cries, but merely gazes blankly at him through filmy brown eyes . . . (*Wall Street Journal*, August 14, 1981).

When I read this I saw it all over again, and realized that he was speaking about my future neighbors. The article is a masterful piece of reporting and one of the most balanced descriptions of the Maryknoll work I have read or heard.

Wednesday, October 28

This afternoon at three o'clock, my sister called from Holland to tell me that my sister-in-law had given birth to a daughter who was diagnosed as suffering from Down syndrome. A week ago I wrote about having seen a Down syndrome child in the house of Pete Ruggere's neighbors; yesterday I read about that child in the *Wall Street Journal*; today I have a niece who suffers from the same disease. I called Holland and talked to Heiltjen, my sister-in-law. The baby, she told me, had been born five hours previously, and the doctors had told her immediately about the child's handicap. "With Laura, our lives will be very different from now on," she said. My brother Laurent was not in the hospital when I called, but my sister as well as Heiltjen told me how distressed he was.

I still find it hard to appropriate this news. I cannot think about much else than this little child who will become the center of my brother and my sister-in-law's lives and will bring them into a world of which they have never dreamt. It will be a world of constant care and attention; a world of very small progressions;

a world of new feelings, emotions, and thoughts; a world of affections that come from places invisible in "normal" people.

I know that Laurent and Heiltjen's love is being tested, not only their love for their new child but even more their love for each other and for their two-year-old daughter Sarah. I pray tonight for them that they will be able to grow in love because of Laura, and that they will discover in her the presence of God in their lives.

Laura is going to be important for all of us in the family. We have never had a "weak" person among us. We all are hardworking, ambitious, and successful people who seldom have had to experience powerlessness. Now Laura enters and tells us a totally new story, a story of weakness, brokenness, vulnerability, and total dependency. Laura, who always will be a child, will teach us the way of Christ as no one will ever be able to do.

I hope and pray that I can be of some support to Laurent and Heiltjen in their long journey with Laura, and that Laura will bring all of us closer together and closer to God.

Thursday, October 29

Tonight the Dominican priest, John Risley, spoke at the institute about the Puebla Documents. These are the public statements that were the result of the 1978 Latin American Bishops' Conference in Puebla, Mexico. The main point he made was that the Church had made a definite choice for the poor. Thus, he said, Puebla brought good news for the poor but bad news for those who hold power and do not want to give it up. The lively discussion that followed revealed various opinions about the implications of such a "preferential option" and about the theology of liberation in general.

One thought hit me in the midst of all the viewpoints, opinions, and ideas that were expressed. It was the thought that the poor themselves are the best evangelizers. I have already met a few very simple people here who revealed to me God's presence in life in a way nobody else could. During breakfast this morning I spoke to Lucha, one of the maids working in the institute. We did not speak about God or religion, but her smile, her kindness, the way she corrected my Spanish, and her stories about her children created a sense of spiritual jealousy in me. I kept thinking: "I wish I had the purity of heart of this woman, I wish I could be as simple, open, and gentle as she is. I wish I could be as in touch." But then I realized that maybe even she didn't know what she was giving me. Thus my ministry to her is to allow her to show me the Lord and gratefully to acknowledge what I am receiving.

True liberation is freeing people from the bonds that have prevented them from giving their gifts to others. This is not only true for individual people but also—particularly—for ethnic groups. What does mission to the Indians really mean? Isn't it foremost to discover with them their own deep religiosity, their profound faith in God's active presence in history, and their understanding of the mystery of nature that surrounds them?

It is hard for me to accept that the best I can do is probably not to give but to receive. By receiving in a true and open way, those who give to me can become aware of their own gifts. After all, we come to recognize our own gifts in the eyes of those who receive them gratefully. Gratitude thus becomes the central virtue of a missionary. And what else is the Eucharistic life than a life of gratitude?

Friday, October 30

Today Gerry McCrane, the director of the language school, gave a presentation to the newcomers. In his gentle and pastoral way he offered us an opportunity to share our struggles in adapting ourselves to a new culture.

One theme that came up was the re-emergence of long-forgotten conflicts. In displacing ourselves into a new and unfamiliar milieu, old, unresolved conflicts often start asking for attention. When our traditional defense systems no longer are available and we are not able to control our own world, we often find ourselves experiencing again the feelings of childhood. The inability to express ourselves in words as well as the realization that everyone around us seems to understand life much better than we do, puts us in a situation quite similar to that of a child who has to struggle through a world of adults.

This return to childhood emotions and behavior could be a real opportunity for mental and spiritual growth. Most of the psychotherapies I have been exposed to were attempts to help me relive those times when immature ways of coping with stress found their origin. Once I could re-encounter the experience that led me to choose a primitive coping device, I was also able to choose a more mature response. Thus I could let go of behavior that was the source of my suffering. A good psychotherapist is a person who creates the environment in which such mature behavioral choices can be made.

Going to a different culture, in which I find myself again like a child, can become a true psychotherapeutic opportunity. Not everyone is in the position or has the support to use such an opportunity. I have seen much self-righteous, condescending, and even offensive behavior by foreigners towards the people in their host country. Remarks about the laziness, stupidity, and disorganization of Peruvians or Bolivians usually say a lot more about the one who makes such remarks than about Peruvians or Bolivians. Most of the labels by which we pigeonhole people are ways to cope with our own anxiety and insecurity. Many people who suddenly find themselves in a totally unfamiliar milieu decide quickly to label that which is strange to them instead of confronting their own fears and vulnerabilities.

But we can also use the new opportunity for our own healing. When we walk around in a strange milieu, speaking the language haltingly, and feeling out of control and like fools, we can come in touch with a part of ourselves that usually remains hidden behind the thick walls of our defenses. We can come to experience our basic vulnerability, our need for others, our deep-seated feelings of ignorance and inadequacy, and our fundamental dependency. Instead of running away from these scary feelings, we can live through them together and learn that our true value as human beings has its seat far beyond our competence and accomplishments.

One of the most rewarding aspects of living in a strange land is the experience of being loved not for what we can do, but for who we are. When we become aware that our stuttering, failing, vulnerable selves are loved even when we hardly progress, we can let go of our compulsion to prove ourselves and be free to live with others in a fellowship of the weak. That is true healing.

This psychological perspective on culture shock can open up for us a new understanding of God's grace and our vocation to live graceful lives. In the presence of God, we are totally naked, broken, sinful, and dependent, and we realize that we can do nothing, absolutely nothing, without him. When we are willing to confess our true condition, God will embrace us with his love, a love so deep, intimate, and strong that it enables us to make all things new. I am convinced that, for Christians, culture shock can be an opportunity not only for psychological healing but also for conversion.

What moves me most in reflecting on these opportunities is that they lead us to the heart of ministry and mission. The more I think about the meaning of living and acting in the name of Christ, the more I realize that what I have to offer to others is not my intelligence, skill, power, influence, or connections, but my own human brokenness through which the love of God can manifest itself. The celebrant in Leonard Bernstein's *Mass* says: "Glass shines brighter when it's broken. . . . I never noticed that." This, to me, is what ministry and mission are all about. Ministry is entering with our human brokenness into communion with others and speaking a word of hope. This hope is not based on any power to solve the problems of those with whom we live, but on the love of God, which becomes visible when we let go of our fears of being out of control and enter into his presence in a shared confession of weakness.

This is a hard vocation. It goes against the grain of our need for self-affirmation, self-fulfillment, and self-realization. It is a call to true humility. I, therefore, think that for those who are pulled away from their familiar surroundings and brought into a strange land where they feel again like babies, the Lord offers a unique chance not only for personal conversion but also for an authentic ministry.

Saturday, October 31

During the last few days, I have been thinking about the significance of gratitude in mission work. Gratitude is becoming increasingly important for those who want to bring the good news of the Kingdom to others. For a long time, the predominant attitude of the missioners was that they had to bring the knowledge of the Gospel to poor, ignorant people and thus offer light in their darkness. In such a view, there is not much room for gratitude.

As the missionary attitude changed, however, and more and more missioners came to see their task as helping others to recognize their own God-given talents, and thus to claim the good news for themselves, gratitude became much more than an occasional "thanks be to God." Gratitude is the attitude which enables us to receive the hidden gifts of those we want to serve and to make these gifts visible to the community as a source of celebration.

There is little doubt that jealousy, rivalry, anger, and resentment dominate our society much more than gratitude. Most people are afraid to make themselves available to others. They fear that they will be manipulated and exploited. They choose the safe way of hiding themselves and thus remaining unnoticed and anonymous. But in such a milieu of suspicion and fear, no community can develop and no good news can become visible.

True missioners are people who are hunting for the Divine treasure hidden in the heart of the people to whom they want to make the Good News known. They always expect to see the beauty and truth of God shining through those with whom they live and work.

The great paradox of ministry, therefore, is that we minister above all with our weakness, a weakness that invites us to receive from those to whom we go. The more in touch we are with our own need for healing and salvation, the more open we are to receive in gratitude what others have to offer us. The true skill of ministry is to help fearful and often oppressed men and women become aware of their own gifts, by receiving them in gratitude. In that sense, ministry becomes the skill of active dependency: willing to be dependent on what others have to give but often do not realize they have. By receiving in gratitude what we have helped others to discover in themselves, we enable them to claim for themselves full membership in the human and Christian community. Only those who truly believe that they have something to offer can experience themselves as spiritually adult. As long as someone feels that he or she is only an object of someone else's generosity, no dialogue, no mutuality, and no authentic community can exist.

As ministers, we share with all other human beings—especially those who have elaborate education and training—the desire to be in control, to tell others what to do and how to think. But if we want to follow Christ and "have his mind," we are called to empty ourselves of these privileges and become servants of the people. True servants depend on those whom they serve. They are called to live lives in which others guide them, often to places they would rather not go.

In different ways, these thoughts have been part of my understanding of ministry for over a decade. But here in Bolivia, in a different milieu, these ideas have taken deeper root; I no longer consider them romantic or sentimental. There is a danger of interpreting these thoughts about gratitude as a requirement to have certain concrete emotions towards others. But how can I feel grateful when I see so many poor, tired, and often apathetic people? My first response is: "How can I give them food, a house, an education, and a job?"

What then is it that we do receive in ministry? Is it the hidden insights and skills of those to whom we want to bear witness? Maybe so . . . but that can never be the true source of our own growth. Seeing how a person slowly becomes aware of his or her own capacities might make us happy for awhile, but that is not enough for a grateful life. A grateful life is a life in which we come to see that the Lord himself is the gift. The mystery of ministry is that the Lord is to be found where we minister. That is what Jesus tells us when he says: "Insofar as you did this to one of the least of these brothers of mine, you did it to me" (Matt. 25:40). Our care for people thus becomes the way to meet the Lord. The more we give, help, support, guide, counsel, and visit, the more we receive, not just similar gifts, but the Lord himself. To go to the poor is to go to the Lord. Living this truth in our daily life makes it possible to care for people without conditions, without hesitation, without suspicion, or without the need for immediate rewards. With this sacred knowledge, we can avoid becoming burned out.

The goal of education and formation for the ministry is continually to recognize the Lord's voice, his face, and his touch in every person we meet. As long as we live, the Lord wants to reveal to us more of himself. As long as we minister, we can expect the Lord to make himself known to us in ways we have not yet experienced. God himself became flesh for us so that we would be able to receive him every time we find ourselves serving another human being.

The question, however, is not only what are we receiving, but who is the receiver? Is it just *I*, with my unique capacity to see or hear, while others remain blind and deaf? No, because to see or to hear God is not a human possibility. It is a divine sensitivity. It is the Spirit of God in us who gives us eyes to see and ears to hear, who allows us to see and hear God in every person we serve. God is thus not only the gift, but also the receiver. Just as it is not we who pray, but the Spirit in us, so it is not we who receive but the Spirit in us.

Gratitude is not just a psychological disposition, but a virtue. Gratitude is an intimate participation in the Divine Life itself. The Spirit of God in us recognizes God in the world. The eyes and ears by which we can see God in others are in fact spiritual sensitivities that allow us to receive our neighbor as a messenger of God himself.

This theological perspective on gratitude makes it clear why it is so crucial that we pray: through prayer we become aware of the life of God within us and it is this God within us who allows us to recognize the God among us. When we have met our Lord in the silent intimacy of our prayer, then we will also meet him in the *campo*, in the market, and in the town square. But when we have not met him in the center of our own hearts, we cannot expect to meet him in the busyness of our daily lives. Gratitude is God receiving God in and through the human interaction of ministry. This viewpoint explains why true ministers, true missionaries, are always also contemplatives. Seeing God in the world and making him visible to each other is the core of ministry as well as the core of the contemplative life.

Today, Reformation Day, a group of North American Lutheran ministers is visiting the institute. They are traveling through Latin America in order to evaluate their mission work. They come with open minds and hearts. Their vision is very much in tune with the vision of Maryknoll, and their main question is: "How can we work together to make and fulfill our common call to evangelize the nations?"

I was invited to attend the meeting, and I felt part of an extremely important new form of ecumenism: cooperation in the missions between the Roman Catholic and the Lutheran communities. To set the tone, Gerry McCrane gave all of us the following words, written by a third world bishop for those who come as missioners to Latin America.

Walk with Us in Our Search

Help us discover our own riches; don't judge us poor because we lack what you have.

Help us discover our chains; don't judge us slaves by the type of shackles you wear.

Be patient with us as a people; don't judge us backward simply because we don't follow your stride.

Be patient with our pace; don't judge us lazy simply because we can't follow your tempo.

Be patient with our symbols; don't judge us ignorant because we can't read your signs.

Be with us and proclaim the richness of your life which you can share with us.

Be with us and be open to what we can give.

Be with us as a companion who walks with us—neither behind nor in front—in our search for life and ultimately for God!

These words not only point toward a contemporary missionary spirituality, but also offer a base for true ecumenism in Latin America. Because, whether we are Lutherans or Roman Catholics, we first of all must listen to the people to whom we come; it is they who will show us the way to Christian unity.

2

November

NEW FACES AND VOICES

■

Sunday, November 1, All Saints Day

THIS MORNING I went with Brian Clark, a journalist for the *Modesto* [California] *Bee,* and with Simon, a Redemptorist brother, to Mass in the Church of Santa Ana. The Dominican priest, Oscar Uzin, celebrated the Eucharist. In a simple, clear, and convincing way, he explained the meaning of All Saints Day: "We do not concentrate today on spiritual heroes, but on people who are saints by loving one another, caring for one another, forgiving one another in their normal, everyday lives. We are celebrating the saints among us who do not have haloes above their heads but who, formed and inspired by the gospel, can make the interest of others more important than their own."

I felt at home in this simple Sunday liturgy. The church was packed with people, young and old, men and women, Cochabambinos and foreigners. Everybody was attentive and many went to communion. It was easy to feel part of this celebration, and, as always in situations like this, I marvel at the universal appeal of the words of Our Lord.

Tonight I was looking at the new moon and the bright stars decorating the wide skies of Bolivia. The air was cool and pleasant. Ernie, an eighty-two-year-old man from Rhode Island, joined me. After a moment of silence, he said: "Nice climate here; if the government were the same, everything would be all right."

Monday, November 2, All Souls Day

Throughout Latin America, All Souls Day is a special feast, the day in which people pay tribute to and enter into communion with those who have died. The place where this celebration of the lasting bonds with the dead can be experienced is the cemetery.

For me, the day started quietly. I spent an hour in the early morning in silent prayer for my mother and all the family members and friends who had died over the last years. From that intimate center, I let the eyes of my mind wander into wider and wider circles. I first saw the many acquaintances in my own little world who are no longer with me, then I thought about the many whose deaths I had learned of through newspapers, radio, and television, and finally I saw the thousands and thousands who had lost their lives through hunger and violence and whose names would always remain unknown to me. Suddenly, I found myself surrounded by a crowd of people who had been cruelly snatched away from life without a prayer, a word of consolation, or even a kiss on the forehead. To all of these I was intimately linked—so intimately that their total freedom had come to depend more and more on this ongoing connection stretching out far beyond the boundary of death. Indeed, part of the meaning of life for the living is our opportunity to pray for the full liberation of those who died before us.

With these thoughts, I began a busy day, which included a visit to the doctor and four classes in Spanish. At 2:30 P.M. I was free to join some friends for a visit to the cemetery of Cochabamba. What I saw there I will never forget. Thousands of people were sitting and walking around the graves as though they were camping with their beloved ones who had died. All types of sounds were mingled together: the sound of boys praying aloud, the sound of a trumpet, the sound of friendly conversations, the sounds of laughter and tears. Was this a gigantic picnic, a massive wake, a city-wide prayer service, a feast, a reunion, a day of repentance, or a celebration of continuing brotherhood and sisterhood? It obviously was all of that and much, much more. Something became visible at that cemetery that defied our usual distinctions between sorrow and joy, mourning and feasting, eating and fasting, praying and playing, and, most of all, living and dying. The people who came together at the cemetery revealed a reality that cannot be grasped by any of the categories that we use to define our daily experiences.

One sad exception remained: the distinction between the rich and the poor. We entered the cemetery through a large gate inscribed with the words, *Fiat Voluntas Tua* ("Your Will Be Done"); but after having passed the large monumental graves and the huge walls with square niches, we soon found ourselves in an open field covered with small wooden crosses that marked the rudimentary graves of the poor. And when we left the official cemetery through a small gate in the back wall, we came upon a large sandy stretch of land where hundreds of people who could not pay for even the simplest spot had claimed a place where they could bury their relatives and visit them. Sister Jeri Cashman, who had lived in Cochabamba for quite some time, explained that after five years the bodies of the poor are removed and burned to make a place for others. A large pit in which you could see pieces of skulls and bones showed that this burning of the poor was a daily event.

Somehow, I felt much more at home in the open field than between the monuments and the walls with niches. Wherever we walked people looked at us with friendly smiles, as if they were grateful that we had come. They appeared to be at a party. Each grave was surrounded by people who had spread a blanket over the grave and covered it with food: bananas, oranges, and all forms of *urpo*, a special bread baked for this day. Often the centerpiece was a cake in the form of a man or woman, representing the one who was buried under the blanket. At one place I saw a large bread, standing up in the form of a man with uniform and gun, indicating that the family was mourning the death of a soldier. Sister Jeri explained: "The people bring all sorts of food to the graves, often the food their deceased relatives most liked, and then they have a meal with them and thus continue to stay in touch."

What caught my attention most of all were the praying boys. In pairs, ten- to twelve-year-old boys walked all over the cemetery with large white sacks over their shoulders. One of each couple had a small booklet. They went from grave to grave asking if the people would let them pray. When the answer was yes, they knelt down in front of the grave, one boy loudly reciting the litany printed in his booklet, the other responding even more loudly every ten seconds: "Let us praise the Lord in the Blessed Sacrament of the altar and the Virgin Mary conceived without original sin." It was clear that the boys had hardly any idea what they were saying, but their eyes were tightly closed and their hands devoutly folded. All over the cemetery the boys' voices sounded in a strangely pleasant rhythm that seemed to unite all that was happening into one great prayer. The members of the family themselves did not utter a word; that was the boys' task. After they had finished their booklet, the boys rose from their knees and opened their sacks to receive the pay for their prayers: a banana, a few cookies, a piece of cake, or whatever they could get. Then they went on to the next grave, while another couple of boys took their place. And so it went on the whole day. When the fruit and the bread had vanished from the blankets into the boys' sacks, fresh food was brought and put on the grave, often arranged in a decorative way.

At one place, I saw an old and inebriated man urging a family to let him pray for their dead. After some pleading, he received permission. He started to say an Our Father and a Hail Mary, but he was so drunk that he could hardly finish it. When he received only one cookie for his prayers, he said with some indigna-tion in his voice: "Is that all?" The head of the family said "Yes," and signaled two boys to take over his poorly performed task. Having watched this scene for a while, I introduced myself to the family. When they heard I was a Dutch priest, they lost all their initial reservation and told me all I wanted to know. "Who is buried here?" I asked. "My sister-in-law," answered a dark young man. "She died five months ago in childbirth." Then he introduced me to his widowed brother and three little children, who were sitting quietly around the grave. The other members of the family just looked on. After some more exchanges, I knelt down on the graveside, said some silent prayers, and blessed the living and the dead. When I rose, the two brothers asked me with some anxiety: "What did you pray?" I said: "I prayed that the Lord will lead your wife and sister-in-law into his home, that he will give new strength and courage to all the members of your family, and that he will bring peace to your country." Everyone expressed a sense of relief and gratitude. "Thank you very much, thank you, thank you," they said as they shook my hand with affection.

When I left the cemetery, many thoughts ran through my mind. What had I witnessed? What did all of this mean? Most central to all the impressions I had received was the impression that I had seen something very deep, old, basic, and human. The gatherings around the graves, the food on the blankets, the human-shaped breads, the praying boys, the exchange of gifts, and the all-pervading spirit of gentleness and hospitality: all of that seemed to come from ages past, even from far beyond the time when the Gospel of Jesus was first brought to Latin America. Most of the inhabitants of Cochabamba are Quechua Indians, and their Christianity is pervaded with the religious convictions and practices of the Quechua culture. Although Our Fathers and Hail Marys are constantly re-cited, it seemed that they only partially express the power of Indian spirituality.

I felt very much part of a mystery that cannot simply be observed and understood, and I started to sympathize even more with the sisters and priests who, after many years in Bolivia, say: "We still can only partially grasp the depth of the Quechua soul." One image stayed uppermost in my mind. It was the image of the boys receiving food for their prayers. The food put on the graves to be eaten with the dead was given to those who prayed for them. In front of my eyes I saw how prayers became food and food became prayers. I saw how little boys who had to struggle to survive received life from the dead, and how the dead received hope from the little children who prayed for the salvation of their souls. I saw a profound communion between the living and the dead, an intimacy expressed in words and gestures whose significance easily escapes our practical and often skeptical minds. The little children, as well as some of the older blind and crippled people, were allowed to enter into communication with the dead, while the adults remained silent, watched, and handed out gifts. "Out of the mouths of babes" we hear the truth, and by them the mysteries of life are revealed to us.

When I returned home, I knew that the Indians had given me a glimpse of a reality that mostly remains hidden in my rational, well-planned, and well-protected life. I had heard voices, seen faces, and touched hands revealing a divine love in which the living and the dead can find a safe home. In the evening I celebrated the Eucharist with friends in the language school. It seemed to me that all who had been part of this day—my family members and friends for whom I had prayed in the early morning, the medical doctor, the students and teachers, the Indian people of Cochabamba and their dead, as well as all the people who live and die on this earth—were gathered around the table. When the bread and the cup, the body and blood of Our Lord, were shared, I felt even more a part of the mysterious interchange I had witnessed in the cemetery. Yes, we all are one people loved by One Lord who became food and drink for us all and thus took away whatever may separate the living from the dead.

Tuesday, November 3

Tonight I saw the movie *All Quiet on the Western Front,* which shows how the members of a German platoon are physically and mentally destroyed in the trenches of the First World War. It brought home the insanity of young German men killing young French men without knowing why.

Meanwhile, the world powers are preparing for a war so massive and devastating that there won't be many left to tell the story or make a movie of it. Samuel Cohen, the father of the neutron bomb, does not believe that a third world war can be avoided. In an interview published on the first of November in *Los Tiempos,* the Catholic daily newspaper printed in La Paz, Cohen expresses his pride in having invented this instrument that "kills but does not destroy." He says, "I never think 'my God, what did I invent?' I am conscious that this bomb is the most selective weapon ever invented. A weapon such as this never existed." In response to the question: "Do you believe that we will have another war?" he says: "Yes . . . I consider this simply to be part of human nature: struggle, death and war . . . and in all wars both parties will take in hand all the possible arms. . . . Nuclear weapons will be used in their total potential."

Reading this after having seen *All Quiet on the Western Front,* I try to imagine the horrible quiet that will hover over our planet if Cohen's prediction comes true. Will there be anyone to mourn the dead or to consider the rebuilding of a human community? The only words that can offer comfort are the words Jesus spoke: "Stay awake, praying at all times for the strength to survive all that is going to happen, and to stand with confidence before the Son of Man" (Luke 21:36). O Lord, have mercy on us.

Wednesday, November 4

Tonight Ed Moore, a Maryknoll priest who was involved in leadership training in Guatemala, and Tom Henehan, a Maryknoller who is doing similar work in Santiago, Chile, shared their ideas and experiences with the students of the language school. One thing was clear to me: those who are trained in leadership roles quickly become targets of the oppressors. When politicians realize that the Indians are no longer passive, dependent beings who can be exploited, but have become a people educated to speak with a clear voice, they respond with oppression, torture, and murder. I was struck with the fact that often education means preparation for martyrdom. This is no argument for not educating. Those who have become aware of the nature of their captivity and have seen what is necessary to change the system never regret what they have learned, even though their knowledge may cost them their lives.

One of Ed's observations helped me see how quickly politics enters the picture. Many young people who have been trained as evangelizers, health promoters, or social-change agents soon become aware of the political nature of the physical, mental, and spiritual poverty of their people. This awareness frequently leads them to enter directly into the political arena; they strive to become mayor of their town or to acquire other political offices.

Another observation made by Tom explained why foreign missioners are so frequently accused of political involvement. In general, they are the ones who work most closely with the poor, the homeless, and the jobless, because they are the only ones who can afford to do so. The local pastoral workers need to earn money to survive, not only for themselves but also for parents and siblings who look to them for support. Thus they are forced to accept income-producing jobs such as teaching in grade school, high school, or university. Foreign missioners, on the other hand, are supported by their congregations at home, and thus have the freedom to live and work with the poor. Thus it is quite understandable that many oppressive governments make the foreign priests, sisters, and lay missioners the target of their hostility and condemn them as communist subversives.

Meanwhile, I try to remember that Jesus was killed as a subversive. God, who became human, submitted himself to the manipulation and oppression of the political powers of his time. He died under the accusation of being the enemy of the ruling class. It was not without reason that Pilate placed above Jesus' head the charge: "This is Jesus, the King of the Jews." Can we be true Christians without being considered to be subversives in the eyes of the oppressors?

Thursday, November 5

I am reading a fascinating chapter from Jerry Mander's book *Four Arguments for the Elimination of Television*. The main idea is: "We evolve into the images we carry in our minds. We become what we see. And in today's America, what most of us see is one hell of a lot of television."

I had heard stories about Vietnam veterans who, during their first real battle, thought that it was just another war movie and were shocked when those they killed did not stand up and walk away. I had read that Vincent van Gogh saw the real world as an imitation of the paintings he saw in the museum. I had noticed how children often are more excited about the repeated advertisements on television than about the movie they interrupt. But I had never fully thought through the enormous impact of the artificially imposed images on my thoughts, feelings, and actions. When it is true that the image you carry in your mind can affect your physical, mental, and emotional life, then it becomes a crucial question as to which images we expose ourselves or allow ourselves to be exposed.

All of this is important to me because it has profound spiritual implications. Prayer also has much to do with imagining. When I bring myself into the presence of God, I imagine him in many ways: as a loving father, a supporting sister, a caring mother, a severe teacher, an honest judge, a fellow traveler, an intimate friend, a gentle healer, a challenging leader, a demanding taskmaster. All these "personalities" create images in my mind that affect not only what I think, but also how I actually experience myself. I believe that true prayer makes us into what we imagine. To pray to God leads to becoming like God.

When Saint Ignatius proposes that we use all our senses in our meditation, he does more than offer a technique to help us concentrate on the mysteries of God's revelation. He wants us to imagine the reality of the divine as fully as possible so that we can slowly be divinized by that reality. Divinization is, indeed, the goal of all prayer and meditation. This divinization allows St. Paul to say: "I live now not with my own life but with the life of Christ who lives in me" (Gal. 2:20).

The more we come to depend on the images offered to us by those who try to distract us, entertain us, use us for their purposes, and make us conform to the demands of a consumer society, the easier it is for us to lose our identity. These imposed images actually make us into the world which they represent, a world of hatred, violence, lust, greed, manipulation, and oppression. But when we believe that we are created in the image of God himself and come to realize that Christ came to let us reimagine this, then meditation and prayer can lead us to our true identity.

These considerations reveal the intimate bond between ministry and the life of prayer and meditation. Because what else is ministry than witnessing to him whom "we have heard, and we have seen with our own eyes; . . . watched and touched with our hands" (1 John 1:1)? Ministry is the manifestation in our own person of the presence of Christ in the world. The more fully we have imagined who we truly are and the more our true identity becomes visible, the more we become living witnesses of Jesus Christ. This means much more than speaking and acting in the Name of Him who came to us long ago. It means that our words and actions themselves become a manifestation of the living Christ here and now.

Latin America offers us the image of the suffering Christ. The poor we see every day, the stories about deportation, torture, and murder we hear every day, and the undernourished children we touch every day, reveal to us the suffering Christ hidden within us. When we allow this image of the suffering Christ within us to grow into its full maturity, then ministry to the poor and oppressed becomes a real possibility; because then we can indeed hear, see, and touch him within us as well as among us. Thus prayer becomes ministry and ministry becomes prayer. Once we have seen the suffering Christ within us, we will see him wherever we see people in pain. Once we have seen the suffering Christ among us, we will recognize him in our innermost self. Thus we come to experience that the first commandment to love God with all your heart, with all your soul and with all your mind, resembles indeed the second: "You must love your neighbor as yourself" (Matt. 22:39–40).

Friday, November 6

Tonight the students and staff of the language school celebrated a special Eucharist of solidarity with the Church in the prelature of Juli in Peru. Bill McCarthy, the Maryknoller who came from Lima to attend a conference here, was the main celebrant; and Sister Lourdes, who works in Juli and is currently studying Aymara (the language of the Aymara Indians, who live in the Altiplano), gave the homily and sang a Spanish song, which she composed herself. A small sculpture of an Indian carrying a heavy load on his back, a plate with incense, flowers, and a candle were placed in the center of the circle to symbolize the suffering, the prayers, and the hope of the poor in Juli. There also was a broken glass and a stone to remind us of the violence that has occurred there recently.

The main reason for this celebration was to call attention to the day of prayer that will take place in Juli on November fifteenth. On that day, Christians from all over Peru will come to Juli to make a prayerful response to the first signs of persecution of the Church in Peru. Sister Lourdes herself was present at the Institute for Rural Education when it was attacked by forty masked men.

As I listened to Bill's explanation of the symbols and to Lourdes' words about fear, hope, and the importance of being faithful, I could not prevent myself from thinking that all of this might be the beginning of a confrontation that can take on dimensions much greater than we now can imagine. What will result from the demonstration on November fifteenth? There are many people who hate the Church because of its support for the poor. Will they see the day of prayer as a reason to intensify the oppression or as a challenge to conversion? It is hard to say. Protest is required by our faithfulness to the poor. But nobody knows if things will become better or worse. I fear the worst, but hope that November fifteenth will make it clear that the Church won't back off from its promises to support the poor at all times.

The songs were joyful, the readings hopeful, and the sharing of the Body and Blood of Our Lord a true expression of community. The celebration allowed us to remind ourselves that we are already part of the kingdom even though we are still living in the valley of tears. It is becoming clearer to me every day that one of the greatest gifts offered to Christians is the possibility of celebrating not only their newly found freedom, but also the captivity to which they are still subjected. In the Christian community, joy and sorrow are never separated. Our joy witnesses to the awareness that nothing can separate us from the Lord of life, our sorrow reminds us that the way of the Lord of life is the way of the cross.

Saturday, November 7

Today was a day filled with letter writing. I wrote to my brother and his wife to express to them my support and love as they struggle to offer a safe and loving home to their little daughter Laura. I wrote to my aunt and uncle to offer them a word of comfort as they grieve for the death of their daughter Rosemarie, who died a few years after they lost their daughter Magdaleen. I wrote to my priest friend, Henny, who lost both of his parents within a few weeks. I wrote to my cousin who lost her husband shortly before she gave birth to her second child.

I now feel tired and emotionally drained. As I let all these pains in the lives of my family and friends enter into my heart, I wondered how I could offer true comfort. How could I ever enter into their pain and offer hope from that place?

How could I enter into real solidarity with them? But then I slowly realized that I do not have to be like them or to carry their burdens, but that our Lord, my Lord and their Lord, has carried all human burdens and was crushed by them, so that we could receive his Spirit, the comforter. I realize now that my first task is to pray that this comforting Spirit will reach the hearts and minds of all those to whom I have written today. I hope that my halting and stuttering letters will be received as an expression of my sincere prayer that what is beyond my ability to touch can be touched by the consoling and healing power of the God whose name is Love.

Monday, November 9

Today I found new living quarters. During the weekend I had become aware that I was speaking too much English and that I needed a total immersion in the Spanish language.

The Quiroga family, who live about a half-hour walk from the institute, offered me their generous hospitality. It is a joy to be here. Mr. and Mrs. Quiroga are very kind and quite willing to correct my Spanish, and their twelve-year-old son, Rodolfito, is excited to have someone in the house with whom he can practice his English.

Rodolfo Senior and his wife, Nancy, lived for eight years in Miami. During that time they learned some English, although the predominantly Cuban population did not encourage them to practice it. But because their son went to school there, he became much more fluent in English than his parents. When the family returned to Bolivia more than four years ago, Rodolfito continued in an English-speaking grade school. Although he now goes to the Spanish-speaking Catholic high school in Cochabamba, he continues to practice his English on the American guests who come to his home. Rodolfo is a businessman in Cochabamba, and Nancy is an enthusiastic shortwave radio amateur, who speaks daily with people from all over the world: Indonesia, Thailand, Poland, Holland, the States, and many other countries.

One of the best parts of living with the Quiroga family is that they all like to talk. I am always surrounded by Spanish sounds, and I hope that these sounds will become more and more familiar to me.

Tuesday, November 10

Last night Rodolfo Quiroga told me the story of his life. He was born in Oruro, the city of the tin mines. His parents were simple, hardworking people. Five of their nine children died during their first months. "Poor climate and poor medical help," Rodolfo explained.

When Rodolfo was eight years old, the son of the owner of the house in which they lived, a seventeen-year-old boy known for his morbid desire to hurt animals, walked into the house with a pistol and killed Rodolfo's ten-year-old brother. Rodolfo's parents were out of their minds with grief. For many days his father woke up during the night, walked around the house with a gun, and spoke wildly about revenge. But when he realized that he still had a caring wife and three boys who needed him, he slowly became a different man. While he had always been a fervent atheist and was married under the condition that the Church would have nothing to do with him and his family, he suddenly turned to God in his grief and became a man who committed his life to prayer, charity, and the spiritual well-being of his family. Both he and his wife started to go to church every day. Soon afterwards, their three sons were baptized and received their first communion. The house of this simple family became a place of faith and hope.

Alex, one of the sons, studied philosophy with the Jesuits for some years and contemplated joining their Society; but he had to leave because of poor health. Alex is currently a professor of Spanish literature in Massachusetts, a very active Christian who introduced the Marriage Encounter movement in Cochabamba. Max, the second son, is an accountant, who after many years in La Paz moved to Cochabamba to give his sickly wife a better climate in which to live. Rodolfo, my host, joined the religious congregation of the Servites for a few years, but had to leave them to support his family when his mother became ill. He married Nancy soon after his return home. Their first two children died. A few years after Rodolfito was born, they adopted a boy who died unexpectedly in his third month of life. Now their twelve-year-old son Rodolfito is the center of their life.

I was moved by this story and the simple and loving way in which Rodolfo told it. For him it was God's story as much as his own. It was a story about suffering, but a suffering in which God had become present and shown his love. When Rodolfo told me his life, he seemed to be speaking more about God's love than about his own struggles. His voice was full of gratitude and praise. No anger, no resentment, no feelings of revenge. He spoke with the quick knowledge that God has guided his life and will continue to do so, no matter what happens.

Wednesday, November 11

Last night Rodolfo celebrated his fifty-second birthday. To me it seemed like an old-fashioned Dutch birthday party. Family and friends kept coming during the evening to congratulate Rodolfo and his wife. As it got later, the circle became larger, the conversation more animated and the voices louder. Everyone was happy and everyone was everyone else's entertainment. No television, radio, music, or slides; just good lively exchanges of home news, town news, and family news, real or made up for the occasion. The food and wine led to the traditional birthday cake which was—to my surprise—welcomed with the American song "Happy Birthday to You."

The evening was of special interest to me because I had a long conversation with Peter, the recently ordained Polish priest who is studying with me at language school and had become a friend of the Quiroga family. Peter's story moved me and awoke in me emotions that had remained hidden for a long time.

During all of his life, Peter had lived in Poland. As a teenager he was not very religious, but he was a good youth leader. A Dominican priest evoked in him the desire for the priesthood. First he thought about becoming a Dominican; but a short time before entering the Dominican novitiate, he met a priest of the Divine Word Society who spoke to him about their missions. Peter felt that this was a providential encounter and he decided to join the Divine Word Society in the hope that one day he could be a missionary in Japan, Korea, or Taiwan. Six months ago, Peter was ordained. But instead of being sent to any of the countries he hoped for, his superiors sent him to Bolivia to learn Spanish in preparation for three years of mission work in Paraguay.

Peter impressed me deeply from the moment I first saw him among the other students of the language school. He has a fine, youthful face that makes him look like a very tender boy; he does not speak one word of English, but his Spanish is remarkable for the short time he has been studying it. Although there is one other Polish priest and two Polish sisters in the institute, he avoids them; he is determined not to utter one Polish word before Christmas. As a result, he learns Spanish faster than anyone else I know.

The first thing Peter expressed to me was a deep sadness that mothers in Poland no longer have the necessary food for their newborn babies. There is such a lack of milk, butter, and other crucial nutrients that the number of abortions in Catholic Poland is staggering. "It is terrible," Peter kept saying. "It is the great sin of our nation. In the few months since I have been a priest, I have heard the confession of so many men and women who agonize over their inability to care for children. But abortion is no solution."

And slowly Peter revealed to me his deep faith, which is intimately connected with his love for his people. "We in Poland desire only two types of freedom: freedom from sin and freedom from foreign domination. Every father and every mother speaks to their children about these freedoms, which are more important for us than food, a house, or material success." With strong emotion, Peter spoke about the faith of his people. "Being Polish and being Catholic is the same for us. We are not interested in politics, in war, in power. We have never started a war. What we desire is to live a life close to God and the Virgin Mother. There is no house in Poland without a picture of Our Lady of Czestochowa, and, I tell you, miracles happen every day to those who bring their sufferings to her. And the Communists? They have the power, they give away the key positions, they make all the decisions, they rule the country. But the heart of the thirty million Poles is not with them. The people pray, the people go to Mass, the people come together in their houses for religious instruction, and that is where you come to understand the Polish soul."

When Peter spoke about John Paul II, I could sense strong feelings surge up in him. John Paul was given to his people to offer them new courage and a new hope for freedom. I came to see in Peter's eyes that John Paul was indeed the mysterious answer of God to decades of fervent Polish prayers. Since John Paul had become Pope, hundreds of young people had entered seminaries and religious life. Now there are thirty major seminaries and each has at least one hundred students. Talking about John Paul, Peter said: "When he was shot, most people in the world were reading the papers or watching television to follow the events, but the Poles all went to their churches and prayed." Moreover, Peter was convinced that without John Paul there would probably have been no Solidarity movement. Peter said: "The Poles listened to every word John Paul said during his visit to Poland. He always spoke about the Spirit of God that all of us have received and that is the basis of our true freedom. His words gave us strength, self-confidence, and the courage to claim our own rights. I think indeed that John Paul had a lot to do with the origin of Solidarity, not directly, but certainly indirectly."

There was not a trace of triumphalism in Peter's voice. It was clear that he spoke as a man who had suffered oppression, exploitation, and hunger although I felt that at times he overlooked some important questions (such as the suffering of Polish Jews in the past and the present), he radiated a simple solid faith that allowed him to speak about God, Jesus, Mary, the Church, and the Pope with an intimacy and familiarity that made me jealous.

He told me about his departure. His father and mother told him: "You are a priest now; be sure to pray always, wherever you are; never let a day go by without saying the rosary." Peter had tears in his eyes when he told me this. "If I just had a little bit of my parents' faith! They are such simple, poor, and faithful people. They truly know what counts. They do not want me to be important, powerful, successful. The only thing they hope is that I will be a man of prayer who leads others closer to God. They know nothing about Bolivia or Paraguay, but they pray for me and for all the people I am sent to."

Peter opened deep places in me. His whole being radiated commitment to God and to his Church, and I sensed that I was in the presence of a man of faith, a faith that I had not seen for a long time. And somewhere, too, Peter gave me a new glimpse of that remarkable—and often disturbing—holy man, John Paul II.

Thursday, November 12

It suddenly hit me. The United States wants war! It is frightening to write this sentence down, but during the last week the thought that the Reagan Administration is not only preparing for the possibility of a war, but is even directly moving towards it, kept haunting me. For a few days, the idea of an approaching war in which a destruction of life and culture would take place such as history has never witnessed kept me restless during the day and sleepless during the night. Looking at the movements of the U.S. government from the perspective of this utterly poor, helpless, and dependent country is a quite different experience than looking at it from within the United States. Living in the United States allows you to maintain the illusion that the arms race, the joint military exercises in Egypt, the sale of the AWACS planes to Saudi Arabia, and especially the Cancun conference in Mexico, are all movements to keep the peace. But living here in Bolivia, surrounded by increasing poverty and human misery, the face of the United States becomes uglier and uglier as the days progress.

What frightens me most is the shift in the popular expectation of war. Although there is no Hitler raving about the superiority of the Aryan race, although there is no visible advantage to any country to become involved in an international conflict, the majority of the American people expect a world war in the near future and few believe that an all-out nuclear holocaust can be avoided.

During the last few weeks, most of the U.S. weeklies as well as the major foreign publications have filled their pages with speculations about an impending war. What most frightens me is the predominantly military responses of the U.S. government to the main problems in the world. *Newsweek* (November 9, 1981) writes: "Reagan had relied mainly on a display of military might: his White House has struck arms deals with El Salvador, Venezuela, and Pakistan, promised to speed up arms shipments to Egypt and the Sudan and invited China to shop at America's weapons bazaar." Behind this show of power is the desire to give the American people the sense of being in control. One of Reagan's top advisers says: "The bottom line is that America is tired of being shoved around and [Reagan has] taken care of that." But the more I think about the lack of genuine diplomacy between Moscow and Washington, the growing tensions in Poland, the extremely fragile situation in the Middle East, the increasing U.S. support to South Africa, and the blatant U.S. help to the "authoritarian" right-wing military regimes in the Southern hemisphere to counteract the so-called totalitarian influence of Cuba in Central America—all of this in the context of the biggest "peacetime" military buildup in the history of the United States—the more I wonder whether there is any serious attempt to ensure peace. I fear that the increasing economic problems not only of the third world countries but also of the United States and Europe may become the occasion to try out some of the apocalyptic toys on which the Pentagon relies so much. Even after Vietnam, we seem to believe that weapons can make peace. They can certainly make war, but today a war no longer can have peace at the other end, only total annihilation.

Meanwhile, words remain extremely dangerous. We now hear words about a nuclear warning attack, words about occupying Cuba or invading Nicaragua. Such words by people in power, with their subsequent denials, create an ongoing atmosphere of anxiety and may eventually lead to mistakes, the consequences of which cannot be overestimated.

It is in the context of this international situation that Christians have to make their choice for peace. Personally, I sometimes feel so engulfed by the political realities that I wonder if a world conflict can be avoided. The main question for me is: Do I "have the strength to survive all that is going to happen, and to stand with confidence before the Son of Man" (Luke 21:36)? Or will I allow myself and others to be so overwhelmed by all these wars and rumors of war that we will die of fear as we await what menaces the world? Am I really ready to encounter my Lord when he comes in a "cloud with power and great glory" (Luke 21: 26–27)?

How much time and energy we spend in understanding, analyzing, discussing, and evaluating the socioeconomic and political status of our globe, and how little of our hearts and minds is occupied to prepare ourselves for the day of the Lord, which will be sprung on us suddenly, "like a trap" (Luke 21:35). Prayer, meditation, fasting, communal life, care for the sick, the dying, the hungry, and the fearful, are they really in the center of our lives as Christian people? The world is coming to an end, probably by our own doing, and this will happen this week, this decade, this century, or millions of years in the future; but the certainty of an end should give us the strength to announce boldly and fearlessly that those who hold on to the Lord of life will not be harmed but have eternal life. But woe to us when, on the day of the Lord, "hearts will be coarsened with debauchery and drunkenness and the cares of life" (Luke 21:34).

All of this suggests to me the urgent need for a spirituality that takes the end of things very seriously, not a spirituality of withdrawal, nor of blindness to the powers of the world, but a spirituality that allows us to live in this world without belonging to it, a spirituality that allows us to taste the joy and peace of the divine life even when we are surrounded by the powers and principalities of evil, death, and destruction. I wonder if a spirituality of liberation does not need to be deepened by a spirituality of exile or captivity. I wonder if a spirituality that focuses on the alleviation of poverty should not be deepened by a spirituality that allows people to continue their lives when their poverty only increases. I wonder if a spirituality that encourages peacemaking should not be deepened by a spirituality that allows us to remain faithful when the only things we see are dying children, burning houses, and the total destruction of our civilization. May God prevent any of these horrors from taking place, may we do all that is possible to prevent them, but may we never lose our faith when "great misery [descends] on the land and wrath on this people, . . . [when there are] signs in the sun and moon and stars, . . . [when] nations [are] in agony, bewildered by the clamor of the ocean and its waves" (Luke 21:24–26). I pray that we will not be swept away by our own curiosity, sensationalism, and panic, but remain attentive to Him who comes and will say: "Come, you whom my Father has blessed, take for your heritage the kingdom prepared for you since the foundation of the world" (Matt. 25:34–35).

Friday, November 13

One of the best articles I have read about the plight of the Latin American Church was published in Lent 1981 in the *National Catholic Reporter*. It is written by an anonymous American priest working in Bolivia. The author preferred to remain anonymous in order to prevent reprisals against himself and those with whom he works. From the depth of his heart he cries out to his fellow Christians in the United States, begging them to listen, to understand and to act. He writes:

> What we see is this. The documents of the Latin American bishops' meetings at both Medellin and Puebla . . . condemn "liberal capitalism" by name along with atheistic communism and ideologies of national security. Neither the U.S. Catholic bishops nor priests, with rare exceptions, teach the implications of this doctrine in the ethical formation of U.S. Catholics. We think this is a grave dereliction of duty which has terrible human consequences.
>
> We see these consequences every day. Assassination, physical and psychological torture and rape are the ordinary judicial means of inquiry in our countries. These intelligence skills have been taught for 35 years to more than 80,000 Latin American military and police forces as counter-insurgent and anti-terrorist tactics to keep the "Communists" from invading our economic sphere of influence. You would want proof? Get names and addresses from the bishops of Chile, Brazil, Argentina, Bolivia, El Salvador, etc., as well as from Amnesty International.
>
> Latin Americans do not want to be satellites of the superpowers, neither of Russia nor the United States. They want to be free of economic and political colonialism. And they are not permitted to be. By force and physical violence, every normal avenue of social and political change is closed to them. Or must we accept the opinion that violence is the only "normal" path to a healthy human society? . . .
>
> For the first time in their tortured history, Salvadoreans, Guatemalans, Peruvians, Brazilians, etc., want the right to be themselves. They want the right to make their own mistakes in their own path to maturity as a people with identity and responsibility. No one can stop this march of history. . . .
>
> Latin America in the year 2000 will have 500 million people, half of them under 21 with creative energy and youthful aspirations. The United States, with its own anti-life culture which considers children as the enemy of conspicuous consumption, will be a nation of old people and old ideas, spent, sterile, wasted and without a future. . . .
>
> The coming generations of young Latin Americans will hate the people of the United States if we continue our greedy ways. How long can we keep these hordes controlled to provide us with our more than comfortable lifestyle if they learn how to read and write?

After these words, this anonymous author addresses himself to parishioners, bishops, and priests, theologians and intellectuals, men and women religious, union members and workers, and finally to the young:

> Do not sell your faith or your freedom to maintain the antique shop called "western civilization." Whatever it may have been in the 18th and 19th

centuries, it has not been for the 20th. And it offers no hope to youth for their century, the 21st. . . . The political and economic systems, theories and practices we have seen for 35 years offer nothing but a musty nostalgia. The smell of death is upon them. . . .

We, your mission representatives, do not ask you to wallow in unproductive guilt. We ask you to change your priorities. And the priorities of our nation. You will then be free. And so will millions of others whose slavery and poverty are now the basis of your good life. How can people of conscience and faith be at peace with themselves or their society knowing what their comfort costs others?

And he concludes with these powerful words:

As for ourselves, we know that we now have, no security and no protection from either our host countries or the colonial power of the United States government always acting behind the scenes. We have no arms except the armor of faith and the shield of hope. We are free as never before to give witness to the life of Jesus as did the sisters in El Salvador. "We are cursed and we bless. . . ." We are condemned as "subversives," "agitators," "Communists," "foreigners" wherever we unmask the idolatry of money and power. We are imprisoned, tortured, expelled, or killed for living the gospel. . . . Our mission task now is to tell the Americans to convert, to "let my people go," to seek a just and fraternal human life with the poor of Latin America and the world. Or to see the United States destroy itself, its youth and its future, by stupid, selfish, useless, endless greed and violence. There is no liberation, no resurrection without conversion and the death of old ways ("A Cry for Latin America," *National Catholic Reporter*, April 17, 1981).

Living here in Bolivia, seeing the tired faces of the women who carry their heavy burdens to the market, seeing the undernourished children, seeing miserable fruit vendors and beggars and realizing that things are getting worse and worse day after day, I know that this cry from and for Latin America doesn't hold any sentimentality, sensationalism, or false rhetoric.

Saturday, November 14

As the days and weeks pass by and I come to know the students of the language school better, I realize more and more how insecure, fearful, and often lonely many of us are. Not only do we continue to hope for mail from "home," but we also continue to be submerged by the powers around us. At home we at least had our own niche in life, our own little place where we could feel useful and admired. Here none of that is present. Here we are in a world that did not invite us, in which we can hardly express ourselves and which constantly reminds us of our powerlessness. And still, we know that we are sent here, that God wants us here, and that it is here that we have to work out our salvation.

The more these strong and often conflicting feelings come to the surface, the more I realize how much we need each other. Mission work is not a task for individuals. The Lord sent his disciples into the world in small groups, not as individual heroes or pioneers. We are sent out together, so that together—gathered by One Lord—we can make him present in this world.

Many of us are eager to go out and to start working as soon as possible, with or without words! It is certainly a sign of zeal, good will, great energy, and generosity. But maybe we should first of all look at each other, recognize each other's suffering and come together as a living body to pray, and to share our joys and hopes, our fears and pains. This experience of belonging to each other by our common love for Our Lord and our common awareness of our task can create the space where God's Spirit will descend and from where we can go out in many directions without ever feeling alone. After all, the first and most important witness is to them who can say of us: "See how they love each other."

Tuesday, November 17

I spent the afternoon with the children of the Catholic orphanage called Gotas de Leche (Drops of Milk). The children were so starved for affection that they fought with each other for the privilege of touching me.

How little do we really know the power of physical touch. These boys and girls only wanted one thing: to be touched, hugged, stroked, and caressed. Probably most adults have the same needs but no longer have the innocence and unself-consciousness to express them. Sometimes I see humanity as a sea of people starving for affection, tenderness, care, love, acceptance, forgiveness, and gentleness. Everyone seems to cry: "Please love me." The cry becomes louder and the response so inaudible that people kill each other and themselves in despair. The little orphans tell more than they know. If we don't love one another, we kill one another. There's no middle road.

Wednesday, November 18

My move to the Quiroga family hasn't made my prayer life easier. I spend much time going back and forth to the language institute, have a hard time keeping up with my four classes every day, and feel more tired than usual. The last two weeks I was not able to spend much time in prayer and had to limit myself to my breviary and the Eucharist. Life without prayer weakens my spirit. I have to start looking for a new rhythm. At least I know the difference between days with ample time for prayer and days that are hurried and restless.

Nobody has to prove to me that prayer makes a difference. Without prayer I become irritable, tired, heavy of heart, and I lose the Spirit who directs my attention to the needs of others instead of my own. Without prayer, my attention moves to my own preoccupation. I become cranky and spiteful and often I experience resentment and a desire for revenge.

I am surprised that I allow the language training to become so important that my prayer life takes a second place to it. It seems that when there are no urgent things to do, I create them myself, and when there are no deadlines to meet, I organize them for myself. That is a clear form of self-deception. The powers that try to keep me from simply being with God have a seductive quality. Something as simple as a language course can play demon with me. Why speak different languages if my heart remains dry and angry, upset and lonely? Everything is so obvious. To reach the obvious, I have to struggle. It is the struggle that Our Lord himself came to share.

Thursday, November 19

In times of testing, God and the demon seem close together. Today I felt this more strongly than on other days. After classes I went to downtown Cochabamba to pick up Rodolfo's bicycle, which he was willing to lend me. As I biked through town and saw groups of young men loitering around the street corners and waiting for the next movie to start; as I walked through the bookstores stacked with magazines about violence, sex, and gossip; and as I saw the endless advertisements for unnecessary items imported mostly from Germany and the United States, I had the feeling of being surrounded by powers much greater than myself. I felt the seductive powers of sin all around me and got a glimpse of the truth that all the horrendous evils which plague our world—hunger, the nuclear arms race, torture, exploitation, rape, child abuse, and all forms of oppression—have their small and sometimes unnoticed beginnings in the human heart. The demon is very patient in the way he goes about his destructive work. I felt the darkness of the world all around me.

After some aimless wandering, I biked to the small Carmelite convent on Avertida America, close to the house of my hosts. A friendly Carmelite sister spoke to me in the chapel and told me that I would be welcome at any hour to come there to pray or celebrate the Eucharist. She radiated a spirit of joy and peace. She told me about the light that shines into the darkness without saying a word about it. As I looked around, I saw the statues of St. Teresa of Avila and St. Thérèse of Lisieux. Suddenly it seemed to me that these two women were talking to me as they had never before. They spoke of another world. As I knelt down in the small and simple chapel, I knew that this place was filled with God's presence. I felt the prayers that had been said there day and night.

After returning from the Carmelite sisters, I read the life of St. Thérèse of Lisieux in *Ten Christians*, a book that I had taken with me on my journey. Thérèse's unconditional love for Christ spoke to me in a new way. She dedicated her life to the missions and she considered herself a missionary in her hidden convent. She reminded me that true mission means being sent into the world as Christ was sent into the world: in total surrender to God's will.

My visit to the Carmelite sisters helped me realize again that where the demon is, God is not far away; and where God shows his presence, the demon does not remain absent very long. There is always a choice to be made between the power of life and the power of death. I myself have to make that choice. Nobody else, not even God, will make that choice for me.

Friday, November 20

This morning at 8:30 Gerry McCrane and Sister Lourdes gave a report to the students at the language school about their journey to Peru. They participated in the day of prayer in Juli on November fifteenth organized in response to the recent attacks on the local church. It was a moving report. Gerry and Lourdes told how five thousand poor *campesinos* walked from the house where the first attack took place to the cathedral. They showed how the Church of Juli had truly become the Church of the people. The people had grown aware over the years that the Church had become something other than a wealthy institution that tries to maintain the status quo. This transition was not as obvious as it might seem. Many of the organizers of the day of prayer had wondered what the response would be. Would people come and join in the pilgrimage? Would there be violence from those who had already shown their hostility by destruction and death threats? Would people get hurt in the crowds? What would be the response of those bishops who like to keep things quiet and who consider such actions provocative? These and many other questions had occupied the mind of Alberto Koenigsknecht, the prelate of Juli, and of his collaborators. The issue had been: "Are we doing more harm than good by calling the people of Peru to a public manifestation of their religious commitment in the face of a beginning persecution?"

But Sunday, November fifteenth, had been a day of solidarity for the poor, a day of sincere prayer, a day of mutual encouragement, and a day of recommitment to the work in Juli. Gerry, who had been pastor in Juli for many years, showed great joy as he gave his report: "It was such a source of gratitude to see that, after many years of hard pastoral work, the people had come to see and believe that they themselves are the Church and that they were willing to offer up a day good for planting to show it." And Lourdes told with excitement how hundreds of *campesinos* had worked together to prepare this day. Small pamphlets about the meaning of this special pilgrimage had been studied in the different parishes during the weeks preceding the day of prayer, and many hours had been spent to make this day not so much a protest against hostile behavior as a witness for Christ living in the people of the Juli prelature. The Eucharist, celebrated on the square in front of the cathedral, had been a true Aymara feast. Many Aymara symbols had been integrated into the celebration; this was not a Latin ritual imposed on poor Indians, but a true manifestation of the spirituality of the Aymara people.

I was glad to hear this story of faith and hope. For awhile I had thought about going with Gerry and Lourdes myself, but felt that language training had to remain my priority for the short time I am in Bolivia. Meanwhile, I wonder with some apprehension if this is the last word we will hear about the prelature of Juli. Where God's love becomes very visible, the forces of evil usually do not long remain hidden. Is the day in Juli the end of a short experience of persecution or the beginning of a long road of suffering on which the faith of many will be tested? I pray that all who work there and will work there will have the strength and the courage to be faithful.

Saturday, November 21

God exists. When I can say this with all that I am, I have the "gnosis" (the knowledge of God) about which St. John speaks and the "Memoria Dei" (the memory of God) about which St. Basil writes. To say with all that we have, think, feel, and are: "God exists," is the most world-shattering statement that a human being can make. When we make that statement, all the distinctions between intellectual, emotional, affective, and spiritual understanding fall away and there is only one truth left to acclaim: God exists. When we say this from the heart, everything trembles in heaven and on earth. Because when God exists, all that *is* flows from him. When I want to know if I ever have come to the true knowledge, the gnosis, of God's existence, I have simply to allow myself to become aware of how I experience myself. It doesn't take much to realize that I am constantly with myself. I am aware of all of the various parts of my body, and I "know" when I am hurting and when not. I am aware of my desire for food and clothing and shelter. I am aware of my sexual urges and my need for intimacy and community. I am aware of my feelings of pity, compassion, and solidarity, my ability to be of service and my hope to give a helping hand. I am aware of my intellectual, physical, and artistic skills and my drive to use them. I am aware of my anger, my lust, my feelings of revenge and resentment, and even at times of my desire to harm. Indeed, what is central to me is: *I exist.* My own existence fills me, and wherever I turn I find myself again locked in my own self-awareness: I exist. Although experiences of hatred are different from experiences of love, and although a desire for power is different from a desire to serve, they all are the same insofar as they identify *my* existence as what *really* counts.

However, as soon as I say, "God exists," my existence no longer can remain in the center, because the essence of the knowledge of God reveals my own existence as deriving its total being from his. That is the true conversion experience. I no longer let the knowledge of my existence be the center from which I derive, project, deduct, or intuit the existence of God; I suddenly or slowly find my own existence revealed to me in and through the knowledge of God. Then it becomes real for me that I can love myself and my neighbor only because God has loved me first. The life-converting experience is not the discovery that I have choices to make that determine the way I live out my existence, but the awareness that my existence itself is not in the center. Once I "know" God, that is, once I experience his love as the love in which all my human experiences are anchored, I can only desire one thing: to be in that love. "Being" anywhere else, then, is shown to be illusory and eventually lethal.

All of these reflections have taken a new urgency for me, during these weeks in Bolivia. It slowly dawned on me that so much, if not most, of our energy and attention goes to the question of our own existence. We wonder how we are doing, how we feel, how we will serve in Latin America, and how we will organize our next day, weekend, year, or decade. We try hard to make responsible and moral choices that give us a sense that at least we are searching in the right direction. But all of this, the good as well as the bad, the responsible as well as the irresponsible, the acts of lust as well as the acts of service, lose their power over us when we realize that God exists, before and after, in the past and in the future, now and forever, and that in and through the knowledge of that divine existence I might get a small glimpse of why there is an I and a he, she, we, and they. Then all questions have only one answer: God. What am I supposed to think about? About God, because all thoughts find their creative power in him. What am I supposed to say? His Word, because all my words are fruitful to the degree that they are a reflection of his. What am I supposed to do? His will, because his will is the loving desire that gave existence to all that is, myself included.

Is it better to be in Bolivia, in Peru, in the United States, or in Holland? Is it better to give a glass of water to a thirsty child or to work on a new world order in which children will no longer beg for water? Is it better to read a book or to walk on the street, to write a letter or bind the wounds of a dying man? Is it better to do this or that, say this or that, think about this or that? All these questions suddenly appear to me as false preoccupations, as a captivity in the illusory concern about my own existence, as an expression of my sick supposition that God depends on me, that his existence is derived from mine.

Nothing is real without deriving its reality from God. This was the great discovery of St. Francis when he suddenly saw the whole world in God's hands and wondered why God didn't drop it. St. Augustine, St. Teresa of Avila, St. John Vianney, and all the saints are saints precisely because for them the order of being was turned around and they saw, felt, and—above all—knew with their heart that outside God nothing is, nothing breathes, nothing moves, and nothing lives.

This makes me aware that the basis of all ministry rests not in the moral life but in the mystical life. The issue is not to live as well as we can, but to let our life be one that finds its source in the Divine Life.

God exists, and the meaning of all that I am depends totally on that knowledge. I wonder constantly if I am genuinely allowing my life to be determined by that truth. Maybe part of my reason for hesitating to embrace this truth fully is that it challenges me to give up all control over my life and to let God be God, my God, the God of my neighbor, and the God of all creation. But I also realize that as long as I do not "do" this, my life is an illusion and most of my energy is spoiled in trying to keep that illusion going.

Does all of this mean that my thoughts, plans, projects, and ideas no longer matter? That conclusion has been drawn by people who used the spiritual life as a way to manipulate others and that conclusion has led, sadly enough, to false views on asceticism, obedience, surrender to God's will, and certain forms of self-denial. The converted person does not say that nothing matters anymore, but that everything that is happens in God and that he is the dwelling place where we come to know the true order of things. Instead of saying: "Nothing matters any more, since I know that God exists," the converted person says: "All is now clothed in divine light and therefore nothing can be unimportant." The converted person sees, hears, and understands with a divine eye, a divine ear, a divine heart. The converted person knows himself or herself and all the world in God. The converted person *is* where God is, and from that place everything matters: giving water, clothing the naked, working for a new world order, saying a prayer, smiling at a child, reading a book, and sleeping in peace. All has become different while all remains the same.

Somehow I feel that all these reflections are important for me in a time during which I have to make some very concrete decisions. The "nothing matters" and the "everything matters" should never be separated in a time such as this. What brings them together is the unceasing cry coming from the heart: "God exists."

Sunday, November 22

This morning for two hours I played with the little boys and girls at the state orphanage. This orphanage is much worse than Drops of Milk, the Catholic orphanage. About a hundred little kids were running around in a poorly kept stony yard surrounded by a large fence. The kids jumped all over me trying to be touched, to attract attention, to play, and to be lifted up. What struck me most was their explicit interest in my body. They kept stroking my forehead, saying, "What a large forehead!" They wanted to see my teeth, my tongue, and kept comparing the size of their hands and fingers with mine. Their fascination with a large person moved me. One six-year-old looked at me and said, "A grown man!" For her I symbolized a world from which she is excluded. These children see mostly other children. They have very few adults around who can help them see beyond themselves. Very soon I was transformed into a climbing tree. The kids tried to climb over my knees, chest, and shoulders to the top, and at one point there was a line of ten little ones waiting for their turn to climb the big man.

I fell in love with a little deaf-mute boy who was able with his expressive hands and eyes to explain to me whatever he wanted me to do. Everytime I did something—connecting a cord to his toy, making a knot in his piece of rope, tying his shoes—he gave me a big smile and put his arms around me.

None of these children has a home. The food they receive is minimal, the attention meager, and the education poor. What will become of them? Who will give them what they need? In a poor country the children always suffer the most.

In the afternoon I celebrated the feast of Christ the King with the Carmelite sisters. The children were on my mind when I took the bread and wine and said: "This is my body, this is my blood." The Lord became flesh and blood for these children; so they could touch him, hug him, kiss him, stroke him. And thus he is their friend, their brother. Jesus died naked on the cross with the words above his head: "This is the King of the Jews." Many of the kids walked around naked, jumping in and out of a cement tub of water, and running up to me to be hugged and kissed and to let my hands touch their skin and squeeze their little bodies. The naked King on the Cross and the naked kids in Cochabamba belong together. The God who is love stands with the children who crave love. I knew that I had seen my King again. He seems to say: "Come back. I will be here every day, every week, every year. I stay here because I became body and blood for them. Come and touch me."

Monday, November 23

Rodolfo Quiroga could hardly be a less political man. He never attends any meetings other than those of the Christian Family Movement, and he spends all his free time with his wife and son. He enjoys taking care of his flowers, making little repairs in his house, and joining his wife in her ham radio hobby. He is one of the most homebound men I have ever met and his conversations focus on his family, his religion, and occasionally—and somewhat reluctantly—on his business.

And yet a little over a year ago, at two o'clock one morning, a group of armed men appeared at his door and asked for entrance. When Rodolfo refused to let them in, they broke open his front door, forced him into their car, and took him off to prison. Nancy, Rodolfito, and the maid, Marcelita, were left in fear and confusion. Early the next day, with the influence of her friends, Nancy got access to the head of the police and was able to find out what had happened and where Rodolfo was. It turned out that a family member with whom they had a long-standing personal conflict had called the military authorities and told them that Rodolfo was a Communist and was using his house for a conspiracy with his leftist friends to overthrow the government. The reaction had been immediate. The paramilitary police—mostly Argentinians trained in sinister duties and hired by the Bolivian government—were called and sent off to arrest Rodolfo. With brute force, they entered his house and took him to an overcrowded prison cell.

When Nancy spoke to the head of the police, one of his first questions was, "Do you know anyone who might like to harm your husband?" When Nancy told him about the conflict with the family member, the officer recognized that this was the same story he had already heard from Rodolfo himself and he told her about the phone call and the accusations. Since the Quirogas have many influential friends in Cochabamba, excuses were quickly made and within two hours Rodolfo was set free. The police officer even offered Nancy breakfast, but nobody offered to pay for the damage to the house.

This story might be read as a comedy of errors, but it illustrates one of the most familiar aspects of Latin American politics, the intimate connection between political and family conflicts. I think it will be hard ever to understand the complex political situations in Latin America without realizing how often old and bitter family conflicts are intermingled with the uses of political power. Objectively, nobody could be less likely to be considered a Communist, a political agitator, a conspirator, or even a public figure than Rodolfo, but he came close to being tortured or killed because of his alleged involvement in a fictitious political event.

All of this reminded me of the story of Dr. Joel Filártiga, my Paraguayan friend, whose seventeen-year-old son was tortured to death in 1976 to silence his own political resistance. Dr. Filártiga is a longtime opponent of the dictatorship of General Alfredo Stroessner. He publicly—through writing and drawing—criticizes his government. But his son would never have been abducted and cruelly murdered if the police inspector Americo Peña, who supervised the torture of the boy with electric shocks, had not also had a long-standing conflict with the Filártiga family.

In small countries such as Paraguay and Bolivia, there are only a few candidates for political office, and these few frequently have as many personal conflicts between themselves as political differences. Often it is difficult to figure out who is against whom and for what reason. The word "Communist" always comes in as a handy word to get the guns out of the closet, but it might well be that an unpaid loan or an offensive word is the real reason for destroying someone's life.

Little Rodolfito now is terribly afraid to be alone in the house. He bites his nails and worries about going away from home without his parents. The sight of his father being dragged out of his home continues to haunt him. Meanwhile, Nancy and Rodolfo endure many sleepless nights wondering what the next move of their enemy will be. I have begun to see why they both spend so many hours during the weekend playing with their ham radio and talking to friendly people from other parts of the world: it is safe company and a good distraction.

Tuesday, November 24

Tonight Sister Maria Rieckelman spoke about the problems of acculturation. She gave a fine presentation about the many psychological struggles we can experience when we try to find a home in a new culture.

She mentioned Erich Fromm's remark that our two main fears are of losing control and of becoming isolated. I keep experiencing these fears every time I make a move, major or minor, and I wonder if I am getting any better in dealing with them. I find myself with the same old struggles every time I am in a new and unfamiliar milieu. In particular, the experience of isolation keeps returning, not in a lessening but in an increasing degree. Becoming older makes the experience of isolation much more familiar—maybe simply because of sheer repetition—but not less painful.

So, maybe the question is not how to cope better, but how slowly to allow my unchanging character to become a way of humility and surrender to God. As I recognize my fears of being left alone and my desire for a sense of belonging, I may gradually give up my attempts to fill my loneliness and be ready to recognize with my heart that God is Emmanuel, "God-with-us," and that I belong to him before anything or anyone else.

And so a new vision of maturity may emerge; not a vision in which I am more and more able to deal with my own pains, but in which I am more willing to let my Lord deal with them. After all, maturation in a spiritual sense is a growing willingness to stretch out my arms, to have a belt put round me and to be led where I would rather not go (John 21:18).

Wednesday, November 25

For two weeks the workers in the tin mines in Huanuni have been on strike to force recognition of their union. Solidarity strikes in other mines soon followed and finally, two days ago, about twelve women from the families of arrested labor leaders went on a hunger strike.

The response of the government was harsh and violent. Many workers were picked up during the night and put in prison, gas and food supplies to the city of Huanuni were cut off, newspapers were kept from circulating, striking workers were fired, and *campesinos* in need of work were sent into the mines. Since it was evident that the workers were not going to give up easily, it seemed for a while that the government was losing control over the situation and that there might be a new coup to break the deadlock. The miners asked the church to mediate. Archbishop Manrique and the Apostolic Nuncio agreed. Finally, a settlement was reached in which all arrested miners would be set free. A government commission will study the issue of recognition of the unions.

Today the Bolivian newspapers announced that the conflict has been solved. Neither the miners nor the government seems to have won. The emphasis during the strike shifted from the recognition of the union to the release of its leaders. The labor leaders will be free, but recognition of the unions will probably be long in coming. The only good thing is that more violence and repression were avoided. The oppressed and exploited miners will most likely not be better off than before. Hundreds of people have suffered terribly during the last few weeks, a suffering that will be kept out of the papers and yet will become part of the quiet and anonymous suffering of this country.

Thursday, November 26

Thanksgiving Day! There is probably no day I liked so much in the United States as this day. I can remember clearly all the Thanksgiving Days I celebrated in the last ten years. It was always a day of being together with friends, and truly a day of saying thanks. In many ways, it struck me as a more spiritual or religious day than Christmas: no gifts, few commercial preparations, just a coming together to express gratitude for life and all the blessings we have received.

Today I miss being in the United States, as do many people here at the language institute. I could feel it at the dinner table and also in the mood during the breaks between classes.

Still, what is important is to be grateful today and to give thanks. I am more and more convinced that gratitude is one of the most sublime of human emotions. It is an emotion that reaches out far beyond our own self to God, to all of creation, to the people who gave us life, love, and care. It is an emotion in which we experience our dependencies as a gift and realize that in the celebration of our dependencies we become most aware of who we truly are: a small but precious part of creation and above all of the human family. On this day we can say: It is good "just" to be human and it is in our common humanity that we can recognize God's love.

Friday, November 27

A psychology of education must exist which describes the up and down phases a student experiences in learning a new language. This week I felt as though I had not learned a thing since I came here. I experienced myself as stuttering worse than ever, as making the same basic mistakes as when I came here five weeks ago, and as still unable to know what people are talking about when they are not talking to me. I also noticed that expressions and constructions that a few weeks ago seemed quite obvious and even simple to me suddenly became real problems again. A small comfort was the realization of how terribly hard the English language is for Spanish-speaking people. Nancy Quiroga made me aware that *una cerveza* (a beer), *un pájaro* (a bird), and *un oso* (a bear) sounded to her all the same in English.

Saturday, November 28

Today is the last day of the liturgical year and tonight at the language school we will have a three-hour prayer vigil for justice and peace to start the advent season. I am happy for the occasion to pray together with the students and teachers. Though our only reason for being together is to become more able to reveal the presence of God in this world, we seldom have expressed this publicly in common worship.

We all know how far we are from a just and peaceful world. Ireland is on the brink of a civil war, Poland is uncertain whether the Russians will invade, Iran is tortured by weekly executions of hundreds of its own people and its war with Iraq, Guatemala is flooded with terror, El Salvador is being destroyed by oppression and civil war, Nicaragua is more and more insecure about its future, the United States is selling arms all over the world, Europe is in turmoil about the increase of nuclear arms on its territory, the Middle East is more explosive than ever, and the peoples of many Asian, African, and Latin American countries are threatened by malnutrition and starvation. The four beasts of which the Prophet Daniel speaks in his vision are running wild over this world.

There is a good reason to pray, especially for us who have come together from all parts of this world to be peacemakers. We know we cannot make peace with our own hands. We know that we are in the service of the King of Peace who one day will appear on the clouds. To him the kingdom, the power, and the glory will be given, and people of all languages and nations will serve him. We know that he will defeat all the beasts and that his power will be eternal and that his kingdom will never be destroyed (see Daniel 7:14). But we, too, are subject to the temptations of this world, the temptations of greed and lust, violence and revenge, hatred and destruction. We are not immune to the powers of the beasts. Therefore we have to help each other to keep our hearts and minds directed toward the Son of Man, so that we will recognize him when he comes and will be free to stand with confidence before him (see Luke 21:36). We have to keep ourselves and each other anchored in his words, because "heaven and earth will pass away, but my words will never pass away" (Luke 21:33). It is on that eternal Word, who became flesh and lived among us, that our hope is built.

Sunday, November 29

It is Advent again. In his sermon this morning, Oscar Uzin said: Be alert, be alert, so that you will be able to recognize your Lord in your husband, your wife, your parents, your children, your friends, your teachers, but also in all that you read in the daily papers. The Lord is coming, always coming. Be alert to his coming. When you have ears to hear and eyes to see, you will recognize him at any moment of your life. Life is Advent; life is recognizing the coming of the Lord.

In Bolivia the Advent symbols are different from those I am used to. In the past, Advent always meant to me the shortening of days, the approach of winter, and the time in which nature became darker and colder until the day of light. But now I have to learn to wait for the coming of the Lord while spring becomes summer and the light increases day by day. Now Advent means the coming of hot days with their fertile showers. Now Advent is the time during which schools are closed and children play on the streets. Now Advent means a time of blossoming trees and first fruits. And so the symbols of Easter become symbols of Christmas. Maybe my first Advent in the southern part of our planet will reveal to me new things about the mystery of God's becoming flesh among us. Until now, nature has only told me half of the story of God's incarnation; now the other half can be told.

But I have to listen, quietly, patiently, and with inner expectation. Nature can only tell me its other half of the story when I am ready to hear it, when my heart is not so full of false images and unnecessary preoccupations that there is no place left to receive the good news I have not yet heard.

Still I keep making my mistakes. Tonight I went with Richard and Theresa to *The Stuntman*, a movie about the making of a film. The movie was so filled with images of greed and lust, manipulation and exploitation, fearful and painful sensations, that it filled all the empty spaces that could have been blessed by the spirit of Advent. The film showed me how human beings are willing to waste their money, time, energy, and most precious intellectual and emotional talents to create a product that will fill the eyes and ears of thousands of people with images that can only damage the gentleness that lies dormant in our innermost being and asks to be awakened by a Divine touch.

Why did I go to this spectacle with Richard and Theresa? Richard is a kind Englishman who just returned from years of work with cooperatives in Africa, and Theresa is an Australian woman with great interest in music and handicrafts. Both hope to work together in Latin America and come to know better the beauty of this land and its people.

To be together, why did we need this violent and intrusive film? We could have spent our time so much better listening to each other's stories than watching the stuntman's tricks. Why do we keep missing the most obvious signs of God's coming and allow our hearts to be filled with all those things that keep suggesting, not that the Lord is coming, but that nothing will happen unless we make it happen.

I hope and pray that Advent will not be filled with stuntmen, but with the Spirit of him who invites us to listen carefully to the sounds of the New Earth that are manifesting themselves in the midst of the old.

Monday, November 30

St. Ignatius of Loyola was converted by reading the lives of the saints. I can understand this quite well, because everytime I read the life of a saint I experience a powerful call to conversion. Every man or woman who lives the Christian life to the full cannot but exercise a deep influence on everyone he or she meets. What continues to fascinate me is that those whose whole mind and heart were directed to God had the greatest impact on other people, while those who tried very hard to be influential were quickly forgotten.

When I met Mother Teresa in Rome, I saw immediately that her inner attention was focused constantly on Jesus. It seemed that she saw only him and through him came to see the poorest of the poor to whom she has dedicated her life. She never answers the many psychological and socioeconomic questions brought to her on the level they are raised. She answers them with a logic, from a perspective, and in a place that remains unfamiliar to most of us. It is a divine logic, a divine perspective, a divine place. That is why many find her simplistic, naive, and out of touch with the "real problems." Like Jesus himself, she challenges her listeners to move with her to that place from where things can be seen as God sees them.

When I explained to her all my problems and struggles with elaborate details and asked for her insights, she simply said: "If you spend one hour a day in contemplative prayer and never do anything which you know is wrong, you will be all right." With these words she answered none as well as all of my problems at the same time. It was now up to me to be willing to move to the place where that answer could be heard.

All these thoughts have come to me since I have been reading Boniface Hanley's book *Ten Christians*. In this book, Hanley offers simple but penetrating portraits of Pierre Toussaints, Damien de Veuster, Frederic Ozanam, Maximilian Kolbe, Teresa of Calcutta, St. Francis of Assisi, St. John Bosco, Rose Hawthorne Lathtop, Joseph Cardinal Cardijn, and St. Thérèse of Lisieux.

Reading these short biographies is like stepping out of this world and back into it again under the guidance of these concrete human beings. They all are much like me, but also different. They all know the struggles I know, but they are living with them in a different way. They all loved the world, but it was a world they came to see through God's eyes.

After having read such biographies, Ignatius could no longer continue his old life. He had seen how he could live when he was willing to take the risk of total surrender to the love of God.

3

December

A LAND OF MARTYRS

∎

Tuesday, December 1

LIVING WITH THE Quiroga family has helped me understand the struggle of Bolivian life. Every day I see more pain and tears under the surface of this seemingly happy and successful family. A few days ago, Nancy told me that little Rodolfito was not their biological son, but their adopted child. After her miscarriage, Nancy and Rodolfo wanted to adopt a child; but in Bolivia this is not easy. Nancy mentioned her desire to one of her ham radio friends, a medical doctor from another Latin American country with whom she had regular radio contacts. One day he told her that he knew of a little baby boy who needed caring parents. Nancy and Rodolfo went to visit the doctor and took the little boy home.

In Bolivia, however, having an adopted child, or being one, is looked down on as something unusual and strange. Soon Nancy and Rodolfo became fearful that their enemies would use their knowledge of the adoption to harm them. Their greatest concern was that the boy would find out from hostile people that he was not his parents' real child. They wanted to be sure that they themselves would explain to their son how and why they adopted him. This was the main reason for which Nancy and Rodolfo left the country and settled with their son in Miami, to give the boy a peaceful and quiet youth. Only when Rodolfito was old enough to understand that he had a truly safe home and that he was chosen by his parents out of love did they return to their country.

Their return did not bring them the peace they desired. Since their enemies had not left, they soon were exposed to the attack and imprisonment I wrote about on November twenty-third. Although Nancy and Rodolfo clearly want to live in their own country, I doubt that they will do so for long. Their son was so Americanized during his six years in the United States that he not only prefers hamburgers, french fries, soft drinks, and pancakes above anything Bolivian, but also dreams about a future in the land of his childhood memories.

All these things—the intense dedication to the short-wave radio, the six years in the United States, the nighttime intrusion of the paramilitary forces, the boy's fear of being away from his parents and Nancy and Rodolfo's intense concern for the well-being of their son—seem to fit together like the pieces of a strange puzzle.

Wednesday, December 2

"A shoot shall sprout from the stump of Jesse, and from his roots a bud shall blossom. The spirit of the LORD shall rest upon him . . . " (Isa. 11:1–2).

These words from last night's liturgy have stayed with me during the day. Our salvation comes from something small, tender, and vulnerable, something hardly noticeable. God, who is the Creator of the Universe, comes to us in smallness, weakness, and hiddenness.

I find this a hopeful message. Somehow, I keep expecting loud and impressive events to convince me and others of God's saving power; but over and over again, I am reminded that spectacles, power plays, and big events are the ways of the world. Our temptation is to be distracted by them and made blind to the "shoot that shall sprout from the stump."

When I have no eyes for the small signs of God's presence—the smile of a baby, the carefree play of children, the words of encouragement and gestures of love offered by friends—I will always remain tempted to despair.

The small child of Bethlehem, the unknown young man of Nazareth, the rejected preacher, the naked man on the cross, *he* asks for my full attention. The work of our salvation takes place in the midst of a world that continues to shout, scream, and overwhelm us with its claims and promises. But the promise is hidden in the shoot that sprouts from the stump, a shoot that hardly anyone notices.

I remember seeing a film on the human misery and devastation brought by the bomb on Hiroshima. Among all the scenes of terror and despair, emerged one image of a man quietly writing a word in calligraphy. All his attention was directed to writing that one word. That image made this gruesome film a hopeful film. Isn't that what God is doing? Writing his Word in the midst of our dark world?

Thursday, December 3

Tonight we celebrated the first anniversary of the martyrdom of Ita Ford, Maura Clark, Jean Donovan, and Dorothy Kazel, the American churchwomen who were raped, tortured, and murdered in El Salvador. Many sisters and priests from the United States, along with their Bolivian and American friends, came together in the parish church of Cala Cala to pray for their sisters who died such a violent and cruel death. It was a moving service in which faith and hope dominated the sadness about the tragic loss.

For me, the most moving part of the service was the reading of the martyrology by Father Jon Sobrino, one of the leading theologians in Latin America. He lives in El Salvador and is deeply involved in the struggle of the Church there. With restraint, he called out the names of the men and women who have been murdered in Latin America during the last decade. As he let the years pass in front of our minds, the numbers of martyrs increased. And every time he finished the list of victims of one particular year, all the people in church responded with a loud: *"Presente."* Yes, indeed, those who had given their lives for the liberation of the poor were still present in the minds and hearts of the people they came to serve. As the list of names grew—1971, 1972, 1973 . . . until 1981—the word *presente* became louder and clearer.

As I listened I realized that Ita, Maura, Dorothy, and Jean were just a few in the growing number of Christians who died as witnesses for the suffering Christ in Latin America. Hundreds and thousands of men and women in El Salvador, Guatemala, Nicaragua, Chile, Argentina, Brazil, Bolivia, as well as in the other countries of Central and South America, have died violent deaths during the last decade—and, for the most part, we do not even know their names. It suddenly struck me that with the thousands of Latin Americans who died, there are few with Anglo-Saxon names. The courage of those few North Americans who came to live and die with their brothers and sisters in South and Central America is a hopeful reminder that God's love transcends all human-made boundaries.

Friday, December 4

After last night's service in memory and honor of the martyrs of El Salvador, Jon Sobrino came to the language school for an informal discussion.

There were about fifteen people sitting in a circle listening to Jon's story. Seldom have I heard a story that touched me so deeply. Most of the facts he told I had heard about at one place or another, and most of the explanations he offered were familiar to me. But to hear the story of the horrendous suffering of the Salvadoran people, told by a man who witnessed it all and was involved in the struggle, is an experience that cannot be compared to reading news reports.

The first thing Jon Sobrino did was simply to state the facts. He kept stressing how tempting it is to deny the truth, to deal with it only partially or to present it in a soft way. We need to face the truth of the mass murders that destroy the lives of thousands of civilians, men, women, and children; of the indiscriminate killings to terrorize the poor; and of the selective and well-planned elimination of the leaders of the opposition, whether they are church leaders or political leaders. At least thirty thousand people have been killed in El Salvador during the last two years, and this is a conservative estimate.

The Church in El Salvador is far from united in the face of these barbarities. Jon Sobrino worked closely with Archbishop Oscar Romero, and now he is in close touch with his successor, Acting Bishop Arturo Rivera y Damas. He spoke with great love and sympathy about these men, but left no doubt that they were exceptions. Most of the Salvadoran bishops show little sympathy for Romero's prophetic behavior, which cost him his life. The people might revere him as a saint, but his fellow bishops certainly do not. When some people asked one of the bishops to protest against the torture of one of his priests, he said: "I cannot do this, since he is not tortured as a priest but as a leftist." This bishop is also *vicarius castrensis,* army bishop, and continued to be present as the Church's representative at military functions.

Hearing this, I felt a profound sadness. It is precisely this inner division of the Church that makes a united confrontation of the powers of evil so hard.

I asked Jon Sobrino to say a little more about himself. "Why are you still alive?" I asked. He confessed that his international notoriety was probably his best safeguard. "The military resent deeply all the publicity around their actions in the international press. I am the only theologian of El Salvador who is known outside the country, and my death would create more problems than it would solve. The great indignation in the United States that followed the death of the four American women in December 1980 was very embarrassing to them. They do not want to see this repeated."

Jon Sobrino encouraged me to come to El Salvador and visit his community. "We won't have much time for you," he said, "because there are fewer and fewer priests and sisters to do the work that needs to be done. But we certainly appreciate visits from foreigners, because it is a way of being protected."

I was impressed by Jon Sobrino. His directness, his honesty, his deep faith, his fidelity to the Church, and his great openness to everyone who shows interest in the Church of El Salvador were signs of hope. But the many tensions of the last years have also wounded him. He told us, "People often speak about the beautiful and spiritual victory of the martyrs in El Salvador, but don't forget that the Church in El Salvador is systematically being destroyed and nobody knows how it will end. The only thing we have is our naked hope."

Saturday, December 5

This morning Sister Fran, a Maryknoll Sister who has lived in Bolivia for many years, invited me to celebrate the Eucharist for the blind people with whom she works regularly. With ten blind women and one blind man, we sat in a circle around a table. The first two readings and the responsory psalms were read by the women from their braille sheets, which Fran had prepared for them. After the Gospel reading, there was a lively discussion about baptism and confirmation in response to the story about the baptism of John and the baptism of Jesus. We sang to the accompaniment of an accordian. We listened to words about God's love spoken by those who have inner eyes. Their faith gave me strength and comfort. "Happy the pure in heart: they shall see God" (Matt. 5:8).

Monday, December 7

After seven weeks at the language institute, I am distressed at how superficial the interaction between students and teachers remains. Maybe this is just my own feeling, but I have not experienced an increase in community between the people at the institute. The atmosphere is pleasant, friendly, and mostly sympathetic, but it is clear that everyone has his or her own agenda and thinks primarily about what lies beyond the institute. Students come to learn a new language as quickly as possible and then move on to the "real thing." In that sense, the institute is very much like a seminary where students endure their studies in order to enter the professional world.

I experienced it in my own seminary years and saw it at Notre Dame, at the North American College, at Yale Divinity School, and at many other places. Everywhere there was the tendency to live, act, and think as if the real life is not here but there, not now but later. This tendency makes the formation of community so difficult, if not impossible. Community develops where we experience that something significant is taking place *where we are*. It is the fruit of the intimate knowledge that we are together, not because of a common need—such as to learn a language—but because we are called together to help make God's presence visible in the world. Only to the degree that we have this knowledge of God's call can we transcend our own immediate needs and point together to him who is greater than these needs.

I do not know if I will be alive tomorrow, next week, or next year. Therefore today is always more important than tomorrow. We have to be able to say each day, "This is the day the Lord has made, let us rejoice and be glad." If we all would die on the last day of our language training, nobody should have to say, "I wasted my time." The language training itself should have enough inner validity to make its usefulness secondary.

There are people from all over the world at this school, and together we represent a treasure house of knowledge, experience, human struggle, and, most of all, of faith, hope, and love. If these mental and spiritual talents could be brought into the light we all would have a beautiful space in which our life together could become an ongoing expression of worship and gratitude. Indeed, we could then experience the kingdom of God among us and thus find the strength to go out to serve people in pain.

But our own fears, insecurities, anxieties, and suspicions continue to interfere with our vocation and push us into small cliques of people in which we find some alleviation of our inner tensions. We quickly fall into the temptation of gossip and divisive words and actions, and before we know it we are imitating all the patterns of the world that we want to change by our ministry. This is the irony and tragedy of most theological and ministerial education. It is therefore not surprising that few will find "out there" what they could not find "right here."

Tuesday, December 8

During the celebration of the Eucharist in honor of the Immaculate Conception of Mary, the mother of God, Sister Lourdes offered a moving meditation. She helped me see Mary through the eyes of the poor people of the third world. Mary experienced uncertainty and insecurity when she said yes to the angel. She knew what oppression was when she didn't find a hospitable place to give birth to Jesus. She knew the sufferings of the mothers who see their children being thrown in the air and pierced by bayonets; she lived as a refugee in a strange land with a strange language and strange customs; she knew what it means to have a child who does not follow the regular ways of life but creates turmoil wherever he goes; she felt the loneliness of the widow and the agony of seeing her only son being executed. Indeed, Mary is the woman who stands next to all the poor, oppressed, and lonely women of our time. And when she continues to speak to people it is the simple and the poor to whom she appears: Juan Diego, the simple old Mexican Indian of Guadalupe; Bernadette, the poor sickly girl in Lourdes; Lucia, Jacinta, and Francesco, the unspectacular children in Fatima.

Every word in Scripture about Mary points to her intimate connection with all who are forgotten, rejected, despised, and pushed aside. She joyfully proclaims: "He has cast down the mighty from their thrones, and has lifted up the lowly. He has filled the hungry with good things, and the rich he has sent away empty" (Luke 1:52–53). These words today have taken on so much power and strength that, in a country like El Salvador, they are considered subversive and can lead to torture or death. Mary is the mother of the living, the new Eve, the woman who lives deeply in the heart of the Latin American people. She gives hope, inspires the fight for freedom, and challenges us to live with an unconditional trust in God's love.

Wednesday, December 9

Psalm 42 remains a source of strength to me. I prayed this psalm many, many times while my mother was dying, and every time since that week in October 1978 it has returned to me in times of distress.

> Like the deer that yearns
> for running streams,
> so my soul is yearning
> for you, my God . . . .
> Why are you cast down my soul,
> Why groan within me?
> Hope in God; I will praise him still,
> my savior and my God.

When I read this psalm last Monday during my morning prayer, I noticed that the psalm-prayer that followed it entered into my soul with an unusual power, so much so that it has stayed with me during the last few days. The prayer says:

> Father in heaven, when your strength takes possession of us we no longer say: Why are you cast down, my soul? So now that the surging waves of our indignation have passed over us, let us feel the healing calm of your

forgiveness. Inspire us to yearn for you always, like the deer for running streams, until you satisfy every longing in heaven.

The words "let us feel the healing calm of your forgiveness" are words that I want to hold onto, because if I desire anything, it is the healing calm of God's forgiveness. The longer I live, the more I am aware of my sinfulness, faithlessness, lack of courage, narrow-mindedness; the more I feel the surging waves of greed, lust, violence, and indignation roaring in my innermost self. Growing older has not made life with God easier. In fact, it has become harder to experience his presence, to feel his love, to taste his goodness, to touch his caring hands. Oh how much do I pray that he will let me know through all my senses that his love is more real than my sins and my cowardice, how much do I want to see the light in darkness, and how much do I wait for the day that he will order the surging waves to calm down, and how much do I wait to hear his voice, which says: "Why are you afraid, man of little faith? I am with you always."

Friday, December 11

Every morning at 6:45 I go to the small convent of the Carmelite Sisters for an hour of prayer and meditation. I say "every morning," but there are exceptions. Fatigue, busyness, and preoccupations often serve as arguments for not going. Yet without this one-hour-a-day for God, my life loses its coherency and I start experiencing my days as a series of random incidents and accidents.

My hour in the Carmelite chapel is more important than I can fully know myself. It is not an hour of deep prayer, nor a time in which I experience a special closeness to God; it is not a period of serious attentiveness to the divine mysteries. I wish it were! On the contrary, it is full of distractions, inner restlessness, sleepiness, confusion, and boredom. It seldom, if ever, pleases my senses. But the simple fact of being for one hour in the presence of the Lord and of showing him all that I feel, think, sense, and experience, without trying to hide anything, must please him. Somehow, somewhere, I know that he loves me, even though I do not feel that love as I can feel a human embrace, even though I do not hear a voice as I hear human words of consolation, even though I do not see a smile as I can see a human face. Still the Lord speaks to me, looks at me, and embraces me there, where I am still unable to notice it. The only way I become aware of his presence is in that remarkable desire to return to that quiet chapel and be there without any real satisfaction. Yes, I notice, maybe only retrospectively, that my days and weeks are different days and weeks when they are held together by these regular "useless" times. God is greater than my senses, greater than my thoughts, greater than my heart. I do believe that he touches me in places that are unknown even to myself. I seldom can point directly to these places; but when I feel this inner pull to return again to that hidden hour of prayer, I realize that something is happening that is so deep that it becomes like the riverbed through which the waters can safely flow and find their way to the open sea.

Saturday, December 12

Today we celebrated with Sister Lourdes and Sister Martha the 150th anniversary of the Sisters of Mercy. It was an important celebration for me, since it reminded me of the fact that "the preferential option for the poor," about which we speak so much today in the missionary circles of Latin America, is nothing new and original.

A reading from *Trinity,* by Leon Uris, offered a vivid description of the hunger, illness, misery, and agony of the Irish people in the year 1831, the year in which Catherine McAuley founded the Sisters of Mercy. Catherine's main purpose in those days was to assist the poor, the ill, and the dying, and offer some relief to the victims of Ireland's famine. To help the poor, and preferably the poorest of the poor, is not an invention of Mother Teresa nor a new idea that has been propagated by the church of Latin America since Medellin or Puebla. This call has lived in the heart of the Church ever since the Lord died in total poverty on the cross. Time and time again this call is revitalized and lived out in new ways. St. Basil heard this call when he organized communities to work for the sick and the poor in the fourth century. St. Francis heard this call in the thirteenth century, St. Vincent de Paul heard it in the sixteenth century, and many others have heard it since.

It was good to realize that the Sisters of Mercy, who now form the largest English-speaking congregation of religious women in the world, find their origin in Catherine McAuley's desire to serve the poorest of the poor. Her fervent hope was to make God's mercy visible to the people by simple, direct, and efficient service to those in need.

No congregation today attracts as many people as the Missionaries of Charity of Mother Teresa, who is for the twentieth century what Catherine McAuley was for the nineteenth, St. Vincent de Paul for the sixteenth, St. Francis for the thirteenth, and St. Basil for the fourth century. Every time we see the crucified Lord again in the wretched of our cities, in the refugee camps, and on the desolated deserts and plains of our world, our faith becomes new again.

Sunday, December 13

Newspapers and radio broadcasts are all announcing the frightening news that the government of Poland has declared a state of martial law. The leaders of Solidarity, Poland's new labor movement, have been arrested; churches, cinemas, and theaters closed; people cannot leave their houses during most hours of the day; the military controls the streets of Warsaw; telephone, radio, and television communications have been broken off; and the whole country lives anxiously awaiting what will come next.

Will the Russians invade? What will be the response of China and the United States? Will the people of Poland rise up in protest? Will this be the beginning of a long suffering of the Polish people or even of many peoples? Will this be the beginning of the third World War?

I saw Peter, the young Polish priest, for a moment. He was nervous, tense, and especially angry at the Communists who without hesitation had accused Solidarity and the Church of causing all the problems. He realized that he was excluded, that he would not be able to call his family, to hear any reliable news, or to get any idea about the fate of his many Polish friends. How powerless and isolated he must feel.

I pray that we all will be able to know what God wants us to do in the midst of this increasing tension and anxiety. I pray for Peter and his people, I pray for John Paul II, to whom many look for leadership in this critical moment, and I pray that we will be faithful to Our Lord and to each other in this hour of darkness.

Monday, December 14

Today is the feast of St. John of the Cross, the sixteenth-century Spanish mystic who speaks to me with great power. Not only did St. John experience oppression, humiliation, and imprisonment in his attempts to reform the Carmelite Order, but in the midst of his agony he experienced God's love as a purifying flame and was able to express this love in the most profound mystical poetry.

St. John reveals the intimate connection between resistance and contemplation. He reminds us that true resistance against the powers of destruction can be a lifelong commitment only when it is fed by an ardent love for the God of justice and peace. The ultimate goal of true resistance is not simply to do away with poverty, injustice, and oppression, but to make visible the all-restoring love of God. The true mystic always searches for this Divine knowledge in the midst of darkness. St. John sings "the Song of the Soul delighted by the Knowledge of God" *(el cantar del alma que se huelga de conocer a Dios)*. He sings this song "though it is night" *(aunque es noche)*.

In the midst of our darkness—darkness in Poland, Ireland, Afghanistan, Iran, and in most Latin American countries; darkness in the broken, hungry, and fearful families; darkness in the hearts of millions who feel impotent and powerless in the face of the powers and principalities; and spiritual darkness in the countless souls who cannot see, feel, or understand that there is any love for them—in the midst of this darkness, St. John of the Cross sings of a light too bright for our eyes to see. In this divine Light we find the source of our whole being. In this Light we live, even when we cannot grasp it. This Light sets us free to resist all evil and to be faithful in the darkness, always waiting for the day in which God's presence will be revealed to us in all its glory.

Tuesday, December 15

Yesterday, a group of twelve Bolivian workers started a hunger strike in the cathedral. They are asking for a general amnesty for all the Bolivian workers who have been exiled from the country or jailed as political prisoners, for the recognition of their unions, and for the implementation of the human rights guaranteed by the national constitution.

The workers have refused to leave the cathedral to enter into dialogue with the prefect of Cochabamba. Afraid of being arrested, they seek the protection of the Church. A commission representing the prefect is now shuttling between the cathedral and *prefectura,* but so far nothing has been accomplished.

The hunger strikers are supported by large groups of workers. In La Paz and other cities, similar hunger strikes are being organized. The frustration, disappointment, and hostility of the Bolivian workers have been growing ever since the miners' strike. Large general strikes may follow and may prompt violence and oppression by the military regime. Christmas may be far from peaceful this year.

There are many parallels between the situations in Poland and Bolivia. The Bolivian workers have not been able to organize themselves in the way the Polish workers have, but with their determination it is unlikely they will give up their demands easily. In the coming days, the tension and anxiety most likely will increase. In a bankrupt country with a corrupt government, all this will probably lead to more repression, more poverty, and more misery for those who are already close to the bottom.

Wednesday, December 16

Tonight I gave the last of three advent meditations on compassion. During a meeting in November, Ralph Davila had asked for more student initiatives to strengthen the community life of the institute. On that occasion I offered to lead a series of reflections that might be of help to people in their preparation for Christmas.

When I look back at the three meetings, I know that I made a mistake. I should not have offered to give these meditations, but should have stuck to my decision to be a student and not to give any lectures, talks, courses, or presentations during my stay in Latin America. These meditations came forth more from my need to be useful than from any real need existing in the students or staff of the institute.

The three evenings never created any spiritual enthusiasm, and I experienced them in the way I had experienced many obligatory clerical days of recollection in the past, when people came more to please the bishop, the superior, or the speaker than to renew their own spirit. Some few people expressed an honest appreciation; but nothing really "happened." Events like these are little more than ways to maintain the status quo. They do not really help us take a step forward in our committed life together. I have seldom felt so little contact with people as with those who came to these meetings. The fact that Gerry and others expressed their concern that I not let the meetings last longer than the scheduled hour symbolized for me that there was little participation from the heart. As so often happens in clerical circles, obligation won out over desire.

My words remained words coming from far away and did not become life-giving words. I am learning that I am in another world, and that words that can renew minds and hearts at one time and place might have a dulling and even deadening effect at another time and place. I have learned that this is not a time for speaking but for listening; not a time for initiatives but for waiting; not a time to offer leadership but a time to let go of old and cherished ideas and to become poor in spirit. Since we can learn from our mistakes, I might as well use this experience as a way to recall that these are times to be silent.

Thursday, December 17

In preparation for my language classes I had to analyze a short story by the Spanish poet and novelist Carmen Corde. In this story a young mother discovers shortly after the birth of her baby boy that the child is blind. She calls her family together and says, "I do not want my child to know that he is blind!" She insists that from that point on everyone use a language in which words such as "light," "color," and "sight" are avoided. The child grows up believing that he is like everyone else until a strange girl jumps over the fence of the garden and uses all the forbidden words.

I think that this story symbolizes much of our behavior. We all seek to hide what is strange and painful and to act as if things are as usual. We say, "Let us act as if there were no problems, no abnormalities, no pains, no wounds, no failures, no illnesses." In my own life I have experienced the power of this urge to hide, an urge that often is more harmful than what it tries to conceal.

Every time I have had the courage or gave others the courage to face their blindness, their mental anguish, or their spiritual agony and let others become part of the struggle, new creative energies became available and the basis of community was laid. Fear, shame, and guilt often make us stay in our isolation and prevent us from realizing that our handicap, whatever it is, can always become the way to an intimate and healing fellowship in which we come to know one another as humans.

After all, everyone shares the handicap of mortality. Our individual physical, emotional, and spiritual failures are but symptoms of this disease. Only when we use these symptoms of mortality to form a fellowship of the weak can hope emerge. It is in the confession of our brokenness that the real strength of new and everlasting life can be affirmed and made visible.

Friday, December 18

This was my last day of language school. When I think about my eight weeks of classes, I have reason enough to be grateful. I do not think that there is any better way to learn Spanish than the way the institute has worked it out. Most impressive are the competence, the dedication, and the flexibility of the teachers. Every two weeks I worked with a different team of four teachers. Daily I had two individual classes with sophisticated language drills, one conversation class together with

Brian Clark, and one grammar class with a small group of six students. It was a nice balance between intense individual work and more relaxing work with other students. After I finished the three basic textbooks, I asked for more attention for my personal language problems and thus my last two weeks were even more tailored to my needs than the first six weeks.

I was impressed by the way the teachers prepared their classes. They prepared the material of the lessons well, but they also tried to help the individual students with their personal struggles with the language. Ernestina, for instance, gave me a series of special exercises to train me in the use of the different past tenses, and made up many complicated sentences to help me distinguish between the use of *por* and *para*, two words I kept mixing up.

During my short time here I had fourteen different teachers. With this helpful change of teachers every two weeks, I never had a chance to get bored. Different teachers had different styles of working, different ways of expressing themselves, different personal interests, and often also a different way of relating to me. Some were formal and stayed close to the book, others enjoyed little mental excursions. Some used the blackboard a lot and appealed to my desire to see things written down. Others tried hard to train my ear and help me hear Spanish sounds better. Some kept the conversation to familiar household matters; others didn't hesitate to become involved in controversial political, social, and religious subjects. But everyone had something significant to offer and did so with great generosity and dedication. One of the most impressive traits of all the staff members of the institute—teachers, librarians, and secretaries—was their insistence on correcting students on the spot. Since I seldom uttered a sentence without at least two mistakes, I offered them all many opportunities to do their work.

Did I learn the language? I can only say that I gave it a good start, and that another three months is probably necessary to approach fluency in it. On the other hand, I do not have the energy or the motivation to continue at this moment. Eight weeks of intensive training is about as much as I can take in one stretch. I am happy that I am not returning to an English-speaking world but can go to Peru and continue to practice Spanish every day.

If I decide to dedicate a few years of my life to full-time work in Latin America, I probably will have to return to the institute for a few more months of language training. I especially would like to be able to write in Spanish. That certainly would take some extra work. For the time being, however, it seems better to leave the school and let the people of Peru become my teachers.

Saturday, December 19

This morning I went to the cathedral to meet the hunger strikers. I expected that it would be hard to get close to them and to have a conversation, yet I found the church open and unguarded with plenty of people going in and out. In a small sectioned-off area of the large cathedral, the hunger strikers lay on mattresses and blankets, slept, read the newspaper, or talked with visitors and medical aides.

During the last few days their number had increased from twelve to forty-eight and about a thousand other workers of MANACO, the largest factory of Cochabamba, had joined them in a separate, supportive hunger strike.

Two men in their late twenties were eager to talk to me. "We are not giving up until the government takes our request seriously," they said. "It is not enough that the government recognizes the unions, we won't stop this hunger strike until the government offers a general amnesty. Thousands of Bolivians live as exiles outside their country since the coup of Garcia Meza on July 18, 1980. We want them to be free to return to their homes and families."

Just a few days earlier, the government had declared that there would be no amnesty this Christmas; but the workers and students in the cathedral made it clear that they would not eat anything until they had accomplished their goals. "Monday our families will join us in the strike if nothing has changed by then. It is going to be very serious."

Meanwhile, aides were walking around giving liquids to the strikers. Sister Mary-Jean, the Vincentian nun from the States who is the newly elected head of the school of nursing in Cochabamba, goes regularly to the cathedral to take the blood pressure of the strikers and to keep an eye on their physical condition. She told me yesterday that the liquid they gave the strikers contained sugar to reduce danger to their health. Nevertheless, the strike is now already five days old, and some of the men are visibly weakening.

"Are you a priest?" they asked. "Yes," I replied. It was clear that the workers had put all their hope in the support of the Church and in the religious sensitivities of the Bolivian people. They said: "The new church (they mean the church that made a preferential option for the poor) gives us much support. Many priests and sisters are on our side and Monsignor Walter Rosales (Vicar General of the Diocese and the highest church authority until the newly appointed bishop is installed) comes regularly to visit us." When I left them they thanked me for my visit and added jokingly: "Write about us in the Dutch papers."

How will Christmas be in Bolivia this year? The rumors are that all the banks will be on strike on Monday to show support for the strikers. Meanwhile, I am struck by the irony that President Reagan offers words of support and sympathy to the Polish labor union Solidarity but refuses any support for the workers in Latin America. The power that criticizes and condemns oppression of the working class when it comes from the Communist regimes ignores, denies, or even encourages the same oppression when it results from the military regimes in Latin America. The issue for Reagan is obviously not, "When are people oppressed?" but, "Who is the oppressor?" The oppressors of the exploitative regimes in Latin America are called "our friends," the oppressors in Poland and Russia are called "our enemies." It seems indeed that the Church today is one of the few institutions in the world willing to defend human rights regardless of who the oppressor is.

Sunday, December 20

The Church is speaking loudly today. Pope John Paul II sent a delegation to Poland to visit Church and government leaders in order to find a nonviolent solution to the increasing conflict. It seems, from the latest newscasts, that the Pope is seriously considering going to Poland himself.

Meanwhile, the bishops of Bolivia wrote a strong Christmas message asking the government to restore the confidence of the Bolivian people in their leaders and to offer a broad political amnesty. "We ask those responsible for the public cause, to restore the faith of the people, which they lost after so many deceptions. The Spirit of justice and true love for the country which transcends the interests of individuals and groups has to be able to return to the people a renewed hope in those who have the responsibility in concrete circumstances. We ask the supreme government for a broad political amnesty, that will open the way to reconciliation of all the Bolivians."

In the midst of all the conflicts, wars, and rumors of war, these strong voices offer hope and encouragement. Although we have to admit that peace and justice have not won the field during the last ten years, we can rejoice in the fact that the voice of the Lord of peace and justice is heard clearer than ever. I pray that many people who are poor and oppressed will find comfort and consolation when they hear this voice, and will find the strength to work together for a better world.

Monday, December 21

The hunger strikers gave up. Nothing has changed. During the weekend, it became clear that there was absolutely no chance that the government would give in, and that the only possible outcome would be bloodshed and the useless loss of lives. The political analysts, who are trusted by the strikers, persuaded them that the continuation of their hunger strike would only bring misery to themselves and their families.

I tried to understand this sudden change by talking to different people. I concluded from all the comments that the position of the government is so weak that a general amnesty would simply mean suicide for the present government. Bringing the many Bolivian exiles back into the country would change the balance of power so drastically that the present government would have no chance of surviving.

Meanwhile, the economic situation of the country is so bad that any promise to offer better financial conditions to the workers would be empty. Many industries lack the funds to offer the expected Christmas bonus and everyone expects the Bolivian peso to drop in value significantly during the first week of January. The official exchange rate is 25 pesos for a dollar, but at any exchange office I can easily get 35 pesos or more. Meanwhile, it remains impossible for the Bolivians to buy dollars. For those who have debts in the States—as the Quiroga family has—this means a growing financial crisis. Rodolfo bought many goods in the States to sell in his store. Now the Bolivians have no money to buy his articles, and his debts to the U.S. banks increase by the rapid devaluation of the peso. This is a quick way to bankruptcy.

I am sad to witness yet another example of the powerlessness of the poor. The military personnel have large salaries and are allowed to buy goods in special military stores for very low prices. Meanwhile, the poor get less and less for their money and most have to let Christmas pass without being able to give any presents to their children. While the president of the country gives patriotic speeches about love of country, unity of the people, and cooperation between all to save the country from disintegration, it is clear that he and his political friends are protecting their wealth gathered by cocaine traffic and other forms of contraband by giving money and guns to those who are willing to protect their privileged position. The Bolivian army exists not to defend the country against outside invaders, but to defend the wealthy few against the poor and the hungry.

Many of the intelligent people who could provide leadership and change the situation give up, leave the country, and become doctors, lawyers, and businessmen in the United States or in Europe. It is a tragedy that today, in Chicago alone, there are a large number of Bolivian M.D.s while the most basic medical care is lacking in large parts of their own country.

Where is the peace and joy of Christmas? In the United States, in Russia, in Poland, in Ireland, in El Salvador, Guatemala, Nicaragua, or Bolivia? Indeed, "The word was the true light that enlightens all men; and he was coming into the world. He was in the world that had its being through him and the world did not know him. He came in his own domain and his own people did not accept him" (John 1:9–11).

Tuesday, December 22

In the midst of all the bad news from Poland and Bolivia, the familiar words from the Song of Zechariah suddenly have an unusual power:

> The God of Israel has raised up for us
> a savior who will free us from our foes,
> from the hands of all who hate us.
> He will give light to those in darkness,
> those who dwell in the shadow of death
> and guide us into the way of peace.

How often have I spoken these words as if they were little more than the expression of an ancient and pious Jew! But here in Bolivia, with the alarming news from Poland covering the front pages of the newspapers, they sound as a call to rebellion, as an invitation to follow a new leader who will throw off the yoke of oppression.

I should not forget that when Zechariah raised his voice Judea and Samaria were occupied territories and that the Jews felt about the Romans as the Dutch felt about the Germans during World War II, and as most Poles feel about the Russians today. Zechariah's song doesn't leave politics behind. In fact, it was difficult for the Jews of Jesus' time to make a distinction between religion and politics. Jesus himself was executed as a political enemy, as someone who claimed to be King of the Jews.

In Latin America, the Good News of the Gospel is a threat to those who oppress and exploit the people. To take the words of the Gospel seriously would mean political suicide for most rulers. The words "God has raised up for us a savior who will free us from our foes" ring out less a note of piety than a call to resistance.

Wednesday, December 23

It has been raining the whole day. I had expected a hot Christmas with cloudless skies and a burning sun, but heavy clouds hang over the Cochabamba valley and people walk hastily in raincoats and with umbrellas, jumping over pools of water and trying to escape the splashes of water caused by the fast-driving buses.

I did my Christmas shopping today: two books about jet planes and space travel for Rodolfito, a Spanish metal cross for Rodolfo and Nancy, a brooch and bracelet for Marcelita, and a few things for the Christmas guests in the Quiroga home.

I also wanted to do something special for Christmas. In Rodolfo's store, I had seen little cars and dolls that would make good presents for the boys and girls of the state orphanage I visited last month. So I asked a friend for the telephone number of the orphanage and called the director to tell her about my plan to give all the kids a Christmas gift. The director was very excited about my plan, but when I asked her, "How many kids do you have?" she said, "Seventy-seven girls between twelve and eighteen." Suddenly, I realized that my friend had given me the number of the wrong orphanage. The cars and dolls from Rodolfo's store probably would not please the teenage girls of the orphanage I now was talking with. But I decided to be brave. I acted as if all were normal and promised the unknown director to appear on Christmas afternoon with gifts for seventy-seven teenage girls.

As soon as I told Rodolfo about my mistake and challenged him to be inventive, he and his staff went to work and came up with games, perfumes, mirrors, brushes, and all sorts of other things that—as they assured me—would certainly please girls between twelve and eighteen. On the twenty-fifth we all will go to the orphanage, and I wonder what the response will be.

Meanwhile, I am looking forward to my first Christmas in the summer.

Thursday, December 24

The most important part of this day for me was the celebration of Vespers and Mass of the Vigil of Christmas. At five o'clock in the afternoon, Sister Fran and I went to the small Carmelite convent and experienced the quiet joy of Christmas with the sisters. It was very quiet and peaceful, a simple and restful service. In the midst of the many activities in preparation for Christmas and surrounded by so many political and socioeconomic anxieties, this celebration was a true oasis. The joyful alertness of the twelve sisters offered Fran and me an opportunity to come in touch with the still and deep presence of God in our lives. I read the genealogy of Jesus Christ as St. Matthew gives it in the first chapter of his Gospel. The many names from Abraham to Jesus are certainly not names of saints. They are names of men and women who struggled hard with the powers of evil, sometimes more successfully than others, and who have experienced love, hatred, joy, pain, reward, and punishment, like ourselves. It is these men and women who form the story of which God himself wanted to become part. God, so it seems, inserted himself in our own tiresome and often exhausting journey and became a fellow traveler. When Jesus joined the sad and deeply disappointed disciples on their road to Emmaus and opened their eyes so that they could see what was happening, he revealed what it means that God is a God with us.

God came to us because he wanted to join us on the road, to listen to our story, and to help us realize that we are not walking in circles but moving towards the house of peace and joy. This is the great mystery of Christmas that continues to give us comfort and consolation: we are not alone on our journey. The God of love who gave us life sent us his only Son to be with us at all times and in all places, so that we never have to feel lost in our struggles but always can trust that he walks with us.

The challenge is to let God be who he wants to be. A part of us clings to our aloneness and does not allow God to touch us where we are most in pain. Often we hide from him precisely those places in ourselves where we feel guilty, ashamed, confused, and lost. Thus we do not give him a chance to be with us where we feel most alone.

Christmas is the renewed invitation not to be afraid and to let him—whose love is greater than our own hearts and minds can comprehend—be our companion.

Friday, December 25

Peter, the Polish priest, and I presided together over the midnight Mass in Temporal. Temporal is a section of Cochabamba that does not have its own church. The Marist brothers have a large school there and on Sundays and feastdays they convert their auditorium into a worship hall. Over the years, the brothers have developed quite a parish. Although they have no regular priest, they usually manage to convince one of the priest-students of the language institute to do the fixed parts of the Mass, while they take care of everything else: preparations, music, sermon, and all the details necessary for a good liturgy. The only thing they require of the priest is that he can read Spanish in an acceptable way.

We all gathered on the playground of the school. As I looked out from the steps of the auditorium over the more than three hundred people gathered there, I realized again how mysteriously God keeps calling us together from so many parts of the world. Although most people were Bolivians, and most of them from Temporal, there were brothers from Spain, visitors from the United States, Peter from Poland, and myself from Holland. And while we all are so aware of the conflicts and wars that result from the ethnic and geographic divisions between people, a celebration like this reveals again that God did not create these divisions but wants his people to come together in unity and peace.

This joyful celebration unfolded with mystery and a few surprises, the first of which announced itself as a mechanical bird hidden in the Christmas tree! A large silver ball produced loud bird calls at regular intervals and the layman who acted as deacon during the liturgy was so enchanted with this gadget that he turned it on at the most unusual moments. Just before the Marist brother started his sermon, the deacon walked up to the tree and made the "metal bird" sing its songs. The brother didn't seem to mind. He just raised his voice and competed happily with the bird, who interrupted every second sentence of his sermon with its calls. When the brother invited me to add a few words to his, I first sent the deacon up to the tree to shut the bird up. My Spanish is bad enough; I don't need an artificial bird to punctuate it.

The lights went out during communion, a second surprise. The electricity fails regularly in Bolivia, but this interruption created more confusion than usual. Luckily, many people had Christmas candles with them, and thus we were able to continue and finish the service without many problems. The singing of *Noche de Paz* ("Silent Night") by candlelight added to the Christmas mood.

The third surprise—at least for me—was that quite a few boys and girls made their first communion during the Mass. They were festively dressed and looked happy in their new suits and dresses and with their large candles and white rosaries in their hands. I found it difficult to combine the celebration of Christmas with the celebration of the first communion, and to pay sufficient attention to both celebrations during the service, but nobody else seemed to share my problem and thus I tried to go with it as best I could.

Finally there were the *"niños"* (baby Jesus dolls). While celebrating the Eucharist, Peter and I were surrounded by baby dolls, small and large, naked and elaborately dressed, lying on simple cushions or hidden in large glass cases. I never saw so many Jesus-babies together in my life. I soon found out that it belongs to the folk tradition that the baby Jesus has to hear Mass on Christmas day. Therefore families take their Christmas child out of his stable and bring him to church. After Mass, Peter and I were busy for quite awhile blessing all the dolls and giving ample attention to the different ways the baby Jesus looked.

But whatever the surprises were, all the people were happy, joyful, and pleased with this holy night, and everyone went home saying or shouting to each other: *"Feliz Navidad!"* or *"Felices Pascuas de Navidad!"* When I looked up to the sky, I saw a splendid firmament richly decorated with bright stars singing their praises to the newborn child. And we, little people with our candles, rosaries, and dolls, smiled at the heavens and heard the song again: "Glory to God in the highest heaven, and peace to men and women and children who enjoy his favor."

This afternoon we went to the state orphanage, taking with us our gifts from Rodolfo's store. Rodolfo had decided to make his own contribution, and had added to the gifts seventy-seven yellow T-shirts that a Japanese perfume factory had sent him as a form of advertisement. At 5 P.M. Rodolfo, Nancy, Rodolfito, and I drove to the outskirts of Cochabamba and, after a few wrong turns, located the orphanage.

We were greeted with enthusiasm, for the girls had been waiting with great expectation. Immediately Rodolfo began to give everybody in the house one of his yellow T-shirts. One went to a little eight-year-old boy who happened to be visiting his sister that afternoon. Raphaelito was so tiny that I lifted him up and stood him on the table to put on his T-shirt, which went all the way down to his bare feet. With his brown face and big dark eyes staring out from above his long yellow dress he looked like a little cupid. When the girls saw him standing there rather forlornly on top of the table they all began to laugh. At that moment big tears came rolling down Raphaelito's round cheeks and he burst out in sobs. It took us a while to console him, and he needed a few more presents to dry his tears.

What an irony! Here I was trying to make everybody happy and the first result was a tearful boy surrounded by seventy-seven laughing girls. But soon all was forgotten and everyone was excited with the gifts. We talked, sang songs, and played games. When we left we were escorted by Raphaelito and all the girls to the gate and lavishly thanked with handshakes, embraces, and kisses. As we drove away we saw a happy crowd with waving arms wishing us good-bye.

The laughter of Raphaelito and the girls also made us mindful of their unmentioned rejection and loneliness. This joyful interruption in their lives had brought us closer to the sadness of their permanent condition. As we returned to our comfortable home, they stayed in their lonely house; as we are surrounded by the care of family and friends, they wonder if anyone cares.

True ministry goes far beyond the giving of gifts. It requires giving of self. That is the way of him who did not cling to his privileges but emptied himself to share our struggles. When God's way becomes known to us, and practiced by us, hope emerges for Raphaelito and the girls in the orphanage.

Saturday, December 26

At three o'clock Sister Mary-Jean picked me up with her Toyota jeep to take me to the Quechua town of Morochata for the weekend. Her friends Sister Ann and Sister Delia, who run the parish in Morochata, had asked her urgently to look for a priest to hear confessions, to celebrate the Eucharist for the children who were receiving their first communion, and to assist in seven marriages. Sister Mary-Jean, whom I had come to admire as a forthright, courageous, and very lively person, convinced me that to accept her invitation would not only be good for the parish of Morochata, but even more so for me. "You will see fabulous landscapes, you will be excited about the llamas in the high mountains, you will love the people of Morochata, and most of all you will discover what the missionary life is really about." Well, this certainly was an invitation I could not refuse! By three thirty we had left the highway and were slowly curving our way up to the top of the mountains. After a while we could overlook the valley of Cochabamba. What a magnificent view! Dark clouds hung above the city, but the sun found enough space between them to throw floods of radiant light into the valley. As we came higher, we gradually entered into the clouds until we were driving in a heavy mist. As soon as we passed the large cross planted on the top, we could see the clouds breaking and had some glimpses of the little villages below on the other side of the mountain. Mary-Jean drove her jeep carefully through the seemingly endless hairpin turns marked by many small crosses, reminding us of the people who had lost their lives on this dangerous road.

It took us about an hour to make our descent into Morochata. "I am sorry that we didn't see many llamas," Mary-Jean said, "but I promise you will see a lot of them tomorrow on your way back." I hoped she was right.

The priests of the diocese of Dubuque, Iowa, who live and work at St. Raphael's parish in Cochabamba had often mentioned Morochata to me. It was the place where their friend Raymond Herman was murdered six years ago. In different places I had seen pictures of Ray Herman, a young-looking, handsome priest. Why was he murdered? Nobody could answer that question satisfactorily, but everyone agrees that his four years of pastoral work for the poor *campesinos* was the main cause.

About thirty years ago, Morochata was a small, flourishing town. Many wealthy landowners had their houses and managed the *campesinos* from there. The large church and the pleasant central square remind visitors of these old days. There was so much going on in this little town that the rich citizens decided to build a small hotel to accommodate their many visitors. But all of that changed when Victor Paz Estenssoro came to power in Bolivia and initiated a radical agrarian reform in 1952, making the *campesinos* owners of their land and terminating the ages-old system of *latifundios* (large landholdings), on which the farmers were little more than slaves.

Soon the wealthy landowners realized that Morochata could no longer offer them the comfort they desired. Gradually, they all moved away, leaving the town to the poor *campesinos*, who discovered that the land reform did not bring them the promised prosperity. The little pieces of land they now owned soon were divided between their many children. The *campesinos* lack of experience and education, combined with the failure of the government to provide adequate loans for machinery and fertilizer, prevented them from developing a decent economic base.

The hotel, which was under construction when the land reform started, was never finished, and its skeleton only reminded the people of Morochata that their town was once a center of attraction for those who had money and power. In 1971, Raymond Herman came to Morochata to become its pastor. Ray was a diocesan priest from Iowa who had worked for many years in Cochabamba. Hardworking, fully dedicated to his people, concerned for nothing but their physical and spiritual well-being, Ray was as apolitical as one can be, and stayed far from the intrigues that characterize the history of Bolivia. He was deeply loved by his people, by the poor and destitute, and also by those who euphemistically could be called middle class.

When Ray saw the half-finished hotel, he immediately thought: "This should be a hospital." For many years he worked hard to collect funds and find support for his plan, and finally, in October 1975, the building was finished and ready to be opened to receive its first patients.

On the morning of October 20, 1975, the day after the dedication of the hospital, Don Pascual Villarroel, Ray's sacristan, bookkeeper, and teacher of cathechetics, was waiting for Ray to say Mass. Noticing the absence of the jeep, he thought that Ray had probably gone on an errand and would soon be back; but when he found his alarm clock on the ground outside of the rectory, he started to feel very nervous. Finally, he went to Ray's bedroom, knocked on the door, and entered. At first he thought that the priest lay in deep sleep, since he could see only his hair outside the sheet. When he could not wake him up, he carefully pulled away the sheet, and saw an unspeakable horror. Ray had been strangled and two bullets were shot through his head; he had been brutally tortured.

Four hours later, Don Pascual reached Cochabamba to tell Leon, the pastor of St. Raphael, the tragic news. It took him a long time before he was able to say that something demonic had happened. Don Pascual hardly could say what he really had seen.

The autopsy performed on Ray's body made it clear that the murder could never have been done by one man. A group of people must have entered his bedroom around 2:00 A.M., torturing and killing him. They took the jeep and many things from his room and made it look like an "ordinary" robbery; but if anything is clear, it is that this was a well-planned assassination that had little to do with robbing a priest.

When I saw Ray's bedroom and heard the story, I asked again: "Why?" The answer to that question, summarized from different people's remarks, was: "We don't know. Some people say that the truck drivers did it because Ray was trying to find cheaper ways for the *campesinos* to bring their products to town. Others say that Ray's serious attempt to help raise the standard of living of the poor— the hospital was a symbol of that—had made him the enemy of those who are in control, and that the order to kill him came from very high up."

I asked what happened afterwards. "Nothing really," one of the people said. "Two men were arrested and put in jail, but soon they were allowed to escape. The Bolivian as well as the American governments have covered up the whole event and even today, six years later, nobody knows the true story."

I walked around the church and the little square. The young people sitting on benches greeted me in a friendly way. From the house in which the sisters live, I had a splendid view of Morochata and the mountains that surrounded it. Everything looked so peaceful and serene. But the demonic force of evil had reached this little town too. People knew it. Next Friday would have been Ray's birthday, and people from all directions have come to be sure that there will be a celebration in his memory. He was very much loved; but here those who are loved as he was are seldom destined to live very long. They are reminders of a world that has not yet been realized.

Sunday, December 27

This morning at eight o'clock I celebrated the Mass for Cecilio, Bernardo, Rolando, Linder, and Alejandro, who were receiving their first communion. Well-dressed and well-groomed, they sat in the first pew with rosaries and candles in their hands while parents, godparents, friends, and parishioners filled the church to be part of the occasion.

Most of the boys were twelve or thirteen years old. So the story of Jesus who went with his parents to Jerusalem and stayed there "among the doctors, listening to them and asking them questions," seemed appropriate for the occasion. I enjoyed explaining this story to them, asking them questions about it, and giving them some idea of the great mystery that this Jesus who once was a boy like them, now comes to them as their lasting guide and support in the sacrament of bread and wine. Everyone was radiant, joyful, and grateful; and when the boys came to the house of the sisters for the traditional cup of hot chocolate, they all looked like little princes, even though their real status was more like that of the poor shepherds of Bethlehem.

The weddings took place at ten o'clock. Don Pascual had placed the seven couples and their *padrinos* (the best men and maids of honor) in a large circle around the altar. Since practically no one spoke Spanish, Don Pascual led the service of the word and the whole wedding ceremony in Quechua. I just tried to follow the ceremony as well as I could and did whatever Don Pascual asked me to do.

After the traditional questions and the exchange of vows, some special rites took place. First there was the blessing and exchange of rings. This proved more complicated than I expected, since it took a while to find a finger on which the rings would fit. (Obviously, these rings had known other couples.) Then I took a handful of coins from a plate and gave them to the groom to make him aware of his responsibility to provide for his family. The groom let all these coins fall into the hands of his bride to show her that he would share all his wealth with her, and the bride then flung the coins back on the plate to make it clear that after all money was not the most important thing in their life together.

After this ritual, the *padrinos* put a thin chain around their heads, which Don Pascual then covered with a red velvet cloth. I handed them a burning candle.

Seven times these rituals were repeated. During all of this, the seven couples looked extremely serious; I could not get one little smile from any of them. They had waited in great anticipation for this moment, and for them this was certainly not a moment for smiles or laughter. One couple must have been in their forties. They never had been able to afford a wedding and had to wait many years before they had the money to offer to their friends the fiesta that forms an essential part of the event.

In the Indian culture, no couple will marry in the church without having lived together for some time and without being sure that the woman will be able to bear children. The church ceremony is more an affirmation by the community of their relationship than a beginning of a new life together. When the church becomes involved, the couple has already proven to each other, their friends, and their community that there is a real basis to their union.

What struck me most before, during, and after the event was the lack of any expression of affection whatsoever between the grooms and the brides. They hardly talked to each other; they did not touch each other except when the ritual demanded it. Not one kiss was ever exchanged. Pascual had to remind them repeatedly during the exchange of vows to look at each other, and even that seemed hard for them. When I asked Ann about this later, she said: "Even in their homes, husband and wife seldom show affection to each other, but both are expressive in their love for their children: they play with them, hug them, kiss them, and touch them constantly."

After the wedding ceremony, I celebrated the Eucharist in Spanish and gave to all who were just married and to their *padrinos* the Body and Blood of Christ. Everyone participated intensely in all that took place, even though probably none of them would be able to explain anything about the Eucharist. But their belief in God's presence during this sacred hour could be read from their dark faces.

At twelve o'clock, when I thought that it was all over, Ann said to me: "I have a little surprise for you: there are thirteen little babies to be baptized! Their parents and godparents are waiting for you in the church. I decided to surprise you with it, because if I had told you before, you might not have come!" There was a lot of action and noise around the baptismal font. Every time a baby cried too loudly for Ann's taste, she asked the godmother to give the baby back to the mother, who then immediately gave her breast to the little one. It always worked. Meanwhile, I went from baby to baby with oil and signed their chests with the sign of the cross. Then, one by one they came to the font and, as I poured the water over their heads, they usually protested with loud cries. After thirteen baptisms, we had quite a noisy crowd! But everyone smiled and laughed and showed their gratitude.

"There is one more thing I want you to do," said Ann, when the people had left the church. "There is a lady here who lost her only son of sixteen years last month. His name was Walter. She wants you to go with her to the cemetery, pray with her, and bless the grave." I found the woman sitting on a bench in the village square. As I touched her, she started to cry bitterly. It was a sad story. Last month, Walter went to Cochabamba with a truck loaded with produce and people. As usual, the younger boys were standing on the running board of the truck holding onto the door. At one point, Walter lost his balance and fell from the truck without the driver noticing. He fell between the wheels and was crushed by the back tires of the truck. They took him in the truck in the hope of reaching the hospital in Cochabamba in time, but he died on the way.

Ann and I drove with Walter's mother in the jeep to the small cemetery behind the hospital. There we found the little niche where Walter's body was laid. We prayed and I sprinkled the place with holy water and we cried. "He was my only son, and he was such a good boy," his mother said with tears in her eyes. Ann told me how helpful Walter had been in the parish and how everyone was shocked by his death.

I couldn't keep my eyes from the woman's face, a gentle and deep face that had known much suffering. She had given birth to eight children: seven girls and Walter. When I stood in front of the grave I had a feeling of powerlessness and a strong desire to call Walter back to life. "Why can't I give Walter back to his mother?" I asked myself. But then I realized that my ministry lay more in powerlessness than in power; I could give her only my tears.

At four o'clock, we were on our way back around the many curves, and at five we reached the top again. And there they were! A large herd of beautiful llamas. We stopped the jeep and walked close to where they stood. They stretched their large necks and looked at us with curious eyes. It was a moving encounter, high up in the mountains where there are hardly any human beings. The llamas stared at us, making it clear that we really didn't belong there.

When we descended into the Cochabamba valley, we noticed how the heavy rain had washed away parts of the road. But Mary-Jean kept her jeep on the path, and at six o'clock we rolled into the city again.

I was very tired, but happy. Mary-Jean had been right when she said that I would see fabulous landscapes, would be excited about the llamas in the high mountains, would love the people of Morochata, and most of all would discover what the missionary life is really about.

Monday, December 28

Although the house of the Quiroga family is richly decorated during this Christmas season, and although Rodolfo and Nancy offered a festive dinner to their family and friends, these days have not been peaceful for them.

On the morning of December 24, when Rodolfo and Rodolfito came to the store to start their day of work, hoping that this last day before Christmas would give them some good business, a man was waiting for them with a court order. At first, Rodolfo thought it was a customer who wanted to buy Christmas gifts; but he soon realized that the family member who had sent him to prison last year was trying to do the same again. The hatred of this man must be of a satanic quality; he had chosen Christmas Eve to do as much harm as possible to Rodolfo. The court order contained many accusations; but since most offices are closed on the day before Christmas, and lawyers and judges do not work during these feast days, there was a real chance that Rodolfo would have to go to prison until the authorities could hear his case.

The man who confronted Rodolfo at his store did not allow him to call Nancy or to warn anybody. He and another man took him immediately to the court-house, leaving little Rodolfito crying in the street with the keys of the store in his hands. When the personnel of the store arrived, the boy told them what had happened. They immediately called Nancy, who rushed to their lawyer; together they went quickly to the courthouse. Meanwhile, other influential friends were informed, and they all soon appeared at the same place to keep Rodolfo out of prison. By noon, things had been "clarified," and Rodolfo could return to his work.

"This is the third Christmas he has tried to destroy," said Nancy. Although Rodolfo was spared from having to spend the holidays in prison, the whole event robbed him of his inner tranquility and made it hard for him to celebrate freely the feast of Christ's birth. He had to spend much of his time contacting lawyers, witnesses, and friends to convince the court that the whole thing was another attempt of his enemy to destroy his family life, and his peace.

Today the tension finally diminished. Rodolfo and Nancy came home with smiles on their faces, telling me that the lawyers had been able to convince the court that this was a setup without any other basis than personal hatred.

"How can this man get court orders to arrest you?" I asked. "He is very wealthy," Rodolfo said, "and here in Bolivia you can buy anything, even judges and witnesses."

Wednesday, December 30

Tonight I visited the Albergue San Vicente with Gerry McCrane. It is a shelter for young boys of Cochabamba who live on the streets, shine shoes, wash cars, and steal to survive. For many years the Vincentian Sister Anne Marie Branson, who has spent most of her religious life in Bolivia, dreamt about a house where these street urchins could find a home. She felt strongly that this is the type of work Vincent de Paul, the founder of the Vincentians, would have been most interested in. She had seen many of these little boys in the streets in Cochabamba, had talked with them, and had become aware of their dehumanized existence.

Finally, in April of this year, some old buildings and some money became available, and Sister Anne Marie started her new work. She went to the boys and invited them to come to her Albergue San Vicente. Within a few weeks, she had thirty regulars. The boys come in the evening, get a warm meal, receive some personal attention, stay for the night, and go back on the streets after a decent breakfast. The stories of these boys are tragic. An eight-year-old boy was simply thrown out of the house when his mother remarried. He was able to get on a truck and come to Cochabamba. He had been roaming the streets for three years until Sister Anne picked him up and gave him a home. Another boy, ten years old, said: "My mother took me to the market, went to the bathroom, and never came back." Every boy has a painful story to tell.

Sister Anne Marie said: "There must be at least two hundred of these boys on the streets of Cochabamba, but I have room for only thirty. Often the boys come home at night with a street friend, and then I try to give him a mattress for the night. My dream is to build a larger dormitory, so I can help more of these poor kids."

The building where Sister Anne Marie works is simple and poor: one large room filled with beds, a small place to eat, and a kitchen. Sister Anne Marie does the cooking—mostly soup with bread—and tries to help the boys live together in some peace. It is a hard job. These boys are so preoccupied with surviving that they do not afford themselves the luxury of being kind, generous, or peaceful. "The whole world is their enemy," Anne Marie says. "What can you expect? Now they at least eat together without fighting, and I am trying to give them some tranquility and quiet during the night."

As soon as Gerry and I came in, two boys noticed our dirty shoes, pulled out their shoeshine boxes, and gave us a free shoeshine. I was moved when they adamantly refused to accept money for their work. Anne Marie was trying to teach them that some people are your friends and you want to help them without asking for money. "I am trying to get some of them to go to school again," Anne Marie said, "but it is hard for them. They are not used to any discipline, and many of them have so little ego that it is hard for them to apply themselves to any task that asks for endurance. Moreover, it is practically impossible for them to trust anyone. They have no experience of a trusting relationship. For as long as they can remember the world has been hostile to them. I am hoping to get some more professional help, a mental health team, that could assist these boys to develop some confidence in themselves and others."

One boy came in with a bleeding foot. Anne Marie gave him some instructions on how to wash his feet with hot water and disinfectants and how to put on a bandage.

As we walked through the dormitory, a little boy of seven years old stood on his bed neatly dressed in blue jeans and a colorful shirt. He had received these clothes as a Christmas gift and was trying them on before going to bed, because the next day he had to help serve at a dinner being given by some rich people. Eagerly he was looking forward to the occasion.

"Oh, it is just band-aid work," Anne Marie said. "We do not even touch the real problem, but at least we may help a few boys."

I had heard a lot about the street boys in Lima, and they had often been on my mind. I was happy to see at least one place and to meet one person who had responded to the inexhaustible needs of these children and had shown them that not everyone is an enemy.

4

January

IN PABLO AND SOPHIA'S HOUSE

■

Friday, January 1

TODAY WAS FILLED WITH PACKING, saying goodbye, paying quick visits to people to say thanks, returning books, umbrellas, raincoats, and the many other little things that I had borrowed.

At eleven-thirty, we celebrated a liturgy with a few old and a few new students. Gerry McCrane was there with Antonio, his close friend. Happily, Lucha and Albina and the two cooks of the institute also joined. So here we were: five Bolivian women, one Bolivian man, a few Americans, two Irishmen, a Filipino, and a Dutchman. For some, Spanish was their only language. For some, Spanish was a second language. For others, Spanish was just becoming their language. And for a few, Spanish was the great unknown. So we made it a bilingual event with readings both in English and in Spanish and with a dialogue homily and prayers in whatever language the person most easily could speak.

All in all, it was a good last day in Bolivia. I spent a quiet evening with Gerry in his room and felt grateful for his friendship and generous hospitality. As I go to bed I can truly say thank you to the friends in the institute, to the Quirogas, to the Carmelite Sisters, and most of all to the Lord of all people who brought me here.

Saturday, January 2
Lima, Peru

Peter, Gerry, and Fran came with me to the airport to be with me at the hour of departure. Peter will soon start his work in Paraguay, while still suffering from the news that comes from Poland. Gerry will continue to work hard at the institute to make it more and more a center for missionary formation, and Fran will continue to explore pastoral work with the blind and will become an active worker in the parish of Cala Cala. They are three committed people whom I now know as true friends.

Now I am back again in the house where I lived for a week in October. The first person I met was Raymond Brown, the biblical scholar, who is here to attend the Faith and Order Conference of the World Council of Churches. Next week he will come to the house to give a series of talks to the Maryknollers in Lima.

Sunday, January 3

This afternoon I had tea in downtown Miraflores (a section of Lima) with John and Kathy Goldstein. John is a Lutheran minister, Kathy is a nurse; and both are preparing themselves to work as Lutheran missionaries in Cuzco. Our conversation made me aware of how spoiled I am. I am living with a supportive missionary community, well-equipped to help newcomers in getting settled. But John and Kathy had to find their way into a new culture, a new country, and a new type of work all by themselves. They studied Spanish and Quechua in Cochabamba, and now are struggling to find their way to Cuzco. For the last two months, they have been trying to get through all the red tape to obtain permanent residency in Peru, to have their Land Rover fixed, to find good doctors for Kathy (who is expecting a baby in February), and to find an apartment in Cuzco. The months have been very tiring for both, but now it seems that they are ready to move from Lima to Cuzco; Kathy by plane and John with a friend in the Land Rover. Next Sunday, they hope to start their missionary work in Cuzco. "What are you going to do there?" I asked. "We don't know yet," John replied. "It is a totally new place for us. We have to see what others are doing there and see where we can fit in. Kathy can always find work as a nurse, but I, as a pastor, will have to wait and see what is the best way to start a Lutheran mission."

I suddenly realized how lonely they both must feel. Two young people, just out of school, in an unfamiliar country, sent to start a new mission. "It is so frustrating to have to wait so long to get anything done," John said. "Yes," Kathy agreed. "Especially since we are expecting our first baby in a few weeks. It would be so good to have a place that we could call home. Now we live in a small hostel and eat out every night in a different place."

When we said farewell, they said: "Be sure to come to Cuzco to see the baby!" After all I had heard about their struggle, I felt especially eager to celebrate their new joy with them. "You can expect me in Cuzco soon," I said. I feel it is a firm promise.

Monday, January 4

Today Claude Pomerleau and Don McNeill arrived. While I was at breakfast, Claude appeared. I knew he was coming, but somehow he surprised me, as he always does, with the easygoing, smiling way in which he walked into the house. Claude is a Holy Cross priest who teaches political science at Notre Dame University. We have been friends for many years, and whenever there is a chance to meet we grab it. Claude was asked to come to Chile for a month to explore the possibility of starting a Notre Dame extension program in Santiago. He is exceptionally well-informed about the social, economic, and political situation in Latin America. He has been central in the development of my interests here.

Around midnight Don, who heads the Center for Experiential Learning at Notre Dame, arrived. He has just spent two weeks in Chile visiting the Holy Cross Associates, laymen and laywomen who give two years of their lives to work in the missions. Don is a strategist and planner. Without his concrete recommendations and suggestions, I would never have come here. It was he who first suggested that I come to Peru, and he put me in touch with the Mary-knoll community.

Claude and Don are close friends, and the idea of visiting me in Peru had captured their imagination. The three of us certainly have a lot to discuss. Yet, more important to me is the awareness of having two close friends who have come to help me start my new life.

Tuesday, January 5

At noon, Don, Claude, and I met Bob Plasker in downtown Lima. Bob, a Holy Cross priest and a close friend of Don's, works with a pastoral team in Canto Grande, a huge *barrio* on the outskirts of Lima.

What struck me most was the contrast between the two forms of ministry to which we were exposed. Bob took us to lunch in Le Sillon Missionaire, one of the most elegant restaurants I have ever seen. It is run by Les Travailleuses Mis-sionaires de l'Immaculée (the Missionary Workers of the Immaculate Mother of God), a community of French women who have similar restaurants in Italy, Upper Volta, the Philippines, Argentina, and New Caledonia.

When we entered, we were greeted kindly by a tall, striking, black sister from Upper Volta who led us to our table and explained a little bit about their ministry. "We want to offer people a milieu where they can taste not only good food, but also something of true Christian hospitality." When I looked around, I soon realized that many bishops, priests, and religious people in Lima come there to enjoy this peaceful hospitality. The surroundings were pleasant. An old mansion with a lovely courtyard had been tastefully converted into a dining space, and while we ate a delicious lunch, baroque music filled the large area and gave us the impression of being transported from the busy streetlife of Lima to a peaceful garden. It was a form of ministry we had not anticipated but Claude, Don, Bob, and I felt grateful for this moment of luxury on our way to Canto Grande.

In Canto Grande, Bob showed us another type of ministry. It took us twenty minutes in a taxi to reach the center of the "desert-city." The word "desert-city" seems the best word to describe this huge new development at the outskirts of Lima; "About a hundred thousand people have come to live here during the last ten years," Bob explained. "Most of them came from the country, lived for some time with friends or relatives in town, and then settled here. You can see the different phases. First they build something like a hut of matted bamboo, and then, over the years, they start earning a little money. They buy bricks, build walls, and slowly transform their huts into small houses. It may take them many years to reach the luxury of a house. Sometimes a fire destroys it all. Fires are especially devastating when there is no water."

I kept thinking about a desert. Yellow sand was all you could see. Trucks, cars, and gusts of wind created a lot of hot dust. The dwellings lacked the two main commodities of modern living—electricity and running water. In front of most houses stone water containers were built to provide the families with washing and drinking water. Large water trucks came daily to Canto Grande to sell water. In many houses there were oil lamps or candles; but most people went to bed with the sun.

Bob and his fellow priests live in a small wooden house in the heart of Canto Grande. It is very simple, but with the help of some plants and a simple rug it looked quite cozy to me.

Bob's understanding of ministry was simply "living with the people, as the people." Instead of a church, he has used different places spread over a large area to celebrate Mass and to conduct other pastoral activities. There was a small pastoral center where the Sunday services are held and where the different work groups have their meeting spaces. The parish committee on human rights is very active and regularly publishes small folders on the rights and urgent needs of the people. On October 20, 1980, this committee, together with many other local groups, organized a march to the center of town to call the attention of the government to the serious problems of Canto Grande: health, energy, transportation, and education. On October 23, the Senate responded and declared the valley of Canto Grande a *zona de emergencia* (emergency zone).

Bob and his fellow workers see it as their main task to work with the people, to make them aware that the Gospel of Jesus Christ supports the poor in their struggle for basic human rights, and to join them in this struggle.

In the short time we were in Canto Grande, we met many good and generous people. They showed hope and a strong will to work for their future. When we walked home through the dark, guided by no other light than the moon, we were grateful to have been able to witness this ministry of solidarity.

Wednesday, January 6

Today Don, Claude, and I did some sightseeing in downtown Lima. One of the churches we saw was the Jesuit Church of San Pedro. A talkative Jesuit brother told us about the busy life of the parish. Daily Masses are celebrated at 7:00 A.M., 8:00 A.M., 9:00 A.M., 10:00 A.M., and every hour afterward until the final mass at 7:30 P.M. "Many people come here," the brother said. "And there are always long rows of people who want to go to confession." While we were standing there talking with the brother, people kept entering and leaving the church. It was clear that at this time of year the main attraction was not the confessional but the Nativity scene, built in one of the side chapels. It was quite a sight. Not only was there the manger with the child and his parents, but around it were landscapes with hills, rivers, waterfalls, and bridges. There were little village scenes with women washing their clothes in the river. There were large herds of sheep and llamas. There were houses in which the lights were going on and off. There were medieval castles and humble straw dwelling places. It was not surprising that many parents took their children there to see the Christmas event laid out in miniature in front of them. But this was not all. In front of a house in which the Angel Gabriel announced to Mary that she was going to become the Mother of God was an American police car, with a policewoman keeping an eye on Mary's house. "We put the car there five years ago," the Jesuit brother explained. "It gives a little touch of modern life. Jesus was born for all people and for all times, and in our time there are many police cars to protect us. We even have permanent police protection for the church." When we looked outside on the little square in front of the church, we saw indeed a white police car and two policemen watching the entrance of the church. It seemed, however, that the police car and the policewoman had not been enough to give the Christmas scene a contemporary flavor. This year a jet plane had been added to fly in circles above the Christmas landscape. By some ingenious mechanism the plane was able to come low and then pull up again, sometimes coming quite close to the shepherds and the Magi, but never close enough to create an accident. "Some people feel that that plane is a little much," the brother said, "but others like it a lot. It is part of our time."

To me it all seemed a little strange, as it was so far from the world of Canto Grande, but it was a genuine expression of the mixture of the Indian, colonial, and technological worlds that underlies the predicament of Peruvian life. Piety and poverty, modern aspirations, realism and sentimentalism, humor and mystery—they all are part of the world of the Peruvian people who continue to celebrate the birth of their Savior.

Thursday, January 7

This morning Claude left for Chile and tonight Don went back to the States. It was good to be together, to deepen our friendship, and to reflect on the new directions our lives are taking. It is strange that after sixteen years of friendship we find ourselves together in Peru, a place none of us thought much about when we met for the first time at Notre Dame. It is a testimony to a radical change of thinking and feeling that has taken place in us all. It is a source of comfort to me to know that in the midst of our inner and outer changes, our friendship has grown. That offers hope for the future.

Friday, January 8

Four hundred and twelve years ago, on January 9, 1570, Servan de Cerezuela arrived in Lima to open a Tribunal of the Inquisition. My stay in Lima offers me my first direct confrontation with the reality of the Inquisition. The Inquisition in Lima was active over a period of two hundred and fifty years. Artifacts from its history are displayed in the Museum of the Inquisition, which I visited with Don and Claude. It shows large paintings of the autos-da-fé, displays lists with crimes and punishments, shows the dungeons in which the prisoners were held, and has a large torture chamber in which, with the help of lifesize mannequins, the visitor can witness the ecclesiastical cruelties of these days.

The museum, which is the only one in Lima where you can enter without paying, was set up to make a forceful anticlerical statement. The museum guard kept saying to us: "This was the work of the priests." All the torturers were dressed in Dominican habits. In one place we saw a plastic Dominican dismembering a prisoner stretched out on a table. At another place we met a Dominican forcing water into a prisoner's body, thus slowly choking him to death. In another scene a priest was flagellating a man, whose head was locked into a wooden block. Besides these cruelties we were exposed to a vivid presentation of hangings, feet burnings, and starvation, all executed by the "servants of God."

As the guard kept repeating that *"los curas"* (the priests) had done all this, Claude finally responded, "And today the military has taken over their job." He did not realize that just then a man in uniform had entered the museum and heard the remark. The man acted as if he had not heard but said politely: "Good afternoon."

Since my visit to this house of torture, I have been reading about the Inquisition. The evaluation of this shameful episode in the history of the Church varies widely. Henry Charles Lea writes, "The colony was kept [by the Inquisition] in a constant state of disquiet, the orderly course of government was well-nigh impossible, intellectual, commercial, and industrial development were impeded, universal distrust of one's neighbor was commanded by ordinary prudence, and the population lived with the sense of evil ever impending over the head of everyone. That there was any real danger to the faith in Peru is absurd. Possibly the Tribunal may have been of some service in repressing the prevalence of bigamy among laymen and of solicitation among the clergy, but the fact that these two offenses remained to the last so prominent in its calendar would show that it accomplished little. In the repression of the practices which were regarded as implying a pact with the demon, the Inquisition may be said to have virtually accomplished nothing. It would be difficult to find, in the annals of human misgovernment, a parallel case in which so little was accomplished at so great a cost as by the Inquisition under Spanish institutions" (Frederick B. Pike, ed., *On the Conflict between Church and State in Latin America* [New York: Knopf, 1964], p. 52).

This evaluation stands in contrast with the evaluation of Salvador de Madariaga, who writes: "the Holy Office of the Inquisition kept its prestige intact with many of the learned, and its popularity alive with the masses, particularly in the capitals such as Lima and in Mexico, where its processions and autos-da-fé were eagerly awaited festivals. The auto-da-fé was above all a pageant of human drama and of colour—human drama because rich and poor alike, when guilty, could be seen under the eyes of poor and rich pass in the procession humbled and crushed under the weight of error and sin; colour because the ceremonies, processions, and settings were carefully staged sights, with the purple silk of the bishops, the black, white, and blue gowns of the monks, the scarlet velvets and blue damasks of viceroys and high officials. . . . The Inquisition was a part of that strange and wonderful life of the Indies, one of the rare periods of History which have succeeded in creating that elusive virtue—a style" (Pike, pp. 63–64).

Lea and de Madariaga are voices on the extremes of a wide spectrum of opinions about the Inquisition. Personally, I see the Museum of the Inquisition as a powerful reminder of how quickly we human beings are ready to torture each other and to do so often in the preposterous assumption that we are acting in the name of God.

Compared with the torture going on in many Latin American countries today, and compared with the thousands of people who have been mutilated and killed during the last few years, the victims of the Inquisition seem few. But the realization that the Church could encourage and participate in creating ways to cause an excruciating and slow death for those whom it considered dangerous, sinners, heretics, or apostates, can only be a reason for repentance and humble confession and a constant reminder that what we now condemn with strong voices was an intimate part of the Church's daily life only two centuries ago.

Saturday, January 9

Letters are gifts, often greater than the writers realize. Ever since I left the United States, I have experienced a deep hunger for lifegiving letters—letters from very close friends who have little to ask and little to inform me of, but who simply speak about bonds of friendship, love, care, and prayer. I am overwhelmed by a letter that says: "We think of you, pray for you, and we want you to know that we love you." I have never experienced the power of such letters as strongly as during these last months. They directly affect my spiritual, emotional, and even physical life. They influence my prayers, my inner feelings, and even my breathing and heartbeat.

"The Word was made flesh, he lived among us" (John 1:14). These words by St. John received new life for me during my last months here. A word of love sent to me by a friend can indeed become flesh and bridge long distances of time and space. Such a word can heal pains, bind wounds, and often give new life. Such a word can even restore a faltering faith and make me aware that in the community of love, the incarnation of the divine love can be realized wherever we are.

Monday, January 11

Yesterday Jim and Mary Ann Roemer arrived. Jim is dean of students at Notre Dame. He and Mary Ann are dear friends of Don McNeill, and they stopped by for a day on their way from Santiago to South Bend. Today Jim, Mary Ann, and

I visited three of Lima's downtown churches. The manifold representation of the suffering Christ became an overwhelming impression. I saw many statues of Jesus sitting in a chair covered with a velvet purple cloak, his head crowned with thorns, streaks of blood covering his face. I saw a painting of Jesus lying naked on the floor, his whole body covered with stripes from the flagellating whip. I saw one altar with a lifesize Jesus figure with the eyes of a man driven mad by torture. It was so frightening that I could not look at it longer than a few seconds. But most haunting of all was a huge altar surrounded by six niches in which Jesus was portrayed in different states of anguish: bound to a pillar, lying on the ground, sitting on a rock, and so on, always naked and covered with blood. All these niches were surrounded by rich golden ornaments—so much so that the whole wall became like a solid gold icon portraying the most abject forms of human suffering.

Men and women from all ages and backgrounds gazed at these morbid Christ figures, some kneeling, some standing, some with crossed fingers, some with their arms stretched out in a pleading gesture. This is the Christ the Spanish conquistadors introduced to the Indians. This is the Christ to whom the people of Peru have prayed during the last five centuries. This is the Christ to whom they bring their own pains and suffering.

Nowhere did I see a sign of the resurrection, nowhere was I reminded of the truth that Christ overcame sin and death and rose victorious from the grave. All was Good Friday. Easter was absent.

I asked a priest about all of this. "Yes," he said. "On Good Friday the churches are packed and thousands of people go to confession, but Easter here seems like a quiet, ordinary Sunday. This is a penitential people."

When we came to the third church, Mary Ann couldn't look at any more. The contrast between the abundance of gold and the tortured bodies of Jesus figures repulsed her. She left the church and waited outside until Jim and I had walked from altar to altar.

The nearly exclusive emphasis on the tortured body of Christ strikes me as a perversion of the Good News into a morbid story that intimidates, frightens, and even subdues people but does not liberate them. I wonder how much of this has also been part of my own religious history, although more subtly. Maybe deep in my psyche I too know more about the deformed Jesus than about the risen Christ.

Tuesday, January 12

At four o'clock in the morning, Jim and Mary Ann Roemer left the house to catch an early flight to Miami. Pete Byrne and I set our alarm clocks early so we could say goodbye. We both felt grateful for their visit and joyful to know them as friends.

This was Ray Brown's day. He gave two splendid lectures on the variety of Christian communities in the post-apostolic period. Ray carefully interpreted the post-Pauline literature (the pastoral letters, the letters to the Ephesians and Colossians, and the writings of Luke) in the morning, and First Peter, Matthew's Gospel, and John's writings in the afternoon. In a convincing and clear way, he presented us with the different styles of the common life at the end of the first century and showed us the various implications for our present-day ministry.

I had to come all the way to Lima, Peru, to hear Ray Brown, who was practically my neighbor in the United States. But it certainly was worth it. Ray made me aware of how much I had allowed the pastoral letters to determine my view of the Church, a church in which structure and good organization dominate. The church life as presented by the other biblical literature—more mystical, more spiritual, more egalitarian—had really never entered into my understanding of the Church during my formative years.

I hope and pray that those who prepare themselves for the priesthood will have incorporated more deeply and personally the different church styles that Ray presented today, and will give hope for an even more multiform life in the church.

Wednesday, January 13

Next week Pete Byrne is leaving for Hong Kong, where the regional superiors of Maryknoll will meet to report on the events in the different regions and to discuss issues of general importance for the society.

In preparation for his trip, Pete called the Maryknollers of Lima together. From this valuable meeting, I received an overview of the variety of missionary activities currently taking place in Peru.

Of most interest to me was the discussion about missioners participating in projects that were cosponsored by the Agency for International Development (AID). AID is a United States government agency that offers financial help to development projects in different countries. Obviously, such aid is given only when the project is in line with the general objectives of the State Department. It was clear from the discussion that Maryknoll did not in any way want its missionary goals to be connected with, or influenced by, the goals of United States foreign policy. Thus a strong statement was sent to the meeting in Hong Kong, declaring that the Maryknoll Missionary Society should not participate in any projects that received money from AID.

This important statement shows a growing hesitation on the part of U.S. church people to be connected with United States government policies. There was a time when being a good Catholic and being loyal to the U.S. government were closely connected. But today, being a Christian and being a loyal patriot are no longer necessarily the same, and the Catholic Church is less and less eager to identify itself with the American "cause." This is clear not only in the Maryknoll statement, but also in the recent statements of U.S. bishops concerning both United States foreign policy in Central America and the nuclear arms race.

It took a long time to move away from the "Constantinian connection," but the Reagan policies have certainly helped to speed up the process of disconnecting.

Thursday, January 14

Tonight I finally moved to Pamplona Alta. I have now been in Peru for twelve days, and I have needed all that time to get oriented, meet different Maryknollers, get a feel for the region, and organize my own affairs. It is good to move away from the comfortable American climate of the center-house into the Peruvian world.

Pete Ruggere drove me in his blue Volkswagen to my new living quarters with the Oscco-Moreno family. They are his neighbors, and with their help he has built a pleasant room on top of the roof of their house. The word "roof" is a euphemism since this house, like many of the houses in the area, is only half-finished. Construction continues at a variable rate depending on money, need, and time. My little room, therefore, might better be seen as the first room built on the second floor. Since nothing else is finished on the second floor, I have in fact a large terrace looking out over the many houses of the neighborhood. My room consists of four brick walls—painted pink ("the only color I had") by our neighbor Octavio—and a roof made of sheets of metal. There is a door and a window, but the wind and the dust have free access to my home since the builders left a lot of open spaces where walls, window, door, and roof meet. With virtually no rain here and with little cold weather, my small place seems quite comfortable and pleasant.

I often have thought about having a *poustinia* or small building for prayer on the marketplace, and this new place seems to be just that. It is like a monk's cell between a large sea of houses and people.

I was warmly welcomed by the downstairs family of Sophia and Pablo and their three children, Pablito, Maria, and Johnny. They all showed great kindness to me, and the kids were soon hanging on my arms and legs.

Pete Ruggere, Tom Burns, and Larry Rich live in the next house. There I can go at any time to wash, use the bathroom, eat, listen to music, or watch television. Their house is a section of the house in which Octavio and his wife and eleven children live. The space looks very small to me, and I wonder where and how they all live and sleep. But last night at ten o'clock nobody seemed to be sleeping. Kids of all ages kept walking in, out, and around, usually accompanied by a few dogs. Everyone is open, smiling, friendly, and obviously quite poor.

Friday, January 15

Today I came to know my new family a little better. I played with Johnny, Maria, and Pablito, took some photographs of them, let them show me the different neighborhood stores, and took them to Mass at night. I also talked a little with Pablo and his wife, Sophia. Pablo works as a butcher in the large market of Ciudad de Dios, and Sophia takes care of the family. The house consists of three dark rooms with walls of gray cement. One room functions as the kitchen, the other as the children's bedroom, and the third serves as living room, dining room, television room, and bedroom for Pablo and Sophia.

From talking with Pablo, I learned that the two most treasured items in the house are the television and the refrigerator. When I came home from Mass with the three children, Pablo was standing on the street corner talking with a neighbor. When he saw me, he said: "Father, we are talking about the robberies on our street. At night, robbers drive their cars up, climb on the roof, and enter the house from above. They are after our televisions and refrigerators. The few things we have, they try to take away from us! It is becoming an unsafe place here."

A noticeable fear could be heard in Pablo's voice. A little later Sophia joined in the conversation, saying: "Can you believe it? They steal from the poor, those *rateros.*" For a moment, I thought that *rateros* meant "rats," but a rat is *una rata.* Usually *ratero* means pickpocket, but here it is used for thief.

The Oscco-Moreno family is poor, but not miserable. The children are well cared for, seem to be healthy, and are playful. Pablo has a job and seems to make enough to give his family the basics. The television and the refrigerator show that they make a little more than their neighbors. Their daily life is very simple. They seem to keep pretty much to themselves. Johnny is never far from his thirteen-year-old brother, Pablito, and always gives him a hand when they walk together. Maria, who is ten years old, spends more time with her mother. It is a simple, but happy family; but not without the fears and anxieties of most poor people. I do not think they are eager churchgoers, but the walls show many pictures of Jesus, Joseph, and Mary. I am glad to live with these people. They teach me about life in ways no books can.

Saturday, January 16

My home in Pamplona Alta is about a fifteen-minute walk from the church of Ciudad de Dios. When people say, "I am going to the city," they do not mean the center of Lima, but the place where the first invasion of poor people took place in 1954, and where Cardinal Cushing built the large church that is staffed by Maryknoll.

Tonight I walked to the church; and when I got there, I saw large groups of people in the parish office as well as in the church. The office was filled with people who came to register for baptism, first communion, or marriage; and the church was filled with parents, godparents, and children waiting for a baptismal ceremony. I attended the baptisms. At first, I thought that only babies were being baptized, but soon I saw teenagers walking up with their parents and godparents to the baptismal font. When people started to lift up these boys and girls like babies, "Padre Carlos"—the Maryknoller Charles Murray—told them that they could stand on their own feet and only needed to incline their heads to be baptized. Before doing so, however, Charles asked them some questions about their faith to make them aware that they were no longer babies, but could answer for themselves.

After Charles had baptized about twenty babies and children, Pete Ruggere walked up to him and said: "There is a wedding here at seven o'clock, and it is already ten past!" Ten minutes later, Charles had finished the baptisms and the church was again filled with the family and friends of the couple to be married. An hour later, another couple was married and the church filled anew with people. Meanwhile, the staff in the office was busy filling out forms, answering questions, advising about preparation for first communion and marriage, and trying to help with whatever problem came up.

To me it all seemed hectic, even chaotic. But for Charles, Pete, and Tom, the priests of Ciudad de Dios, it was just another Saturday night.

Talking about this seemingly busy parish, Pete said, "There are one hundred and twenty thousand people living in this parish. We reach only about 5 percent of them." There is room for at least ten churches within the boundaries of the present parish. Many invasions of people over the last thirty years have made this one of the most populated areas of Lima, and the long lines of people waiting at the parish office testify to the tragic lack of pastoral personnel and facilities in the "City of God."

Sunday, January 17

This morning at nine o'clock I celebrated the Eucharist in the Church of Ciudad de Dios and preached. Preaching for very poor people is an activity that forces you to be honest with yourself. I kept asking myself: "What do I really have to say to these people?" I had the feeling that they had more to say to me than I to them. I thought: "Who am I to think that I can say anything of value in this situation. I have never been poor, I have never had to struggle with survival as these people have, and I do not even know their language!" And yet I knew that I was here to preach and that none of my hesitations was a valid reason not to preach. That, I am sure, is part of the mystery of being sent. I prayed that somehow God would touch the hearts of the people through my own broken words.

The Gospel told the story about Andrew and another disciple of John who followed Jesus. Jesus said: "What are you looking for?" They said: "Rabbi, where do you live?" When Jesus said: "Come and see," they stayed with him. Later, Andrew shared what they had seen and heard with his brother Simon, and so Simon came to Jesus. This story offers three important verbs to reflect upon: to look for, to stay, and to share. When we search for God, stay with him, and share what we have seen with others, we become aware of the unique way that Jesus calls us. A vocation is not a privilege of priests and sisters. Every human being is called by Jesus in a unique way. But we have to be looking for God, we have to be willing to spend time with him, and we must allow others to become part of our spiritual discoveries. The three Spanish words—*buscar, quedar,* and *compartir*—helped me to articulate what I wanted to say.

I wanted to help the people realize that they are important in God's eyes, and that they are called as much as any other human being. I hope that—in between all my broken Spanish—people sensed at least that I took them seriously, and that God certainly does. But when I am honest, I have to confess that the youth choir with its liberation songs received a lot more attention than I did with my sermon. The powerful songs led by a fervent university student, Javier, seemed in this instance to express the spirit of the people better than the words of a foreigner.

Monday, January 18

Every day I see and hear a little more about the different forms of pastoral care in this immense parish. Today I saw the "parish kiosk" and "the library."

On Monday mornings from 9:00 to 12:00, Tom Burns goes to his little kiosk, which he built in one of the small markets in the parish. This market consists of about two hundred stalls where vegetables, fruit, and cloth are sold, and here people from the neighborhood come for their daily shopping. It is not a flourishing place. Since the vendors can only sell small quantities, their prices are high compared to those of the large market in Ciudad de Dios. Among all these little stalls, Tom has his *kiosko parroquial* (parish kiosk). With a smile, he tells me that his motto is: *"Aqui no se venden verduras, sino verdades"* ("Here we sell not vegetables but truths"). As we arrived at the *kiosko*, people greeted us with big smiles. Tom's first task is to unlock the place and open the wooden shutters. It looks just like a small newspaper stand, the only difference being that instead of buying newspapers, you can enter it and talk with a priest.

The loudspeaker of the market announces that "Padre Tomas" has arrived and welcomes visitors. It was a slow morning. One person came to talk about the first communion of his child. Another asked for help to get his daughter into high school, and someone else had marriage plans to talk about.

While Tom received his parishioners, I walked around the area with Sister Mary Kay, whom we met in the market. She offered to show me her library, a little old medical dispensary that was no longer used as such. "We had the building and wanted to put it to good use," Mary Kay explained. "We wondered if we could make it available to the schoolchildren, who have no books with which to study. We didn't realize that we had struck a pastoral gold mine. We often had wondered how to reach the youth, and we had not been very successful. But when we opened this little library, we suddenly found ourselves surrounded by hundreds of boys and girls eager to learn." It was a small operation, but very effective. Every day after school, the children come, take out the book that the teacher has recommended, and study it in the reading room. No book can be taken home; all the studying takes place in the library itself. The children themselves tell the staff what books they need most, and thus slowly a library has been formed geared to the needs of the children. History, geography, mathematics, and religion were well represented. There also were quire a few classic stories in comic strip form, which proved to be quite popular. The whole collection was kept in a small room and could fit on a dozen shelves, but more than a thousand young people are being helped by this mini-library.

I asked Sister Mary Kay, "How do students normally study?" She answered, "By taking notes in class and studying them. The children and the schools are too poor to have books. All education is note-taking." I asked again: "Was there any way for these kids to read books before this library existed?" "Yes," Mary Kay answered, "But they had to go to downtown Lima and stand in line for hours to use a book for awhile, and very few had the time, the opportunity, and the motivation to do so."

While we were talking, a group of teenagers was having a mathematics class in the reading room. Mary Kay told me, "Many students have problems with mathematics. So, during the summer, we hire a mathematics teacher to help the students catch up. It is a very popular class."

What most impressed me was the great eagerness to learn. Education was clearly seen as *the* way to get out of poverty and to move ahead in life. I could see on the faces of the students how seriously they took their classes. Keeping order was obviously no problem for the teacher.

"We never were fully aware of this need," Mary Kay said. "We have worked here for many years and only accidentally hit on this ministry. When we started this library, we wondered if anyone would use it. Now we have more than one thousand regular users, and we meet more young people than ever before. We are very excited about it."

As we walked back to the marketplace, we heard the loudspeaker announce a course for adults in Peruvian history: seven lectures and a trip to the anthropological Museum in Lima. Price: 100 *soles* (20 cents). "That is one of the courses we have organized. It is quite popular," Mary Kay said.

We found Tom alone in his kiosk reading a book about the Kingdom of God. It suddenly hit me that Tom and Mary Kay had given me a better understanding of Jesus' words, "The Kingdom of God is among you."

Tuesday, January 19

Tomorrow a two-day conference on El Salvador starts in Lima, organized by the Social Democrats. Although they are almost unknown in the United States, the Social Democrats are a powerful political force throughout Europe and the third world. There are more than seventy social democratic parties, and about twenty-five of these are exercising power—among them, the parties of Helmut Schmidt in Germany and François Mitterrand in France. The Social Democrats have nothing to do with the Communists, who look at them as nothing more than another form of bourgeois political liberalism.

All the world's social democratic parties have joined together in an organization called the Socialist International. Under its president, Willy Brandt, it has made a great effort in recent years to give support to democracy and liberation movements throughout the third world. It supported, for instance, the Sandinista struggle against the dictatorship of Anastasio Somoza. In Europe and in many circles of the third world, the Social Democrats are well known and greatly respected. It is for these reasons that the Lima meeting is so important.

Some members of the United States delegation to the conference visited the parish this afternoon. Robert Drinan, S.J., former United States congressman; Joe Eldridge, director of the Washington Office in Latin America (WOLA); and Larry Burns, the key person of the Council of Hemispheric Affairs (COHA). WOLA and COHA are two highly regarded human rights organizations that work out of Washington, D.C. Regrettably, the visitors did not have enough time to come to my neighborhood, so I missed meeting them. Tom Burns, who will attend the conference as a representative of Maryknoll, showed them a little of Ciudad de Dios and answered some of their questions.

Wednesday, January 20

Can we truly live with the poor? Although I live with them and share their life to some extent, I am far from poor. During the noon hour, I walk to the rectory in Ciudad de Dios and eat a good meal prepared by a good cook, and one day a week I go to the Maryknoll center house in Miraflores to take a shower, sleep in, and have a day of relaxation.

So my living with the poor hardly makes me poor. Should it be different? Some say yes, some say no. Some feel that to be a priest for the poor, you should be no different from them, others say that such is not realistic or even authentic.

I have been here only one week, and thus am unable to have an opinion, but I know one thing: right now I would be physically, mentally, and spiritually unable to survive without the opportunity to break away from it all once in awhile. All the functions of life, which previously hardly required attention, are complicated and time-consuming operations here: washing, cooking, writing, cleaning, and so on. The winds cover everything with thick layers of dust; water has to be hauled up in buckets from below and boiled to be drinkable; there is seldom a moment of privacy, with kids walking in and out all the time, and the thousands of loud sounds make silence a faraway dream. I love living here, but I am also glad that I can escape it for two hours a day and for one day a week. Living here not only makes me aware that I have never been poor, but also that my whole way of being, thinking, feeling, and acting is molded by a culture radically different from the one I live in now. I am surrounded by so many safety systems that I would not be allowed to become truly poor. If I were to become seriously ill, I would be sent back to the United States and given the best possible treatment. As soon as my life or health were really threatened, I would have many people around me willing to protect me.

At this moment, I feel that a certain realism is necessary. I am not poor as my neighbors are. I will never be and will not ever be allowed to be by those who sent me here. I have to accept my own history and live out my vocation, without denying that history. On the other hand, I realize that the way of Christ is a self-emptying way. What that precisely means in my own concrete life will probably remain a lifelong question.

I am writing all this from my comfortable room in the center house in Miraflores, where I have a day off. I enjoyed my shower, I am glad to receive mail and have a dust-free desk on which to answer it, and I look forward to reading a book, seeing a movie, and talking to friends about religion, politics, and "home." But I am also happy that tomorrow I can return to Pablito, Johnny, and Maria and play with them in Pamplona Alta.

Thursday, January 21

The conference of the Social Democrats on El Salvador ended today. Tom Burns, who attended all the meetings as a Maryknoll representative, and Larry Rich, who attended as a journalist for *Noticias Aliadas* (Latin American Press), both felt optimistic about the strong statement issued against United States military intervention and against elections without negotiations. Moreover, a feeling emerged that this conference had created a powerful human rights platform in Latin America.

Friday, January 22

This afternoon Sister Pam and I visited several families with retarded children. Trained in special education, Pam has worked for many years with the physically and mentally handicapped.

Pam came to Pamplona Alta to continue the work that Sister Mariana had started. After many years of patient work, Sister Mariana had built a small school for children who need special education and had identified the families with handicapped children. While doing this difficult and often ungratifying ministry, she herself was fighting cancer in her own body. Finally, she realized that she was losing the battle and had to return to the United States. In July 1981 she died.

One of the consolations during her last months of life was that someone would continue her work. When Sister Pam arrived, she found a well-organized card system with all the names and addresses of the families who needed special attention.

As we walked through the sandy streets, Pam said: "I am only visiting those children who are too handicapped to be able to go to the school." We visited a twelve-year-old girl who is unable to speak, hardly able to walk, and totally dependent for all basic life functions on her mother and two brothers. We visited a little six-year-old boy, one of eleven children, who suffers from cerebral palsy and cannot speak. We visited a three-year-old boy who has regular convulsions and seems to be getting worse as he grows older. We visited an extremely retarded thirteen-year-old girl who, as a result of the dysfunction of her glands, had grown so fat that a huge chair had to be built for her. And so we went from house to house.

All these people lived in extreme poverty. Many of the dank, humid hovels looked worse than stables, they were filled with naked children and terrible smells, and lacked any sanitary facilities. In one house, a four-year-old retarded girl who refused to wear clothes kept ripping off any dress they tried to put on her. She was living naked on a cement floor surrounded by chickens and dogs, making strange, inarticulate noises.

"One of the problems I have," Pam said, "Is to get the cooperation of the family in the treatment of these retarded children. It is so hard to convince the parents to do regular exercises with their children and thus to help them in the development of their muscles." I soon saw how right she was. When we visited an eighteen-month-old child with Down syndrome, we realized that the baby always lay on her back and was not developing the muscles necessary to lift her head, to reach out her arms, or to strengthen her legs. Pam said: "I keep telling her mother and older sisters to teach her to walk and to help her lift up her head, but they simply don't do it. Every time I come here, I find the little girl again on her back in bed. As you can see, she is less developed than her five-month-old brother. It is so hard to convince people that something can really be done for retarded children. Parents tend to give up soon and neglect their retarded children. They do not really believe that any help is possible."

My walks with Sister Pam gave me a glimpse of the larger dimensions of poverty. Poverty is so much more than lack of money, lack of food, or lack of decent living quarters. Poverty creates marginal people, people who are separated from that whole network of ideas, services, facilities, and opportunities that support human beings in times of crisis. When the poor get sick, have handicapped children, or are the victims of an accident, no help seems available. The poor are left to their own minimal resources.

It suddenly hit me how crucial it is for the poor to organize themselves into supportive communities. But for people who struggle day after day just to survive, little energy remains to build these necessary networks.

Saturday, January 23

Pam and I continued our visits today. In one house we met a little two-year-old girl whose face and left hand were terribly deformed as a result of a fire. While the mother was away from home, her bamboo-matted house caught on fire and the burning roof fell on the baby, who was lying alone on the bed. The doctors were able to save the child's life, but they did not perform surgery to restore her face and hand. The mother, an energetic and intelligent woman, went many times to the hospital to ask for further treatment but was sent back again and again with the message that there was no bed available.

Pam said: "When I saw this girl, I realized that a further delay of surgery would make it more and more difficult to restore her face and hand. So I went to a group of wealthy women in Lima who want to help poor sick children and pleaded with them to accept this child. They finally promised to take her on and now I hope that we can find a private clinic where surgery can be done. Without ample financial support, nothing is going to happen."

This seemed to be a typical story. Good medical care is out of the reach of the poor, and many poor people do not even try to find it. Often they do not have the time, the opportunity, or the transportation to go to a good hospital; and frequently they cannot pay for the medicines the doctors prescribe.

Parents simply do not have the time and energy to give the necessary attention to their handicapped child. In one of the houses we found a totally paralyzed three-year-old boy lying on his parents' bed. His little brothers and sisters were playing around the house. Both parents were absent. The father works from 7:00 A.M. to 11:00 P.M. on odd jobs to earn enough to keep his family alive, and the mother goes far distances every day to bring her husband his lunch and to do the necessary errands for the family. When Pam told the mother that she had to do daily exercises with her little boy to help him develop his leg, arm, and neck muscles, she simply said: "I cannot do it. I do not have the time for that work."

In another house, Pam had come across a fourteen-year-old boy, Alfredo, who had had meningitis when he was twelve and had been in the hospital for one year. He was partially paralyzed but had a good mind. Since he had come home, however, he stayed in bed watching television all day. He had become totally passive. Pam said: "It took me endless visits to get the boy to talk, to read, and to do some schoolwork." When Pam and I entered the house, he was sitting in a chair with a book. It was more than Pam had expected. With some difficulty, Alfredo talked with me. Together we read a story about David and Absalom and tried to discuss some of the questions at the end of the story. Alfredo had no difficulties in grasping the content of the story; but I realized that, without constant personal support, he would probably not be motivated enough to do regular homework. With both parents absent most of the time, it is unlikely that he will come far in developing his muscles as well as his mind.

Wherever we went, we came across similar situations: poor, overburdened people unable to give the members of their family the basic help they need and unable to afford the help that is available to the happy few.

Sunday, January 24

Today I became fifty years old. I am glad that I can celebrate this birthday in the parish of Ciudad de Dios and with my family in Pamplona Alta. I hope that by concluding here half a century of living, I am perhaps moving toward a new way of living and working in the future.

There were small celebrations at different moments during the day. Father Charles announced my birthday to the people in church at the nine o'clock Mass, which I celebrated. As a result, I received several hundred kisses and embraces from the people after Mass. At noontime Father John Eudes, the abbot of the

Genesee Abbey, and Kay, Eileen, and Virginia, friends from New Haven, surprised me with their congratulations by phone After dinner there was the traditional birthday cake with candles, and at 6:00 P.M. I brought a cake to my family to have a little *fiesta* with them. Pablito, Johnny, and Maria sang "Happy Birthday," I blew out the candle (which I had put into the cake myself), and Sophia made some coffee. Together we watched the cartoons on television, and Johnny beat me in a game of checkers.

Later Charles, Pete, Tom, Larry, and I went out for a pizza; and there Charles asked me the difficult question: "How does it feel to be fifty?"

"How does it feel?" If feels quiet and peaceful. I am here with good, simple, and affectionate people; I sense that God wants me to be here; and this fills me with a simple joy. The words of Paul to the Corinthians, which we read during Mass today, expressed my feelings very well: "Our time is growing short. . . . Those who mourn should live as though they had nothing to mourn for; those who are enjoying life should live as though there were nothing to laugh about . . . " (1 Cor. 7:29–30).

I felt a little of this "spiritual indifference." Within a few years (five, ten, twenty, or thirty) I will no longer be on this earth. The thought of this does not frighten me but fills me with a quiet peace. I am a small part of life, a human being in the midst of thousands of other human beings. It is good to be young, to grow old, and to die. It is good to live with others, and to die with others. God became flesh to share with us in this simple living and dying and thus made it good. I can feel today that it is good to be and especially to be one of many. What counts are not the special and unique accomplishments in life that make me different from others, but the basic experiences of sadness and joy, pain and healing, which make me part of humanity. The time is indeed growing short for me, but that knowledge sets me free to prevent mourning from depressing me and joy from exciting me. Mourning and joy can now both deepen my quiet desire for the day when I realize that the many kisses and embraces I received today were simple incarnations of the eternal embrace of the Lord himself.

Monday, January 25

This afternoon Betty Evans presented a lecture on the history of Peru, the first in a mini-course offered to the women of Pamplona Alta and organized by the women's commission of the Center of the People's Culture.

Betty Evans—a Peruvian teacher married to an Englishman—gave a lively presentation with slides about the formation of the Inca culture in Peru. The thirty or so women, who had come from different sections of Pamplona Alta to the public soup kitchen in the little market where Tom has his kiosk, showed great interest in Betty's talk and a strong desire to learn about their own past. Some came because their children had questions they couldn't answer, others because they simply felt a need to know more about their own history. Everyone came to meet other women and to become aware of common interests, needs, and roots. Betty designed the course to help the women understand better why they live the way they live, and what factors have played a role in the development of their present socioeconomic situation.

After the lecture, Mary Kay told me that when the children were asked to draw pictures of their families, many depicted the father drunk or fighting, and the mother doing all the heavy work. Mary Kay said: "Betty is going to talk with these children to get a better idea of the way they experience their parents." I began to see how a course for women about their own history could be an important tool in the slow process of human liberation.

Wednesday, January 27

Anyone who has lived awhile in one of the poor sections of Lima tends to warn visiting friends against robbers and pickpockets. "Do not wear your watch visibly on the bus, someone will rip it off;" "Be sure to have a second pair of glasses, someone might pull your glasses from your head to sell the frame;" "Do not let your purse hang loosely from your shoulders, someone might cut the straps and run away with all your money and your papers;" and so on. Such warnings can be heard every day, often coupled with dramatic stories to show that the warnings are necessary.

Today, however, I heard a story about the consequences not of carelessness but of hypervigilance. A nun who had lived in Lima for quite some time had a friend visiting her. One afternoon, when this friend wanted to go shopping in the market, her experienced host said: "Now, be careful on the buses and in the market place. Before you know it, they will grab your money, your purse, and your watch. Be sure to take your watch off and put it in your purse and hold your purse tight under your arm."

Thus warned, the sister went on her way. The bus was crowded as always, and she had to push her way into it, always conscious of the potential robbers around her. While the bus was moving, and the sister was holding on to the handle to keep her balance, she suddenly noticed her watch on the bare arm of a young man leaning against her.

Overcome by the awareness that after all the warnings she had not been able to avoid being robbed, and furious at the shameless thief, she screamed: "You stole my watch, give it back immediately." While saying this, she pulled out her pen and pushed it right into the man's cheek. The reaction was quick. The man, frightened by the aggressive nun, and realizing (without understanding her English) that she meant business, quickly took off the watch and gave it to her.

Meanwhile, the bus had come to a stop and this gave the sister the opportunity to get off immediately. She had become so nervous that her only desire was to get home. When she returned to her friend's house with her watch still tightly grasped in her hand, her friend said: "But how, in heaven's name, did this man ever get into your purse?" "I don't know," was the puzzled answer.

Then the sister opened her purse and found her watch tucked safely between her notebooks and papers. In total consternation, she cried out: "My God, now I have two watches—and one of them I stole!" Her hypervigilance had turned her into a robber.

Sometimes we may be more frightened of people than we need to be. Maybe on her next trip to the market, the sister should wear a watch on each arm so that at least one will be stolen.

Thursday, January 28

If anything has affected me deeply since I have been living in Pamplona Alta, it has been the children. I have realized that since my eighteenth year I have not been around children. The seminary, the university, and all the teaching positions that followed were the worlds of young adults, worlds in which children and old people hardly entered. Yet here I am surrounded by boys and girls running up to me, giving me kisses, climbing up to my shoulders, throwing balls at me, and constantly asking for some sign of interest in their lives.

The children always challenge me to live in the present. They want me to be with them here and now, and they find it hard to understand that I might have other things to do or to think about. After all my experiences with psychotherapy, I suddenly have discovered the great healing power of children. Every time Pablito, Johnny, and Maria run up to welcome me, pick up my suitcase, and bring me to my "roof-room," I marvel at their ability to be fully present to me. Their uninhibited expression of affection and their willingness to receive it pull me directly into the moment and invite me to celebrate life where it is found. Whereas in the past coming home meant time to study, to write letters, and to prepare for classes, it now first of all means time to play.

In the beginning, I had to get used to finding a little boy under my bed, a little girl in my closet, and a teenager under my table, but now I am disappointed when I find my friends asleep at night. I did not know what to expect when I came to Pamplona Alta. I wondered how the poverty, the lack of good food and good housing would affect me; I was afraid of becoming depressed by the misery I would see. But God showed me something else first: affectionate, open, and playful children who are telling me about love and life in ways no book was ever able to do. I now realize that only when I can enter with the children into their joy will I be able to enter also with them into their poverty and pain. God obviously wants me to walk into the world of suffering with a little child on each hand.

Friday, January 29

Charles, Tom, Pete, Sister Marge, and I went to the beach today. Charles explained: "When there are five Fridays in a month, we cancel our team meeting on the fifth Friday and go to the beach to swim and to have a good meal." We drove to Punta Hermosa, about a half-hour north of Lima. Huge waves came rolling up to the beach in rapid succession. Compared with the waves of the Atlantic Ocean, these waves were immense. It was great fun to try to "catch a wave" at the right time and to be carried in on its crest. I failed most of the time, and often found myself spinning under a wall of water, wondering where I would emerge. I found that not only the children but the waves of the Pacific have healing power! They wash away my preoccupations and make me smile in gratitude to him who led his people through the Red Sea and the Jordan and calmed the storms on the lake.

Saturday, January 30

Dust is probably my greatest physical problem here. Wherever I turn, I encounter dust. Walking on the sandy street, I am always surrounded by small clouds of dust, and when a car passes the dust becomes like a heavy fog that vanishes only slowly. Everything in my room is covered with a layer of fine dust. When I want to write a letter, I first blow the dust away; when I want to drink tea, I have first to wash the dust off the cup; and when I want to go to sleep, I have first to shake the dust from the covers and the sheets. It settles in my hair, ears, and nose. It crawls into my socks, shirts, and pants; and it creeps in between the pages of the books I am reading. Since it is quite humid here, the dust sticks easily to whatever it lands on. This gives me a nearly permanent desire for a shower. Only the realization that the pleasure of feeling clean would probably not last longer than five minutes has helped me to develop a certain indifference to this dustbowl.

For the many people who like to keep their houses, their bodies, and their small children clean and fresh-looking, dust remains a resolute enemy. The only hope is that the water pipeline that has recently been built to Pamplona Alta will enable trees, plants, and grass to grow fast enough so that within a decade its people will win the war against the dust.

Sunday, January 31

The Gospel of this Sunday touches a sensitive nerve in me. It speaks about the authority with which Jesus speaks, heals, and exorcises demons. People who saw Jesus said: "What is this? A new teaching, taught with authority!" When Jesus addressed the people, his words had healing power and even were able to make evil spirits obey.

All of this stands in contrast to my own experience in preaching here. I wonder if anyone is really listening, and I often experience my words as totally powerless. This morning, while I was trying to say a few things with conviction, I found myself face to face with a man who was sound asleep. He was sitting in the corner of the first pew and kept reminding me, in his passive state, that my words had absolutely no authority for him.

The most important question for me is not, "How do I touch people?" but, "How do I live the word I am speaking?" In Jesus, no division existed between his words and his actions, between what he said and what he did. Jesus' words were his action, his words were events. They not only spoke about changes, cures, new life, but they actually created them. In this sense, Jesus is truly the Word made flesh; in that Word all is created and by that Word all is recreated.

Saintliness means living without division between word and action. If I would truly live in my own life the word I am speaking, my spoken words would become actions, and miracles would happen whenever I opened my mouth. The Gospel of today thus confronts me not so much with a question about pastoral tactics or strategy, but with an invitation to deep personal conversion.

5

February

AN INNER AND OUTER STRUGGLE

•

Monday, February 1

THE NIGHTS IN Pamplona Alta are filled with loud sounds. Until late at night, music from different parties pours through the many holes in my little room. Around 2:00 A.M., buses come to the neighborhood to pick up the merchants to take them to the warehouses where they buy the products which they will sell later in the day in the market. Since the people are afraid to wait outside of their houses with money in their pockets, the bus drivers blow their horns loudly to tell the people of their arrival. From 2:00 to 3:00 A.M., these loud sounds of the dilapidated buses fill the air. Shortly after 4:00 A.M., the roosters start their calls; and by 6:00 A.M. the bread-carrying boy blows his whistles to sell his fresh-baked loaves. Strangely enough, it is quite peaceful between 6:00 and 8:00 A.M. But then the huge loudspeaker of a neighboring school blasts the national anthem over the roofs and makes everyone part of the first instructions to the children.

Parties, buses, roosters, breadboys, and loudspeakers keep the sounds floating through the night and the early morning. During my first weeks here, I thought I would never get used to it; but now these sounds have become a familiar background noise that no longer interrupts my sleep, my prayers, or my reading, but simply reminds me in my roof-room that I am in the middle of a world of people who have to struggle not only hard, but also loudly in order to survive.

Tuesday, February 2

Today we celebrate the presentation of our Lord in the temple. I have been thinking about this mysterious event. Mary and Joseph took Jesus to Jerusalem "to present him to the Lord" and to offer the Lord the sacrifice of the poor, "a pair of turtledoves or two young pigeons." There in the temple they met two old people, Simeon and Anna, who sensed the sacredness of the moment and spoke words about the child that astounded his parents.

Every time I try to meditate on a sacred event such as this, I find myself tempted to think about it in an intellectual way. But today I realized more strongly than ever before that I simply have to be there. I have to travel with Mary and Joseph to Jerusalem, walk with them on the busy temple square, join the thousands of simple people in offering their simple gifts, feel somewhat lost and awed by it all, and listen to two unknown old people who have something to say, something that sounds very strange and even frightening. Why do I want more? Why do I want to add a comment to it all? It is as if I want to keep some distance. But the story is so simple, so crystal clear, so unpretentious. I do not have to do anything with it. I do not have to explain or examine these events. I simply have to step into them and allow them to surround me, to leave me silent. I do not have to master or capture them. I have only to be carried by them to places where I am as small, quiet, and inconspicuous as the child of Mary and Joseph.

Something of that happened to me as I went through the day. I kept seeing Simeon and Anna; and instead of disregarding them as two pious old church mice who disturbed me with their aggressive predictions, I sat down for a while and allowed them to speak and me to listen. I heard Simeon and Anna many times over during the day, and I suddenly realized that they have been trying to speak to me for a long time.

Wednesday, February 3

Writing letters has become extremely important for me during this long absence from home. I have discovered in myself a growing freedom to express to my friends my feelings simply and directly. A deep change is taking place in me as I write down what is most joyful and most painful for me. I find myself hardly interested in telling about the daily events of my outer life, but strongly compelled to share openly, even nakedly, what is happening within me. I no longer feel that I have anything to lose: all I have I can give. Writing letters is becoming a way of self-emptying, of being nothing more and nothing less than someone who wants to give and receive love. It seems that the poor people of Pamplona Alta have taught me this. They keep telling me without words: "All you have is yourself, so do not hide it from those you love."

Thursday, February 4

When I first came to Lima, Bill McCarthy invited me to visit his house in Andahuaylas. I met Bill for the first time a few years ago at Yale, when he spent a sabbatical year there. Bill McCarthy is a Maryknoller who spent most of his professional life teaching church history at the Maryknoll seminary in New York state. Although he entered the Maryknoll society to become a missioner, he found himself for many years teaching future missioners at home. But after his sabbatical at Yale, Bill asked to be sent to the missions. He went to Cochabamba for language training and after that joined Joe, a young Maryknoller, to start a new mission in Andahuaylas, a seven-year-old *barrio* in eastern Lima.

Today I saw Bill's new house and got some impressions of the neighborhood and the pastoral work Bill and Joe are developing. Ten years ago, Andahuaylas was still a large hacienda at the outskirts of Lima. Now it is a *pueblo joven* (young town) with hundreds of small houses under construction. It looks very much like Pamplona Alta but as yet has neither running water nor electricity. Most of the people try to earn their living as *ambulantes,* walking vendors in the market place.

Bill and Joe, with the help of Lucho, the catechist, are trying to develop small Christian "base" communities. They go around visiting people in their homes and encouraging them to meet regularly with people from their block, discussing common problems in the light of the Gospel, studying the Scriptures, and praying.

"How do you motivate people to form such a community?" I asked. Bill answered: "Well, we first explain to people that the Church started in the homes of people and not in church buildings. We read from the Acts of the Apostles and suggest that just as the apostles built the Church in the first century in the Middle East, so we can build the Church now, in the twentieth century."

It was an effort that required much patience and perseverance. "It is very slow work," Bill said. "The people who live here work long hours and when they come home from the market, they often are so tired that they do not have the energy to have meetings and to study and pray. On their few free days, they like to rest and play soccer. It is important for us to understand their condition." In addition to the different basic communities, which were slowly developing, Bill, Joe, and Lucho also started two liturgical centers for the Sunday Eucharist. One was in the chapel of the former owner of the hacienda, and the other was in an open lot that was set aside for the future church. Attendance was low: thirty people at one place, ten at the other. "We are just beginning," Bill said, "and we are still groping for the right way to be pastors here."

This short visit created in me a desire to learn how to build a church from the ground up, to let the people themselves give shape and form to their own Christian life. This approach is far from the old triumphalism of the gold-decorated churches in downtown Lima, far from the church of great visibility and power. A very humble and inconspicuous church builds upon the rock of faith, hope, and love.

Friday, February 5

Unexpectedly, I am experiencing a deep depression. Perhaps the days of friendly greetings and introductions have kept me on an artificial level of contentment that prevented me from acknowledging my deep-seated feeling of uselessness. The depression seems to hit me from all sides at once. I have very little strength to deal with it. The most pervasive feeling is that of being an outsider, someone who doesn't have a home, who is tolerated by his surroundings but not accepted, liked but not loved. I experience myself as a stuttering, superfluous presence and the people around me as indifferent, distant, cold, uninterested, and at times hostile. The men, women, and children I see on the streets seem to be so far from me that I despair when I think of them as people to whom I am sent. I crave personal attention and affection. The life in a parish suddenly strikes me as cool, mechanical, and routine. I cannot find a person with whom I can go beyond asking informative questions. I desire friendships, a moment of personal attention, a little interest in my individual experiences. The world around me appears to me as a complex pattern of words, actions, and responses in which I am caught, an entrapping net of baptisms, weddings, masses, and meetings. Meanwhile, I keep hearing: "This is the way we do things here. You should just try to become part of it. If you have problems, just stay with it and you will find out that our ways are the best."

The fact that my feelings are so general and touch practically everything I see, hear, or do, shows that I am dealing with a genuine depression and not with critical observations. I have little control over it. It feels like a form of possession. I try to pray for deliverance, but prayer does not bring any relief. It even appears dark and frightening. What else can I do but wait?

Saturday, February 6

The emotions of loneliness, isolation, and separation are as strong today as they were yesterday. It seems as if the depression has not lost any of its intensity. In fact, it has become worse. My mind keeps asking: "Why does nobody show me any personal attention?" My sensation that my feelings, experiences, history, and character are irrelevant to the people I meet, and that I am primarily used as a body that can take over routine functions, keeps ripping me apart from the inside. What I am craving is not so much recognition, praise, or admiration, as simple friendship. There may be some around me, but I cannot perceive or receive it. Within me lies a deadness that leaves me cold, tired, and rigid.

I attended a small workshop given by Pete Ruggere and Tom Burns about the basic meaning of being a Christian, but little of what was said reached my heart. I realized that the only thing I really wanted was a handshake, an embrace, a kiss, or a smile; I received none. Finally, I fell asleep in the late afternoon to escape it all.

Sunday, February 7

In times of depression, one of the few things to hold onto is a schedule. When there is little inner vitality, the outer order of the day allows me to continue to function somewhat coherently. It is like a scaffolding put around a building that needs restoration.

I got up at 6:30 A.M. and assisted Charles in the 7:00 o'clock Mass. At 9:00 A.M. I celebrated Mass myself and gave a sermon. From 10:30 to 12:30, I wrote a few letters. After lunch, at 2:00 P.M., Tom took me to a little fund-raising fiesta in Los Angeles, one of the sections of Pamplona Alta. The small Christian community there wants to build a chapel and decided to have a mini-fiesta on one of the street corners. They had games to play and food to buy. I picked up Pablito, Johnny, Maria, and her little girlfriend so they could try out the food and the games. They had a good time.

At 7:00 P.M. I was back at the parish and attended a short meeting in which two couples who had just finished a marriage encounter were welcomed home by other couples. Around 9:00 Charles, Tom, Pete, Larry, Patricia, a visiting Mercy Sister, and I went out to have a pizza. At 11:00 I was back home. I prayed my evening prayers and went to bed. The events of this "uneventful" day kept me mentally alive. I feel I am simply waiting for the day and the hour that the cloud of depression will pass by and I can see the sun again.

Monday, February 8

Today a two-week summer course in theological reflection began in downtown Lima. It is the twelfth time that this course, inspired and directed by Gustavo Gutiérrez, has been held. It is one of the most significant yearly events in the church in Lima. This year, three thousand "pastoral agents" are participating. People come not only from all the districts of Peru, but also from Chile, Brazil, Colombia, Ecuador, Paraguay, Uruguay, Argentina, Panama, and Nicaragua. It is a young, vital, and enthusiastic student body.

The summer course has three levels. The first level is an introductory theology course. The second and third levels have different emphases each year. This year, the second-level course deals with Christology and the third-level course with Spirituality.

I decided to take the course on Spirituality. From 3:00 to 5:00 P.M. there are discussion groups, and from 5:30 to 8:00 P.M. lectures. Gustavo Gutiérrez gave the first two lectures tonight. He discussed Christian spirituality under three headings: (1) living according to the Spirit; (2) the encounter with Christ; and (3) a global way of life.

Gustavo is a lively teacher. Holding a microphone in one hand and gesturing vigorously with the other, he takes his audience through theological hills and valleys and shows one fascinating panorama after the other. Impatiently, he shuffles his papers and complains that he cannot say it all in a few hours. He gives the impression of a man who has an enormous treasure to share and is continually frustrated that he cannot show his gifts all at once. But in a short time he is able to give his listeners a desire for theological understanding, offer them challenging perspectives, and make them aware of the privilege of being a Christian today. One of the points that stuck with me was his view on the interior life. The interior life, Gustavo said, does not refer to the psychological reality that one reaches through introspection, but is the life lived free from the constraining power of the law in the Pauline sense. It is a life free to love. Thus the spiritual life is the place of true freedom. When we are able to throw off the compulsions and coercions that come from outside of us and can allow the Holy Spirit, God's love, to be our only guide, then we can live a truly free, interior, and spiritual life.

Tuesday, February 9

Gustavo's lecture today was entitled "The Journey of a People in Search of God." It was a brilliant treatment of a spirituality of leaving, walking, and entering: the people of God are called to leave their situation of slavery and walk through the desert in order to enter the land of freedom, where they can own the land and live in justice and peace.

In the light of many biblical texts, Gustavo explored the meaning of this journey of freedom. His main assertion was that the search for God *is* the search for freedom, and that the search for freedom *is* the search for God. Many people who are deeply involved in the struggle for water, for light, for schools, and for health care do not perceive this as a search for God. And many who attend churches, walk in processions, and bless their houses with holy water do not experience this as part of a struggle for freedom. This is not uncommon. Even the Hebrews who left Egypt did not fully understand the meaning of the events in which they were participating. It is precisely in the reflection on the events of the people that the search for God and the struggle for liberty are connected and can deepen each other.

Of particular importance to me was Gustavo's notion that the journey of the people is not a journey from nothing to something, but from something to something. When we speak about a movement from slavery to freedom, from scarcity to possession, and from exploitation to justice, we should not think and act as if freedom, possession, and justice are only on one end of the polarities. In fact, in Egypt there existed freedom, possessions, and justice. That is why at times the Hebrews wanted to return to Egypt, and that too is the reason why a desire for full freedom, possession, and justice could grow. You can only desire what you already know or have in some measure.

This, therefore, also means that the search for God is a search for him whom we have already met, and who has already shown us his mercy and love. The desire for God makes us aware that we already know him.

For me, these thoughts are important because they point to a ministry that first of all recognizes the gifts of God that are already present. It is by acknowledging these gifts and lifting them up as signs of God's presence in our midst that we can start leaving, walking, and entering. The journey is not a journey of despairing people who have never seen God nor tasted freedom; rather, it is a journey of hopeful people, who know that God is with them and will lead them to a freedom of which they have already tasted the first fruits.

Wednesday, February 10

I continue to be impressed by the thousands of people who are actively participating in the summer course. They are not only people from all parts of Latin

America, but also from very different stages and walks of life. There are quite a few priests and sisters, mostly Americans, British, and Irish; but the majority of this assembly is made up of people who have been born and raised in the poor *barrios* and have become active pastoral agents in the process of liberation. They know their own people and they have learned to think with one eye on the Gospel and one eye on the plight of their compatriots. In the Latin American Church, the people themselves are showing the direction in which to go. They are open and hospitable to strangers who want to participate, but the struggle is theirs and they themselves provide the leadership.

Many of these people are very young. They work in their different districts as catechists, social workers, project coordinators, and so on. All of them are steeped in the Bible; with it they live and struggle. They have come to think of themselves as the people of God called to the promised land. They all know it will be a long, arduous, and often painful journey; but they also know that no worldly powers can make them give up their struggle and return to the state of submission and resignation from which they came.

In his lecture today, Manuel Diaz Mateos, S.J., developed a spirituality of the marginal person and the stranger. He pointed to Abel (the weak one), Noah, Job, Ruth, the innocent children, the widows, the publicans, and the Samaritans as proof of God's special love and attention for those who live on the periphery of society and who are considered weak. For me, this presentation opened up a vision of ministry that I keep losing, although I am constantly called back to it. It is the vision that ministry means first of all searching for God where people are lost, confused, broken, and poor. Often I have gone to such people to bring them back to God, to the sacraments, and to the church. But that is acting and living as if God is where I am, and as if my first task is to bring others to my place. When, however, God is with the poor and marginal, then I have to dare to go there, live there, and find him there. I now realize that I can be with people without having to make them think my thoughts and say my words. I can be free to listen and slowly to discern where God shows his merciful face to me.

Thursday, February 11

Every day of the summer course, the students meet for two hours in "commissions," discussion groups in which the lectures of the previous day are discussed and appropriated. I am a member of a discussion group with twenty participants. We are a very interesting little community. The majority are Peruvians, but there are two Chileans, a Uruguayan, a Nicaraguan, a Swiss, and myself. All of these people are active in some form of pastoral care, and most of them are leaders in their own communities.

The discussions are extremely poignant, with little abstract thinking going on. People constantly test the ideas presented in the lectures against their own daily experiences and try to let these experiences be their source of ongoing theological reflections. Some of these experiences are harsh. They are experiences of harassment, exploitation, imprisonment, and torture. Everyone is aware that the road to liberation is rough and uncharted, asking for a commitment that goes as far as the willingness to sacrifice one's life. It is overwhelming for me to hear these young men and women speak so directly and articulately about their love for Jesus Christ, their desire to give everything to the realization of his Kingdom, their willingness to be and remain poor with the poor, and their joy to be chosen for this great task of liberation. There is little sentimentality and little piety. The word that dominates all the discussions is *la lucha*, the struggle.

Today the main topic was prayer. Within a few minutes, the growing charismatic movement (Neo-Pentecostalism) became the main subject. Most participants considered the charismatic movement as appealing primarily to the middle- and upper-class youth; as offering a spiritual experience without social consequences; as closely linked to other conservative organizations such as the *cursillistas*, as a spiritual weapon in the hands of the oppressing classes. People didn't hesitate to say that prayer, as seen and practiced in many charismatic groups, was not Christian prayer since it does not come from nor lead to the *lucha* for the liberation of God's people.

Reflecting on this discussion, I feel quite uncomfortable. The sweeping generalizations about the charismatic movement seem to deny the need of many people to find a still point in their lives where they can listen to the voice of God in the midst of a sad and war-ridden world. This desire for inner tranquility and the direct experience of God's Spirit can become a form of escape from the struggle for liberation, but it does not have to be that way.

During my one-semester stay in Rome, I participated actively in a charismatic prayer group at the Gregorian University. In many ways it kept me spiritually alive during that time. I never experienced this prayer group as an escape mechanism, but as a source of spiritual revitalization that freed me from many fears and compulsions and allowed me to dedicate myself more generously to the service of others.

I even have the feeling that those who want to be active in the struggle for freedom for a lifetime will need an increasingly strong and personal experience of the presence of the Spirit of God in their lives. I would not be surprised if, within a few years, a search for new disciplines of prayer were to occupy the minds of many Christians who struggle with the poor for liberation. I hope that the division between the charismatic movement and the liberation movement will not grow so wide that it creates a *lucha* within the Christian community.

Friday, February 12

The lectures given yesterday and today were disappointing; they consisted of many words but few connections with daily experiences. One speaker spoke eloquently about compassion as the most important attribute of Jesus, and another talked about the centrality of contemplation in the history of Christian spirituality. Each covered a huge area of Christian thought, but neither was able to touch his audience. It was sad to see how everyone had a hard time staying awake during lectures on such life-giving realities as compassion and contemplation.

The discussion group showed a lot more vitality. We were asked to list core traits of a Latin American spirituality. Fifteen aspects of Christian spirituality were written on the blackboard and everyone was asked to choose three that were most important for Latin America today. Everyone agreed that "compassion" had too many passive connotations. Some argued that, in a world in which the largest part of the population is oppressed and exploited, the word compassion sounds too personalistic and suggests a sentimental acceptance of the status quo. However, when people started to choose the three most important traits, many still considered compassion an essential quality in the struggle for liberation. After much discussion, we came to the conclusion that every Christian is called to a radical commitment to establish the Kingdom of God on earth, and that for the Latin American Christian this means a compassionate struggle to liberate the poor. Everyone stressed that this formulation was inadequate and did not cover the whole of a Christian spirituality for Latin America, but nobody denied that this formulation captured the main thrust of the "New Church."

I was struck by the repeated use of the word *lucha*. This word is used to counteract a passive and fatalistic stance towards the misery of the masses and to stress the urgency of an active—even aggressive—involvement in the war against poverty, oppression, and exploitation. However, I tried to locate a concrete idea of this *lucha* in the daily life of the Christian community, and of the Christian strategy of this struggle. In the absence of such a concrete idea and strategy, there is a danger that the struggle for the full liberation of the people will be narrowed down to a "fight for rights." This type of *lucha* can easily lead to a fanaticism no longer guided by the joy and peace of God's Kingdom, but by a human instinct seeking to replace one form of oppression with another.

Saturday, February 13

Over the week, my depression has worn off a bit. It has not been lifted or healed, but it has lost its most painful edges in the midst of the summer course. I was helped by the insight that I had to move directly and aggressively in the direction I want to go. Waiting to be shown the best people to meet, the best places to visit, the best events to become part of, only feeds my depression. I am sure that I will find my direction in life when I search actively, move around with open eyes and ears, ask questions, and—in the midst of all that—pray constantly to discover God's will. The Lord searches for me, I am sure, but only when I search for him too will I encounter him and will his word for me become clear. Every time I slip into another depression, I notice that I have given up the struggle to find God and have fallen back into an attitude of spiteful waiting.

Sunday, February 14

In Peru, people celebrate Carnival by throwing water at each other. Innocent passersby are often surprised by a shower, and buses and cars with open windows make attractive targets for water-throwers. A few years ago, this was causing so many accidents that the government decided that the only Carnival days were the four Sundays of February, disregarding the date of Ash Wednesday.

My friends had instructed me to wear old clothes on these wet Sundays. Wherever I went today I saw little groups of teenagers on the street corners ready to attack any dry person with anything that can hold water: balloons, pots and pans, and even large buckets. I also noticed eager water-throwers perched on the roofs to surprise people entering and leaving the buildings. Some people simply decide to stay home during Carnival. One of the parish choirs decided not to sing today, because they don't like to sing in church while soaking wet.

I took a bus to Las Flores, a large *barrio* on the southern outskirts of Lima, to visit a community of English Benedictines. Unlike many other buses I had ridden on here, there were few broken windows on this bus, but at every stop people getting on or off were thoroughly drenched. Everyone seemed to enjoy the game, although even well-dressed people looked like drowned cats as they stepped on the bus. The driver tried to escape the water-throwing youths by stopping between official stops to let people off and by letting people on at any place they raised their hands. He played the game with a good spirit. He lost a few and won a few.

Most people, from very young to very old, take it all with good-natured laughter. "As long as they don't put paint in the water," a woman said to me, "it's a lot of fun. It is so hot here anyhow that you are dry again before you are home." I made it to the monks moist but not wet.

Monday, February 15

During the last few years, I have received several letters from Marist Sister Teresa asking for money to help some Peruvian ex-prisoners. Today Sister Teresa took me to Lurigancho, the huge prison where she works. It is hard to describe what I saw, heard, and smelled during my four hours in Lurigancho. I want to record at least some of my impressions.

Lurigancho is a world within a world. About four thousand men live inside a small area surrounded by huge walls and watchtowers. They are there for reasons varying from murder to buying cocaine on the street. The majority of these men have never been sentenced and have no idea when their case will come to court or how long they will have to stay behind those walls. Some have been there for a few months, others for more than seven years; some are there for the first time, others old regulars for whom Lurigancho has become a second home. Some seem friendly and gentle, others silent and menacing.

Lurigancho impressed me as a microcosm of the extremes in life. Within the prison I visited several small libraries with helpful librarians. Everywhere were men weaving baskets, playing ball, sleeping in the sun, and standing on corners talking together. Less visible but no less real are the knives, guns, and drugs hidden in the corners, closets, and cells. What do these men do? For most of them there is no work, no way to keep busy except weaving baskets. Yet much activity goes on. Gangs fight each other, prisoners kill each other, groups pray together, men study together. There are meek, quiet, and unassuming people; there are also aggressive and dangerous men who are feared, avoided, or kept under control.

What struck me first was the enormous chaos. Once we had made our way through the gates, it seemed that all discipline was gone. Since most of the thirteen huge cellblocks were open, we could walk freely in, out, and through. Prisoners were walking around with little restriction and behaved as if they were in charge. Most of them were naked from the waist up; many just wore swimming trunks. Some showed big scars on their bodies, the result of self-inflicted cuts that had put them in the hospital and allowed them to escape from torture. The food consists of bread in the morning, rice and beans in the afternoon, and soup in the evening. It is brought in huge containers and put on the patio of the cellblock for anyone who wants it. But many feed themselves in other ways. They get money from their visitors and buy food from the different black market stores or bars.

There is as much horror, cruelty, and violence as there is friendliness, human play, and simple village life. One of the most surprising things to me was that all the prisoners can receive visitors two times a week. During visiting days the population practically doubles. Women come with large baskets of food, some to bring it to their imprisoned relatives, others to sell it to those who have money. One cellblock looked like a lively market place. There were different food stands, and all over the place groups of people were sitting on the floor, talking or playing cards. It was not all that different from the marketplace in Ciudad de Dios.

Prisoners can take their wives or girlfriends to their cells with them. Cellmates simply stay away for a few hours, and when one of them has a visitor the favor is returned. Most prisoners live together according to the area of town or the district they come from. The nature of their crime seems to have little to do with the company they keep; first offenders often live together with experienced killers.

Often cellblocks fight with each other. Walls get broken down, windows smashed, and when there is enough alcohol around, people get wounded or killed. Once in a while things get so far out of hand that the *guardia republicana*, the police force, moves in. On February 2 the police carried out a wild and indiscriminately brutal assault on one cellblock. Tear gas was used and random shooting took place. During the four-hour rampage prisoners were severely beaten, tortured, and wounded. When it was all over, three men were dead.

While talking about all this, one of the prisoners brought me to a little flower garden he had carefully cultivated. Proudly he showed me the lovely roses that had just come out. It has hard for me to put it all together. But that is Lurigancho.

On our walk, we passed a pavilion that we could not enter. "That is where the homosexuals live together," one of my prisoner-guides told me. I saw a lot of prisoners hanging around the building and gazing through the fence into the open lot. I suddenly felt as though I were at a zoo. One prisoner said: "Look, those are the gays." It was clear to me that they were really talking about transvestites. There is a lot of sex between men in Lurigancho, but in this section lived the real "queens," who had asked to be together to have some degree of freedom from harassment. They were locked up by their own wish more than by that of any prison authority. I have never seen humans look at caged people in such a way. It made me feel something very dark and evil.

Finally, Teresa led me to the pavilion of the foreigners. It was located at some distance from the other cellblocks we had just seen. When we went in, I had the strange sensation of walking into an exclusive country club. On the open patio, blond young men in tiny swimming suits were playing racquetball or sunbathing on a towel. Their tanned and well-fed bodies were a stark contrast to the dark, scarred bodies of the poor Peruvians I had just visited. These were prosperous, middle-class Europeans, Americans, or Australians who came from a world light-years away from the dark, dirty cells of the other pavilions. A minute after I entered, I met a young Dutchman who was glad to meet fellow countryman and to speak his mother tongue. He gave me the grand tour. The main living space consisted of a huge, open hall where people spent most of their time. The atmosphere was that of an exposition hall. In the center stood workbenches where people could do a little carpentry. Scattered about were stands where food and drinks were sold, and all over the place people were playing cards, chess, and checkers. The place looked clean and well-kept—more like an amusement park than a prison. My Dutch guide showed me his bedroom. It was a small wooden room with two bunkbeds. "I paid $200 for it," the Dutchman explained. "You can get anything here when you pay for it." He introduced me to his roommate, a tall, good-looking American from Washington, D.C. "It doesn't look too bad here," I said. "Oh no," they responded. "In fact it's quite all right here, except that you're locked up and don't know for how long."

I soon found out that they both were arrested because of drugs. "I sold some drugs to an undercover policeman, and that got me here," the Dutchman said. As he and his American friend talked more, I got the picture. Since they had been arrested on drug charges, they now have to buy their way out, and legal help is extremely expensive. Every step of the way can cost a fortune. But money came from Holland or the United States through the embassies. The American was lucky to have his wife in Lima, who could visit two times a week and bring in all the food they wanted. "We don't touch the prison food," the Dutchman said. "My American friend's wife brings us steaks and good soup, and we make our own meals." I asked how they spend their time. "We read a lot and play games, talk and sit in the sun," they said. "And here we can get any drugs we want."

I had never expected this strange island of decadence in the center of the Lurigancho prison. If I ever saw discrimination, it was here. The poor lived in miserable poverty, the wealthy built their own country club, and these two worlds lived side by side behind the prison walls.

But this living side by side was not as simple as it might seem. At night the foreigners had to protect their domain against attacks from the poor pavilions. My hosts explained: "We had to organize our own guard to keep the others from our roof and to prevent them from breaking in and stealing our stuff."

When we were let out through the heavy gates and stepped onto the bus to go home, I knew that only a very simple, pure, and holy person would be able to work with these men for any length of time. Just being there for four hours had made me see that Teresa must be such a person. She moved in this world without fear, open, practical, unsentimental, and with a deep sense of God's love. She saw it all clearly, but was not entangled in it. The men knew that she was one of the few who had no second motives. She was just there to be of help and that was all. Surrounded by the complexity of the dark world, the simple love of God can easily be discerned.

Tuesday, February 16

Today I went to the airport to pick up some galley proofs that were sent to me by my publisher through one of the airlines. Naively, I thought that it would be a matter of a few minutes. But when I got to the cargo area I received some papers to take to a network of offices, officials, cash registers, and desks that was more complex than I have experienced before in my life. Every time I had made it through one hoop, another awaited me. A sea of people, as nervous and confused as I, added to the endless waiting. Meanwhile, young boys offered to do it all for me for some money, trying to convince me that they knew the right way to the package. However, I clung to my growing stack of documents with the anxiety of a man whose life is in danger. Finally, after three hours, I made it to the warehouse where I could see the package. An hour later, a man from customs came with some more documents and let me open the package and identify the galleys. For a moment I thought that now I could take them home with me, but I soon found out that I was only halfway through the process. Two more payments had to be made, and at least three more offices with long waiting lines had to be visited. At that time, I gave in to the boys and gave them the money to do the work for me. They took my papers and gave me their I.D., and I left the airport with their promise that tomorrow morning I would get my package.

David Ritter, a Jefferson City, Missouri, priest who has worked in Peru for three years and who drove me to the airport for this "quick errand," prevented me from going crazy in the midst of it all. He smiled and laughed about it and explained how this way of doing things gave work and money to many Peruvians, and gave me a chance to practice my patience.

I am amazed how hard it is to just take things the Peruvian way, use my time to talk with people, practice my Spanish, and simply flow with the stream. After all, I might profit more from waiting than from being waited on. My frustration, anger, anxiety, and impatience, however, clearly showed me how far I truly am from enjoying solidarity with the poor!

Wednesday, February 17

After two more hours of running from office to office, talking to an endless succession of people, and paying more tips, I finally got my package. Then I returned to the course on spirituality and listened to Gustavo Gutiérrez's lecture on the "traits of a contemporary spirituality in Latin America." It was the most impressive presentation of the course so far, and it brought together many of the themes that have occupied our minds during the last ten days.

Gustavo stressed the "eruption of the poor into the history of Latin America." The suffering poor have become the pastoral agents who point to a new way of being Christian, a new spirituality, characterized by a call to conversion not only of individual people, but of the church as a whole. This conversion promises a way of living in which effectiveness is sought in a climate of grace. Such a climate allows us to experience a real joy that comes forth from suffering, helps us to live as "spiritual infants" with the poor while fighting against poverty, and makes it possible to find freedom in a communal life. Although all of these are among the classical themes of a Christian spirituality, they have found new articulation and meaning in the context of the eruption of the poor.

What struck me most was Gustavo's ability to integrate a spirituality of struggle for freedom with a spirituality of personal growth. He placed great emphasis on the importance of personal friendship, affective relationships, "useless" prayer, and intimate joy as essential elements of a true struggle for liberation.

The method Gustavo used was of special interest to me. As the source for his spirituality, he used documents that came forth from the suffering church in Latin America. A text written by a Christian community in Lima, declarations by the bishops of Guatemala and Chile, sermons of Bishop Romero of El Salvador, letters by Rutilio Grande, Nestor Paz, and Louis Espinal, and statements by the mothers of the "vanished ones" all formed the sources from which Gustavo developed a spirituality for Latin America. It was a powerful example of reflection on the suffering experienced in persecution and martyrdom. I was not surprised, therefore, with the warm and enthusiastic reception that Gustavo's vision met. He is a genuine theologian, a man who breaks the bread of God's word for thousands of people and offers hope, courage, and confidence.

Thursday, February 18

What does it mean to live a religious life in Latin America? During the last months I have often asked myself: Would it be possible to live with a small group of dedicated people in the midst of a *pueblo joven* and practice there the disciplines of prayer and meditation in such a way that the group would become a center of hope for the neighborhood?

What I see now are many dedicated and generous people involved in different projects. They are very busy, distracted, pressured, and restless, and often very tired. They hardly have time and space for each other, let alone for spiritual reading, theological reflection, sharing of religious experiences, mental prayer, the liturgy of the hours, or any other religious practice.

But how would it be if, in the midst of the very poor, a small group of men and women created a space for people to celebrate God's presence? How would it be if, instead of running in all directions, these men and women could draw others into prayer, silence, reflection, sharing of experiences, and singing God's praise? Maybe it is just a romantic dream, but it is a dream that continues to press itself on me.

Friday, February 19

This was the last day of the summer course. At seven-thirty, Bishop German Schmitz celebrated a festive liturgy with the three thousand students and teachers of the course. There was a general mood of gratitude. All the people I spoke with communicated a real excitement about having been part of this event and a desire to go back to work and share with others the new insights and experiences that the course had offered.

Among the hundreds of ideas that passed through my mind in the past days, one in particular has stayed with me. It is the simple thought that true theological reflection can convert a paralyzing experience into an experience of hope. That seemed to me what this course had done for many. Most of the students work with the poor, often in depressing, discouraging, and even agonizing circumstances. The reflections of the course gave us a consciousness of a divine and liberating presence in the midst of it all and freed us from fatalism and despair. We came to experience that agony really means struggle, and that God is in that struggle with us. And so a new joy could grow, and we could become aware that it is a privilege to work with the poor and suffer with them for a new world.

Thus the final liturgy could be a genuine celebration, a lifting up of God's presence among us and among the poor, and an expression of gratitude for what we had seen with our own eyes, heard with our own ears, and touched with our own hands (1 John 1:1).

Saturday, February 20

Gratitude is one of the most visible characteristics of the poor I have come to know. I am always surrounded by words of thanks: "thanks for your visit, your blessing, your sermon, your prayer, your gifts, your presence with us." Even the smallest and most necessary goods are a reason for gratitude. This all-pervading gratitude is the basis for celebration. Not only are the poor grateful for life, but they also celebrate life constantly. A visit, a reunion, a simple meeting are always like little celebrations. Every time a new gift is recognized, there are songs or toasts, words of congratulation, or something to eat and drink. And every gift is shared. "Have a drink, take some fruit, eat our bread" is the response to every visit I make, and this is what I see people do for each other. All of life is a gift, a gift to be celebrated, a gift to be shared.

Thus the poor are a eucharistic people, people who know to say thanks to God, to life, to each other. They may not come to Mass, they may not participate in many church celebrations. But in their hearts they are deeply religious, because for them all of life is a long fiesta with God.

Sunday, February 21

After more than a month in Pamplona Alta, I have come to believe strongly that a "pastoral presence" is more important than any plan or project. This conviction has grown out of the observation that, more than anything else, people want you to share their lives. This afternoon I simply walked to where I heard music. About six blocks from where I live, I soon saw people dancing around a tree and cutting it down bit by bit. It proved to be a carnival celebration that is popular in the jungle of Peru, and that some emigrants had transported to Pamplona Alta.

Although nobody knew me, it didn't take long for people to offer me a drink and to make me part of their fiesta. One member of the band told me without blinking an eye that he was a drug dealer and had just imported a kilo of "cocaine pasta" from Colombia. He said: "I look simple and poor, but I have a good business and make enough money to go to the World Cup games in Spain." When I told him that I had met a lot of drug buyers and drug dealers in the Lurigancho prison, he was hardly impressed. It seemed that he worked for the drug underworld, and that he was so well protected that his frankness about this business was not any real risk for him.

Besides this drug dealer, there were many others who wanted to tell me their stories, some jokingly, others seriously, some heavily inebriated, others with a clear mind. What struck me most of all was the easy way in which these Peruvians received me and let me be one of them.

More and more, the desire grows in me simply to walk around, greet people, enter their homes, sit on their doorsteps, play ball, throw water, and be known as someone who wants to live with them. It is a privilege to have the time and the freedom to practice this simple ministry of presence. Still, it is not as simple as it seems. My own desire to be useful, to do something significant, or to be part of some impressive project is so strong that soon my time is taken up by meetings, conferences, study groups, and workshops that prevent me from walking the streets. It is difficult not to have plans, not to organize people around an urgent cause, and not to feel that you are working directly for social progress. But I wonder more and more if the first thing shouldn't be to know people by name, to eat and to drink with them, to listen to their stories and tell your own, and to let them know with words, handshakes, and hugs that you do not simply like them, but truly love them.

If I ever decide to live in Peru for a long time, I think I should stay in one place and spend the first year doing little more than participating in the daily Peruvian life. A ministry of word and sacrament has to grow from a deep solidarity with the people. Contemplation is essential to ministry, and listening to people's lives and receiving them in a prayerful heart is true contemplation. I have little doubt that out of this contemplation it will become clear how the good news of the Gospel has to be announced, and how the healing presence of God needs to be made manifest among his people.

The greatest news of all is that God is with his people, that he is truly present. What greater ministry, then, can be practiced than a ministry that reflects this divine presence? Any why worry? If God is with his own, his own will show me the way.

Monday, February 22

I am still fascinated with the question of what it would be like to be living with two or three brothers or sisters in the midst of one of the *barrios* of Lima, praying together at regular hours, walking the streets, visiting the homes, spending one day in study and reflection, practicing hospitality whenever possible, and celebrating the mysteries of God's presence. The core of this idea is that of living among the people to learn from them. This might sound romantic and sentimental, but in fact it requires discipline to allow the people to become our teachers. With such discipline, all that we see and hear can become a rich source for locating the presence of God among his people.

It would be a ministry of presence, but an active, articulate, considered presence. It would be a mutual ministry of continuous receiving and giving. It would be contemplation and action, celebration and liberation, study and work, ascetic and festive, fraternal and hospitable. I am convinced that there are at this moment young, idealistic, well-trained theological students who would be very open to such a ministry. Is this idea a dream, a fantasy, an illusion, or something worth pursuing? I will let it rest for a while and see what happens with this little seed that I put into the ground of my own search to serve God.

Tuesday, February 23

Villa Salvador is a section of Lima that in 1971 was nothing but a bare desert, dry, sandy, isolated, and inhospitable. Now, eleven years later, three hundred thousand people have found a home there. It has been a hard and painful struggle for the people to make the desert into a city, but now they are proud of what they have accomplished. There is a water supply, electricity, many schools, and a slowly improving transportation system that takes the workers to their factories and offices.

Today I visited Eugene Kirk, an Irish priest who has lived in Villa Salvador for the last eight years. I also visited two "little brothers of Jesus," the Frenchman Jacinto and the Basque José, who founded one of their fraternities there. What most struck me during the long conversations with Eugene, Jacinto, and José was that they considered the simple act of staying with the people the core of their ministry. Eugene began in Villa Salvador by living in a small shack and setting up a little carpentry shop. Slowly but surely he got to know many people and was able to build a Christian community that today is strong and vital. Jacinto works in a small furniture factory and commutes two hours a day with thousands of others. José works in a carpenter's shop in the neighborhood. During the weekends, Jacinto and José stay around the house to receive visitors and help the neighbors with whatever needs they have. Eugene, Jacinto, and José have small chapels in their houses and live as contemplatives in the midst of a sea of humans.

It was a joy to spend a day with these men. They are simple, good men who enjoy their life with the people immensely. They work hard, yet they seem to have time for anyone and anything. They feel at home in this desert-city and they speak easily about the great privilege of being allowed to live and work as members of the community of Villa Salvador.

There is a great and holy mystery here, the mystery of the incarnation lived in simple ways. I saw an Irishman, a Basque, and a Frenchman thanking and praising God daily for being given the opportunity to be with the people of God. The many little children walking in and out of their dwellings made me realize how close the Lord is to all of them.

Wednesday, February 24

Ash Wednesday. During the last weeks, I have slowly become aware of what my Lenten practice might be. It might be the development of some type of "holy indifference" toward the many small rejections I am subject to, and a growing attachment to the Lord and his passion.

I am constantly surprised at how hard it is for me to deal with the little rejections that people inflict on each other day by day. I feel this even more strongly now that I am living in a country where I am so dependent on introductions and invitations. It is hard to meet people, to see projects, or to learn about current issues if you are not explicitly brought in touch with them. During the last month, I kept hearing about many interesting events only when they were past! Why didn't anyone tell me about them? Why wasn't I invited? Why was nobody willing to make me aware of them? How should *I* know? I do not think that there is any hostility towards me. Everyone thinks that everyone knows, and nobody takes the initiative to extend a personal invitation. Thus I feel welcome and not welcome at the same time. Nobody objects to my presence, but nobody is very glad about it either.

This atmosphere often leaves me with a feeling of being rejected and left alone. When I swallow these rejections, I get quickly depressed and lonely; then I am in danger of becoming resentful and even vengeful. But it is such an institutional problem that I can hardly imagine that I can ever be without it. The Catholic Church, wherever I have seen it operate, from the Vatican to the parishes in the *barrios* of Peru, tends to make the personal subservient to the institutional. There is always a need for priests to say Masses, baptize, and marry, and anyone who can do that in a responsible way is always "welcome." There are so many things to do that good workers can easily be placed. At the same time, there are so many people asking for services, so many activities to participate in and meetings to attend, that it is difficult to pay attention to the intimate interpersonal aspects of existence. And thus the paradox becomes that those who preach love and defend the values of family life, friendship, and mutual support find themselves often living lonely lives in busy rectories.

Is there a solution to this? When I see the people I am working with, I doubt there is one. They are all deeply committed, hardworking, and caring people. They will all give their lives for their people. They are full of enthusiasm and pastoral energy. But they too are part of an enormous institution that has such a pervasive influence on their way of being that it is practically impossible to escape the loneliness it breeds.

But maybe all of this is the other side of a deep mystery, the mystery that we have no lasting dwelling place on this earth and that only God loves us the way we desire to be loved. Maybe all these small rejections are reminders that I am a traveler on the way to a sacred place where God holds me in the palm of his hand. Maybe I do have to become a little more indifferent towards all these ups and downs, ins and outs, of personal relationships and learn to rest more deeply in him who knows and loves me more than I know and love myself.

Thursday, February 25

Today, I realized that the question of where to live and what to do is really insignificant compared to the question of how to keep the eyes of my heart focused on the Lord. I can be teaching at Yale, working in the bakery at the Genesee Abbey, or walking around with poor children in Peru and feel totally useless, miserable, and depressed in all these situations. I am sure of it, because it has happened. There is not such a thing as the right place or the right job. I can be happy and unhappy in all situations. I am sure of it, because I have been. I have felt distraught and joyful in situations of abundance as well as poverty, in situations of popularity and anonymity, in situations of success and failure. The difference was never based on the situation itself, but always on my state of mind and heart. When I knew that I was walking with the Lord, I always felt happy and at peace. When I was entangled in my own complaints and emotional needs, I always felt restless and divided.

It is a simple truth that comes to me in a time when I have to decide about my future. Coming to Lima or not for five, ten, or twenty years is no great decision. Turning fully, unconditionally, and without fear to the Lord *is*. I am sure this awareness sets me free to look around here without much worrying and binds me to the holy call to pray unceasingly.

Friday, February 26

Rose Dominique and Rose Timothy, two Maryknoll sisters, are the directors of a small downtown office, the Centro de Creatividad y Cambio (The Center for Creativity and Change). Their work could be seen as a nonecclesiastical ministry through which they reach many different groups of people, non-Christians as well as Christians. This center is a grass-roots organization to work for a new society. Its members publish pamphlets and booklets to draw attention to urgent problems concerning health, education, and youth, and to suggest strategies for change. The "Roses" pay special attention to the plight of Peruvian women. They felt that working within the traditional church structures was not the best way to strive for the liberation of women; so they set up shop for themselves while continuing to offer their services to parishes and church groups when asked.

This morning I talked for an hour with Sister Rose Dominique. Her sharp and compassionate understanding of the Peruvian situation helped me to articulate some of my own feelings of which I had been only vaguely aware. What impressed me most was her observation that the leaders in the theology of liberation had little sympathy with or understanding of the issues that touch the oppressed situation of the women in the church. Rose remarked: "In this Catholic country, it is very hard to change the predominantly clerical way in which the Church works. The liberation theologians are very much Church people, and they have a hard time considering our concern for women as a real part of their struggle for liberation."

I feel that she was talking about something that I had noticed but had found hard to pinpoint. The obvious and overwhelming need for socioeconomic liberation and the undeniable presence of immense poverty creates a situation in which women's issues are easily seen as a distraction, especially in a clerical, male-dominated Church. I had felt this in many little ways. After living for many years in an interdenominational and interconfessional setting, I could feel the strong dominating influence of a Church that is the only real religious power. And even the most progressive and liberated people in that Church are still marked, mostly unconsciously, by this clerical, male-dominated way of thinking and living.

Saturday, February 27

During the last few weeks I have been asking myself and others if I was learning enough about pastoral ministry during my stay in Pamplona Alta. I love the family I live with, I enjoy celebrating the Eucharist with the people, I am moved when I bring Communion to the sick, and I appreciate my weekly meetings with the lectors, but I have not really become a part of the pastoral team. Most things that happen remain unknown to me, and somehow I am getting the message that it is more a bother than a help to make me part of the daily life of the parish. I had hoped to participate in youth-group meetings, to visit the little communities in some of the sections of the parish, to help out in preparations for the sacraments of baptism and matrimony and—in general—to share actively in the ministry of the parish. Now I feel that I am standing in the center of a busy square wondering in which direction everyone is going. Last week I discussed my feelings with Tom, but it seems hard to make me part of things.

The whole situation is quite understandable. People are busy, and there are so many short-term visitors that it becomes fatiguing to keep introducing them over and over again to the daily goings-on in the parish. I have come to the conclusion that I have learned as much as I can and that I had better try to discover some new areas of ministry outside of Pamplona Alta before I leave Peru. In order to be able to make a responsible decision about my future, I need more experience than I can get here.

So this afternoon I explained to Charles and Tom that I felt it was better to move back to the center house in Miraflores and to start visiting people and places from there. It was hard to say good-bye to Sophia, Johnny, Pablito, and Maria. Living with them was, undoubtedly, the most important experience of my time here. Their affection and friendship were gifts for which I will always remain grateful. We ate some ice cream together, and Johnny and Pablito helped me carry my suitcases to the bus. When I stood on the steps of the bus and saw them waving good-bye, I felt a real pain and prayed that somehow I would be able to see them again as happy and mature adults. I waved back and shouted: *"Adiós, hasta la vista, gracias por todo."*

Sunday, February 28

This morning at 11:00 I had a good visit with Bishop German Schmitz, one of the auxiliary bishops of Lima. His main responsibility is the young towns in the southern part of Lima. I wanted to express to him some of the ideas that have developed in my mind during the last month and get his response. I explained my desire to live in a poor section of Lima—alone or with a few others—and to try to articulate the rich spiritual gifts of the people. My short stay with Sophia, Pablo, and the children had given me a glimpse of the presence of God with the poor. What a joy it would be to make this divine presence visible not only to them but also to the many nonpoor people who sincerely search for light in their darkness! A life of prayer and hospitality among the poor, to discover and express their gifts, is slowly presenting itself as a vocation to me.

Bishop Schmitz responded warmly, even enthusiastically, to this idea. But he felt that something more was needed. He said: "There is such a need for spiritual growth and formation among the poor that you would offer a real service with retreats and days of recollection for the people. They are too tied down to their homes to travel far for days of reflection and study. But if an opportunity for this arose in their own neighborhood, they would gladly respond." Bishop Schmitz kept stressing that his idea was not really different from mine. He only wanted to "complete the picture" based on his own understanding of the need of the people.

I felt affirmed in this conversation, and I have a sense that something is becoming visible that might prove to be more than just a fantasy. Bishop Schmitz suggested that I discuss my ideas a little more with others, and then present them to the Cardinal of Lima. He made it clear that he could not yet give his permission and that the Cardinal needed to be consulted before any action was taken. But that is not my problem at this time. I am far from that phase. At this moment I was happy to have a sympathetic response from a Peruvian bishop.

6

March

THE OUTLINES OF A VISION

∎

Monday, March 1

SISTER REBECCA, one of the Marist sisters, took me this morning to Larco Herrera, a huge mental hospital in Lima. Rebecca had worked in the Lurigancho prison, and also had access to the pavilion of the mentally ill prisoners who are sent to this hospital.

We spent most of the morning with Manuel and Luis, two prisoner-patients. Both are intelligent and articulate people who in no way showed any signs of being criminals or mentally ill. They took us around their pavilion, introduced us to their fellow inmates, and explained everything we wanted to know. We also spoke with the psychologist of the section, a friendly man who received us and our guides with great hospitality and discussed the difficult situation of his patients. Most of them were never sentenced, and nobody could say how long they would remain locked up. We also talked a bit to the *guardia republicana*, the armed guards who surround this little section of the hospital, since it is a prison as well.

Although the place, which houses thirty-eight patients, was extremely poor; although the patients had nothing to keep them busy; although the justice system in Peru is so bureaucratic and complex that these men may be there for many years without any attention to their case, the atmosphere was very humane. Guards, doctors, and patients treated each other amiably, talked freely, and showed a remarkable openness to each other. Somehow, the Peruvian friendliness and hospitality have taken some of the sharp edges off the suffering of these men. One of the guards even allowed Luis to bring us to the main gate. He walked along with us and was as much a part of the party as Rebecca, Luis, and myself.

Poverty, injustice, misery, and loneliness were all present; but in the midst of it all I saw an expression of humanity I have never seen in any mental hospital before. While we walked to the gate, I noticed that Luis was playing with scissors and a piece of silver paper from a pack of cigarettes. Just before we said good-bye, he offered me a lovely silver flower that he had quickly made while walking. This gesture captured the poignancy and paradox of my visit. I embraced him and for a moment all was good, very good.

Tuesday, March 2

This morning I visited the Centro Bartolome de las Casas with Bill McCarthy. A three-story building on Ricardo Bentin street in Rimac, it is the heart of the liberation theology movement. I had heard so much about it that I expected a large building, with many people and classrooms, full of activity. Instead, I saw a very simple house in a suburb of Lima. Gustavo Gutiérrez, who founded the center, was not in; but Alberto Maguina, one of the staff members, received us kindly and told us all we wanted to know.

The center is an independent institute with a small staff of sociologists and theologians who dedicate themselves to sociotheological studies and to the formation and continuing education of pastoral agents in Peru. Their work is divided into four main areas: (1) popular religiosity; (2) the daily life of the poor; (3) the poor as protagonists of their own history; and (4) Church and Society. Under these four titles, different subjects are studied.

One of the subjects under the heading of "popular religiosity" is "the moral sense of the poor." Such a theme is prepared by the staff in a pre-workshop, in which all the available literature is studied and methodological questions are dealt with. Then a year-long workshop is set up, in which about forty people participate. These people are mostly grass-roots workers, men and women who live and work with the poor and can offer their observations and experience as sources for reflection. After a year, the results of the workshops are summarized and made available to a larger circle of pastoral workers. Some of the work of the center finds its way into *Páginas,* the widely read monthly magazine edited by Carmen Lora, or in the publications of Centro de Estudios y Publicaciones (CEP), directed by Pedro de Guchtenere.

What is most striking about this center of higher studies is that it stays close to the daily life of the people. It practices theology by reflecting critically on socioeconomic, political, and ecclesiastical events, and by evaluating these events in the light of the Gospel and the teachings of the Church. There is a large library of classical theological sources and documents of past and present events in Church and state. It is clear that these are continually consulted and studied with the concrete problems of the day in mind.

What makes liberation theology so original, challenging, and radical is not so much its conceptual content as its method of working. A true liberation theologian is not just someone who thinks about liberation, but someone whose thought grows out of a life of solidarity with those who are poor and oppressed. The most impressive aspect of the Centro Bartolome de las Casas is that those who come and work there are men and women whose knowledge has grown from an intimate participation in the daily life of the people who struggle for freedom.

Thus the center reveals one of the oldest of truths: that *theologia* is not primarily a way of thinking, but a way of living. Liberation theologians do not think themselves into a new way of living, but live themselves into a new way of thinking.

Wednesday, March 3

This morning I had a pleasant discussion with David Molineau, the new director of *Noticias Aliadas* (Latin American Press). I mentioned to David how impressed I had been with the way the Peruvian people express their faith, their gratitude, their care, their hopes, and their love. I told him that it might be a special task for me to give words to much of the spiritual richness that I saw, but of which the people themselves are hardly aware. David agreed, but added: "Living with the poor not only makes you see the good more clearly, but the evil as well." He told me some stories from his own experience in a Peruvian parish, and illustrated the truth that in a world of poverty, the lines between darkness and light, good and evil, destructiveness and creativity, are much more distinct than in a world of wealth.

One of the temptations of upper-middle-class life is to create large gray areas between good and evil. Wealth takes away the sharp edges of our moral sensitivities and allows a comfortable confusion about sin and virtue. The difference between rich and poor is not that the rich sin more than the poor, but that the rich find it easier to call sin a virtue. When the poor sin, they call it sin; when they see holiness, they identify it as such. This intuitive clarity is often absent from the wealthy, and that absence easily leads to the atrophy of the moral sense.

David helped me see that living with the poor does not keep me away from evil, but it does allow me to see evil in sharper, clearer ways. It does not lead me automatically to the good either, but will help me see good in a brighter light, less hidden and more convincing. Once I can see sin and virtue with this clarity, I will also see sadness and joy, hatred and forgiveness, resentment and gratitude in less nebulous ways.

Thursday, March 4

Not far from the Maryknoll center house is the secretariat of the Latin American section of Pax Romana. This large Catholic student organization is hardly known in the United States, but in Latin America it is one of the most creative and influential forces in recent developments in the Church. Many of the leaders of the liberation theology movement, laymen, laywomen, and priests, received their spiritual formation and inspiration through membership in Pax Romana. For many years, Gustavo Gutiérrez has been the chaplain of UNEC, the Peruvian section of Pax Romana, and layleaders such as Manuel Piqueras, Javier Iguiniz, and Rolando Ames had and still have intimate ties with this Catholic student movement.

I had lunch with the staff today. There were representatives from Brazil, Ecuador, the Dominican Republic, Chile, Spain, and Peru. They told me that I would never understand the meaning and influence of liberation theology without seeing the Catholic student movement as an integral part of its growth. After lunch I talked to Luis Maria Goicoechea, a Basque priest. He told me about the history of Pax Romana, showed me its publication, and gave me some idea of the preparations for the upcoming assembly in Montreal, where the emphasis will be on the poor in the world.

The core of the spirituality of Pax Romana is *La Revisión de Vida*, an ongoing process of evaluation of one's daily life in the light of the Gospel. It is an important discipline that challenges the members to explore how they live out their Christian commitment in the concrete events of each day. The question, "How did I put my life in service of the Kingdom of God today?" invites the active members of the movement (they call themselves *militantes*) to continue to develop, and search for new directions. It is this spiritual flexibility that made it possible for the Latin American Pax Romana to play such a crucial role in the years that followed Vatican II.

Friday, March 5

It is far from easy to be a missioner. One has to live in a different culture, speak a different language, and get used to a different climate, all at great distances from those patterns of life which fit most comfortably. It is not surprising that, for many missioners, life is full of tension, frustration, confusion, anxiety, alienation, and loneliness.

Why do people become missioners? Why do they leave what is familiar and known to live in a milieu that is unfamiliar and unknown? This question has no simple answer. A desire to serve Christ unconditionally, an urge to help the poor, an intellectual interest in another culture, the attraction of adventure, a need to break away from family, a critical insight into the predicament of one's own country, a search for self-affirmation— all these and many other motives can be part of the making of a missioner. Long and arduous formation offers the opportunity for re-alignment and purification of these motives. A sincere desire to work in the service of Jesus Christ and his kingdom should become increasingly central in the mind and heart of a future missioner, although nobody can be expected to be totally altruistic. Not seldom do we come in touch with our hidden drives only after long and hard work in the field. Preparatory formation and training cannot do everything. The issue is not to have perfectly motivated missioners, but missioners who are willing to be purified again and again as they struggle to find their true vocation in life.

The two most damaging motives in the makeup of missioners seem to be guilt and the desire to save. Both form the extremes of a long continuum, both make life in the mission extremely painful. As long as I go to a poor country because I feel guilty about my wealth, whether financial or mental, I am in for a lot of trouble. The problem with guilt is that it is not taken away by work. Hard work for the poor may push my guilt underground for a while, but can never really take it away. Guilt has roots deeper than can be reached through acts of service. On the other hand, the desire to save people from sin, from poverty, or from exploitation can be just as harmful, because the harder one tries the more one is confronted with one's own limitations. Many hardworking men and women have seen the situation getting worse during their missionary career; and if they depended solely on the success of their work, they would quickly lose their sense of self-worth. Although a sense of guilt and a desire to save can be very destructive and depressive for missioners, I do not think that we are ever totally free from either. We feel guilty and we desire to bring about change. These experiences will always play a part in our daily life.

The great challenge, however, is to live and work out of gratitude. The Lord took on our guilt and saved us. In him the Divine work has been accomplished. The human missionary task is to give visibility to the Divine work in the midst of our daily existence. When we can come to realize that our guilt has been taken away and that only God saves, then we are free to serve, then we can live truly humble lives. Clinging to guilt is resisting God's grace, wanting to be a savior, competing with God's own being. Both are forms of idolatry and make missionary work very hard and eventually impossible.

Humility is the real Christian virtue. It means staying close to the ground (*humus*), to people, to everyday life, to what is happening with all its down-to-earthness. It is the virtue that opens our eyes for the presence of God on the earth and allows us to live grateful lives. The poor themselves are the first to help us recognize true humility and gratitude. They can make a receptive missioner a truly happy person.

Saturday, March 6

Today I met Javier Iguiniz. During the last few weeks, I had heard his name mentioned different times, always with great respect and sympathy. Javier is professor of Economics at the Catholic University in Lima, and a very committed and active collaborator of the Centro Bartolome de las Casas. He has known Gustavo Gutiérrez since his years as a student, and has become increasingly involved in the liberation theology movement.

One of the most interesting things Javier said to me was that liberation theology was a way of thinking and working in close relationship with and in obedience to the *movimiento poular*, the movement of the people. He contrasted the individualistic academic world that I come from, characterized by the principles of competition and "publish or perish," with the slow, patient, and communal way of working of the people who meet at the Centro Bartolome de las Casas.

"We are not interested in creating a new theology, we are not trying to confront traditional church structures. We are not hoping for quick radical changes. No, we want to listen carefully and patiently to the movement of the people and slowly identify those elements that lead to progress. We want to work as church participants in an age-old process of living, thinking, celebrating, and worshiping, and then give form and shape to what really belongs to the movement of God's people."

Javier was very aware of the fact that he belonged to the Church, which works slowly and gradually but in which sudden eruptions can make drastic change possible. Such eruptions, although they cannot be organized, need to be recognized, understood, evaluated, and made part of the larger movement of the Church. "We have thousands of ideas, insights, and visions. We talk about them, exchange them, and play with them. Often they seem very significant, but most of them are shelved, usually for many years. A few of these ideas, insights, and visions may later reappear and prove to be substantial. But it can be a long time before we know if we are in touch with something that really belongs to the movement."

Javier showed me—without explicitly saying so—a theology of doing theology. He was extremely critical of "theological heroism." He did not believe in simply publishing all the good ideas that come up. He kept stressing the need for humble, slow, faithful work in obedience to the people who are to be served. He said: "Many of the poor are still very close to the Council of Trent in their spirituality. If we do not understand this, our concern for their liberation cannot be a true Christian service."

Javier was sympathetic to my desire to live with the people, but strongly urged me to continue my academic work. The greatest need, he felt, was not for more pastoral workers but for people who could help articulate, evaluate, systematize, and communicate what is going on in the pastoral field. "We need people who can conceptualize what they live and connect it with the larger tradition of the Church." He warned me against romanticism: "It is quite possible to live with the people without being part of the movement of the people, and that movement you might find as much in the university as in the *barrio*."

My general impression was that Javier did not discourage me in my desire to come to Peru, but he did want to make me aware that the way of doing theology here would require a great faithfulness to the slow-moving Church of the people.

Sunday, March 7

Rose Timothy and Rose Dominique invited me to come to Caja de Agua, a large barrio in the North Zone of Lima where they live. I arrived at 8:00 A.M. and went straight to the rectory. There I met Matias Sienbenaller, the pastor of Caja de Agua and the Vicar of the whole North Zone. Matias is a diocesan priest from Luxembourg who has worked in Lima for the last sixteen years. He is highly respected and admired by many and has been a creative and patient leader since he arrived in Peru.

Matias had not the faintest idea who this poorly-Spanish-speaking stranger was that walked into his house at 8:00 A.M. on Sunday morning. He seemed suspicious in the beginning, and didn't know how to respond. He offered me a cup of coffee and asked many questions. After awhile, he relaxed and showed interest in my search for a vocation in Peru. He said that he had very little time for me at this moment, but invited me to come back and stay with him for a few days so that he could give me a better perspective on the possibilities of coming to Peru. He felt that my experience so far had been far too limited, and that I needed a broader vision to be able to make a responsible decision.

I immediately realized that I had met a man who has much to offer. Since he is a diocesan priest from Europe—as I am—with much experience in Peru, I felt a strong desire to spend more time with him.

Monday, March 8
Cuzco, Peru

During these last weeks, the Maryknollers Michael Briggs and Paul Kavanaugh were staying in the Center house. Both are working in the Altiplano, the high mountain plane around Lake Titicaca, and have come to Lima for their altitude leave, a much-needed time to recuperate from the physical stresses of "high living."

Talking with them has increased my desire to see more of Peru than Lima. They convinced me that to know only Lima would give me a very one-sided impression, not only of Peru, but also of the pastoral work in Peru. Before returning to their missions, Mike and Paul planned to attend a two-week course in Cuzco for all the pastoral workers of the region of the Southern Andes. They invited me to join them.

So this morning we flew from Lima to Cuzco and settled in at the Instituto de Pastoral Andina (the Pastoral Institute of the Andes). Since the course does not start until tomorrow morning, I had the whole day to look around Cuzco. Cuzco is like a precious pearl set in a lovely green valley. The many trees, the fresh pastures, and the green-covered mountains offered a dramatic change from the dry and dusty hills of Pamplona Alta. Set in the pure blue sky, a bright sun threw its light over the small city. The central square of Cuzco is of unusual beauty. The imposing facades of the cathedral and the Church of the Compañia are flanked by pleasant galleries with shops, restaurants, bars, and bookstores.

Paul and I walked around town for a few hours and enjoyed the busy life in this Quechua town. The dark faces of the people, the stores with beautiful Indian handicrafts, the old Inca walls in which huge stones interlock with meticulous precision, and the many memories of the Inca empire all made me aware that Cuzco explains much of the glory and agony of present-day Peru.

In the late afternoon we took a cab to the Indian ruins surrounding the city. We saw the old Inca fortress of Sacsahuamán, the sculpted rock of Quenkko, and the ritual baths of Tambomachay. These solemn and sacred sights in the midst of splendid green mountains gave me the desire to spend some quiet days there meditating on the mystery and misery of human history. I soon realized that the splendid churches in downtown Cuzco were built with the stones from these old Indian temples and fortresses. The main concern of the Spaniards had been to destroy the pagan world and to show triumphantly the victory of the Christian faith. The Indian people were only reluctantly recognized as human beings. It would take centuries to acknowledge their rich spiritual heritage. Only recently has mission come to mean something other than a spiritual conquest.

In Cuzco, all can be seen together: the solemn faces of the Inca gods, the glory and the shame of a Christianity proclaimed with the support of the sword, the living faith of the people who have brought their Indian heritage and their new religion together into a deeply rooted spirituality, and the poverty and oppression of a people that has never fully regained its freedom.

Tuesday, March 9

Rolando Ames, a political scientist at the Catholic University in Lima, is leading the first three days of the course. The lectures are on the *Coyuntura Política-Eclesiástica*, the status of Church and politics in Peru.

In his brilliant lectures, Rolando brought together many of the pieces of information, insight, hearsay, and gossip that I had gathered during the last two months. Many things fell into place. Rolando described the years 1976 to 1978 as the period during which a new revolutionary consciousness developed that affected the whole nation. This new consciousness provided the climate for a new way to preach the gospel and deeply influenced the pastoral work of the Peruvian Church. This period has now passed. Today the Church has to continue to work in a different political climate. With the popular movement no longer as clearly visible, an increasing pragmatism has emerged that makes the poor less militant and the left less clear about its direction.

Rolando affirmed in a concrete way what Xavier told me on Saturday, namely that it is crucial for every pastoral worker to keep in close touch with the political ups and downs of Peru. The problems of 1971 and those of 1982 might look much the same; there is still poverty, malnutrition, lack of educational facilities, poor medical care, and a great need for a more developed knowledge of the Christian faith. Why, then, is there a need to enter into the complexity of daily politics? Rolando's answer is that even when the problems seem the same, the spiritual tone can be very different. The understanding of this tone is essential for the work of a Christian who really wants to serve the people. To ignore the political movements of a country such as Peru is to ignore the realities that determine the hope or despair of the people.

During the past few years, Peru has shifted toward a growing dependence on international capitalism. All the emphasis is on promoting export of those materials that serve the needs of the large transnational corporations. This means less support for local and national enterprises, and thus less work and money for Peruvian workers and companies. Since the transnational corporations don't see any profit coming from capital invested in people's projects (educational, agrarian, or industrial) these "economics" offer little optimism to the people.

How then can we form true communities of hope in the midst of this political reality? That is the question that touches the heart of pastoral care in this country.

Wednesday, March 10

Rolando Ames helped us to identify today the major developments within the Peruvian Church over the last thirty years. In many ways, they reflect the tumultuous events within the Church in all of Latin America.

Three main phases can be distinguished. First of all, the Church distanced itself from the ruling class—or the oligarchy, as it is called in Latin America. Until the fifties, the Latin American Church lived and worked hand in glove with the ruling class. The *haciendas,* where owner and priest were both considered as bosses by those who worked the land, were vivid manifestation of the connection between the Church and the oligarchy. But in 1958, an official church document appeared in which the *orden oligárquico* (rule by oligarchy) was called unjust. It was the first sign of a movement in the Church that called attention to the plight of the poor and oppressed.

In the second phase, the Church moved from a general sympathy for the poor to an active defense of their rights. The Vatican Council had set the tone which made this development possible, but the Conference of the Latin American Bishops in Medellin in 1968 gave it shape. In Medellin, the Church formulated the "preferential option for the poor" and thus defined itself as a Church that supports oppressed people in their struggle for liberation. In many ways, the statements of Medellin went far beyond the psychological state of mind of most of the bishops there present. But the decision by the Church as a body to speak directly and officially in defense of the poor, oppressed, and exploited peoples of Latin America meant the birth of a new Church. By calling the order that causes the rampant injustices "sinful," the Church had committed itself—at least in principle—to the struggle for a new social order.

This radical change in self-definition made the Latin American Church of the seventies a Church drenched by the blood of martyrs. In Argentina, Brazil, Chile, El Salvador, Guatemala, and many other countries, thousands of Christians lost their lives as a consequence of their commitment to this new Church. Although direct persecution did not take place in Peru, the option for the poor has led to many conflicts between the Church and the Peruvian ruling class.

The third phase has just begun, the phase in which an ecclesial counter-reaction is taking shape. During the seventies, the opposition within the Church itself against a new direction had remained dormant. But in the beginning of the eighties, a new and well-organized conservatism that divides the Church into two camps has become visible. One of the preparatory documents for the Latin American Bishops' Conference in Puebla, published in 1979, opened this third phase. The document describes the task of the Church as guiding the unavoidable transition of the Latin American society from a rural to an industrial society. It stressed the necessity of preventing the secularism that resulted from a similar transition in France during the last century, and it pointed to the bishops of Latin America as those who have to secure the faith in this time of change.

Today, the conservative forces in the Church in Peru are well-established. Because the hierarchy can no longer follow one line, the episcopal documents have become compromises between two opposing directions. Whereas, a few years ago, the Peruvian bishops could still issue strongly prophetic statements in the spirit of Medellin, the latest publications of the Peruvian Bishops' Conference show ambiguity, ambivalence, and paralysis.

Rolando showed how hard it will be for many who found their faith in the new church to continue in the struggle and not become discouraged. But he was convinced that the new conservatism is a passing phase to test and purify the new commitment to the poor, from which there is no return.

Friday, March 12

Tonight George-Ann Potter, assistant director of Catholic Relief Services in Peru, invited me to dinner. She also invited Rolando Ramos, a Peruvian priest who works in Amparaes (Calca province). Although I had never met (or even heard of) Rolando, an immediate sense of friendship developed between us. It seemed to me that here was the priest I had been looking for. He combined a deep, contemplative spirit with a strong commitment to service among the poor. He radiated faith in the presence of God among the people, hope for the liberation of the poor, and love for all he meets. Being in his presence felt like being in the presence of a man of God, a pastor and prophet.

Rolando's parish is four hours away from Cuzco. He serves a large group of small villages that can be reached only on horseback or on foot. He lives the life of the poor and participates fully in their daily struggles. He lives this hard life with gladness, because he can see, hear, and touch the Lord in his people and feels deeply grateful for that privilege.

I guess that my joy in knowing Rolando has something to do with my difficulties in relating to the people in the course. I find the participants tough and even harsh. They have so identified themselves with the *lucha* that they permit little space for personal interchange. They are good and honest people, but difficult to get to know. They work diligently, not only in their parishes but also in this course. They are serious, intense, and deeply concerned men and women.

When I met Rolando and experienced his personal warmth, his kindness, and his spiritual freedom, I was suddenly able to come in touch with the feelings of oppression that I myself was experiencing in the course. Rolando invited me to come to his parish and to live with him for as long as I wanted. There I would be able to experience that it was possible to be fully involved in the struggle for the poor while at the same time remaining sensitive to the personal and interpersonal quality of life. That explains my immediate feelings of closeness to him.

Saturday, March 13

For the last few days, the course has dealt primarily with the new agricultural law. A lawyer from Lima came to explain the law, and triggered a lively debate about the way the poor *campesinos* would be affected by it. Most pastoral workers felt that this law was simply one more way in which the poor would be made poorer. The law opened the way for rich people who had lost their land during the agrarian reform to reclaim it. One of the French pastoral workers presented an alternative law that would serve the poor farmer. This law had been formulated by the *campesinos* themselves, with the help of leftist lawyers and economists.

When I reflect on these legal debates and discussions, I become strongly aware of the new style of this liberation-oriented Church. It would have taken an outsider a long time to find out that this was a group of priests, nuns, and Catholic laymen and laywomen dedicated to the preaching of the Gospel. The style of the dialogue, the fervor of the discussions, and the ideological language suggested a meeting of a political party rather than a church group. I feel that this is true not only for the formal sessions, but also for the informal relationships between the participants—during meals and coffee breaks. Yet these men and women from France, Spain, Italy, and the United States have left their countries to serve the poor of Peru in the name of the Lord Jesus Christ. Their religious dedication has led them into the lives of the poor. Therefore the sophisticated and highly critical analysis of the new agrarian law was for them not purely political but a necessary step in the struggle for freedom for the people of God.

Yet two Churches are gradually developing in Peru, and they are at the point where they are no longer able to talk to each other. On the one side is the Church that speaks primarily about God, with little reference to the daily reality in which the people live; on the other side is the Church that speaks primarily about the struggle of the people for freedom, with little reference to the Divine mysteries to which this struggle points. The distance between these Churches is growing. This morning I went to the Cathedral of Cuzco, and when I walked from altar to altar and statue to statue and listened to the monotone voice of a priest saying Mass, I suddenly felt a deep pain. I would never feel at home any more in this traditional Church, but will I ever in the Church of the *lucha*?

Sunday, March 14

George-Ann Potter and her guest, Anne Lise Timmerman, vice-president of Caritas in Denmark, invited me to join them on a trip to the sacred valley of the Incas.

The majestic beauty of this valley impressed me; the Urubamba River, surrounded by fertile cornfields and green-covered mountain ranges, filled me with awe. Along the road small groups of Indians guiding cattle carried their loads of wood. These small, dark, silent people with faces carved by nature and hard work evoked in me a sense of the sacred.

In their silence, they spoke of centuries of care for the land, of a mysterious intimacy with nature, of an unceasing prayer to the God who has made their land fertile, and of a knowledge that we in our Volkswagen would never be able to grasp. The valley was filled with a holy silence: no advertisements along the roads, no factories or modern houses, no loudspeakers or shouting vendors. Even the busy market of the little town of Pisac seemed covered with this sacred quietness.

We bought a few artifacts in the marketplace, attended Mass in the Pisac Church, and visited an agricultural school for *campesinos*. We talked about all sorts of things, had a pleasant dinner, and struggled for an hour to change a tire. But none of our activity could disturb the sacred silence of this valley of the Incas. When we came back to Cuzco I felt refreshed, renewed, and grateful to the Indian people for this healing gift of silence.

Monday, March 15

Today the last part of the course began. After three days about the political and ecclesial state of affairs in Peru, and two days about the new agrarian law and its possible alternatives, the emphasis now shifts to a spirituality of liberation. Gustavo Gutiérrez flew into Cuzco from Lima this morning, and will be our guide in a four-day workshop. Just as in the summer course in Lima, Gustavo's presence had a vitalizing effect. Many of us showed signs of fatigue after six days of intense discussions, but Gustavo unleashed new energies and engendered new enthusiasm.

Two ideas in Gustavo's presentations impressed me deeply. The first focused on the Gospel terms, which have passed through the filter of individualism and thus have been spiritualized and sentimentalized. The word "poor" has come to mean "humble," the word "rich," "proud." Terms like "the children," "the blind," "the sinner" have lost their historical meaning and have been "translated" into ahistorical, asocial and apolitical words. Thus, "child," which in the New Testament refers to an insignificant, marginal, and oppressed human being, has become an expression for simplicity, innocence, and spontaneity. Jesus' call to become "like children" has been passed through the filter of individualism and has thus been romanticized.

This explains how the idea of a spiritual combat has lost its social, political, and economic quality and now refers only to an inner struggle. Gustavo showed us an example of how the Magnificat is mostly read in a very individualistic way and has lost its radical, social dimensions in the minds of most contemporary Christians. In the Magnificat, Mary proclaims: "[The Lord God] has shown the strength of his arm, he has scattered the proud in their conceit. He has cast down the mighty from their thrones and has lifted up the lowly." These words have a concrete historical, socio-economic, and political meaning; the interpretations that relate these words exclusively to the inner life of pride and humility rob them of their real power.

A second idea that touched me in Gustavo's presentation was that affection, tenderness, solitude are not to be rejected by those who struggle for the freedom of the people. There is a danger that these important realities of the Christian life are considered by the "revolutionaries" as soft and useless for the struggle. But Gustavo made it clear that love for the people is essential for a true Christian revolution. Those who do not value tenderness and gentleness will eventually lose their commitment to the struggle for liberation.

This observation was extremely important to me, especially in the context of my earlier feelings about the participants in this course. Someone mentioned to me that "new fighters" in the struggle for liberation often are tense, harsh, and unfeeling, but that those who have been in the struggle for a long time are gentle, caring, and affectionate people who have been able to integrate the most personal with the most social. Gustavo himself is certainly an "old fighter."

Tuesday, March 16

Today Gustavo showed how the eruption of the poor has dramatic implications for our spirituality. The new and concrete pastoral concerns that came out of the involvement with the poor have dramatically challenged the traditional ways of living the spiritual life. But those who have gone through this crisis and tasted it to the full have also come to realize that, even though the experience of a break with the past remains a reality, so too does continuity. In fact, as Gustavo remarked, the full immersion in the struggle makes us rediscover the basic spiritual values that also undergirded the "old-fashioned" seminary spirituality. Humility, faithfulness, obedience, purity—these and many other traditional values are being rediscovered in the midst of the work with the poor.

One example of this rediscovery of traditional values is the renewed understanding of humility. In the spirituality of the past there was little place for conflict; but anyone who really becomes involved in the daily lives and struggles of the poor cannot avoid moments and periods of conflict. Experiences of abandonment, despair, and deep anguish can enter into the spiritual life itself. It can even lead to a struggle and confrontation with God, who does not seem to make his presence known. Thus a spirituality marked by the struggle for liberation can lead to an experience of deep darkness, which will require true humility. It is this humility that enables us to continue in the struggle, even when we see little progress, to be faithful even when we experience only darkness, to stay with the people even when we ourselves feel abandoned.

I am moved by this new understanding of humility, precisely because it is so old! It has deep connections with the humility of Jeremiah, who confronts God in the midst of his confusion, and with the humility of John of the Cross, who stays faithful in the darkness. Thus the new spirituality of liberation opens us to the mystical life as an essential part of the pastoral task given to us by the people themselves.

Wednesday, March 17

After lunch, I had an opportunity to spend some time with Gustavo Gutiérrez and to ask his advice about a possible long stay in Peru. He was extremely concrete in his advice. He said that it would be a good thing for me to come to Peru for a long time, live in a parish in Lima, do some pastoral work, get to know as much as possible the pastoral people of the city, and join a theological reflection group in the Centro Bartolome de las Casas. In many ways, his suggestions were similar to those of Xavier Iguiniz and Rolando Ames.

I feel far from making a decision of this nature. The many shifts in my emotions and my feelings of being a lonely bystander indicate that this is not the right time to accept Gustavo's invitation.

I am happy that I do not have to decide now, and that I can take more time to let things develop in me. It probably will be a gradual process of discernment. I will be at home here only when I experience my stay as a vocation, a call from God, and from the people. At this moment, the call is not clear. I will have to bring my search more directly into the presence of God and pray more fervently for light.

Thursday, March 18

Yesterday I read the so-called Santa Fe document. It is an analysis written in 1980 by a group of Latin American experts of the Republican Party, to formulate the new policy for the United States towards Latin America in anticipation of Ronald Reagan's presidency.

The third proposition of the second part reads: "The foreign policy of the United States must start to confront (and not simply respond after the facts) the theology of liberation as it is used in Latin America by the clergy of the 'liberation theology'."

This proposition is clarified by the following explanation:

> In Latin America, the role of the Church is vital for the concept of political freedom. Regrettably, the Marxist-Leninist forces have used the Church as a political weapon against private property and the capitalist system of production, by infiltrating the religious community with ideas which are more Communist than Christian (Translated from the French publication *Dial: diffusion de l'information sur l'Amérique Latine*, January 28, 1982).

Although these words show a lack of understanding of liberation theology, they disclose that those who were setting the guidelines for the greatest power in the world consider theology a real threat. The simple fact that theology is taken that seriously by people whose primary concern is to obtain and maintain first place among all the powers of the world is among the greatest compliments to theology I have ever heard.

There is a little man in Peru, a man without any power, who lives in a *barrio* with poor people and who wrote a book. In this book he simply reclaimed the basic Christian truth that God became human to bring good news to the poor, new light to the blind, and liberty to the captives. Ten years later this book and the movement it started are considered dangerous by the greatest power on earth. When I look at this little man, Gustavo, and think about the tall Ronald Reagan, I see David standing before Goliath again with no more weapon than a little stone, called *A Theology of Liberation*.

Friday, March 19

The Cuzco course is over. Last night we celebrated the Eucharist together in a way I will never forget. It was a celebration in which all the joys and the pains of the struggle for the liberation of the poor were brought together and lifted up together with the bread and the wine as a sacrifice of praise. It was a powerful spiritual experience, serious yet glad, realistic yet hopeful, very militant yet peaceful. It was for me the most prayerful moment of the course.

During his last presentation, Gustavo made an interesting observation. He remarked that the Christians of Latin America had passed from a traditional to a revolutionary understanding of their faith without going through a modernistic phase. One person in whom this process could be seen was Archbishop Oscar Romero of El Salvador. This traditional churchman became a true revolutionary through his direct contact with the suffering people without ever rejecting or even criticizing his traditional past. In fact, his traditional understanding of God's presence in history was the basis and source of his courageous protest against the exploitation and oppression of the people in El Salvador. What is true of Bishop Romero is true of most Latin American Christians who joined the movement for liberation. Their traditional understanding of the teachings of the Church was never a hindrance to their conversion. On the contrary, it was the basis for change.

Here we see an important difference between the Latin American situation and the situation in Western Europe and in some parts of the United States. Latin America did not go through a stage of secularization. In Europe, many liberation movements have an antireligious, antichurch, and anticlerical character. That is not the case today in Latin America. Most people who have joined liberation movements in Latin America are deeply believing Christians who look to the Church for guidance and support. Many Europeans who come to Latin America to know more about the people's movement for liberation are surprised and often impressed by the Christian commitment they encounter in the revolutionaries with whom they speak. Europeans often feel that the Church has lost credibility and relevance in the struggle for a new world. But here they discover that the Church is one of the main sources of inspiration in the struggle.

The closing Eucharist of the course made this clear to me. The texts of Scripture, the prayers of petition and thanks, the offering of the gifts, the sharing of the bread and the cup, and the hymns of praise were an integral part of all that had been said during the last two weeks. The Eucharist was not tacked on to the course because all the participants were Christians. No, the Eucharist was the most powerful and the most radical expression of what this whole course was about. It became a powerful call to go out again and continue in the struggle of the people of God.

Saturday, March 20

Now that the course is finished, I am living with my Lutheran friends John and Kathy Goldstein in Cuzco.

It is wonderful to stay with friends in a "homey" house, to have a good bed, good conversation, and free time to write, to play with John and Kathy's five-week-old son, Peter Isaac, and to make little trips to the center of Cuzco. The difference between the intense atmosphere at the Pastoral Institute and the relaxed and friendly family atmosphere in the Goldstein's home has really struck me. It is the difference between quick meals on long tables with eighty people and leisurely meals around the kitchen table, between introducing yourself every moment to a new person and being in a familiar place, between always talking about Church and society and talking about the little things of daily life, between the hectic eagerness of celibates and the sustained concern of a father and a mother for their newborn child. All these differences make me very glad to be with my friends and to take it easy for a while.

Monday, March 22

During the last few days, I have been deeply disturbed by the news of the murder of four fellow Dutchmen in El Salvador. Koos Koster, Hans Lodewijk, Jan Kornelius Kuiper, and Johannes Willemsen were members of a Dutch television team sent to El Salvador to report on the political situation in the weeks before the elections. The radio mentions the official explanation of the Salvadoran government, which says that the four Dutchmen were caught in a crossfire between government troops and guerrilla fighters. The radio also mentions that another Dutch reporter refutes this explanation and says that the four were murdered by a military unit.

The Peruvian paper *El Diario* gives a detailed report of the murders. It says that the four Dutchmen had just finished their work and were on the way to the airport of Lloapango in their car, loaded with equipment and just-finished films. Near the detour of Santa Rosa, before the turn to Chalatenango, they were intercepted by a military truck. A group of soldiers of the fourth brigade of the infantry forced the four Dutchmen to board their truck, hitting them with the butts of their rifles. A little further, the prisoners were let out and machine-gunned down with total disregard for the astonished guides who accompanied the four Dutchmen and the people who witnessed the murder from the surrounding thicket. When the soldiers arrived in the *cuartel* of El Paisnal with the four bodies, they reported to their superiors. All the cameras, as well as films showing the daily agony of the Salvadoran people, were immediately destroyed.

In a long analysis of the murders, *El Diario* is of the opinion that "the Argentinian Colonels, who offer their intelligence service to the armed forces of El

Salvador could finally rest since they had finished a hunt that had started nine years ago." With the help of Anibal Aguilar Penarrieta, the president of the Association of Lawyers for Human Rights in Bolivia, *El Diario* was able to reconstruct the journeys through Latin America of the Dutch television team during the last decade. Koos Koster was in Chile during the 1973 coup of General Augusto Pinochet and made an extraordinary film of the attack on the Palace de la Moneda, where President Salvador Allende died. During 1973, 1974, and 1975, Koster was in Peru with his colleagues and made films about the life of the *campesinos*. Later the team came to Argentina, where they made the best available documentary about the thirty thousand "disappeared ones" and the mothers of the Plaza de Mayo. When their shocking film appeared on European television, the Argentinian military started to look for an opportunity to kill them, according to *El Diario*. In 1980, the television crew was in Bolivia documenting the violations of human rights during the military occupation of the Bolivian tin mines. They also revealed the role of Argentina in the Bolivian coups of Garcia Meza and Arce Gomez. But when Arce Gomez ordered their arrest, they had already left Bolivia.

A few weeks ago, *El Diario* says the head of the Salvadoran armed forces traveled to Argentina to work out a plan for selective terrorism. Part of the conversation is supposed to have dealt with the way to eliminate the Dutch reporters in El Salvador. The plan was to authorize the Dutchmen to travel to the interior of El Salvador and to give them apparent freedom of movement. Then they would be arrested under the pretense that their names were found as contact persons on the dead body of a guerrilla fighter. *El Diario* concludes: "With this puerile proof the execution did not have to be delayed long and on the 17th of March they fell, in the same month that two years ago Bishop Oscar Arnulfo Romero was assassinated."

This tragedy has made Holland suffer with the poor and oppressed people of Central America. I hope and pray that this painful compassion will bring the people of El Salvador at least one step closer to peace.

Tuesday, March 23

This is my last day in Cuzco. John, Kathy, and I made a trip to the splendid Inca ruins in the area and to some churches and a museum in town. More than ever before, I was impressed by the majestic beauty of the buildings of the Inca Empire. The gigantic temples, the watchposts, and ritual baths were the work of a people guided by the rule, "Do not lie, do not steal, and do not be lazy," and inspired by a powerful devotion to the Sun God and many other divinities. But, more than before, I was stunned by the total insensitivity of the Spanish conquerors to the culture and religion they found here.

It suddenly hit me how radical Gustavo Gutiérrez's liberation theology really is, because it is a theology that starts with the people and wants to recognize the deep spirituality of the Indians who live in this land. How different from what we saw today on our trip. There we witnessed a centuries-long disregard for any Indian religiosity, and a violent destruction of all that could possibly be a reminder of the Inca Gods. What an incredible pretention, what a cruelty, what a sacrilegious sin committed by people who claimed to come in the name of a God of forgiveness, love, and peace.

I wished I had the time to spend a whole day just sitting on the ruins of Sacsahuamán. These temple ruins overlooking the city of Cuzco, with its many churches built from its stones, make me ask the God of the sun, the moon, the stars, the rainbow, the lightening, the land, and the water to forgive what Christians did in his name.

Maybe the new spirituality of liberation is a creative form of repentance for the sins of our fathers. And I should not forget that these sins are closer to my own heart than I often want to confess. Some form of spiritual colonialism remains a constant temptation.

Wednesday, March 24
Lima, Peru

Today I flew back from Cuzco to Lima. I arrived just in time to commemorate the second anniversary of the martyrdom of Archbishop Oscar Romero of El Salvador. Since his death, tens of thousands of other Salvadorans have been murdered. They are the anonymous martyrs of our day. They are men and women who were killed because, in some way or another, they witnessed for freedom, human dignity, and a new society.

Often we think of martyrs as people who died in defense of their consciously professed faith, but Jesus' words, "What you did for the least of mine, you did for me," point to a true martyrdom in the service of God's people.

In a strange way, I am grateful that it is not only poor anonymous people who are losing their lives, but also well-known churchmen and churchwomen. The death of people like Bishop Romero allows us to lift up the martyrdoms of thousands of unknown *campesinos*, catechists, youth leaders, teachers, priests, and guerrilla fighters, and to make them fruitful for the whole Christian community in Latin America. Bishop Romero's solidarity in death with the poor and oppressed of his country makes him a true bishop, not only in life, but also in death.

We celebrated Bishop Romero's death in the Church of Ciudad de Dios. I am increasingly impressed by the Christian possibility of celebrating not only moments of joy but also moments of pain, thus affirming God's real presence in the thick of our lives. A true Christian always affirms life, because God is the God of life, a life stronger than death and destruction. In him we find no reason to despair. There is always reason to hope, even when our eyes are filled with tears.

Many priests of the southern part of Lima joined Bishop Herman Schmidt in the celebration of the Eucharist. It was good to be back in these now-familiar surroundings. Many parishioners came up to me to express their joy at seeing me again after a few weeks of absence. I felt consoled by those whom I had known only for a short time. This mysterious experience in which grief and joy, gladness and sadness merged brought me to a new understanding of the unity of the death and resurrection of Christ.

Thursday, March 25

John Goldstein had asked me to take a letter to Troy Baretta, the coordinator of the ministry of the Lutheran Church in America (LCA) in Peru. John and Kathy had already made me aware of how hard it is for Protestant missionaries to live and work in Peru. In the beginning of this century, Protestants were still outlawed, and the history of Protestantism shows periods of harsh persecution. Under the influence of a greater religious tolerance in the western world, and of a greater appreciation of the Protestant churches by the Second Vatican Council, outright persecution has stopped and some creative ecumenical dialogue has started. But from my own impressions, it seems that many Catholics have remained suspicious of Protestants, and some even overtly hostile toward them.

Such anti-Protestantism is partly understandable. Most priests have had disturbing experiences with different fundamentalist sects which are known for their fierce anti-Catholic preaching and for their divisive practices. Various evangelical sects—Jehovah's Witnesses, Mormons, Israelites, and similar groups—tend to create divisions between people, arouse an atmosphere of suspicion towards Catholics, and isolate people from their natural bonds with their relatives and friends. The great proliferation of these sometimes fanatic sects has certainly not built an ecumenical atmosphere between Catholics and Protestants.

But this being the case, there remains the fact that Protestantism has as much "right" to be in Peru as Catholicism and that there is, in fact, a relatively large, well-established Peruvian Protestant community. I am shocked by the argument that Catholicism is so much a part of the Peruvian culture that Protestantism, even in its most orthodox forms, can be seen only as robbing people of their own heritage. In the light of the way in which the Spanish destroyed the Indian cultures in Peru and imposed their religion on the people with the force of weapons—and this less than four hundred years ago—it seems quite preposterous to consider Protestantism a threat to the Peruvian culture. Moveover, the historic Catholic missionaries have never hesitated to evangelize alien cultures and to bring the Gospel to people from whom accepting the Good News of Jesus required a radical break with their traditions and customs. The history of the missions to China, Japan, and other well-integrated cultures shows clearly that cultural integrity has certainly not been the main concern of Catholic evangelizers in the past.

My discussions with John and Kathy, with Troy and Anne, and with many other Protestant missionaries from mainline denominations (Lutherans, Methodists, and Episcopalians) in Latin America have convinced me of the urgent need for a new ecumenism in the area of mission and for a much greater humility on the part of Catholics in their relationship with their Protestant brothers and sisters. It seems that there are now enough people on both sides who are open and ready for a creative collaboration.

Friday, March 26

This proved to be a very important day for me. As I had planned before going to Cuzco, I met again with Matias Sienbenaller, the Luxembourgian priest who is pastor in Caja de Agua, one of Lima's *barrios*. This morning as we talked I felt that many pieces of my puzzle began to come together.

I explained to Matias my dream about living among the people, praying with and for them, visiting them in their homes, offering days of retreat and recollection, and gradually helping them to articulate their own spiritual gifts. I asked him if he felt there was a place for me in Peru, how to relate all this to my past in Holland and the United States, and in which way to envision my future. I also shared with him my feelings about the clericalism in Peru, my need for a supportive community, and my search for ways to live a somewhat structured spiritual life with others.

Matias responded with great warmth and concrete suggestions. He gave me a true sense of being called. He offered his own parish as a good place to try out what I was dreaming about. There is a good pastoral team that would offer support, encouragement, and constructive criticism; there is a daily life of communal prayer in the "rectory," a friendly home, and a strong spirit of working together. Moreover, the *barrio* Caja de Agua is close to the center of town and would make it easy to work closely with the people of Centro Bartolome de las Casas and to keep in touch with other pastoral events in town. Important for me was Matias's insistence that I not cut off from all contact with the academic world in the United States. While he stressed that I should commit myself firmly to the Peruvian Church and be willing to work in the service of that Church, he also felt that it would be good to continue to communicate through writing and lecturing to the world from which I come. He therefore encouraged me to stay in touch with the places of theological formation in the States. Some part-time teaching there might be good for me, for the Church in Peru, and for students in the United States. Finally, we talked a little about introductions to the Cardinal of Lima, letters of recommendation, time schedules, and other such things.

It was quite a morning. Just three days before my return to the United States, an appealing, clear, and convincing vocation has started to take form. Many of the things Matias proposed had a certain obviousness to me. The more I thought about them during the day, the more I felt that things fit very well and that I have as much clarity and certainty as I probably will ever have.

I now have to return to my friends in the States and to my bishop in Holland to ask for their responses and advice. Then I should soon be able to make a decision that has a solid basis and that is, I hope, not just an expression of my own will.

Saturday, March 27

My discussion with Matias gave me a sense of closure. My stay in Peru is coming to an end, my impressions of ministry in Peru are starting to show patterns and my future plans are slowly taking some identifiable shape.

As I walked through Lima today, I had the strong sense that this city would become an important place for me in the future. I felt the desire to pray in this city at the different holy places and to ask God's guidance for my future. So I decided to go to the Church of the Lord of the Miracles. I still have vivid memories of my first Sunday in Peru, when I joined the crowd on the Plaza de Armas to welcome the procession of the Lord of the Miracles. This time I had a chance to see the painting on the main altar of the Church. Many people, young and old, men and women, were praying and I felt grateful that I could be there with them. As I looked up to the painting of the crucified Lord and felt the deep devotion of the people surrounding me, I had the feeling of being accepted in Peru. This, indeed, could become my country, my home, my church, and these people could become my fellow Christians, my friends, and my co-workers in the ministry. As my thoughts wandered to the future, I saw myself coming to this Church many times, asking the Lord of the Miracles to bless the people, to give me strength and courage, and to fill me with a spirit of joy and peace.

I also visited the house of St. Rose of Lima, observing where she lived her harsh and ascetic life, and the Church of La Merced, where the Cross of Pedro Urrarte is venerated. The streets and churches of Lima were all filled with people. I felt embraced by a welcoming city, and enjoyed just being carried along from place to place by the crowds. I did not feel like a stranger anymore. I felt more like a guest who was being invited to stay longer. My prayers became part of the murmuring sounds of the thousands who paraded through the streets and in and out of the churches. There was a sense of harmony, of belonging, yes, maybe even of vocation. To find that vocation, I had to come to Peru.

Sunday, March 28

Today during the Eucharist, we read in the letter to the Hebrews: "In the days when [Christ] was in the flesh, he offered prayers and supplications with loud cries and tears to God, who was able to save him from death, and he was heard because of his reverence. Son though he was, he learned obedience from what he suffered; and when perfected, he became the source of eternal salvation for all who obey him" (Heb. 5:7–9).

Jesus learned obedience from what he suffered. This means that the pains and struggles of which Jesus became part made him listen more perfectly to God. In and through his sufferings, he came to know God and could respond to his call. Maybe there are no better words than these to summarize the meaning of the option for the poor. Entering into the suffering of the poor is the way to become obedient, that is, a listener to God. Suffering accepted and shared in love breaks down our selfish defenses and sets us free to accept God's guidance.

After my stay in Bolivia and Peru I think that I have seen, heard, and even tasted the reality of this theology. For me it is no longer an abstract concept. My time with Sophia, Pablo, and their children was an experience that gave me a glimpse of true obedience. Living, working, and playing with them brought me close to a knowledge of God that I had not experienced anywhere before.

But do I really want to know the Lord? Do I really want to listen to him? Do I really want to take up my cross and follow him? Do I really want to dedicate myself to unconditional service?

I look forward to going home tomorrow, to sitting in a comfortable airplane. I like to be welcomed home by friends. I look forward to being back again in my cozy apartment, with my books, my paintings, and my plants. I like showers with hot water, faucets with water you can drink, washing machines that work, and lamps that keep burning. I like cleanliness. But is it there that I will find God? I look forward to being back at the Trappist monastery in upstate New York, to feeling the gentle silence of the contemplative life, singing the psalmodies in the choir, and celebrating the Eucharist with all the monks in the Abbey church. I look forward to walking again in the spacious fields of the Genesee Valley and driving through the woods of Letchworth Park. But is it there that I will find God? Or is he in this dusty, dry, cloud-covered city of Lima, in this confusing, unplanned, and often chaotic conglomeration of people, dogs, and houses? Is he perhaps where the hungry kids play, the old ladies beg, and the shoeshine boys pick your pocket?

I surely have to be where he is. I have to become obedient to him, listen to his voice, and follow him wherever he calls me. Even when I do not like it, even when it is not a way of cleanliness or comfort. Jesus said to Peter: "When you were young you put on your own belt and walked where you liked; but when you grow old you will stretch out your hands, and somebody else will put a belt round you and take you where you would rather not go" (John 21:18). Am I old enough now to be led by the poor, disorganized, unclean, hungry, and uneducated?

Monday, March 29

I am at the Lima airport. It is close to midnight. My flight is leaving at 1:00 A.M. At 6:30 A.M. I will be in Miami, at 10:15 A.M. in Washington, D.C., and at 2:05 P.M. in Rochester, New York. If all goes well, I will be at the Abbey around 3:30 P.M., just in time to celebrate the Eucharist with the monks. It is hard for me to comprehend this huge step from a restless airport in Peru to the restful monastery in upstate New York. My mind cannot yet do what the plane will do.

I feel grateful, deeply grateful. George-Ann Potter and her friend, Stephanie, came to the Maryknoll Center house to say good-bye. That meant a lot to me. We decided to have a little farewell party in a nearby restaurant. John and Cheryl

Hassan, Larry Rich, Betty-Ann Donnelly, and Phil Polaski, Maryknoll lay missioners who happened to be at the Center house, joined in the celebration.

Just before we left the house, the city lights went out. We found our way to the restaurant in the pitch dark and sat around a large table with a candle in the middle. It felt like a mysterious conspiracy of friends.

This spontaneous last-minute get-together was a significant conclusion to my journey that started six months ago. It was as if these good friends were telling me, without planning to do so, that it would be possible to feel truly at home in Peru, to have good friends, to pray together, to share experiences and hopes, and to work in unity for the Kingdom of God. I felt a stronger bond with this small group of people huddled around the candle than I had felt with any other group during my stay in Peru. It felt as if these friends were answering the question that had occupied me during most of my stay here: Will there be a community in Peru that can give me a sense of belonging? Nobody in the casual, unpretentious, and unplanned gathering talked about community, at-homeness, or a sense of belonging, but to me all those present spoke a language that maybe only I could fully interpret. It was in that language that I heard a true invitation to return.

It is midnight now. The plane from Buenos Aires and Santiago has just arrived. I am eager to get on board and head north; but I am also aware that something has happened to me. I sit here and wonder if going north still means going home.

CONCLUSION
A Call to Be Grateful

∎

THE TITLE of this journal summarizes what I found, learned, and heard. The word that I kept hearing, wherever I went, was: *Gracias!* It sounded like the refrain from a long ballad of events. *Gracias a usted, gracias a Dios, muchas gracias*—thank you, thanks be to God, many thanks! I saw thousands of poor and hungry children, I met many young men and women without money, a job, or a decent place to live. I spent long hours with sick, elderly people, and I witnessed more misery and pain than ever before in my life. But, in the midst of it all, that word lifted me again and again to a new realm of seeing and hearing: "*Gracias!* Thanks!"

In many of the families I visited nothing was certain, nothing predictable, nothing totally safe. Maybe there would be food tomorrow, maybe there would be work tomorrow, maybe there would be peace tomorrow. Maybe, maybe not. But whatever is given—money, food, work, a handshake, a smile, a good word, or an embrace—is a reason to rejoice and say *gracias*. What I claim as a right, my friends in Bolivia and Peru received as a gift; what is obvious to me was a joyful surprise to them; what I take for granted, they celebrate in thanksgiving; what for me goes by unnoticed became for them a new occasion to say thanks.

And slowly I learned. I learned what I must have forgotten somewhere in my busy, well-planned, and very "useful" life. I learned that everything that is, is freely given by the God of love. All is grace. Light and water, shelter and food, work and free time, children, parents and grandparents, birth and death—it is all given to us. Why? So that we can say *gracias*, thanks: thanks to God, thanks to each other, thanks to all and everyone.

More than anything else, I learned to say thanks. The familiar expression "let us say grace" now means something very different than saying a few prayers before a meal. It now means lifting up the whole of life into the presence of God and all his people in gratitude.

As I was trying to find an answer to the question: "Does God call me to live and work in Latin America?" I gradually realized that the word *"gracias"* that came from the lips of the people contained the answer. After many centuries of missionary work during which we, the people of the north, tried to give them, the people of the south, what we felt they needed, we have now come to realize that our very first vocation is to receive their gifts to us and say thanks. A treasure lies hidden in the soul of Latin America, a spiritual treasure to be recognized as a gift for us who live in the illusion of power and self-control. It is the treasure of gratitude that can help us to break through the walls of our individual and collective self-righteousness and can prevent us from destroying ourselves and our planet in the futile attempt to hold onto what we consider our own. If I have any vocation in Latin America, it is the vocation to receive from the people the gifts they have to offer us and to bring these gifts back up north for our own conversion and healing. The Maryknoll community in Peru speaks about "reverse mission," suggesting that the movement God wants us to learn is the movement from the south to the north. In the Latin America where countless martyrs have made the suffering Christ visible, a voice that we need to hear more than ever cries out. That voice calls us anew to know with heart and mind that all that is, is given to us as a gift of love, a gift that calls us to make our life into an unceasing act of gratitude.

THE ROAD
TO DAYBREAK

A Spiritual Journey

∎

ACKNOWLEDGMENTS

■

THIS JOURNAL could make it to publication only with the help of many friends. With much gratitude I mention their names.

During the time of writing, Peter Weiskel, who worked for me in Cambridge, Massachusetts, did the first editing on the hand-written text. Margaret Studier spent many hours typing, and Phil Zaeder gave much attention to the use of good English.

When I moved to Canada in August 1986 and decided to condense the long text into a readable book, Richard White offered his assistance in deciding which entries could form the core of a book and which could be deleted. He worked several months to discern the main direction of the seven-hundred-page manuscript by carefully evaluating the various entries.

During the last phase of the work, Michael Plante helped me to put the already condensed text into final form. During that period, Sue Mosteller and Michael Harank offered many suggestions for deletions, additions, and revisions. Connie Ellis, my secretary at Daybreak, was of invaluable help in retyping the whole text, asking permission of different people to publish entries in which their story was told and encouraging me to keep believing in the significance of this journal.

To all these friends I am deeply grateful. Their skillful assistance, their generosity in giving me their time and attention, and their personal interest made it possible to move from a seemingly unmanageable stack of papers to a text that could be presented to Bob Heller, my editor at Doubleday. If ever a personal journal was the result of many people's work, it is *The Road to Daybreak*. I would like the reader of this book to know this and thus share in my gratitude.

CONTENTS

∎

PROLOGUE

■

IN THE LATE SEVENTIES, when I was on the faculty of Yale Divinity School, someone paid me a visit that would radically change my life. At the time it seemed like an uneventful and even inconsequential visit. But as the years went by I started to see it as a response to my prayer: "Lord, show me where you want me to go, and I will follow you."

And so it is that I begin this book with the story of this seemingly unimportant visit. One afternoon the bell of my New Haven apartment rang and a young woman stood at my door. She said, "I am Jan Risse and come to bring you greetings from Jean Vanier." I had heard about Jean Vanier and the L'Arche community for mentally handicapped people, but I had never met him, spoken to him, written him, or been in touch with his work. So I was quite surprised by these greetings and said, "Well, thank you . . . what can I do for you?" She said, "Oh . . . nothing. I just came to bring you the greetings of Jean Vanier." "Yes, I understand," I said, "but I guess you have another reason for your visit." But she insisted, "No, no. I just came to bring you greetings from Jean." It was hard for me to hear her. I kept thinking that her greetings were but the introduction to a request to give a lecture, a retreat, or a sermon or to write an article or a book. Convinced that her bringing greetings wasn't all she came for, I tried once more: "I appreciate hearing from Jean Vanier, but is there anything I can do for you?"

She smiled and said, "Well, can I come in?" I realized then that I hadn't shown much hospitality and said hastily, "Sure, sure, come in . . . but I have to leave soon because I have many appointments at the school." "Oh, you just go ahead," she replied, "and I will spend some quiet time here until you return."

When I returned that evening, I found my table set with a beautiful linen cloth, nice plates and silverware, flowers, a burning candle, and a bottle of wine. I asked, "What is this?" Jan laughed. "Oh, I thought I'd make you a nice meal." "But where did you find all these things?" I asked. She looked at me with a funny expression and said, "In your own kitchen and cupboards . . . you obviously don't use them too often!" It then dawned on me that something unique was happening. A stranger had walked into my home and, without asking me for anything, was showing me my own house.

Jan stayed for a few days and did many more things for me. Then, when she left, she said, "Just remember, Jean Vanier sends his greetings to you." A few years went by. I had completely forgotten about Jan's visit. Then one morning Jean Vanier called and said, "I am making a short silent retreat in Chicago. Would you like to join me?" Again, for a moment, I thought he wanted me to give a talk there. But he insisted. "Henri, it is a *silent* retreat. We can just be together and pray."

Thus Jean and I met. In silence. We spoke a bit, but very little. In the years that followed, I made two visits to his community in France. During my second visit I made a thirty-day retreat and gradually came to the realization that Jan Risse's visit had been the first of a series of events in which Jesus was responding to my prayer to follow him more fully.

But the years between Jan Risse's visit and my decision to become part of L'Arche were tumultuous and full of anxious searching. After ten years at Yale, I felt a deep desire to return to a more basic ministry. My trips to Latin America had set in motion the thought that I might be called to spend the rest of my life among the poor of Bolivia or Peru. So in 1981 I resigned from my teaching position at Yale and went to Bolivia to learn Spanish and to Peru to experience the life of a priest among the poor. My months there were so intense that I decided to keep a journal, which was later published under the title *¡Gracias!* I sincerely tried to discern whether living among the poor in Latin America was the direction to go. Slowly and painfully, I discovered that my spiritual ambitions were different from God's will for me. I had to face the fact that I wasn't capable of doing the work of a missioner in a Spanish-speaking country, that I needed more emotional support than my fellow missioners could offer, that the hard struggle for justice often left me discouraged and dispirited, and that the great variety of tasks and obligations took away my inner composure. It was hard to hear my friends say that I could do more for the South in the North than in the South and that my ability to speak and write was more useful among university students than among the poor. It became quite clear to me that idealism, good intentions, and a desire to serve the poor do not make up a vocation. One needs to be called and sent. The poor of Latin America had not called me; the Christian community had not sent me. My experience in Bolivia and Peru had been very fruitful, but its fruits were not the ones I had expected.

About that time Harvard Divinity School invited me to join their faculty to teach christian spirituality with a special emphasis on the spiritual aspects of liberation theology. I accepted with the conviction that I was called to a "reverse mission," a mission from the South to the North, and that in this way I could realize my desire to serve the church in Latin America. But I soon realized that the students had a greater need for spiritual formation than for information about the burning issues of the Latin American Church, and so my teaching quickly moved to more general areas of the spiritual life. Thus I found myself doing what I had done at Yale, only on a larger scale. Gradually I discovered that Harvard was not the place where I was called to follow Jesus in a more radical way; I was not really happy there, found myself somewhat sulky and complaining, and never felt fully accepted by the faculty or students. The signs were clear that I still had not found the way. In the midst of all my doubts and uncertainties, the voices of Jan Risse, Jean Vanier, and L'Arche gained in strength. When I visited the L'Arche community in France I experienced a sense of at-homeness I had not experienced at Yale, in Latin America, or at Harvard. The noncompetitive life with mentally handicapped people, their gifts of welcoming me regardless of name or prestige, and the persistent invitation to "waste some time" with them opened in me a place that until then had remained unavailable to me, a place where I could hear the gentle invitation of Jesus to dwell with him. My sense of being called to L'Arche was based more on what I had to receive than on what I had to give. Jean Vanier said, "Maybe we can offer you a home here." That, more than anything else, was what my heart desired, even though I had never taken my desire seriously, and that gave me the first inkling that my prayer to follow Jesus more radically was being heard.

The core of this book consists of the spiritual journal I kept during the year between leaving Harvard and joining the L'Arche community of Daybreak in Canada. Most of that year I spent in Trosly-Breuil, where Jean Vanier first founded homes for people with mental handicaps. But I made many excursions to Holland, Germany, Canada, the United States, and other places. When I went to France, my hope was that L'Arche would prove to be the place where I would be called to follow Jesus. But I wasn't sure. In fact, the difference between the life of the university and the life at L'Arche proved to be so profound that I experienced many doubts about whether I would be able to make the jump. These journal notes show the struggle, yes, the spiritual combat connected with the question "How does one follow Jesus unreservedly?" Many of the same pains I expressed in *The Genesee Diary* and ¡*Gracias!* can be found here. The difference is not only the context, but also the direction. In the past I wanted to know where to go. Now I knew where to go, but didn't really want to. Living and working with mentally handicapped people seemed precisely the opposite of what I had been trained and qualified to do. Everything else seemed more reasonable and useful than going to L'Arche. But still . . . Jan Risse, Jean Vanier, my friends at L'Arche, and most of all the handicapped people themselves kept saying, gently but persistently, "Here is a home for you; maybe you need us." All my desires to be useful, successful, and productive revolted. Some of my trips away from L'Arche may have been an expression of that revolt. But whether I knew it at the time or not, they became part of the basic struggle to let go of old ways and to be led to "where I rather would not go" (John 21:18).

In the following pages there are words about L'Arche, about prayer, about living with handicapped people, about art, about city life, about filmmaking, about AIDS, about the conflicts in the church, about Paris, London, San Francisco, and Los Angeles, about Canada and a future there, and about many other small and great people and events. What binds them together in their wide variety is the spiritual struggle to say "yes" to Jesus' invitation "Come and follow me." It is a screaming and kicking "yes" that fills these pages. It is a "yes" emerging from the recognition of my own brokenness and need for radical healing. In the epilogue I try to summarize my experiences during my first year at Daybreak, the L'Arche community in Toronto to which I went after my year in France. Even though I didn't have the time and energy to keep a journal at Daybreak, I still felt the need to describe simply and honestly what happened to me after I had found a home.

The title of this journal, *The Road to Daybreak*, not only refers to the fact that my year in Trosly led me to accept the invitation of the Daybreak community in Toronto. It also refers to my conviction that the experiences described in this journal led me to the beginning of a new life.

Many of these notes speak about confusion, fear, and loneliness, because much of the journey took place in the night. But as I stand at the break of a new day, I am filled with hope. I pray that those who will read this journal will be encouraged in their own spiritual journey and discover that same hope in their own hearts.

1

PARENTS AND CHILDREN

■

A NEW BEGINNING
(Trosly, France; Tuesday, August 13, 1985)

THIS IS THE first day of my new life! Though it sounds melodramatic, I cannot avoid feeling that something significant is starting today. My decision to leave Harvard Divinity School and move to France to live for at least a year with Jean Vanier and his L'Arche community in Trosly took many tears and many sleepless nights. It came after a period of many hesitations and inner debates. But as I drove away from the carriage house which for a year had been the center of my life at Harvard, I felt as if I were moving toward a new freedom. When Madame Vanier, Jean's eighty-seven-year-old mother, threw her arms around me as I stepped into her house this morning, it felt like coming home.

It is so good to be back. Nine months ago I finished a thirty-day retreat here. At the time I had no idea I would be back so soon, but now I know that the retreat prepared me to say good-bye to the academic world and to start looking for a community of people who could lead me closer to the heart of God.

This afternoon I heard something like an inner voice telling me to start keeping a journal again. Even since my trip to Latin America four years ago, I had given up daily writing. But it suddenly dawned on me that this year is going to be a year of prayer, reading, and writing while listening carefully to the inner movements of the spirit and struggling with the question "How do I follow Jesus all the way?" How better to keep in touch with God's work in me than by recording what is happening to me day after day? If this is really going to be a year of discernment, an honest journal might help me as much now as it has in the past.

The enormous contrast between my busy, noisy, and nerve-wracking last days in Cambridge and this utterly quiet, still day in Trosly moves me deeply. As I walked the narrow streets of this little French village this afternoon without seeing a person or hearing a car, I wondered if I were on the same planet. The six-and-a-half-hour night flight from Logan Airport in Boston to Charles de Gaulle Airport in Paris makes the distance between there and here seem so small. But Cambridge and Trosly are much farther apart than a night's flight. They represent two very different worlds: Cambridge—a world of academic intensity, institutional rivalry, intellectual competition, and ever mounting excitement; Trosly—a world of quiet village living, community celebration, the sharing of human vulnerabilities, and an always new invitation to let Jesus be the center of everything.

It is dark now, very dark. Not a sound around me, only the regular beat of the quartz alarm clock Jutta Ayer gave me shortly before I left. The clock reminds me of the world I left behind. Here no one has told me when to get up tomorrow, what to do, or whom to meet: no classes, interviews, or counseling, no last-minute phone calls or visits. Tomorrow is as open as any tomorrow has ever been. What will it bring? Only God knows. The silence whispers, "Go to bed and sleep as long as you want. Nobody will wake you up." I will push the button of my quartz clock to the white dot which reads "signal off." A new life has begun.

THE NAME ABOVE ALL OTHER NAMES
(Wednesday, August 14)

The house in which I live is called "Les Marronniers." I had known the name, but only today did I find out its meaning. Madame Vanier told me that *les marronniers* are the four large chestnut trees standing in front of the house. "Each of them has a different name," she said, "Marc, Luc, Matthew, and Jean," and with a smile she added, "You will understand why I called the one closest to the house Jean."

Names are very important. For a long time I lived with the conviction that Francis Avenue, on which Harvard Divinity School stands, was named after St. Francis. That had somehow given me a little consolation as I walked to work. I must have suppressed my inclination to verify this conviction out of fear of being robbed of another illusion, but one day someone brought me back to earth by informing me that the Francis for whom the street was named was a nineteenth-century Divinity School professor and not my favorite saint. I am sure that no saints gave their names to any of Cambridge's streets or Harvard's houses. Here in Trosly the saints are everywhere and the community for the handicapped is called L'Arche, a constant reminder of Noah's Ark, to which people and animals fled for shelter as the flood covered more and more of the land. L'Arche is indeed the place where many vulnerable men and women who are threatened by the judgmental and violent world in which they live can find a safe place and feel at home.

Names tell stories, most of all the name which is above all other names, the name of Jesus. In his name I am called to live. His name has to become my house, my dwelling place, my refuge, my ark. His name has to start telling the story of being born, growing up, growing old, and dying—revealing a God who loved us so much that he sent his only child to us.

PÈRE THOMAS
(Thursday, August 15)

Today, August 15, the Feast of the Assumption of Our Lady, is a national holiday in France. Although the majority of French people seldom if ever enter a church, they all close their stores and businesses to celebrate this feast day of the Mother of God, to whom France is especially dedicated.

Père Thomas Philippe, a Dominican who twenty years ago started the L'Arche community with Jean Varnier and who is considered its spiritual father, offered a long, fervent homily in honor of Mary's assumption. The hundred and fifty people in the chapel all listened with great attention to the words of this eighty-year-old priest.

I keep hearing more and more about this saintly man. Father Ed O'Connor, who comes here every year from the United States to make a retreat with Père Thomas, calls him the John of the Cross of our time. This sounded rather grandiose at first, but when the Peeters, a Belgian family who invited me to dinner, told me that they had moved to France to be close to Père Thomas, I started to become aware of the extraordinary spiritual gifts of this man. I still have a hard time following his long and intense French sermons, but being in his presence and hearing the way he pronounces the words "Mary," "Our Mother," and "the Blessed Virgin," and speaks of the Assumption as a source of hope for all of us are experiences I cannot forget.

It is a profound experience to be in the presence of someone whom I can hardly understand, but who nevertheless communicates deeply and convincingly the mystery of God's presence among us. It is an especially profound experience since it unites me so intimately with the so-called "retarded" men and women and lets me hear as they do, with the heart. After the Eucharist, Père Thomas shook my hand with great intensity and said, "I entrust my sheep to you, Father." I replied, "I will try my best, but with my French I can assure you my sermons will be a lot shorter!" He smiled.

This afternoon he left for ten days. One of the reasons I came just before his departure was to be able to take his place. One of the women said to me, "Père Thomas cannot be replaced, you know." Nevertheless, in the coming days I will try. Standing in for a saint will not be easy, but then again, God is merciful . . .

DANNY'S PRAYER
(Friday, August 16)

Tonight I spent a wonderful evening with the L'Arche group from Cork, Ireland, who are spending the month of August in Trosly. It is obviously easier for me to be among the Irish than among the French. The language helps, but also the easy camaraderie.

During evening prayer we sang simple songs, we listened to Danny, one of the handicapped men from Cork, who with great difficulty read from Jean Vanier's book *I Meet Jesus,* and we prayed. Danny said, "I love you, Jesus. I do not reject you even when I get nervous once in a while . . . even when I get confused. I love you with my arms, my legs, my head, my heart; I love you and I do not reject you, Jesus. I know that you love me, that you love me so much. I love you too, Jesus." As he prayed I looked at his beautiful, gentle face and saw without any veil or cover his agony as well as his love. Who would not respond to a prayer like that?

I suddenly felt a deep desire to invite all my students from Harvard to sit with me there in that circle. I felt a deep love for all those men and women I had tried to speak to about Jesus and had often failed to touch. I wanted so much for all of them to sit and let Danny tell them about Jesus. I knew they would understand what I had not been able to explain. As I walked home after having kissed everyone good-night, I felt a strange warm pain that had something to do with the many words I was trying to keep together.

L'ARCHE: A LITTLE BIT OF HISTORY
(Saturday, August 17)

Less than a minute's walk from the house where I live is the house where it all started. Above the door hangs a small wooden sign with the word "L'Arche." In that house Jean Vanier went to live twenty years ago with two handicapped men, Raphael and Philippe. Every time I pass that small, unspectacular little house and see the wooden sign above the door, I am moved by the mystery of small acts of faith. When Jean decided to take two handicapped men out of a large institution and bring them into his "ark," he knew he was doing something irreversible. He knew that from that moment on his life would be intimately connected with the lives of these two men. They had no family to which he could send them, nor could he ever return them to the institution from which they came. This was the form of poverty Jean had chosen after much prayer and a long search for a vocation.

When Jean made this decision he was still a professor of philosophy at St. Michael's College in Toronto. He had come to Trosly to visit his spiritual director, Père Thomas Philippe, who had been his guide and friend since the days of his studies at the Institut Catholique in Paris. Under the guidance and inspiration of Père Thomas, Jean was able to leave his successful academic career and embark on a spiritual journey, the end of which was completely invisible. As far as Jean was concerned, living with Raphael and Philippe was to be his vocation. He had no plans to start a large movement, nor was he thinking about an international network of homes for the handicapped. His new life began in this small French village with a humble house and two handicapped men, and with his good friend Père Thomas nearby.

Today, L'Arche is a word that inspires thousands of people all over the world: in France, Belgium, Italy, Spain, Canada, the United States, Mexico, Haiti, Honduras, the Ivory Coast, India, and many other countries. Its vision is a source of hope; its work draws praise from popes, bishops, kings, queens, and presidents. But Jean didn't anticipate any of that when he put the L'Arche sign above the door of his first *foyer*. He just wanted to be poor with the poor.

It sounds very much like stories I have heard before—of Benedict and Scholastica, Francis and Claire, Peter Maurin and Dorothy Day, Catherine de Huyck Doherty and Frère Roger of Taize. "Set your heart on God's kingdom . . . these other things will be given you as well" (Luke 12:31).

PAINFUL BUT PRECIOUS MEMORIES
(Sunday, August 18)

A sunny Sunday! My father came to visit me. Traveling with a friend from Holland to Switzerland, he decided to come through Trosly to see where and how I am living now. He attended the Mass I celebrated for the L'Arche community, ate dinner with some of the members of La Ferme, the contemplative community founded by Père Thomas, visited the Irish group, and had tea with Madame Varnier.

It was a special joy to listen to the stories Madame Varnier and my father had to share. She was born in 1898, my father in 1903, and though their lives have followed quite different courses, they have common memories of a part of history I know only from books. Madame Vanier's experiences at the Canadian embassies in Paris, London, and Algiers and my father's experiences in a Dutch law firm and university were connected by their common experiences of the Second World War.

During the war years seven European governments were in exile in England. During that period the Vaniers lived in London as representatives of the Canadian government. They came to know, often in bomb shelters, Dutch officials who were quite well known to my father.

And here they were, drinking tea in 1985, talking about a time I scarcely remember. They mentioned names of people who were once quite famous but are now forgotten and relived frightening and exhilarating events which are hardly real for latecomers like me.

How strange that this cruel war was the context of my vocation to the priesthood and Jean Vanier's call to a life among the poor. Our parents taught us something about God that is hard to teach to a generation with no memories of bomb shelters, the destruction of large cities like Rotterdam and London, and the constant fear of death.

Seeing and hearing these two strong people speak with each other made me aware of a mystery of human and divine love far beyond words and gestures, revealed here for a moment in a casual encounter over tea.

2

FOLLOWING JESUS

■

LEAVE EVERYTHING BEHIND
AND FOLLOW ME
(Monday, August 19)

THE STORY OF the rich young man, which I read in both French and English during the Eucharist, continues to captivate me. "Jesus looked steadily at him and loved him, and he said, 'There is one thing you lack. Go and sell everything you own and give the money to the poor, and you will have treasures in heaven; then come, follow me.' But his face fell at these words and he went away sad, for he was a man of great wealth" (Mark 10:21–22).

Jesus loved this young man and, as I understand it, desired to have him with him as a disciple. But the young man's life was too complex; he had too many things to worry about, too many affairs to take care of, too many people to relate to. He couldn't let go of his concerns, and thus, disappointed and downcast, he left Jesus. Jesus was sad, the young man was sad, and today I feel sad because I wonder how different his life would have been had he been free enough to follow Jesus. He came, heard, but then left. We never hear of him again. Every year we remember Peter, John, and James, the three disciples Jesus loved so much. But this man, whom Jesus also loved in a special way and also invited to become a witness to the good news, remains unknown. He never became a follower of Jesus and never made his mark on the history of the church as these other disciples did. If Francis of Assisi had remained in business, he would certainly not be remembered so fondly today.

I feel like praying tonight that my life might become simple enough for me to be able to say "yes" when Jesus looks at me with love and invites me to leave everything behind and follow him. Missing that moment would not only sadden Jesus and me but would, in a way, also be a refusal to take my true place in God's work of salvation.

JESSIE'S THREAT
(Friday, August 23)

John Fraser, the European correspondent of the *Globe and Mail*, one of Canada's national newspapers, came to visit Madame Vanier. I was invited for tea. We talked about the people of China, Tibet and the Dalai Lama, the Catholic Church in the Philippines and North Korea, and the Pope's recent visit to Holland. John Fraser is a well-traveled, very knowledgeable journalist who is both a keen observer of world events and a man with a deep personal interest in the religious life.

Among all his stories about world events, John told us a small story about his daughter Jessie. It is this story I will remember most:

One morning when Jessie was four years old, she found a dead sparrow in front of the living room window. The little bird had killed itself by flying into the glass. When Jessie saw the dead bird she was both deeply disturbed and very intrigued. She asked her father, "Where is the bird now?" John said he didn't know. "Why did it die?" she asked again. "Well," John said hesitantly, "because all birds return to the earth." "Oh," said Jessie, "then we have to bury it." A box was found, the little bird was laid in the box, a paper napkin was added as a shroud, and a few minutes later a little procession was formed with Daddy, Mama, Jessie, and her little sister. Daddy carried the box, Jessie the homemade cross. After a grave was dug and the little sparrow was buried, John put a piece of moss over the grave and Jessie planted the cross upon it. Then John asked Jessie, "Do you want to say a prayer?" "Yes," replied Jessie firmly, and after having told her baby sister in no uncertain terms to fold her hands, she prayed: "Dear God, we have buried this little sparrow. Now you be good to her or I will kill you. Amen." As they walked home, John said to Jessie, "You didn't have to threaten God." Jessie answered, "I just wanted to be sure."

Well, among all the stories about the Pope, the Dalai Lama, and the other leaders of this world, Jessie's story told me most about the human heart: compassionate—but ready to kill when afraid. Whether we become merciful people or killers depends very much on who tells us what life is about. John, who had to tell so many stories about violence, murder, oppression, and other human sins, wanted Jessie to learn another story. His deep love for his family made that very clear.

SEEING AND BEING SEEN
(Saturday, August 24)

Today we celebrate the feast of St. Bartholomew. I am struck by the first encounter between Jesus and Bartholomew, who in the Gospel is called Nathanael.

The emphasis is on *seeing.* Jesus said to Nathanael, "Before Philip came to call you, I saw you under the fig tree," and after Nathanael's response: "You are the Son of God," Jesus remarked, "You believe that just because I said I saw you under the fig tree. You will see greater things than that . . . you will see heaven laid open, and above the Son of man, and the angels of God ascending and descending" (John 1:49–51).

The story speaks deeply to me since it raises the questions "Do I want to be seen by Jesus? Do I want to be known by him?" If I do, then a faith can grow which proclaims Jesus as the Son of God. Only such a faith can open my eyes and reveal an open heaven.

Thus, I will see when I am willing to be seen. I will receive new eyes that can see the mysteries of God's own life when I allow God to see me, all of me, even those parts that I myself do not want to see.

O Lord, see me and let me see.

GOD'S CHOICE
(Sunday, August 25)

This morning Jean Varnier was interviewed on French television. I watched the program together with his mother, his brother Bernard, who is visiting for ten days, and Simone, a friend from the L'Arche house of prayer, La Ferme. Although I have heard Jean speak frequently, he said things that struck me as new.

A few minutes into the interview, Jean started to speak about Eric, a severely handicapped eighteen-year-old who had recently died. He mentioned Eric's deep sensitivity. Eric could not speak, walk, or feed himself, but when tension arose between assistants in the house, he banged his head against the wall; and when peace and harmony prevailed, he was joyful and cooperative. "The handicapped often tell us the truth, whether we want to know it or not," Jean remarked, and added with a smile, "It is not always easy to have such a barometer in your house."

As Jean mentioned this, I sensed that there is a deep connection between being seen by God and being seen by handicapped people. Yesterday's Gospel about Jesus seeing Nathanael suddenly held a new depth for me.

It was important for me to be reminded again of this gift of the handicapped. They see through a facade of smiles and friendly words and sense the resentful heart before we ourselves notice it. Often they are capable of unmasking our impatience, irritation, jealousy, and lack of interest and making us honest with ourselves. For them, what really counts is a true relationship, a real friendship, a faithful presence. Many mentally handicapped people experience themselves as a disappointment to their parents, a burden for their families, a nuisance to their friends. To believe that anyone really cares and really loves them is difficult. Their heart registers with extreme sensitivity what is real care and what is false, what is true affection and what is just empty words. Thus, they often reveal to us our own hypocrisies and invite us always to greater sincerity and purer love.

My limited experience with handicapped people has made me see the truth of Jean's observation. Being at L'Arche means many things, but one of them is a call to a greater purity of heart. Indeed, Jesus speaks through the broken hearts of the handicapped, who are considered marginal and useless. But God has chosen them to be the poor through whom he makes his presence known. This is hard to accept in a success- and production-oriented society.

GOD IS NOT IN A HURRY
(Monday, September 2)

When I was wondering what to write about tonight, I realized that I often write about my most immediate concerns, while the deeper stirrings of the spirit remain unrecorded.

Today I was reading *Two Dancers in the Desert,* a book by Charles Lepetit about the life of the spiritual father of the Little Brothers and Sisters of Jesus, Charles de Foucauld. While reading it, I was reminded again of my deepest concern: how to come to a deeper experience of God in my life. I have been very concerned with this question since I feel that my life at Harvard led me in the wrong direction; that is why I finally left. Now that I am free to go the way of prayer, fasting, and solitude, I sense that without a concentrated effort I will transform my life here into another Harvard. I feel a burning desire to preach the Gospel, but I know in my heart that now is the time to pray, to read, to meditate, to be quiet, and to wait until God clearly calls me.

I am happy with the clarity I have. It makes no sense to preach the Gospel when I have allowed no time for my own conversion. This is clearly a time for hiddenness and withdrawal from lecturing and giving retreats, courses, seminars, and workshops. It is a time for being alone with God.

I feel a tension within me. I have only a limited number of years left for active ministry. Why not use them well? Yet one word spoken with a pure heart is worth thousands spoken in a state of spiritual turmoil. Time given to inner renewal is never wasted. God is not in a hurry.

SHEILA CASSIDY'S HOSPICE
(Sunday, September 8)

Sheila Cassidy, the English doctor who was imprisoned and tortured two years after General Pinochet took power in Chile, has written me a fine letter. I have never met her, but our lives have occasionally touched each other's, mostly through our writings.

Today I read her short description of a hospice, and I was so touched by it that I would like to copy some of her words into this journal:

> Medically speaking, hospices exist to provide a service of pain and symptom control for those for whom active anti-cancer treatment is no longer appropriate—there is *always* something that can be done for the dying, even if it's only having the patience and the courage to sit with them. Most lay people imagine that hospices are solemn, rather depressing places where voices are hushed and eyes downcast as patients and their families await the inevitable. Nothing could be further from the truth. Hospice care is about life and love and laughter, for it is founded upon two unshakable beliefs: that life is so precious that each minute should be lived to the full, and that death is quite simply a part of life, to be faced openly and greeted with the

hand outstretched. One of the hallmarks of hospice life is celebration: cakes are baked and champagne uncorked at the first hint of a birthday or anniversary, and administrators, nurses, and volunteers clink glasses with patients and their families.[1]

As I read this, I was struck that much, if not all, that Sheila Cassidy says can be said of L'Arche as well. A hospice is for the dying who cannot be cured of their disease; L'Arche is for the handicapped whose handicap cannot be removed. Both proclaim loudly the preciousness of life and encourage us to face reality with open eyes and outstretched hands. Both are places of celebration in which the certainty of the present is always much more important than the uncertainty of the future. Both are witnesses to the paradox that the most unlikely people are chosen by God to make us see. Sheila Cassidy and Jean Vanier found their vocations in very different ways, but their common faith in Jesus and his Gospel has given them a remarkably similar vision.

LEAVING HARVARD
(Monday, September 9)

My decision to leave Harvard was a difficult one. For many months I was not sure if I would be following or betraying my vocation by leaving. The outer voices kept saying, "You can do so much good here. People need you!" The inner voices kept saying, "What good is it to preach the Gospel to others while losing your own soul?" Finally, I realized that my increasing inner darkness, my feelings of being rejected by some of my students, colleagues, friends, and even God, my inordinate need for affirmation and affection, and my deep sense of not belonging were clear signs that I was not following the way of God's spirit. The fruits of the spirit are not sadness, loneliness, and separation, but joy, solitude, and community. After I decided to leave Harvard, I was surprised that it had taken me so long to come to that decision. As soon as I left, I felt so much inner freedom, so much joy and new energy, that I could look back on my former life as a prison in which I had locked myself.

I feel no regrets about my time in Harvard. Though in a divinity school, I had a real chance to be in a thoroughly secular university environment, and I had the opportunity to experience joy and fear in speaking directly about Jesus. I came to know many students and made some close friends, and saw more clearly than ever my own temptations and weaknesses. I feel warmly toward many of the people I met at Harvard, but now that I have left I also feel compassion for them. I now see so clearly that the ambition to achieve academically that keeps them bound is the same ambition that, without my fully knowing it, kept me bound too.

These thoughts came to me as I was reading one of St. Francis Xavier's letters from his mission field. In his youth he was a student and ambitious lecturer at the University of Paris. There he met Ignatius of Loyola and became one of his first companions. He writes:

> Often I am overcome with the desire to cry out against the universities, especially against the University of Paris . . . and to rage with all my powers like a fool who has lost his senses.
>
> I would cry out against those who are more preoccupied with becoming scientists than with letting people in need profit from their science . . . I am afraid that many who learn their disciplines at the university are more interested in using them to acquire honors, bishoprics, privileges, and high position than in using them for what is just and necessary . . . The common word is: "I will study 'letters' in order to get some good privileged position in the Church, and after that I will live for God." These people are brutes, following the guidance of their sensuality and disordered impulses . . . They do not trust in God, nor do they give themselves completely to him . . . they are afraid that God does not want what they desire and that when they obey him they are forced to abandon their unjustly acquired privileges . . .
>
> How many would be enlightened by the faith of the Gospel if there were some who would put all their effort into finding good people who are willing to make sacrifices to search for and find not what belongs to them, but what belongs to Jesus Christ. In these lands so many people come to faith in Jesus Christ that many times my arms fail me because of the painful work of baptizing them.[2]

Francis Xavier wrote this many years after he had left the university. His new milieu, in which many people asked him to enlighten them with faith, made him see how many of those with whom he had lived and studied had been wasting their talents in the search for power and success and thereby were not available for the work of salvation that needed so urgently to be done.

Little has changed since the sixteenth century. After only a few weeks away from the competitive, ambitious, career-oriented life at Harvard Divinity School, I already feel the desire to say some of the things that Francis Xavier said. But it seems better not to play the prophet. I am not a Francis Xavier, nor do I wish to be. My dominant feeling toward Harvard is not indignation, but gratitude. Notwithstanding its pretentiousness, Harvard was the place where I met some of my most caring friends, where I became most acutely aware of my desire to love Jesus without compromise, and where I discovered my vocation to live and work with mentally handicapped people. Without a Harvard there probably would not have been a L'Arche for me either.

3

DARKNESS AND LIGHT

∙

FEELING REJECTED
(September 10)

A VERY HARD DAY. I have been waiting for my dear friend Jonas, who took me to the airport in Boston and promised to come and visit me in France. Two weeks ago I heard he had indeed left for Paris and was going to visit me at the end of last week. Today I found out that he has already returned to Boston.

It was a very painful discovery. I had anticipated his visit and made all sorts of arrangements to welcome him. Now I feel not only sad at not seeing him, but also hurt and rejected. He did not even send me a note or a card and left me guessing and misguessing for a week.

I had had the impression that he was eager to see me and that one of the reasons he came to France was to be with me. He went to Brussels, Paris, and the Alps, but didn't come to Trosly! What a lesson! When I called him, he explained to me that things had just worked out differently from what he had foreseen, that he couldn't find my phone number, and that he was very tired. Still, I felt deeply hurt.

I now wonder what to do with this experience. Luckily, I am less depressed by it than I used to be in similar circumstances. Ever since I heard that Jonas had returned to Boston, I have been saying to myself, "If you really want to be less visible, less known, try to take this event and use it to become more forgotten, more passed over; be grateful for the occasion. Trust that hiddenness will give you new eyes to see yourself, your world, and your God. People cannot give you new eyes; only the one who loves you without limits."

I said things like this at different times, but it didn't quite work. I prayed for a few quiet moments, asking Jesus to help me not to become angry or bitter, and I tried to do my work as best I could. But I kept going back over the event again and again, constructing reasons for why he should have visited me and why I should feel rejected. It will probably take a while before I can fully forgive Jonas and be grateful for this occasion to grow in the spirit. Meanwhile, I am trying to keep a sense of humor and write a few notes to people who are always close to thinking that I am rejecting them.

Lord, give me the peace and joy that only you can give.

ICONS AND ICONOGRAPHY
(Sunday, September 15)

This afternoon I spent a few hours with Brother Christian Leisy, a monk of Christ in the Desert Monastery at Abiquiu, New Mexico, and Jackie Nelson from Santa Fe. They are both iconographers who have just finished a course with Father Egon Sendler, S.J., the great icon specialist. This occasion gave me a wonderful chance to ask questions about icon making which I had always wanted to ask.

I felt awe for these two humble and receptive people, who told me everything I wanted to know. What impressed me most was their conviction that the renewal of the art of iconography was in fact a renewal of the spiritual life. Not only did Brother Christian and Jackie Nelson exercise their art as a sacred task for which they had to be spiritually prepared, they also saw their work as a way to bring people to faith in the presence of the divine among us. They told me about many people who had found God through their interest in icons.

Icons are not just pious pictures to decorate churches and houses. They are images of Christ and the saints which bring us into contact with the sacred, windows that give us a glimpse of the transcendent. They need to be approached in veneration and with prayer. Only then will they reveal to us the mystery they represent.

Iconography has come to the West mainly from the Orthodox tradition, especially from Russia and Greece. Since the Russian Revolution of 1917, many Orthodox Christians have fled to the West, and through them the holy art of iconography has gradually become more known and appreciated in the Latin Church. Russian and Greek icons have become one of the most important sources of inspiration for my own prayer life. The icon of Our Lady of Vladimir, Rublev's icon of the Holy Trinity, and the nineteenth-century Greek icon of Christ that I obtained in Jerusalem have become integral parts of my life of prayer. I cannot think about the Holy Trinity, Jesus, and Mary without seeing them as the holy iconographers saw them. Icons are certainly one of the most beautiful gifts of the Orthodox Church to the churches of the West.

Brother Christian showed me photographs of the icons he had made and explained to me how he made them. He told me how he prepared the wood, how he mixed egg white with ground colors and made egg tempura, how he covered the surface with many layers of paint, going from the darker colors to the lighter, and how he did all of this in a way faithful to centuries-old iconographic traditions.

I was most moved by the icon of the Lebanese St. Charbel, whose face was one of the most penetrating I had ever seen on an icon. I asked Brother Christian if there were any chance that he could paint an icon of St. Charbel for me. He showed great interest in doing so. He is going to Rome for three years to study theology and prepare himself for the priesthood. He hopes to set up his own icon studio there. If he does, he will paint another Charbel icon for me. It would be a wonderful way for me to stay in communion with this remarkable Lebanese saint and his war-torn country.

A SACRED CONNECTION
(Tuesday, September 17)

Two places in Trosly have a deep connection with each other. They are L'Oratoire and La Forestière. L'Oratoire is a prayer room where the Blessed Sacrament is exposed all day long and where people are always present in silent adoration. The room itself is a large, rather dark space with small kneelers and little mats. The space is divided by a thick stone wall built of heavy grey stone. In the middle of the wall, a large open space is carved in the shape of a semicircle. There the monstrance stands, flanked on each side by three oil lamps. Beautiful fresh flowers are always present. On both sides of the wall people kneel, sit, or lie down in prayer.

In many ways L'Oratoire is the heart of L'Arche. The unceasing silent prayer in the presence of the hidden God who gives himself completely to us in unlimited love is the breath that makes L'Arche possible. Every time I enter L'Oratoire I feel a deep rest coming over me, and even if it is hard for me to pray I feel held there. It is as if the room prays for me. I know of few places where the presence of prayer is so tangible. If I can't pray, I go there so that I can at least breathe air rich with prayer. In L'Oratoire I meet the poverty of God, the God who became flesh and even our food and drink, the God who does not hold back any of his love and who says, "Eat of me, drink of me," the God who is so deeply hidden that he can be recognized only by the eye of faith.

Then there is La Forestière, the foyer where the most handicapped people live with their assistants. The handicapped people in La Forestière cannot walk, speak, or dress themselves. Many cannot feed themselves; some can hardly see or hear. Their bodies are severely distorted and often wracked with intense pain. When I go to La Forestière, I am always struck by the silence. The handicapped and their assistants live a life that in many ways feels monastic. The assistants are very busy with cleaning, cooking, feeding, dressing, or just holding, but they do it all in a very quiet way. Once in a while the quiet is interrupted by a groan, a cry, or a shout, in which the deep agony of the handicapped men and women can be sensed. But mostly there is silence.

If I can truly believe that God loved us so much that he became flesh among us, the people of La Forestière invite me to see how deep that love is. Indeed, here I can meet Jesus, the same Jesus whom I adore in L'Oratoire. Here, too, God is hidden; here, too, is unceasing prayer of simple presence; here, too, is the utmost poverty.

Tony, an Englishman who is also in Trosly for a year, said to me yesterday, "The first great commandment is lived out in L'Oratoire, the second in La Forestière. Here in Trosly you can come to understand what Jesus meant when he said that these commandments resemble each other." I have thought about Tony's words the whole day.

"USELESS" PRAYER
(Wednesday, September 18)

Why should I spend an hour in prayer when I do nothing during that time but think about people I am angry with, people who are angry with me, books I should read and books I should write, and thousands of other silly things that happen to grab my mind for a moment?

The answer is: because God is greater than my mind and my heart, and what is really happening in the house of prayer is not measurable in terms of human success and failure.

What I must do first of all is be faithful. If I believe that the first commandment is to love God with my whole heart, mind, and soul, then I should at least be able to spend one hour a day with nobody else but God. The question as to whether it is helpful, useful, practical, or fruitful is completely irrelevant, since the only reason to love is love itself. Everything else is secondary.

The remarkable thing, however, is that sitting in the presence of God for one hour each morning—day after day, week after week, month after month—in total confusion and with myriad distractions radically changes my life. God, who loves me so much that he sent his only son not to condemn me but to save me, does not leave me waiting in the dark too long. I might think that each hour is useless, but after thirty or sixty or ninety such useless hours, I gradually realize that I was not as alone as I thought; a very small, gentle voice has been speaking to me far beyond my noisy place.

So: Be confident and trust in the Lord.

JOY IN SMALL CORNERS
(Thursday, September 19)

Nathan, a Canadian assistant, invited me tonight for supper at his foyer, Le Surgeon. *Le surgeon* means "the shoot." It is also the French word for "the branches of the vine."

Le Surgeon in Cuise, a neighboring village, is a foyer for severely handicapped people like those at La Forestière. There I met Philippe, Sylvienne, Michelle, Jean-Luc, and Gérard, all people who need total care. Alain was temporarily in the hospital. Nathan told me a little about the daily schedule, much like a monastic schedule, in which every hour is carefully planned.

The days have a strict rhythm: dressing, bathing, eating breakfast, cleaning the house, shopping, cooking and eating dinner, quiet time, Mass, supper, getting ready for bed, and evening prayer. During the morning and afternoon the handicapped men and women spend a few hours in the "workshop," where other helpers do exercises with them to keep them as alert as possible. During these hours the assistants do housework and shopping and have their quiet time. During the night, one of the assistants sleeps close to their six handicapped companions to help them if needed. All the handicapped need different types of medication to maintain their physical and mental balance. The assistants hold frequent meetings with a psychiatrist and psychologist to discuss various complications in this small community.

Living in Le Surgeon requires great discipline and much commitment. It is a humble life in which joy is hidden in small corners, always there to be found but never separate from much pain. The atmosphere in Le Surgeon is peaceful and quiet with no great events or great debates, just simple, steady service, day in and day out. The rewards are small but very real: Philippe smiles, Jean-Luc looks you in the eye, Gérard gives a hug, Michelle sleeps a whole night, Sylvienne says one more word.

Nathan shows me pictures: "Look, this is Gérard when he came out of the institution, and here he is a year later. See the difference? Isn't that wonderful? Look how happy he is!" Indeed, Gérard is happy. He cannot walk, speak, dress, or undress himself, but with his smile he gives you all you could ever want.

During evening prayer one of the assistants reads a passage from Jean Vanier's book *I Walk with Jesus:* "There is an intimate connection between the presence of Jesus in the Eucharist and the presence of Jesus in the deprived person. The deprived person sends us back to Jesus in the Eucharist. To receive the Body of Jesus is to have his eyes and his heart to see him in the poor."

As Nathan drove me home, he said, "Dominique, one of the assistants at Le Surgeon, has decided to enter a contemplative monastery, and another of us is considering doing the same."

After my visit, I could well understand why.

THE PILGRIMS OF EMMAUS
(Saturday, September 21)

Today I went to the Louvre in Paris with Brad Wolcott to see Rembrandt's *The Pilgrims of Emmaus.* Brad and I met for the first time many years ago, when I was teaching at Yale Divinity School and he was finishing his dissertation in French literature. We became friends and lived through many struggles together. After a few years of teaching at St. Lawrence University in upstate New York, Brad decided to come to L'Arche and live here as an assistant in one of the foyers. It is a great joy for me to be so close to Brad again. Seeing *The Pilgrims of Emmaus* together has been our longtime hope.

At first sight, the painting was a disappointment. It was much smaller than I had expected and surrounded by so many other paintings that it was hard to see it as a separate work of art. Maybe I was too familiar with it through reproductions to be genuinely surprised. Brad and I stood in front of it just looking at the event portrayed.

Jesus sits behind the table looking up in prayer while holding a loaf of bread in his hands. On his right, one of the pilgrims leans backwards with his hands folded; while on his left, the other has moved his chair away from the table and gazes with utter attention at Jesus. Behind him a humble servant, obviously unaware of what is happening, reaches forward to put a plate of food on the table. On the table, a bright white cloth only partially covers the heavy table rug. There are very few objects on the table: three pewter plates, a knife, and two small cups. Jesus sits in front of a majestic stone apse flanked by two big, square pillars. On the right side of the painting, the entrance door is visible, and there is a coat stand in the corner over which a cape has been casually thrown. In the left corner of the room, a doglike figure can be seen lying under a bench. The whole painting is in endless varieties of brown: light brown, dark brown, yellow-brown, red-brown, and so on. The source of light is not revealed, but the white tablecloth is the brightest part of the painting.

Brad and I noticed that the bare feet of Jesus and the two pilgrims were painted with great detail. Not so the feet of the servant. Rembrandt obviously wanted us to know about the long, tiring walk they had just made. The large door and the cape on the coat stand were also there to remind us of the journey. These men truly came from somewhere.

As we looked at the painting, many people passed by. One of the guides said, "Look at Jesus' face, in ecstasy, yet so humble." That expressed beautifully what we saw. Jesus' face is full of light, a light which radiates from his head in a cloudlike halo. He does not look at the men around him. His eyes look upward in an expression of intimate communion with the Father. While Jesus is in deep prayer, he yet remains present; he remains the humble servant who came to be among us and show us the way to God.

The longer we looked at the painting, the more we felt drawn into the mystery it expresses. We gradually came to realize that the unoccupied side of the table across from Jesus is the place for the viewers. Brad said, "Now I see that Rembrandt painted the Eucharist, a sacramental event to which we, as we view it, are invited." It suddenly dawned on me how many similarities exist between this painting and Rublev's Trinity icon. There, as here, the white table is the real center. There, as here, the viewer is made a real part of the mystery of the Eucharist. As we continued to let the painting speak to us, we were amazed that we both came to see it more and more as a call to worship Christ in the Eucharist. The hands of Jesus holding the bread on the white altar table are the center not only of the light, but also of the sacramental action. Yet if Jesus were to leave the altar, the bread would still be there. And we would still be able to be with him.

For an instant the museum became a church, the painting a sanctuary, and Rembrandt a priest. All of it told me something about God's hidden presence in the world.

When we walked away from the painting and merged with the crowd of tourists headed for the *Mona Lisa* and the *Venus de Milo,* we felt as if we were returning to a busy street after a time of silent adoration in a holy place.

SHIFTING EMOTIONS
(Monday, September 23)

The depression that hit me when my long-awaited friend Jonas did not come to visit never totally left me. The many things to see, to hear, and to do covered up my darker feelings most of the time, but on various occasions they reappeared above the surface of my daily activities and reminded me of their presence.

This afternoon Jonas suddenly telephoned from the United States. My depression returned to me in full force. "Why didn't you call me? Why didn't you write me? Why didn't you visit me?" He responded, "Hey, wait a moment, that's all past. I want to come visit you in October!" I had a hard time hearing him. I kept nurturing my own hurt feelings and couldn't really appreciate his attempt to let me know that he really wanted to be a caring, loving friend who had not forgotten me.

Only after we discussed dates and places did I start to realize my deafness and gradually hear his faithful friendship. When I laid down the receiver, I felt new peace entering into my innermost self and sensed that my depression was slowly dissolving.

Oh, I am so little in control of my feelings and emotions! Often I have to just let them pass through me and trust that they won't hang around too long. Many other things happened today that could fill pages of this journal, but the few minutes with Jonas on the telephone affected me more than anything else. That is why I want to write about it, although it seems such a miserable subject after *The Pilgrims of Emmaus.* But often the deepest pains are hidden in the smallest corners.

4

FIRST GLIMPSES OF A NEW VOCATION

•

A NEW COMMUNITY
(Toronto, Canada; Tuesday, October 1)

I AM IN Canada for nine days to visit Daybreak, the L'Arche community near Toronto. This is my first day. Joe Egan, the director, welcomed me warmly.

This morning I had a chance to meet all the assistants in their weekly meeting, and tonight I celebrated the Eucharist for all those who have been part of the community longer than two years, the handicapped as well as the assistants. It was interesting to hear Joe say that the distinction between handicapped people and assistants is becoming less important than the distinction between long-term community members and short-term helpers. Joe said that those who have built a real and lasting bond with L'Arche are especially responsible for making visitors, short-term assistants, and new handicapped people feel welcome.

So, indeed, it is a community on a journey, always changing, always adapting itself to new people, always open to surprises, always willing to try new things, but with a solid center of committed people who know the importance of permanency.

MEETING MICHAEL
(Wednesday, October 2)

The Daybreak community is much larger than I had imagined. At the farm, about a thirty-minute drive from downtown Toronto, there are three homes for handicapped people and their assistants. The same land holds the homes of the assistant director, the farm manager, and their families. There is also a large, newly built meeting house, a carpenter's shop, and a large barn. The Daybreak community also includes three homes in the town of Richmond Hill and two in Toronto. The whole community—handicapped people, assistants, and staff—adds up to about eighty persons.

I am living at the "Green House" on the farm, a spacious house for six handicapped people and their assistants. It feels very good to be part of their daily life. Although all the handicapped people do some form of work during the day, they can never be left alone. This became dramatically clear with Michael, a very beautiful young man who suffers from frequent epileptic seizures. Even though he has regular medical care and takes all the necessary medication, he is often overcome by spasmodic attacks that can cause him serious injury. Tonight at the swimming pool in town, when he was left for a minute, he had a seizure, fell and hit his head on the concrete floor, and had to be taken to the hospital. Happily enough, his wound was not very serious and he could come home again soon.

In his slow, stuttering voice, he asked me to pray for him. After we had prayed for a while together, he gave me a big hug and a wonderful smile. Then he told me that he would like to help me say Mass and wear a red stole as I do. Michael may well be much closer to God than I am, and I will surely give him something to wear that makes him aware of how special he is.

PRAYING FOR ROSE
(Thursday, October 3)

After dinner tonight a few of the community went to the chapel to pray for Rose. Rose is a twenty-two-year-old woman but looks like a fourteen-year-old girl, very thin, fragile, very wounded, but exceedingly beautiful. She cannot speak and can hardly walk, but she is a source of joy for all those who are close to her, especially for Mary, who assists her during the day.

Rose has suddenly become very ill and will soon need an operation. So we gathered around a candle and a red rose. Mary showed us some lovely slides of Rose, and then we all prayed for her. When handicapped people pray for handicapped people, God comes very near. The simplicity, directness, and intimacy of their prayer often make me feel like a skeptical bystander. I even feel a certain jealousy of their special gift of prayer. But they do not want me to be jealous. They hugged and kissed me after the prayer, and Michael took me by the hand to the sacristy to show me the red stole he wants to wear.

Lord, give me a heart like these people have so that I may understand more fully the depth of your love.

SLOW TOGETHER IS BETTER
THAN FAST ALONE!
(Friday, October 4)

During the meeting of the long-term assistants, Nick, who works with four handicapped men in the wood shop, spoke about his joys and frustrations. He explained how hard it is to do a job well and at the same time keep the needs of the handicapped men uppermost in mind. He wants to become a skillful and efficient carpenter, but realizes that the products of his work are less important than the growing self-esteem of the men he works with. This requires a lot of patience and a willingness to let others do slowly what you yourself can do rapidly. It means always choosing work in which people much less capable than yourself can participate. It asks for a deep inner conviction that a slow job done together is better than a fast job done alone.

Nick told us how long it had taken him to come to this insight. At first he had been primarily concerned about learning the skills of carpentry from Joe, the director of the wood shop. He was very excited about learning a new trade. But then he came to see that his skills were meant not just to make blackboards, play blocks, and coat hangers for kindergartens, but also and above all to help four handicapped people grow in human dignity and self-reliance.

I found this out myself this afternoon when I went apple picking with Janice, Carol, Adam, Rose, and their assistants. My attitude was to get the apples picked, put them in bags, and go home. But I soon learned that all of that was much less important than to help Rose pick one or two apples, to walk with Janice looking for apples that hang low enough so that she herself can reach them, to compliment Carol on her ability to find good apples, and just to sit beside Adam in his wheelchair under an apple tree and give him a sense of belonging to the group.

We finally collected four bags of apples, but eight people took more than an hour to do it. I could have done the work in half an hour. But efficiency is not L'Arche's most important word. Care is.

GREGORY'S STORY
(Saturday, October 5)

Today I visited the two L'Arche houses in the city, the house on Wolverleigh Boulevard and the house on Avoca Avenue.

At the Wolverleigh house, Gregory, one of the handicapped men in the house, gave a slide show about his own life. It was a very moving experience to hear a thirty-year-old man speak about the difference between his life in an institution and his life in a community. For Gregory, it was the difference between darkness and light, hell and heaven, self-destructive thoughts and a desire to live, between the "dumps" and a home.

When he was four years old, Gregory was taken to a mental institution in Orillia. "I had a stroke that paralyzed my right arm, and my parents brought me to Orillia. They came to see me every three weeks, but I was always sad because I didn't know why they put me there." Gregory showed slides of the dormitory, the dining hall, and the clothes room of the place where he had lived for twenty years, together with hundreds of other mentally handicapped people. He said, "We didn't have any privacy. We didn't even have our own clothes. We always wore clothes that had been worn before by other inmates. It was so lonely, so sad, I often thought of killing myself."

Then he showed slides of his life at Wolverleigh, to which he had come five years before. "Here I am in a store, buying food for the first time. And here I am in the kitchen, cooking my first meal. I was quite nervous, but everyone said they liked it."

Then he showed a slide of all the members of the house, sitting around the table with a candle in the middle. Gregory said, "Here we are all together at evening prayer. We never did such a thing in the institution. Here we are a family."

Gregory's simple but penetrating presentation taught me more about the charism of L'Arche than any article I had read or lecture I had heard. L'Arche offers a home to broken people and gives them a new sense of dignity and self-respect. Gregory made the point and made it stick.

RAYMOND'S ACCIDENT
(Sunday, October 6)

Everyone's mind and heart is with Raymond, who has been hit by a car and seriously injured.

Yesterday afternoon he and Bill were going to take a bus into town when Raymond suddenly crossed busy Yonge Street to reach the bus stop. Bill realized that Raymond had not noticed a car coming and tried to call him back. But Raymond did not hear him and was hit by the car and thrown into the air. At first it seemed that he had only minor fractures. But the X rays showed that many ribs were broken and one of his lungs was perforated. He is now in critical condition at St. Michael's Hospital in Toronto.

The whole community is visibly in anguish over it, especially D.J., the head of the house where Raymond lives, and Bill, who saw it all happen in front of his eyes. I became more acutely aware of the awesome responsibility assumed by people who care for handicapped men and women. On the one hand, you want to protect them as much as possible; on the other hand, you want to give them their independence as much as possible. It is a fine line to walk between these two "wants."

D.J. is a very responsible, caring person. He had felt that Bill and Raymond could travel together without assistance. They had done so for a long time. Now he obviously wonders if he gave them too much independence.

I went twice to St. Michael's Hospital with Kathy Judge to visit Raymond. Although on a respirator and fed intravenously, he was able to respond to our questions with nods. We prayed with him and assured him of our love. It was so sad to see him unable to talk to us. A few times he tried to pull off the respirator to say a few words but had to be restrained from doing so.

If he survives the first forty-eight hours, his chances for recovery are good. But his situation is quite critical. During the Eucharist this morning and the evening prayers in the different homes, all the prayers were for Raymond. These direct, heartfelt, and intense prayers revealed the strong faith of these handicapped people and their assistants. I felt surrounded by a fellowship of the weak. The noisy road in front of the house suddenly sounded like a "roaring lion, looking for someone to devour" (1 Peter 5:8).

O Lord, remember Raymond and give him your light and your joy during these agonizing hours. Please be good to him and all the broken people at Daybreak.

THE AGONY OF PARENTS
(Monday, October 7)

Many things today. An intimate, prayerful liturgy with the assistants, an insightful presentation by Joe Vorstermans, the director of the wood shop, about work with handicapped people, a stimulating exchange among the new assistants about their experiences at Daybreak during the past week, and a lovely dinner and good conversation with Gus, the assistant director, his wife, and his children.

But the overriding concern was Raymond. His situation has deteriorated, and his death seems imminent. At 7:30 P.M. Gus, D.J., and I drove to Toronto, where Joe Egan, the director of Daybreak, joined us. When we got to the hospital we found Raymond so heavily sedated that he could not communicate with us any more. The doctor and nurse said there was still hope but also prepared us for a sudden turn for the worse. Most important of all was our time with Ray's parents.

It is hard for parents to see any child suffer. But to see the suffering of a handicapped child creates an even greater pain. Raymond had lived for years in an institution and had only recently come to Daybreak. Not everyone was convinced yet that Daybreak was the best place for Raymond, and the accident obviously called up feelings not only of guilt, but also of frustration and even anger. Many questions went through our minds concerning road safety, the freedom given to handicapped people, care for Ray, and the wisdom of past decisions.

Guilt feelings separate, divide, alienate; they can lead to anger and hostility. When we all came together in our common concern for Raymond, we were able to express our feelings to each other not only in words, but also in gestures of love and in prayers and stories about our lives. Soon a new community developed. Raymond's father said to Gus and D.J., "You are as much fathers to Raymond as I am," and thus acknowledged our pain. We were able to understand why he had not always been grateful for the work Daybreak had done for his son, and thus acknowledged his deep anguish.

Raymond's situation remains critical. We do not even know if he will survive the night. But all those who love him are united and support each other in their struggle. Not guilt but love guides our concern. And that certainly is a tangible way in which God has responded to our prayers.

A NEW FUTURE DAWNS
(Wednesday, October 9)

I am writing in a plane somewhere between Toronto and Paris. This morning I still wasn't sure if I should return to Trosly today. Raymond's condition remained critical. Last night Joe Egan said, "It might be good if you stay a few more days.

In case Raymond does not survive this crisis, your presence will be very important for all of us." I promised to stay if the community asked me to.

But around 10 A.M. Ray's father called and told us good news: Ray was doing a little better. There was no immediate danger of death. Everyone agreed that I should return to Trosly as planned. At 1 P.M. I went with Kathy and D.J. to the hospital to say good-bye to Raymond and his parents. Raymond was still in the intensive care unit but indeed seemed a little better. He responded with nodding and hand squeezing to our questions, and his fever was clearly less than yesterday. I showed Ray's father how to make the sign of the cross on Ray's forehead. He had never done this before and cried as he signed his son in the name of the Father, the Son, and the Holy Spirit. A father's blessing is so healing.

Kathy, D.J., Ray's parents, and I sat together in the waiting room for a while and talked. We talked about Ray, about guilt and forgiveness, about trips to Paris, about how good it was to have each other's support, about crying and laughing, and about staying in touch and seeing each other again. After we left the hospital, Kathy and D.J. drove me to the airport; at 6:30 P.M. Air France flight 832 was on its way to Paris.

In my nine days at Daybreak I came to feel intimately a part of the intense joys and sorrows of this community of care. I have a deep love for the handicapped men and women and their assistants, who all received me with such warm hospitality. They did not hide anything from me. They allowed me to see their fears and their love. I feel deeply grateful for having been part of it all. I know that these days will deeply affect not only my time in France but also my decisions about the years to come.

5

THE PRIMACY OF THE HEART

∎

WRITING LETTERS
(Trosly; Friday, October 11)

IT FEELS GOOD to be home again, even though the mail seems a little overwhelming. But as I was writing letters today, I realized that writing letters is a much more intimate way of communicating than making phone calls. It may sound strange, but I often feel closer to friends I write to than to friends I speak with by phone.

When I write I think deeply about my friends, I pray for them, I tell them my emotions and feelings. I reflect on our relationship, and I dwell with them in a very personal way. Over the past few months I have come to enjoy letter writing more and more. In the beginning it seemed like a heavy burden, but now it is a relaxing time of the day. It feels like interrupting work for a conversation with a friend.

The beauty of letter writing is that it deepens friendships and makes them more real. I have also discovered that letter writing makes me pray more concretely for my friends. Early in the morning, I spend a little time praying for each person to whom I have written and promised my prayers.

Today I feel surrounded by the friends I am writing to and praying for. Our love for each other is very concrete and life-giving. Thank God for letters, for those who send them, and for those who receive them.

STAYING HOME CAN BE
FOLLOWING, TOO!
(Sunday, October 13)

When Anthony heard Jesus' words to the rich young man, "Go and sell everything you own and give the money to the poor, then come, follow me" (Mark 10:21), he suddenly realized they were meant for him. He sold everything, left his family, and went into the desert. We now consider him the father of Christian

327

monasticism. Today Madame Vanier told me how the same words that had led Anthony to the desert had brought her to L'Arche. After her husband died, she was living in an apartment in Montreal. When she came to visit her son in Trosly, one of the assistants said to her, "Why don't you come to live and work with us?" She answered brusquely, "Mind your own business, young man." But a seed was planted. When she made a retreat later that year to discern her future, she read this Gospel and suddenly felt tears welling up in her. She knew she had to follow the suggestion of the "brash" young man. She left her aristocratic life behind and came to live with her son in the community of L'Arche.

But today the story of the rich young man has a different meaning for her. Her poor health prevents her from traveling. It was her custom to return to Canada each year to visit her sons, Benedict and Michel, but for the first time in fourteen years at L'Arche she was unable to go. Her daughter, Thérèse, had come from England to visit before going to Canada. Madame Vanier's original plan had been to go with Thérèse, but now Thérèse was going alone.

As we read the Gospel story, it became clear that staying home now at eighty-seven had become as hard for her as leaving home at seventy-three. Now, leaving father, mother, brother, and sister to follow Jesus meant accepting the hard fact of no longer being able to visit her children in her own country and realizing that it might never be possible again.

It struck me that selling what you own, leaving your family and friends, and following Jesus is not a once-in-a-lifetime event. You must do it many times and in many different ways. And it certainly does not become easier.

THE SEARCH FOR AFFECTION
(Thursday, October 17)

At 9 A.M. I went to Père Thomas for spiritual direction. I asked him about my need for affection. I told him that getting older had not lessened that need, and that I feared it might prevent rather than help the development of my spiritual life. It took me about five minutes to express my problem. Père Thomas responded with a two-hour answer! It was a sermon, a lecture, and an exhortation, as well as a very personal response to my question. After half an hour I was so tired from trying to grasp fully the meaning of his words, as well as his difficult French, that I interrupted him by saying, "Thank you so much, that gives me enough to think about for a long time." But the good Père gave me another hour and a half of profound ideas and insights that will keep me going forever!

At first I felt overwhelmed by this long theological reflection, but now I realize that Père Thomas wanted to help me to think differently before helping me to feel differently. I will try to write down here at least some of his thoughts.

He started by saying that, for many of us in this highly psychologized culture, affection has become the central concern. We have come to judge ourselves in terms of the affection that is given or refused to us. The media—television, radio, magazines, and advertisements—have strongly reinforced the idea that human affection is what we really need. Being loved, liked, appreciated, praised, acknowledged, recognized, etc.—these are the most desired prizes of life. The lack of these forms of affection can throw us into an abyss of loneliness and depression, and even lead us to suicide. We have developed great sophistication in analyzing the many nuances of our affections and developed a rich language which allows us to express how we feel about ourselves and others at different times and in different situations. We have become highly developed psychological beings, and the range of our emotions and feelings regarding personal and interpersonal experiences has become increasingly wide.

I very much agree with Père Thomas's viewpoint. During my years at Harvard, much was said about the giving of love in its many expressions, as well as about the withholding of love through anger, resentment, and indignation. But the highly nuanced psychological language used, even at the divinity school, made spiritual and theological language sound irrelevant, superficial, and even offensive.

But it is precisely this highly developed psychological consciousness that sometimes prevents us from reaching that place in us where the healing powers are hidden. Père Thomas's greatest gift, as I see it, is his ability to speak about that place and mobilize its hidden gifts. He calls that place the heart.

Tomorrow I will try to write down some of his thoughts about the heart.

THE HEART
(Friday, October 18)

What is the heart? It is the place of trust, a trust that can be called faith, hope, or love, depending on how it is being manifested. Père Thomas sees the trusting heart as the most important characteristic of the human person. It is not so much the ability to think, to reflect, to plan, or to produce that makes us different from the rest of creation, but the ability to trust. It is the heart that makes us truly human.

This vital observation helps explain why we respond with our hearts to our surroundings long before our consciences are developed. Our consciences, which allow us to distinguish between good and evil and thus give us a basis for moral choice, are less in control than our hearts. Père Thomas is convinced that much of the crisis in the life of the Church today is connected with a lack of knowledge of the heart. Much Church discussion today focuses on the morality of human behavior: premarital sex, divorce, homosexuality, birth control, abortion, and so on. Many people have become disillusioned with the Church because of these issues. But when the moral life gets all the attention, we are in danger of forgetting the primacy of the mystical life, which is the life of the heart.

Quite often the suggestion is made that the mystical life, a life in which we enter into a unifying communion with God, is the highest fruit and most precious reward of the moral life. The classical distinctions among the purifying way, the illuminating way, and the unifying way as the three progressively higher levels of the spiritual life have strengthened this suggestion. Thus we have come to see the mystical life as the life of the happy few who reach the prayer of total surrender.

The greatest insight of Père Thomas—an insight in which the best of his theology and the best of his pastoral experience with handicapped people merge— is that the mystical life lies at the beginning of our existence and not just at its end. We are born in intimate communion with the God who created us in love. We belong to God from the moment of our conception. Our heart is that divine gift which allows us to trust not just God, but also our mother, our father, our family, ourselves, and the world. Père Thomas is convinced that very small children have a deep, intuitive knowledge of God, a knowledge of the heart, that sadly is often obscured and even suffocated by the many systems of thought we gradually cultivate. Handicapped people, who have such a limited ability to learn, can let their hearts speak easily and thus reveal a mystical life that for many intelligent people seems unreachable.

By speaking about the heart as the deepest source of the spiritual life, the life of faith, hope, and love, Père Thomas wanted to show me that human affections do not lead us where our hearts want to lead us. The heart is much wider and deeper than our affections. It is before and beyond the distinctions between sorrow and joy, anger and lust, fear and love. It is the place where all is one in God, the place where we truly belong, the place from which we come and to which we always yearn to return.

I now realize that my "simple" question about my affections required a fuller response than I had expected. I need to relearn the central place of the mystical experience in human life.

THE THREE MONKS OF TOLSTOY
(Saturday, October 19)

This afternoon Maria and Louis Tersteeg, friends of mine from Holland, came to Trosly for an afternoon. It was a joy to see them both. We lunched at La Ferme, prayed for a moment in L'Oratoire, had a short visit with Madame Vanier, enjoyed tea with the people at La Forestière, went to Mass with the whole community, and had dinner at Le Val Fleuri, one of the largest and oldest foyers of L'Arche.

Both Maria and Louis were deeply impressed with what they saw and heard. In many ways L'Arche was an eye-opener for them. When we went back to the station in Compiègne, Louis said, "What I will remember most is the three servers during the Eucharist." Maria fully agreed. Seeing three handicapped men in white albs come close to the altar to help Père Thomas prepare the gifts somehow summarized for them the meaning of all they had seen that afternoon.

"They remind me of the three monks in the Tolstoy story," Louis said. As we talked more, the story came back to life:

Three Russian monks lived on a faraway island. Nobody ever went there, but one day their bishop decided to make a pastoral visit. When he arrived he discovered that the monks didn't even know the Lord's Prayer. So he spent all his time and energy teaching them the "Our Father" and then left, satisfied with his pastoral work. But when his ship had left the island and was back in the open sea, he suddenly noticed the three hermits walking on the water—in fact, they were running after the ship! When they reached it they cried, "Dear Father, we have forgotten the prayer you taught us." The bishop, overwhelmed by what he was seeing and hearing, said, "But, dear brothers, how then do you pray?" They answered, "Well, we just say, 'Dear God, there are three of us and there are three of you, have mercy on us!'" The bishop, awestruck by their sanctity and simplicity, said, "Go back to your island and be at peace."

When Louis saw the three handicapped altar servers, this story came immediately to his mind. Like the three monks of Tolstoy, these men may not be able to remember much, but they can be holy enough to walk on water. And that says much about L'Arche.

6

FEELING THE PAIN

■

JOHN'S DEATH
(Thursday, October 24)

MY DEAR FRIEND Rose just called from Oakland, California, to tell me that her son John died yesterday morning at 9:30 A.M. Her voice was full of pain and desolation. "It is so hard, so hard, so hard to keep believing in the midst of all this," she said. "I feel more lost and in anguish than when Dan [her husband] died." I heard her cries, her deep feeling of aloneness, her desperation.

But she also spoke words of consolation: "Oh, Henri, the people of the hospice were so good, loving, and caring. Many are gay or lesbian, and few are part of any church or believe in God, but their love for Johnny was so beautiful, so deep, so generous. Many give up their jobs just to be with their dying brothers and sisters . . . Johnny has been loved to the end . . . I just want you to know." Her words were like drops of hope in a sea of despair, inklings of gratitude in the midst of an overwhelming feeling of loss, flashes of light in a deep darkness.

I said, "Johnny loved you so much and he told me how much your love for him meant to him. Hold on to that. Your pain is deep because you suffered that long journey toward death with him. You and he were so open with each other. You didn't hide anything from each other. You saw and felt his struggle and he saw and felt yours . . . It will be hard for you . . . very hard . . . but I know your love is strong and beautiful."

I didn't know John very well, but a few years ago when I was in San Francisco, Rose introduced me to him and we spent some time together. John told me about his homosexuality and his life in the San Francisco gay community. He did not try to defend his way of living or apologize for it. I remember his great compassion for the people he spoke about, but also his critical remarks about snobbism and capitalism in the San Francisco gay community. He himself was extremely generous. He gave much of his time, money, and energy to people in need and asked very little for himself. Seldom have I known anyone who was so eager to have me understand and learn. He was so nonjudgmental, self-possessed, and honest that I came to think of him as an example of a just man.

Last February, Rose called me in Cambridge to tell me that John was very sick with AIDS. I immediately flew to San Francisco and spent a day with Rose at her home and with John and his friend Mike in the hospital. John asked me to read the Twenty-third Psalm with him. It was the psalm he remembered, the psalm his father had prayed with him. It was a psalm that gave him peace. We prayed the words together several times:

> *The Lord is my shepherd,*
> *there is nothing I shall want.*
> *Fresh and green are the pastures*
> *where he gives me repose.*
> *Near restful waters he leads me*
> *to revive my drooping spirit.*

Tomorrow I want to write a little more about my visit to Rose and John.

JOHN'S AGONY
(Friday, October 25)

My time with John and Rose showed me the ravaging power of AIDS. John could hardly stay quiet for a minute. Like a wild animal caught in a cage, he could find no rest, and his whole body moved in pain. To see his agony and not be able to do anything, to know that he would only get worse, was nearly intolerable. But I was struck by the care which surrounded him. Many AIDS patients are rejected by family and friends. But Rose's love for her son grew stronger every day of his illness. No condemnation, no accusation, no rejection, but love as only a mother can give. And Mike, John's companion, gave every minute of his time and every ounce of his energy to his sick friend. No complaints, no signs of irritation, just faithful presence.

Mike knew that John would die soon. But it could be a week, a month, a year, or longer. He wanted only one thing: for John to feel a little better and be comfortable during the time that was left to him. "I don't believe in God," Mike said, "but if John wants to pray with you, please pray with him. Do anything that is good for John. That's all that matters to me."

After I returned to Cambridge John began to recover somewhat. He left the hospital and found a small apartment where he could live with Mike. People from the hospice came daily to care for John while Mike went to work.

In August I saw John again. He was less restless but suffered from terrible dizziness. "I want to die," he said. "I cannot bear this dizziness any longer." I asked him to accept death when it came, and not to hasten it. We spoke about

Rose's and Mike's love and how much he meant to them. "Try to live for them as long as God wants you to," I said.

He asked me to give him the sacrament of the sick—"the last rites," as he called them. He said, "I was baptized and received my First Communion, and I also want to receive the last rites before I die. Will you give me the sacrament?" He wanted to be alone with me. We sat together at the kitchen table. We prayed the Twenty-third Psalm again. I blessed him, crossed his forehead and hands with sacred oil, and prayed for healing—but also for the grace to die with Christ. Together we said, "Our Father, who art in heaven, hallowed be thy name. Thy kingdom come. Thy will be done on earth as it is in heaven."

He said, "Thank you very much," and added in his typical understated way, "This certainly can't hurt me." Afterwards I talked with Mike for a moment. "I am afraid he won't live into the next year," Mike said. "I can't even imagine what it will mean to be without him." I saw Mike's deep suffering. All the attention was on John, but Mike needed support, too. Rose knew this and gave him all she could.

When Rose called me yesterday, she said, "Mike and I cried the whole afternoon yesterday. We had to. I am so glad that Mike and I can support each other. We both miss him so much."

Today John is being cremated. Tuesday there will be a memorial service. Rose will be there. Mike will be there, and so will most of John's brothers and sisters. I will miss being with them. "Can I do something?" I asked Rose on the phone. "If you wish, send some money to the San Francisco hospice people for their work. When they came to help me wash and anoint John's body and take him away, they told us that Johnny was the fourth person to die from AIDS that day in San Francisco. These people are so loving, so caring, so good . . . they may not all believe in God, but they surely help me to do so."

I thank God for having known John and having come to know in a new way the inexhaustible mystery of human suffering and human love.

SEEING CHRIST
(Saturday, October 26)

For a week now, I have been trying to write a meditation about the icon of Christ the Savior painted by Andrew Rublev. I have not yet been able to write a word, but in fact have experienced an increasing anxiety. I looked at some books on iconography, studied some articles on Rublev's particular style, read through Ian Wilson's book on the Turin Shroud, and let my mind make all sorts of connections but could not find words for writing. I feel tired, even exhausted, because I have spent much mental energy but have found no way to channel it creatively.

I am gradually realizing that what restrains me is the direct confrontation with the face of Jesus. I have written about Rublev's icon of the Trinity and about the icon of Our Lady of Vladimir. Yet writing about the icon of Christ's sacred face is such an awesome undertaking that I wonder if I can really do it.

This afternoon I just looked at this seemingly indescribable icon. I looked at the eyes of Jesus and saw his eyes looking at me. I choked, closed my eyes, and started to pray. I said, "O my God, how can I write about your face? Please give me the words to say what can be said." I read in the Gospels and realized how much is written there about seeing and being seen, about being blind and receiving new sight, and about eyes—human eyes and the eyes of God.

I know I must write about Rublev's icon of Christ because it touches me more than any icon I have ever seen. I must come to know what happens to me when I look at and pray with it. One thing is certain: I have read enough about it. I must simply be present to it, and pray and look and pray and wait and pray and trust. I hope that the right words will come, because if they do, perhaps many will begin to see with me and be touched by those eyes.

A PRAYER TO SEE AND BE SEEN
(Monday, October 28)

O Lord Jesus, I look at you, and my eyes are fixed on your eyes. Your eyes penetrate the eternal mystery of the divine and see the glory of God. They are also the eyes that saw Simon, Andrew, Nathanael, and Levi, the eyes that saw the woman with a hemorrhage, the widow of Nain, the blind, the lame, the lepers, and the hungry crowd, the eyes that saw the sad, rich ruler, the fearful disciples on the lake, and the sorrowful women at the tomb. Your eyes, O Lord, see in one glance the inexhaustible love of God and the seemingly endless agony of all people who have lost faith in that love and are like sheep without a shepherd.

As I look into your eyes, they frighten me because they pierce like flames of fire my innermost being, but they console me as well, because these flames are purifying and healing. Your eyes are so severe yet so loving, so unmasking yet so protecting, so penetrating yet so caressing, so profound yet so intimate, so distant yet so inviting.

I gradually realize that I want to be seen by you, to dwell under your caring gaze, and to grow strong and gentle in your sight. Lord, let me see what you see—the love of God and the suffering of people—so that my eyes may become more and more like yours, eyes that can heal wounded hearts.

NOT MILK, BUT SOLID FOOD
(Tuesday, October 29)

Every Tuesday night I celebrate the Eucharist for the English-speaking assistants of the community. We gather in the small chapel of La Forestière. Not all the English-speaking people can come, but the chapel is quickly filled, especially since a few of the assistants bring a handicapped housemate with them.

I have noticed that these people have little desire for dialogue or discussion, though they do like to pray together, sing together, be silent together, and listen together to a reflection on the Gospel. The assistants are often tired from a long day of work with handicapped men and women, and they want to be nurtured, supported, and cared for.

I must learn a new style of ministry. Few of those who participate in these Tuesday night liturgies need to be convinced of the importance of the Gospels, the centrality of Jesus, or the value of the sacraments. Most have moved beyond that stage. They have discovered Christ; they have made their decision to work with the poor; they have chosen the narrow path.

I still spend much energy convincing them of God's love, calling them to community, and offering them a place to experience the peace of Jesus. That kind of ministry is appropriate in a secular university, where students are fully caught up in the race for achievement. But here there is no urge to success; here time is filled with dressing, feeding, carrying, and just being with those in need. It is a very demanding and tiring way, but there is no rivalry, no degree to be acquired, no honor to be desired—just faithful service.

I do not want to romanticize the young men and women at L'Arche. I am too aware of their struggles, imperfections, and unfulfilled longings. Still, they have made a choice that few have made. Their need is less to be convinced of the importance of that choice than to find encouragement to continue, new perspectives to keep them from falling into a spiritual "rut," and support to remain faithful to what they have already chosen. What they need, to use the words of the apostle Paul, is not milk, but solid food (1 Corinthians 3:2).

This is a new challenge for me. It requires me to develop the art of "spiritual companionship" with these fellow travelers. I now realize that the Gospel of John was written for men and women like these. It was written for mature spiritual persons who do not want to argue about elementary issues, but who want to be introduced into the mysteries of the divine life. I must truly be a man of prayer to be able to respond to this desire.

Tonight we prayed especially for John. I wished I could be with the many who will gather today in California for the memorial service, to express gratitude for having known him. May he now find the love he searched for with so much pain and agony during his short life.

CRIES FOR AFFECTION
(Thursday, October 31)

The November issue of *Messages des Sécours Catholiques,* a monthly newsletter published by a French Catholic organization for emergency relief, is filled with gripping stories about human loneliness. The headline, which I have also seen printed on a poster hanging in many churches, says, "La solitude, Ça existe. La solidarité aussi," which means "Loneliness exists; solidarity, too!" I am moved to see loneliness described as a form of suffering that afflicts not only poor people, prisoners, and the elderly, but also well-educated young adults. Loneliness is first of all a cry for affection. The many letters received by the Sécours Catholiques agency ask not just for food, shelter, money, or a job, but also, and often with greater urgency, for affection.

One letter writer says: "I have a need for affection, for tenderness, but where can I find that in this indifferent world?" Another says: "I have no friends anymore . . . I ask your help to be able to live again with normal people who don't need drugs or alcohol to exist!" Another: "I need someone to help me. I need someone who loves me . . . without that I feel myself slowly dying." Another: "I have never been looked at or listened to. I do not count anymore, I do not exist anymore."[3]

Much suffering in our time is caused by this need for affection. An increasing number of people have no home. They live alone in small rooms hidden away in large cities. When they return from work there is nobody to welcome them, kiss them, embrace them, and ask them, "How was your day?" There is nobody to cry with, laugh with, walk with, eat with, or just sit with.

Michel, eighteen years of age, writes, "Let me appear on radio or television so that I can cry out about the pain of young men who have never been loved, who have been shuffled from place to place, who have never known the love of a family."[4]

This is a cry for a real neighbor, for someone who is willing to be close, who gives not just food, a house, or a job, but the sense of being loved. Where are the people who can offer this closeness to their lonely brothers and sisters?

As I think about these questions, I vividly remember Père Thomas's views about the human need for affection. I agree with his viewpoint that in our psychologized culture, human affection has become a central concern. I also realize more than ever before that a new knowledge of God's unconditional love is needed. But reading these desperate cries for affection, I wonder how this unconditional divine love can be experienced in our media-controlled milieu. One thing is becoming clear to me: God became flesh for us to show us that the way to come in touch with God's love is the human way, in which the limited and partial affection that people can give offers access to the unlimited and complete love that God has poured into the human heart. God's love cannot be found outside this human affection, even when that human affection is tainted by the brokenness of our time.

FORGIVING THE HURT

■

GOING BEYOND FEELINGS
(Sunday, November 3)

TONIGHT JONAS ARRIVED. He came directly from Cambridge and will be here in Trosly for ten days. The depression that hit me when he didn't visit during his September vacation in France has lurked under the surface of my mostly cheerful life.

Jonas's visit is very important to me. It will not be an easy time for me, as I need to find ways to forgive him and deepen our friendship. But I trust that God will help me to go beyond my feelings of rejection and find reconciliation.

SHARING THE GIFTS
(Tuesday, November 5)

Jonas and I spent the day visiting the community. Because he raised many questions from the perspective of a psychologist, I learned much about L'Arche that I had never considered before. I was also reminded of the centrality of "living L'Arche," that is, living in intimate communion with the handicapped. As elsewhere, work is important, the development of behavioral skills is important, health and education are important—but they are all secondary to a life lived together in a community of love. There are doctors, psychologists, psychiatrists, physical therapists, and nurses, but they are all consultants more than leaders. The professionals are here to help the assistants live with the handicapped in a creative, supportive, and healing way.

It is also important that the handicapped people develop as much physical and emotional independence as possible, but never disregarding community life. The central words here are not "equal rights" but rather "sharing the gifts." The handicapped people are different from their assistants, but within their differences lie gifts which need to be discovered, acknowledged, and shared. The handicapped people and the assistants need each other, though sometimes in different ways. Together they seek to form a true fellowship of the weak, always thanking and praising God for the fragile gift of life.

GOOD NEWS FROM DAYBREAK
(Wednesday, November 6)

Sue Mosteller arrived with good news from Daybreak: Raymond left the intensive care unit, Rose's surgery went well, and both are on their way to recovery. She also brought kind words with her from D.J. and from Ray's family.

With Sue, I experienced great joy at this victory over the power of death and I was reminded of the words of the prophet Ezekiel: "Why die, house of Israel? I take no pleasure in the death of anyone . . . so repent and live" (Ezekiel 18:32).

TRUE AMATEURS
(Thursday, November 7)

Jonas and I are having an important week together. We are busy visiting foyers, workshops, and specialists. It feels to me like showing a foreigner my hometown and discovering it myself in the process! Because Jonas raises questions, notices events, and makes comparisons differently from me, he has uncovered a different L'Arche from what I had seen so far.

To Jonas, a psychologist in a large institution for handicapped people, L'Arche is a place where the professional distance that allows people to heal others without getting entangled in their many problems is less visible, even absent. L'Arche might at first seem somewhat amateurish to a professional. Still, the word "amateur" is a word we must recover; it suggests a way to understand the true nature of this distance. The word comes from *amare*, which is Latin for "to love."

Life at L'Arche is built upon love, not simply for handicapped people, but for the God of life revealed to us in Jesus Christ, the rejected man of Nazareth. It is a love based upon the knowledge of the heart, a deep conviction that "nothing, neither death nor life, nor angel, nor prince, nothing that exists, nothing still to come, nor any power or height or depth, nor any created thing can ever come between us and the love of God made visible in Christ Jesus our Lord" (Romans 8:38-39). This love is much more than an emotion or feeling. It is rooted in the fact of God's unlimited love for us. It is this love which allows us to be deeply involved with the suffering of the world without being swallowed up by it. It is this love which enables us to listen to the howls and cries of handicapped people without being possessed by them. It is this love which allows us to be very close without ever losing the distance necessary for us to live healthy, joyful, and peaceful lives.

When our love is rooted in God's love, we can carry the burden of life and discover it to be light. Jesus calls us: "Come to me, all you who labor and are overburdened, and I will give you rest. Shoulder my yoke and learn from me, for I am gentle and humble of heart . . . Yes, my yoke is easy and my burden light" (Matthew 11:28–30). The burden of Jesus is the burden of all human suffering, but when we take on that burden in communion with him, it proves to be light and easy. Personally, I think that living close to handicapped people, as do the L'Arche assistants, is impossible unless one draws upon the love of Christ. Without this love, such a life leads to "burnout." But when this love is deep and strong and constantly nurtured by the community, the handicapped people can become conductors of the vision of that greater love which holds us safely.

Thus a new type of distance develops: not a professional distance, which protects us from getting too close to the world's pain, but a spiritual distance, which allows us to let that pain become a light burden.

STRUGGLING WITH THE NATURE OF FRIENDSHIP
(Friday, November 8)

Maintaining spiritual distance is a more personal matter than I realized yesterday. It is essential to the understanding and living of true friendship. Jonas and I are trying to deal with our friendship. In the beginning we touched upon it only indirectly, but in the past few days we have been able to explore our relationship more directly. It is hard for me to speak of my feelings of being rejected or imposed upon, of my desire for affirmation as well as my need for space, of insecurity and mistrust, of fear and love. But as I entered into these feelings, I also discovered the real problem—expecting from a friend what only Christ can give.

I feel so easily rejected. When a friend does not come, a letter is not written, or an invitation not extended, I begin to feel unwanted and disliked. I gravitate toward dark feelings of low self-esteem and become depressed. Once depressed, I tend to interpret even innocent gestures as proofs of my self-chosen darkness, from which it is harder and harder to return. Looking carefully at this vicious cycle of self-rejection and speaking about it directly with Jonas in a good way to start moving in the opposite direction.

Two things happened when Jonas and I spoke. First, he forced me to move out of the center! He too has a life, he too has his struggles, he too has unfulfilled needs and imperfections. As I tried to understand his life, I felt a deep compassion and a desire to comfort and console him. I no longer felt so strongly the need to judge him for not paying enough attention to me. It is so easy to convince yourself that you are the one who needs all the attention. But once you can see the other concretely in his or her life situation, you can step back a bit from yourself and understand that, in a true friendship, two people make a dance.

Second, I learned afresh that friendship requires a constant willingness to forgive each other for not being Christ and a willingness to ask Christ himself to be the true center. When Christ does not mediate a relationship, that relationship easily becomes demanding, manipulating, oppressive, an arena for many forms of rejection. An unmediated friendship cannot last long; you simply expect too much of the other and cannot offer the other the space he or she needs to grow. Friendship requires closeness, affection, support, and mutual encouragement, but also distance, space to grow, freedom to be different, and solitude. To nurture both aspects of a relationship, we must experience a deeper and more lasting affirmation than any human relationship can offer.

As we struggled with the true nature of our friendship, Jonas and I read Paul's words to the Romans: "We know that by turning everything to their good, God cooperates with all those who love him, with all those whom he has called according to his purpose . . . those he called he justified, and with those he justified he shared his glory" (Romans 8:28–30).

When we truly love God and share in his glory, our relationships lose their compulsive character. We reach out to people not just to receive their affirmation, but also to allow them to participate in the love we have come to know through Jesus. Thus true friendship becomes an expression of a greater love.

It is hard work to remind each other constantly of the truth, but it is worth the effort. Constant mutual forgiveness and a continual openness to the love of God are the disciplines which allow us to grow together in friendship.

THE SMALL SEDUCTIONS OF A SENSUAL WORLD
(Saturday, November 9)

Today Jonas and I spent an afternoon and an evening in Compiègne. We considered going to Paris but were not fully convinced that riding trains and subways, finding a place to stay, and seeing churches and museums would be the best way to conclude our time together at L'Arche. We decided to go to Compiègne and then see if going on to Paris would be attractive to both of us.

In Compiègne it was market day. Thousands of people were walking through the streets, going from stand to stand, looking, arguing, and buying. Parents with their children, small groups of teenagers, single men and women, and elderly couples had all come to town on Saturday to buy for the holiday (Monday, November 11, is Armistice Day), to do their banking, or just to meet friends and have a good time.

Both Jonas and I were struck by the sharp contrast between our quiet, prayerful week in Trosly and our restless, noisy, busy, and crowded afternoon in town. We felt ourselves being distracted, scattered, pulled away from our center, and drawn into the anonymous life of strangers. After a time of peace and joy lived in community, we both experienced a certain inner restlessness and sadness. It seemed as if the city were tempting us with its sensuality: its many colors, movements, things to buy, and people to look at. Jonas spoke about the return of the "desiring mind" after a period of being among the poor and handicapped in a somewhat desire-free way. Our curiosity, which had left us for a while, returned with new force. We both experienced in the people, movements, and places of Compiègne a temptation to lose touch with God's kingdom and be swept up by desires for the many "other things" (Luke 12:31) of this world.

We were glad we could talk about these things. Often such experiences remain hidden and cause much shame and guilt. But by confessing to each other how easily we are seduced by the attractions of the world, we affirmed our true commitment and safeguarded that commitment in each other. I now understand much better why Jesus sent his disciples into the world in groups of two rather than alone. Together, they could maintain the spirit of peace and love they found in his company and could share these gifts with everyone they met.

After four hours in Compiègne, we decided to return to Trosly and have a quiet, prayerful Sunday there. We weren't ready for Paris yet!

A FORGIVEN PERSON FORGIVES
(Monday, November 11)

Often I am not prepared for my morning meditation and end up just sitting in the oratory at 7 A.M. with all kinds of thoughts except the thought my meditation subject suggests to me.

But I simply must stay with it, even when it seems quite pointless. This morning I meditated on God's eagerness to forgive me, revealed in the words of the One Hundred Third Psalm: "As far as the East is from the West, so far does God remove my sin." In the midst of all my distractions, I was touched by God's desire to forgive me again and again. If I return to God with a repentant heart after I have sinned, God is always there to embrace me and let me start afresh. "The Lord is compassion and love, slow to anger and rich in mercy."

It is hard for me to forgive someone who has really offended me, especially when it happens more than once. I begin to doubt the sincerity of the one who asks forgiveness for a second, third, or fourth time. But God does not keep count. God just waits for our return, without resentment or desire for revenge. God wants us home. "The love of the Lord is everlasting."

Maybe the reason it seems hard for me to forgive others is that I do not fully believe that I am a forgiven person. If I could fully accept the truth that I am forgiven and do not have to live in guilt or shame, I would really be free. My freedom would allow me to forgive others seventy times seven times. By not forgiving, I chain myself to a desire to get even, thereby losing my freedom. A forgiven person forgives. This is what we proclaim when we pray, "and forgive us our trespasses as we forgive those who have trespassed against us."

This lifelong struggle lies at the heart of the Christian life.

FORGIVENESS AND FREEDOM
(Tuesday, November 12)

Jonas left this morning. I got up early, broke two wine glasses trying to find my way around the kitchen, made Jonas a sandwich for his train ride, and then walked to his room. We prayed together in the oratory, had a quick breakfast, and discovered that Simone had also made him a sandwich for the train. Barbara picked us up in one of the L'Arche Renaults and drove us to the station. The train to Brussels appeared on the minute. We embraced, said good words to each other, and waved good-bye as the train pulled away. Barbara said, "He is a very nice man. It was good for us that he came. I hope it was also good for him."

Tonight, during the Eucharist for the English-speaking assistants, we heard the words of Jesus: "Forgive your brother from your heart." I spoke about the freedom that forgiveness can bring, and many people said afterwards that my words had touched them deeply. I discovered once again that what is most personal is most universal. Jonas had left, but his leaving was a good leaving that was already bearing fruit.

8

JESUS IN THE CENTER

■

FATHER GEORGE STROHMEYER, the co-founder of L'Arche community in Erie, Pennsylvania, is visiting for a few weeks. This morning I had a chance to speak with him about being a priest for L'Arche.

He told me about his "conversion" when he came to Trosly for the first time. His hours of adoration in front of the Blessed Sacrament and his contacts with Père Thomas were the two main causes behind his more radical turn to Jesus. As he told his story, it became clear that Jesus is at the center of his life. This would seem obvious for a priest, but such is not always the case. George has come to know Jesus in a way few priests have. When he pronounces the name of Jesus you know that he speaks from a deep, intimate encounter. His life has become simpler, more hidden, more rooted, more trusting, more open, more evangelical, and more peaceful. For George, being a priest at L'Arche means leading people— the handicapped and their assistants—always closer to Jesus.

I now know for sure that there is a long, hard journey ahead of me. It is the journey of leaving everything behind for Jesus' sake. I now know that there is a way of living, praying, being with people, caring, eating, drinking, sleeping, reading, and writing in which Jesus is truly the center. I know from Jean Vanier, from Père Thomas, and from the many assistants who live here that this way exists and that I have not fully found it yet.

How do I find it? George gave me the answer: "Be faithful in your adoration." He did not say "prayer" or "meditation" or "contemplation." He kept using the word "adoration." This word makes it clear that all the attention must be on Jesus and not on me. To adore is to be drawn away from my own preoccupations into the presence of Jesus. It means letting go of what I want, desire, and have planned and fully trusting Jesus and his love.

Talking to George creates a certain jealousy in me. It seems as if he stands on the other side of the river and calls me to jump in and swim. But I am afraid; I think I will drown. I think I am not prepared to let go of all the good things on my side of the river. But I also want to be where he is; I sense the freedom, joy, and peace he has found. There is a clarity about him that I lack, an utter simplicity, a total commitment, and a vision that do not come from reading or studying but are a gift from God. I am jealous but also ambivalent, hesitant, and doubting. There is a voice in me that says, "You don't want to become a fanatic, a sectarian, a Jesus freak, a narrow-minded enthusiast . . . you want to remain open to many ways of being, explore many options, be informed about many things . . ." I know that this is not the voice I should trust. It is the voice that keeps me from making a full commitment to Jesus and from truly seeing the way God wants me to be in the world.

To give, not from my wealth but from my want, as the widow of Jerusalem who donated her last coin, that is the great challenge of the Gospel. When I look critically at my life, I find that my generosity always occurs in the context of great wealth. I give some of my money, some of my time, some of my energy, and some of my thoughts to God and others, but enough money, time, energy, and thoughts always remain to maintain my own security. Thus I never really give God a chance to show me his boundless love.

Maybe following George's example is the best I can do: adoring Jesus in the Blessed Sacrament every day, listening more to Père Thomas, and consistently choosing a life among the poor.

RETURNING WITH AN IMPURE HEART
(Sunday, November 17)

For three days I have been meditating on the story of the prodigal son. It is a story about returning. I realize the importance of returning over and over again. My life drifts away from God. I have to return. My heart moves away from my first love. I have to return. My mind wanders to strange images. I have to return. Returning is a lifelong struggle.

It strikes me that the wayward son had rather selfish motivations. He said to himself, "How many of my father's paid servants have more food than they want, and here am I dying of hunger! I will leave this place and go to my father." He didn't return because of a renewed love for his father. No, he returned simply to survive. He had discovered that the way he had chosen was leading him to death. Returning to his father was a necessity for staying alive. He realized that he had sinned, but this realization came about because sin had brought him close to death.

I am moved by the fact that the father didn't require any higher motivation. His love was so total and unconditional that he simply welcomed his son home.

This is a very encouraging thought. God does not require a pure heart before embracing us. Even if we return only because following our desires has failed to bring happiness, God will take us back. Even if we return because being a Christian brings us more peace than being a pagan, God will receive us. Even if we return because our sins did not offer as much satisfaction as we had hoped, God will take us back. Even if we return because we could not make it on our own, God will receive us. God's love does not require any explanations about why we are returning. God is glad to see us home and wants to give us all we desire, just for being home.

In my mind's eye I see Rembrandt's painting *The Return of the Prodigal Son*. The dim-eyed old father holds his returned son close to his chest with an unconditional love. Both of his hands, one strong and masculine, the other gentle and feminine, rest on his son's shoulders. He does not look at his son but feels his young, tired body and lets him rest in his embrace. His immense red cape is like the wings of a mother bird covering her fragile nestling. He seems to think only one thing: "He is back home, and I am so glad to have him with me again."

So why delay? God is standing there with open arms, waiting to embrace me. He won't ask any questions about my past. Just having me back is all he desires.

A JEALOUS LOVE
(Monday, November 18)

I am growing in the awareness that God wants my whole life, not just part of it. It is not enough to give just so much time and attention to God and keep the rest for myself. It is not enough to pray often and deeply and then move from there to my own projects.

As I try to understand why I am still so restless, anxious, and tense, it occurs to me that I have not yet given everything to God. I notice this especially in my greediness for time. I am very concerned to have enough hours to develop my ideas, finish my projects, fulfill my desires. Thus, my life is in fact divided into two parts, a part for God and a part for myself. Thus divided, my life cannot be peaceful.

To return to God means to return to God with all that I am and all that I have. I cannot return to God with just half of my being. As I reflected this morning again on the story of the prodigal son and tried to experience myself in the embrace of the father, I suddenly felt a certain resistance to being embraced so fully and totally. I experienced not only a desire to be embraced, but also a fear of losing my independence. I realized that God's love is a jealous love. God wants not just a part of me, but all of me. Only when I surrender myself completely to God's parental love can I expect to be free from endless distractions, ready to hear the voice of love, and able to recognize my own unique call.

It is going to be a very long road. Every time I pray, I feel the struggle. It is the struggle of letting God be the God of my whole being. It is the struggle to trust that true freedom lies hidden in total surrender to God's love.

Following Jesus is the way to enter into the struggle and find true freedom. The way is the way of the cross, and true freedom is the freedom found in the victory over death. Jesus' total obedience to his Father led him to the cross, and through the cross to a life no longer subject to the competitive games of this world. Jesus held on to nothing, not even to satisfying religious experiences. His words "My God, my God, why have you forsaken me?" give us a glimpse of the complete surrender of Jesus to his Father. Nothing was left for him to cling to. In this complete surrender he found total unity and total freedom.

To me Jesus says, "Come and follow me . . I have come so that you may have life and have it abundantly" (John 10:10).

SEARCHING FOR THE RIGHT WORDS
(Thursday, November 28)

Words, words, words! Tonight we start a "reflection weekend." All day I have been looking in the dictionary to find the French words for a talk I must give tomorrow to all the assistants of the community.

I am also struggling to find a way to maintain some spontaneity while speaking in a foreign language. My desire to make no mistakes can inhibit my freedom of expression. But too many mistakes are distracting and prevent people from hearing the message.

My main problem, however, is on a much deeper level. How do I speak to people whom I perceive to be more converted than I am? I have been asked to speak about hope in the midst of a world full of despair. But what can I say about hope to people whose lives are a living proof of hope? The 250 assistants here at L'Arche have left home, career, and wealth in order to live simple lives with people who are considered useless by the world. This is certainly a radical way of proclaiming hope.

So I feel as if I am carrying coals to Newcastle or, as the Dutch say, "bringing owls to Athens" or, as the French say, "bringing water to the river." But whatever expression you use, it is hard to speak well to the converted! I know I must speak because I have been asked to speak, and proclaiming the Good News is my vocation. In this case, I trust that those who will be listening tomorrow will be able to hear beyond my limping words, will be affirmed in the choices they have already made, and will help me to believe so strongly in my own words that I will find new courage to put them into practice. Occasionally the main fruit of speaking is the conversion of the speaker!

With that hope I can go ahead and let my words do the work for me.

A TRUE EXPERIENCE OF CHURCH
(Friday, November 29)

The reflection weekend is a unique event at L'Arche since it is the only time during the year when the assistants gather without the handicapped people and reflect on their life at L'Arche. It is a retreat, but also a celebration. It is a time to pray, sing, and think, but also a time to get to know each other and feel part of one body.

Because the foyers are spread across four different villages and the assistants must be home most of the time, you never realize how many people work at L'Arche. But last night, during the opening of the reflection weekend, I was struck by how large the community really is. At least 250 men and women came together—young, old, married and single, coming from the most diverse places in the world to be with the poor in spirit. A festive mood prevailed, and everyone was happy to have these days to be together. Most of the handicapped men and women have gone home or to their "special families" so that the assistants can receive all the attention for a change.

I am coming to realize how generous these people, who usually remain hidden in their busy homes with their broken brothers and sisters, really are. As we were together talking, laughing, singing, and praying, I experienced church in the best sense of that word: a people called together to praise God and to serve the poor.

My presentation this morning was well received. Much better than I expected. Nobody seemed to have problems understanding my French, and most people felt that what I said was clear and helped them in their discussions. I spoke about the movement from despair to hope. I described despair as it is visible in interpersonal relationships, in the world at large, and in the Church and I discussed how prayer, resistance, and community are three aspects of a life of hope in the midst of a despairing world.

I feel grateful for the warm response of the assistants. It makes me feel more a part of this community and gives me a sense of having made a small contribution to people who have given me so much.

9

THE IMPORTANT
AND THE URGENT

∎

THE MOST IMPORTANT event of the day for me was the arrival of my co-worker Peter Weiskel. Peter flew from Boston to Brussels this morning and arrived in Compiègne by train at 7 P.M. It is great to have him here for two weeks. Working together with such a great distance between us has not always been easy. And though we have regular contact by letter and phone, our communication is often difficult and at times frustrating. It is hard for Peter to envision my daily life here in France and to feel fully a part of the situations I am describing in this journal. I hope that his two weeks here will make him feel more connected to L'Arche and more able to help me think through some of the concerns I am writing about while here.

THE FIRST GOTHIC ARCH!
(Sunday, December 1)

This afternoon Peter and I attended Vespers in the church of Our Lady of Morienval. Morienval is a small village about a half hour's drive from Trosly.

We were not prepared for this unusual event. About thirty people sang Vespers together for the first Sunday of Advent. Most of them were members of religious orders from the area. The pastor who had organized the simple service told us that no Vespers had been sung in that church since 1745, when the Benedictine sisters, whose abbey church it was, left the area. It was a moving experience to pray with this small group of believers. We reached out over the centuries to those who had preceded us and took up the prayer that had been interrupted for 240 years.

This in itself was unusual enough. But when the service was over and we had a chance to look around, we realized that we had come upon one of the most precious architectural gems in France. Built around 1050 in fine Romanesque style, the church has a central nave, three aisles, and a majestic clock tower. Its wide transepts and semicircular choir are flanked by two elegant, decorative towers. Compared to a cathedral, it is a small, homely church. We were astonished to see an eleventh-century church in such a fine state of preservation. Neither the feudal conflicts of the Middle Ages, nor the French Revolution, nor the First and Second World Wars had done any harm to it. It is undoubtedly one of the best-preserved Romanesque churches in France.

The pastor of the church was eager to tell us about its history. He took us to the apse and showed us that one of the arches was pointed, in contrast to the rounded curves of the other Romanesque arches. As if he were betraying a secret, he whispered, "It is said that this is the first Gothic arch in the world." I was quite impressed to stand at the birthplace of the Gothic style, which would dominate the next several centuries. As a whole, the church was still round, down-to-earth, and simple. But the builder had begun to express an urge to go higher and strive for the heavens!

The pastor turned on all the lights in the church and let the tower bells ring. Suddenly all was light and sound. We felt privileged to have a glimpse of the devotion and faith of people who had lived nine hundred years before us. They sang the same psalms as we did and prayed to the same Lord as we did. We felt once again a joyful, hope-giving connection with the past.

As we left the church, a group of teenagers with a loud portable radio walked through the square, calling us back to the twentieth century. But as we looked at the church again and realized the beauty of this house of prayer, we said to each other, "We really should come back here and pray Vespers again." It seemed the right thing to do. The church was built for prayer.

OUR FRAGMENTED LIVES
(Monday, December 2)

Not much to report today except for many little frustrations, interruptions, and distractions. One of those days that pass without having felt like a real day. Many letters, telephone calls, short visits, little talks, but no real work, no sense of moving, no sense of direction. A day that is so fragmented that it does not seem to come together at all—except perhaps by writing about it!

One of the great gifts of the spiritual life is to know that even days like this are not a total waste. There was still an hour of prayer. There was still the Eucharist, there were still moments of gratitude for the gifts of life. And there is the opportunity to realize that a day like this unites me with thousands, even millions, of people for whom many days are like this, yet who are in no position to do anything about it. So many men, women, and children dream about creative lives; yet because they are not free to shape their own lives, they cannot realize their dreams. I had better pray for them tonight.

CHOOSING WHAT IS IMPORTANT
(Tuesday, December 3)

This morning I spoke with Père André about my restlessness. Père André is a Jesuit priest from Belgium who spends part of the year at Trosly. He directs the Jesuits who make their third year of formation at L'Arche and gives spiritual guidance to many of the assistants. I told him I have the sense of being terribly busy without really feeling that I am moving down the right path. Père André responded by saying that I have to keep a careful eye on the difference between urgent things and important things. If I allow the urgent things to dominate my day, I will never do what is truly important and will always feel dissatisfied. He said, "You will always be surrounded by urgent things. That is part of your character and your way of living. You move from Harvard to Trosly to get away from the busy life, and soon Trosly is as busy for you as Harvard. The issue is not where you are, but how you live wherever you are. For you that means a constant choosing of what is important and a willingness to accept that the urgent things can wait or be left undone."

I know both how right this advice is and how difficult it is for me to put it into practice. I responded, "How do I know what to let go of? Should I not answer my mail, not write that book, not visit or receive these persons, not pray, not spend so much time with handicapped people? What is urgent and what is important?" He said, "You have to decide to whom you want to be obedient."

We talked about the question of obedience a bit. Then he said, "Why don't you let me be your authority. Stop writing books and articles for a while, answer your mail, be good to those who visit you, pray, and just be here at L'Arche without worrying so much."

When I came home, I felt a lot freer. I started to answer letters and felt good about spending my time this way. I could even say to myself, "You are not allowed to do anything else!" My restlessness faded as I went about my work.

THE KNOWLEDGE OF THE HEART
(Wednesday, December 4)

Tonight I was invited to the Oasis foyer to participate in the weekly house meeting and supper. It was a special evening since Daniel, a handicapped man in the foyer, had just learned that his father had died. It requires special care and attention to offer consolation and support to people who express themselves with so much difficulty. The assistants at Oasis wondered how to guide Daniel through this time of grief.

During the house meeting Daniel was the center of attention for a long time. He spoke with difficulty about his grandmother, whose grief over her son's death had touched him deeply. People listened to him with much attention and love. Then Daniel made a surprising proposal. He invited all the members of the foyer to come to his room and pray. This was remarkable since Daniel never joined in evening prayer and was very protective of his privacy. People never just went into his room. But tonight he invited everyone to enter more deeply into his life to be with him in his grief. He placed some candles and small statues on the floor. Pépé, one of the other handicapped men, brought a picture of his deceased mother and put it next to the candles and the statues. I was deeply moved by this gesture of solidarity in grief. Pépé had little to say, but by putting his own mother's photograph on the floor of Daniel's room, he said more than any of us could with our sympathetic words.

The twelve of us huddled together in Daniel's small bedroom and prayed for him, his father, his mother, his grandmother, and his friends. We showed him a picture of Jesus and asked him who it was. "It is Jesus, the hidden one," he answered. For Daniel, Jesus was hard to reach, but tonight this small group of friends made Jesus more tangible than ever before.

As one of the assistants drove me home, she said, "We were worrying about how to help Daniel, but he himself showed us a way nobody else would ever have thought of. The heart knows so much more than the mind!"

HAPPY ARE THE POOR
(Thursday, December 5)

Jean Vanier gave a short talk last Sunday morning at the conclusion of the reflection weekend. He said some things then that have stayed with me the whole week. I now realize that what he said has a special meaning for me, and that I must not let it pass as just another beautiful talk.

Three thoughts have stayed with me. First, Jean said that working and living with handicapped people does not become easier the longer you do it. In fact, it often becomes harder. Jean shared his own struggle with us. He said, "Often I go off in dreams about living and being with the poor, but what the poor need are not my dreams, my beautiful thoughts, my inner reflections, but my concrete presence. There is always the temptation to replace real presence with lovely thoughts about being present."

Second, Jean remarked that we have to move from feelings to conviction. As long as our relationship with handicapped people rests on feelings and emotions, a long-term, lifelong commitment cannot develop. In order to stay with the handicapped even when we do not feel like staying, we need a deep conviction that God has called us to be with the poor, whether that gives us good or bad feelings. Jean expressed gratitude toward the many people who come to L'Arche for a month, six months, or a year. He said it was important for them and for L'Arche. But what is most needed are people who have come to the conviction that they are called to be with the handicapped permanently. This conviction makes a covenant possible, a lasting bond with the poor.

Finally, Jean said that poverty is neither nice nor pleasant. Nobody truly wants to be poor. We all want to move away from poverty. And still . . . God loves the poor in a special way. I was deeply struck with Jean's remark: "Jesus did not say, 'Happy are those who serve the poor,' but 'Happy are the poor.'" Being poor is what Jesus invites us to, and that is much, much harder than serving the poor. The unnoticed, unspectacular, unpraised life in solidarity with people who cannot give anything that makes us feel important is far from attractive. It is the way to poverty. Not an easy way, but God's way, the way of the cross.

These three themes have had a deep impact upon me. God is speaking to me in a way that I cannot just pass by. Jean's thoughts are much more than thoughts for me. They are important themes to consider in my own process of discerning a new direction.

10

POVERTY AND WEALTH

•

MONASTIC LIFE
(Paris; Friday, December 6)

SINCE THIS IS Peter's first visit to Europe, it seemed good to see more than just the little village of Trosly and its surrounding villages. So we decided to spend a day and a half in Paris, enjoy the beauty of this great city, and get a sense of its spiritual life. Tonight we attended Vespers and Mass at the Church of St. Gervais, undoubtedly one of the most remarkable centers of new religious vitality in France.

St. Gervais is the spiritual home of the Monastic Fraternities of Jerusalem. These parallel communities of men and women have chosen the city as their place of prayer, in contrast to the great contemplative orders of the past, which built their monasteries and abbeys in the peaceful countryside.

Being in St. Gervais and praying with the monks and nuns and the several hundred Parisians who had come directly from their work to the service was a deeply moving experience for both Peter and me. The liturgy was both festive and solemn, a real expression of adoration. The monks and nuns wore flowing white robes. The music had a prayerful, polyphonic quality reminiscent of Byzantine rites. There were icons, candles, and incense. People sat on the floor or on small benches. The atmosphere was very quiet, harmonious, prayerful, and peaceful. To come from the busy, restless city streets into the large church, and to be embraced by the simple splendor of the liturgy, was an experience that made a deep impression on both of us.

Peter picked up a flyer describing the spirituality of the brothers and sisters of Jerusalem. There I read:

> Life in the city today is a wilderness for the masses of men and women who live alone, some worrying about the future, some unconcerned, each

unknown to the other. The brothers and sisters of Jerusalem want to live in solidarity with them, just as they are now, and wherever they are. They wish to provide them with some kind of oasis, freely open to all, a silent place alive with prayer, in a spirit of welcome and sharing, where real life means more than mere talking or acting. A peaceful place where all people, whatever their social background, their age, or their outlook on life, are invited to come and share in a common search for God.

At St. Gervais, we found what these words describe. I have often thought about the possibility of living a truly contemplative life in the heart of the city. Is it possible? Or just a romantic dream? At Cambridge I had tried to start something like that among my students. But my own busyness, restlessness, and inner tension showed that I was not yet ready for it. I needed much more inner discipline than I could develop at a highly demanding university. But the Brothers and Sisters of Jerusalem are doing it. Their self-description continues:

They have chosen to live in Paris, that large city made up of ten million people. Through their own experience of the hardships of city life, with its alienations, its struggles, its work, its restraints, they know the stress, the noise of pollution, the joys and the sorrows, the sinfulness, and the holiness of Paris. Together with the people of Paris, they would like to help point out "the signs announcing the kingdom" in a very humble way, but whole-heartedly, at once breaking off with the world and living in communion with it, both keeping apart and sharing with others . . . They choose to be neither Benedictines nor Trappists, nor Carmelites nor Dominicans. They are "city folk" or, in other words, "monks and nuns of Jerusalem."

When we walked out of the church at 7:30 P.M., looking for a place to eat, we saw some familiar faces: people we had met at L'Arche. I realized that this church has become a home for many people, a place to be together in quiet prayer, a center to form a community, and most of all a *foyer* that makes it possible to live in Babylon while remaining in Jerusalem.

PARIS: RICH AND POOR
(*Saturday, December 7*)

As Peter and I walked through Paris today, we were impressed by its abundance as well as by its poverty. The stores, be they bookstores or foodstores, offer a wealth and variety found in few other cities. People throng the city, looking, buying, drinking coffee, having lively conversations, laughing, kissing, and playing.

In the subways, guitarists and singers with portable microphones and loud-speakers join the ride, sing rock songs, and ask for donations. On one train we were treated to a puppet show with a dancing moon, a talking bear, and a sweet melody.

Paris is full of life, movement, art, music, and people of all ages, races, and nationalities. So much is going on—often at the same time—that it is hard not to feel overwhelmed by the enormous variety of impressions. Paris is exhilarating, surprising, exciting, and stimulating, but also very tiring.

We also saw the other side: many poor, hungry people living on the streets, sleeping in subway stations, sitting on church steps begging for money. There are so many unemployed, so many alcoholics, so many drug users, so many mentally and physically ill people that those who want to offer them shelter, food, and counsel can never feel they have finished the task. Amid all the beauty, wealth, and abundance of Paris, there is immense suffering, undeniable loneliness, and unreachable human anguish.

WHERE MISERY AND MERCY MEET
(Trosly; Sunday, December 8)

Every Sunday at 5 P.M. it is Jean Vanier's custom to share with the community come of his reflections on the Gospel. But this year his many travels around the world have made this *partage* (sharing) only an occasional event.

But today he was home. Jean sat on the floor of the hall of Les Marronniers, surrounded by about forty people—some handicapped people, some assistants, and quite a few visitors. He read from the Gospel of St. Luke and then meditated aloud on the words he had just read. Being present at this session felt like being invited to enter into the prayer of a friend. No great theological analysis, no difficult words, no complicated ideas—just a faithful penetration of the word of God.

Jean said many things that moved me. But one sentence stayed with me and has continued to grow in me. He said, "Jesus always leads us to littleness. It is the place where misery and mercy meet. It is the place where we encounter God."

Having seen some of the poverty of Paris and having heard Jean say last Sunday that we are called not just to serve the poor but to *be* poor, I was struck forcefully by his words. To choose the little people, the little joys, the little sorrows, and to trust that it is there that God will come close—that is the hard way of Jesus. Again I felt a deep resistance toward choosing that way.

I am quite willing to work for and even with little people, but I want it to be a great event! Something in me always wants to turn the way of Jesus into a way that is honorable in the eyes of the world. I always want the little way to become the big way. But Jesus' movement toward the places the world wants to move away from cannot be made into a success story.

Every time we think we have touched a place of poverty, we will discover greater poverty beyond that place. There is really no way back to riches, wealth, success, acclaim, and prizes. Beyond physical poverty there is mental poverty, beyond mental poverty there is spiritual poverty, and beyond that there is nothing, nothing but the naked trust that God is mercy.

It is not a way we can walk alone. Only with Jesus can we go to the place where there is nothing but mercy. It is the place from which Jesus cried, "My God, my God, why have you forsaken me?" It is also the place from which Jesus was raised up to new life.

The way of Jesus can be walked only with Jesus. If I want to do it alone, it becomes a form of inverse heroism as fickle as heroism itself. Only Jesus, the Son of God, can walk to that place of total surrender and mercy. He warns us about striking off on our own: "cut off from me, you can do nothing." But he also promises, "Whoever remains in me, with me in him, bears fruit in plenty" (John 15:5).

I now see clearly why action without prayer is so fruitless. It is only in and through prayer that we can become intimately connected with Jesus and find the strength to join him on his way.

SEEING AND HEARING
(Monday, December 9)

Since Peter's arrival I have been more concerned with seeing than with hearing. One of Peter's reasons for spending two weeks here is to make a photographic essay of life at L'Arche in Trosly. So much can be shown that cannot be said. So much can be expressed by a face that cannot be expressed in words. Among handicapped people words are certainly not the most important way of communicating. Often the eyes say more than the mouth.

Peter has taken hundreds of photographs. He moved gradually from catching the beauty and charm of houses, gates, and statues to catching the more hidden beauty and charm of people playing, laughing, eating, and praying together. He was wise to wait a while before making photographs of the men and women living here in community. A relationship of trust must develop before people are willing to be photographed.

It is remarkable how much easier it is to get permission to make a tape recording than to take a photograph. It seems as if taking a picture is experienced as more of an intrusion than recording a voice. Happily, the people here have become more and more at ease with Peter's presence as a photographer and have even started to invite him to their homes and places of work to take pictures. His kindness and patience have made him seem less and less a threat and more and more a friend. We like to show our faces to our friends.

In the Gospels, "to see" and "to hear" are among the most used words. Jesus says to his disciples, "blessed are your eyes because they see, your ears because they hear! In truth I tell you, many prophets and upright people longed to see what you see, and never saw it; to hear what you hear, and never heard it" (Matthew 13:16–17). Seeing and hearing God are the greatest gifts we can receive. Both are ways of knowing, but all through the scriptures I sense that seeing God is the more intimate and personal of the two. This is confirmed by my own experience. A telephone conversation is such a poor way of being together compared to an encounter face to face. And don't we often say on the phone, "I look forward to seeing you soon"? Seeing is better than hearing. It is a lot closer.

While I try to find words that can be heard or read, Peter tries to find images that can be seen. Few people at L'Arche will read what I write or hear what I say, but many will look again and again at the photographs Peter has made.

Peter's presence here is a great gift—not just to me, but to all who will see what he saw and rejoice in the way he saw it.

THE CONSOLATION OF MARY
(Tuesday, December 10)

My prayer life has been quite difficult lately. During my morning meditation I think about a thousand things except God and God's presence in my life. I am worrying, brooding, and agonizing, but not really praying.

To my own surprise the only prayer that offers me some peace and consolation is the prayer to Mary. My meditation on the Annunciation brought me real peace and joy, while reflections on other mysteries could not keep me focused. As I tried to simply be with Mary and listen to her words, "You see before you the Lord's servant; let it happen to me as you have said" (Luke 1:38), I discovered a restful peace. Instead of thinking about these words and trying to understand them, I just listened to them being spoken for me.

Mary is so open, so free, so trusting. She is completely willing to hear words that go far beyond her own comprehension. She knows that the words spoken to her by the angel come from God. She seeks clarification, but she does not question their authority. She senses that the message of Gabriel will radically interrupt her life, and she is afraid, but she does not withdraw. When she hears the words "You will bear a son . . . he will be called the son of the most high," she asks, "But how can this come about, since I have no knowledge of man?" Then she hears what no other human being ever heard: "The Holy Spirit will come upon you and the power of the Most High will cover you with its shadow." She responded with a complete surrender and thus became not only the mother of Jesus but also the mother of all who believe in him. ". . . let it happen to me as you have said" (Luke 1:34–35, 38).

I keep listening to these words as words that summarize the deepest possible response to God's loving action within us. God wants to let the Holy Spirit guide our lives, but are we prepared to let it happen? Just being with Mary and the angel and hearing their words—words which changed the course of history—bring me peace and rest.

I shared this experience with Père André this morning. He said, "Just stay there. Stay with Mary. Trust that she will show you the way. Do not move on as long as you find peace and rest with her. It is clear that she wants your attention. Give it to her, and you will soon understand why it is you are so distracted."

Simple, good, and consoling advice. I do not have to move faster than I can. I have received permission to stay in the place where I am consoled. It is the place where Mary says "Yes" to God's love.

DOING AND BEING
(Thursday, December 12)

Peter left today. He felt increasingly at ease as he came to know the community. I wished he could have stayed longer. It seemed that the twelve days he was here were not enough to finish all the work, meet all the people, and see all the sights. But I am grateful he came. He now has an idea of life at L'Arche here in Trosly. It will certainly help us a lot in our work together in the year ahead. He can now visualize the situation in which I live, recognize the names of persons about whom I write, and explain to those who come to see him in Cambridge how L'Arche lives and works in France. The more than six hundred photographs he made while here will certainly be helpful in telling the story.

I am a little sad that we had so little time to just be together. There always seemed to be something that needed to be done. Even here, in this quiet, sleepy village, time seems to fly. Friendship is such a holy gift, but we give it so little attention. It is so easy to let what needs to be done take priority over what needs to be lived. Friendship is more important than the work we do together. Both Peter and I know and I feel that, but we still don't live it very well.

As the train rolled away from the station, I thought, "He should come back and stay longer, have more time to pray, talk, and just waste time." But I know that I, too, must become a different person to make that happen.

Certainly our time together has deepened our bond and strengthened our love for each other. It is a love that grows by forgiving each other constantly for not yet being who we want to be for each other.

11

A CLEAR CALL

∎

THE CALL
(Friday, December 13)

YESTERDAY WAS NOT only the day on which Peter left, but also the day on which I received a long letter from Daybreak in Canada inviting me to join their community.

The fact that the letter arrived on the same day that Peter left has a great symbolic meaning for me. On August 15, Peter will conclude his work with me and begin his studies in geology; Joe Egan has invited me to begin living with the Daybreak community on August 29. Something is coming to a conclusion; something new is beginning. I realize that my Cambridge period is ending and that I am being asked to move in a new direction.

Joe writes, "This letter comes to you from the Daybreak Community Council and we are asking you to consider coming to live with us in our community of Daybreak . . . We truly feel that you have a gift to bring us. At the same time, our sense is that Daybreak would be a good place for you, too. We would want to support you in your important vocation of writing and speaking by providing you with a home and with a community that will love you and call you to grow."

I am deeply moved by this letter. It is the first time in my life that I have been explicitly called. All my work as priest since my ordination has been a result of my own initiative. My work at the Menninger Clinic, Notre Dame, Yale, and Harvard and in Latin America has been work that I myself chose. It was mostly very satisfying work, but it was always my own choice. Though I was directly responsible to Cardinal Alfrink and Cardinal Willebrands, and though I am now directly responsible to Cardinal Simonis, none of them has ever called me to a specific task. They have always agreed with and supported the choices I made.

But now a community is saying, "We call you to live with us; to give to us and receive from us." I know that Joe's invitation is not a job offer but a genuine call to come and live with the poor. They have no money to offer, no attractive living quarters, no prestige. This is a completely new thing. It is a concrete call to follow Christ, to leave the world of success, accomplishment, and honor, and to trust Jesus and him alone.

Both the assistants and the handicapped people at Daybreak have been consulted—the call comes from the whole community. It is a call made after much prayer and thought. If I ever wanted a concrete sign of Jesus' will for me, this is it.

I feel many hesitations. Living with handicapped people in a new country is not immediately attractive. Still, something tells me that Joe's letter is not just another letter asking me to do something. It is a response to my prayer to Jesus, asking him where to go. So often I have prayed, "Lord, show me your will and I will do it." So here is a response, more concrete and more specific than I ever dared to hope for.

The coming months will be months to grow into a faithful answer. I must speak to Cardinal Simonis in Holland and ask his permission to accept Joe's call. I must pray for the strength and courage to be truly obedient to Jesus, even if he calls me to where I would rather not go.

PRESENT TO THE PRESENT
(Wednesday, December 18)

Just a week after I had bought some postcards with reproductions of paintings by Cézanne, Rainer Maria Rilke's *Letters on Cézanne* was sent to me as a Christmas gift. It is a happy coincidence. Ever since I read *Letters to a Young Poet*, I have felt a deep connection with Rilke. Now he will introduce me to Cézanne, whose paintings I like but have not yet fully seen. Rilke will help me to see.

When Rilke wrote to his wife, Clara, abut Cézanne's painting of Mont Sainte-Victorie, he said, "Not since Moses has anyone seen a mountain so greatly . . . only a saint could be as united with his God as Cézanne was with his work."[5] For Rilke, Cézanne was indeed a mystic who helped us to see reality in a new way. He writes about Cézanne as a painter who "so incorruptibly reduced a reality to its color content that that reality resumed a new existence in a beyond of color, without any previous memories."[6]

Cézanne, in Rilke's view, was able to be fully present to the present and could therefore see reality as it is. This was also Rilke's own desire. He suffered from his inability to be fully in the present and thus see clearly. He writes, "One lives so badly, because one always comes into the present unfinished, unable, distracted. I cannot think back on any time of my life without such reproaches or worse. I believe that the only time I lived without loss were the ten days after Ruth's [Rilke's daughter] birth, when I found reality as indescribable, down to its smallest details, as it surely always is."[7]

Cézanne's paintings revealed to Rilke a man able to live "without loss," totally present to the present, truly seeing. This was Rilke's own search.

I am so glad for this encounter with Rilke and Cézanne because they both bring me closer to the place where true living and true seeing are one.

RIGHT GLORY AND VAIN GLORY
(Thursday, December 19)

There are many small "formation groups" in L'Arche. There are groups on peace, on conflict resolution, on medical issues. There are groups on spirituality, politics, and economics. Jean Vanier asked me to lead a group on the Gospel of John. Tonight we had our third meeting.

We spoke about the word "glory." I have gradually become aware how central this word is in John's Gospel. There is God's glory, the right glory that leads to life. And there is human glory, the vain glory that leads to death. All through his Gospel John shows how we are tempted to prefer vain glory over the glory that comes from God.

This idea did not affect me greatly until I realized that human glory is always connected with some form of competition. Human glory is the result of being considered better, faster, more beautiful, more powerful, or more successful than others. Glory conferred by people is glory which results from being favorably compared to other people. The better our scores on the scoreboard of life, the more glory we receive. This glory comes with upward mobility. The higher we climb on the ladder of success, the more glory we collect. But this same glory also creates our darkness. Human glory, based on competition, leads to rivalry; rivalry carries within it the beginning of violence; and violence is the way to death. Thus human glory proves to be vain glory, false glory, mortal glory.

How then do we come to see and receive God's glory? In his Gospel, John shows that God chose to reveal his glory to us in his humiliation. That is the good, but also disturbing, news. God, in his infinite wisdom, chose to reveal his divinity to us not through competition, but through compassion, that is, through suffering with us. God chose the way of downward mobility. Every time Jesus speaks about being glorified and giving glory, he always refers to his humiliation and death. It is through the way of the cross that Jesus gives glory to God, receives glory from God, and makes God's glory known to us. The glory of the resurrection can never be separated from the glory of the cross. The risen Lord always shows us his wounds.

Thus the glory of God stands in contrast to the glory of people. People seek glory by moving upward. God reveals his glory by moving downward. If we truly want to see the glory of God, we must move downward with Jesus. This is the deepest reason for living in solidarity with poor, oppressed, and handicapped people. They are the ones through whom God's glory can manifest itself to us. They show us the way to God, the way to salvation.

This is what L'Arche is beginning to teach me.

BECOMING FRIENDS
(Saturday, December 21)

Nathan and I are gradually becoming close friends. It is wonderful to experience the birth of a new friendship. I have always considered friendship to be one of the greatest gifts God has given me. It is the most life-giving gift I can imagine. Since I came to Trosly, I have met many wonderful, loving, and caring people. They have been a source of great joy to me. I know that when I leave we will remember each other with gratitude and fondness but will find it hard to sustain lasting relationships of mutual love and support. It is therefore a beautiful experience to discover that out of the many, someone is emerging who is becoming a friend, a new companion in life, a new presence that will last wherever I will go.

Nathan is a Canadian. His parents, who are Baptists, are the founders of "King's Fold," a small retreat center near Calgary. Two years ago Nathan entered the Catholic Church; soon after that he came to L'Arche in Trosly to live and work with the handicapped. He is a man of deep compassion. When I see him with his friends in the foyer, I am deeply moved by the generous affection he shows to men and women who are so deeply broken. It is the fruit of caring for his own handicapped brother, who died a few years ago.

Over the past few months we have gradually come to know each other. I was not aware of how significant our relationship had become for me until he left for a month to visit his family and friends in Canada. I missed his presence greatly and looked forward to his return.

Two days ago he came back, and tonight we went out for supper together. I felt a need to let him know how much I had missed him. I told him that his absence had made me aware of a real affection for him that had grown in me since we had come to know each other. He responded with a strong affirmation of our friendship from his side. As we talked more about past experiences and future plans, it became clear that God had brought us close for a reason. Nathan hopes to begin theological studies in Toronto in September and plans to live at Daybreak during that time. I am filled with gratitude and joy that God is not only calling me to a new country and a new community, but also offering me a new friendship to make it easier to follow that call.

LISTENING TOGETHER
(Sunday, December 22)

Today the Gospel of the Visitation is read in preparation for Christmas. In recent months the story of Mary's visit to her cousin Elizabeth has become very dear to me.

Mary receives the great and shocking news that she is going to become the Mother of the "Son of the Most High." This news is so incomprehensible and so radically interrupts Mary's humble life that she finds herself totally alone. How can Joseph or any of her friends or relatives understand her situation? With whom can she share this most intimate knowledge, which remains inexplicable even to herself?

God does not want her to be alone with the new life given to her. The angel says, "your cousin Elizabeth also, in her old age, has conceived a son, and she whom people called barren is now in her sixth month, for nothing is impossible to God" (Luke 1:36–37).

God offers Mary an intimate, human friend with whom she can share what seems incommunicable. Elizabeth, like Mary, has experienced divine intervention and has been called to a response of faith. She can be with Mary in a way no one else possibly could.

Thus, it is understandable that "Mary set out at that time and went as quickly as she could into the hill country to a town in Judah" (Luke 1:39) to visit Elizabeth.

I am deeply moved by this simple and mysterious encounter. In the midst of an unbelieving, doubting, pragmatic, and cynical world, two women meet each other and affirm in each other the promise given to them. The humanly impossible has happened to them. God has come to them to begin the salvation promised through the ages. Through these two women God has decided to change the course of history. Who could ever understand? Who could ever believe it? Who could ever let it happen? But Mary says, "Let it happen to me," and she immediately realizes that only Elizabeth will be able to affirm her "yes." For three months Mary and Elizabeth live together and encourage each other to truly accept the motherhood given to them. Mary's presence makes Elizabeth more fully aware of becoming the mother of the "prophet of the Most High" (Luke 1:76), and Elizabeth's presence allows Mary to grow in the knowledge of becoming the mother of the "Son of the Most High" (Luke 1:32).

Neither Mary nor Elizabeth had to wait in isolation. They could wait together and thus deepen in each other their faith in God, for whom nothing is impossible. Thus, God's most radical intervention into history was listened to and received in community.

The story of the Visitation teaches me the meaning of friendship and community. How can I ever let God's grace fully work in my life unless I live in a community of people who can affirm it, deepen it, and strengthen it? We cannot live this new life alone. God does not want to isolate us by his grace. On the contrary, he wants us to form new friendships and a new community—holy places where his grace can grow to fullness and bear fruit.

So often new life appears in the Church because of an encounter. Dorothy Day never claimed *The Catholic Worker* as her own invention. She always spoke of it as the fruit of her encounter with Peter Maurin. Jean Vanier never claims that he started L'Arche on his own. He always points to his encounter with Père Thomas Philippe as the true beginning of L'Arche. In such encounters two or more people are able to affirm each other in their gifts and encourage each other to "let it happen to them." In this way, new hope is given to the world.

Elizabeth helped Mary to become the Mother of God. Mary helped Elizabeth to become the mother of her Son's prophet, John the Baptist. God may choose us individually, but he always wants us to come together to allow his choice to come to maturity.

A CHRISTMAS PRAYER
(Monday, December 23)

O Lord, how hard it is to accept your way. You come to me as a small, powerless child born away from home. You live for me as a stranger in your own land. You die for me as a criminal outside the walls of the city, rejected by your own people, misunderstood by your friends, and feeling abandoned by your God.

As I prepare to celebrate your birth, I am trying to feel loved, accepted, and at home in this world, and I am trying to overcome the feelings of alienation and separation which continue to assail me. But I wonder now if my deep sense of homelessness does not bring me closer to you than my occasional feelings of belonging. Where do I truly celebrate your birth: in a cozy home or in an unfamiliar house, among welcoming friends or among unknown strangers, with feelings of well-being or with feelings of loneliness?

I do not have to run away from those experiences that are closest to yours. Just as you do not belong to this world, so I do not belong to this world. Every time I feel this way I have an occasion to be grateful and to embrace you better and taste more fully your joy and peace.

Come, Lord Jesus, and be with me where I feel poorest. I trust that this is the place where you will find your manger and bring your light. Come, Lord Jesus, come.

Amen.

PREPARE!
(Tuesday, December 24)

Père Thomas keeps telling us in his sermons that the days before Christmas must be days of deep prayer to prepare our hearts for the coming of Christ. We must be really ready to receive him. Christ wants to be born in us, but we must be open, willing, receptive, and truly welcoming. To become that way we have Advent and especially the last days before Christmas.

Often, if not daily, I tell myself, "Today I am going to spend some extra time just praying, just waiting expectantly, just sitting quietly." But always the day seems to be consumed by a thousand little things which beg for my attention. When the day is over I feel frustrated, angry, and disappointed with myself.

Especially today! This morning I thought the day was completely free and open for prayer. Now it is evening, and I don't know where the time went. Somehow the externals of Christmas—presents, decorations, short visits—took over and the day drained away like water through a poorly built dike. How hard it is to remember Père André's words about the difference between the urgent and the important!

I often think, "A life is like a day; it goes by so fast. If I am so careless with my days, how can I be careful with my life?" I know that somehow I have not fully come to believe that urgent things can wait while I attend to what is truly important. It finally boils down to a question of deep and strong conviction. Once I am truly convinced that preparing the heart is more important than preparing the Christmas tree, I will be a lot less frustrated at the end of the day.

I wish I had better things to write on Christmas Eve. But better write what is true than what is pious. God is coming. He comes to a restless, somewhat anxious heart. I offer him my frustration and confusion and trust that he will do something with it.

A "DRY" CHRISTMAS
(Wednesday, December 25)

Christmas has arrived again. Night Mass was festive with many green branches, red lights, and white-robed altar boys. The church was packed, the songs sweet, and Père Thomas's sermon moving. The dawn Mass, which I celebrated in English in Madame Vanier's dining room, was simple and quiet. The 11 A.M. day Mass was joyful and rich with many good words from the good Père.

Père Thomas explained that the mystery of Christmas was so deep that the Church needs three Masses to express itself. It is an event that touches our innermost self, our life in family and community, and the whole created order.

There was a big dinner after the day Mass, and we exchanged gifts. In the afternoon I slept a little, talked a little with Madame Vanier and Jo Cork, who had just arrived from the Daybreak community in Canada, and wrote a little.

Everything was there to make a splendid Christmas. But I wasn't really there. I felt like a sympathetic observer. I couldn't force myself to feel differently. It just seemed that I wasn't part of it. At times I even caught myself looking at it all like an unbeliever who wonders what everybody is so busy and excited about. Spiritually, this is a dangerous attitude. It creates a certain sarcasm, cynicism, and depression. But I didn't want or choose it. I just found myself in a mental state that I could not move out of by my own force.

Still, in the midst of it all I saw—even though I did not feel—that this day may prove to be a grace after all. Somehow I realized that songs, music, good feelings, beautiful liturgies, nice presents, big dinners, and many sweet words do not make Christmas. Christmas is saying "yes" to something beyond all emotions and feelings. Christmas is saying "yes" to a hope based on God's initiative, which has nothing to do with what I think or feel. Christmas is believing that the salvation of the world is God's work and not mine. Things will never look just right or feel just right. If they did, someone would be lying. The world is not whole, and today I experienced this fact in my own unhappiness. But it is into this broken world that a child is born who is called Son of the Most High, Prince of Peace, Savior.

I look at him and pray, "Thank you, Lord, that you came, independent of my feelings and thoughts. Your heart is greater than mine." Maybe a "dry" Christmas, a Christmas without much to feel or think, will bring me closer to the true mystery of God-with-us. What it asks is pure, naked faith.

12

GOING HOME

∎

APPREHENSION
(The Netherlands; Thursday, December 26)

AFTER CELEBRATING the Eucharist with Madame Vanier and Jo Cork, Barbara drove me to the railroad station in Compiègne, where I took the train to my home country.

Traveling to my family and friends in Holland fills me with apprehension and a certain fear. Most of those with whom I shared my youth have moved away from the Church and have little connection with anything even vaguely spiritual. Speaking about spiritual things to spiritual people is quite easy. But speaking about God and God's presence in our hearts, our families, and our daily lives to people for whom "God words" are often connected with hurtful memories seems nearly impossible.

So here I am traveling through my own country. I know its language better than any other, but do I have the words to say what I truly want to say? As I go from Rosendaal to Breda to Eindhoven to Helmond, I pray the rosary. The Hail Marys make me aware that I have to be very quiet, very simple, and perhaps very silent.

A SURPRISING VISITOR
(Friday, December 27)

My first day home was good and surprising. Good, because my eighty-two-year-old father welcomed me warmly. He is in good health and good spirits, vitally interested in national and international affairs, and eager to talk about them. Although he had just sold his large judicial library, his reading chair was surrounded with many new books about literature, history, and art. He kept saying, "Have you read this . . . and that . . . and this . . . it is very interesting." It is good to be home, in a house so richly filled with memories of a long and well-lived life.

It was also a surprising day because the mayor of Eindhoven, the city where the Phillips Corporation has its main factories, called to say he wanted to see me. He arrived a few hours later. I had no idea why the mayor of Eindhoven wanted to see me so urgently. I had never heard of him before and did not know that he had heard of me. But he had read one of my books and called my father to ask when I would be home.

Gilles Borrie proved to be a wonderful, warm, and very gentle person who just wanted to speak about the "things of God." It was a heart-to-heart conversation. We spoke about the Church in Holland, about the Trappist life, about prayer, and about our continuing search for God. In the middle of the conversation Gilles's wife called to tell him that his mother had just suffered a stroke and was dying. She was in her nineties but had been very healthy and alert until now. Suddenly our relationship deepened. We became friends in a moment of shock and grief. We prayed together and reflected on this crucial moment of Gilles's life. Then he left with the firm promise to stay in touch.

I was deeply moved that without doing or planning anything, I had been put in touch with a man searching for God and called to accompany him in his grief. It felt as if God wanted to welcome me back to my own country and say, "Don't be too nervous about finding the right language or the right tone, but trust that my spirit will speak through you, even when you are least prepared."

SMART BUT DISTRACTED
(Saturday, December 28)

The most remarkable thing about Holland is its prosperity. Unlike in France, England, or the United States, there are almost no poor people. Wherever you go people look well fed, well dressed, and well housed. This Christmas especially, it seemed that everyone was able to buy what they wanted, eat what they liked, and go where they wished. Countless Dutch people went to Switzerland or Austria to ski; others stayed home eating, drinking, and watching TV, and a few attended well-prepared and carefully orchestrated worship services. The country feels very self-satisfied. There is not much space left, inside or outside, to be with God and God alone.

It is hard to explain why Holland changed from a very pious to a very secular country in one generation. Many reasons can be given. But it seems to me, from just looking around and meeting and speaking to people, that their captivating prosperity is one of the more obvious reasons. People are just very busy—eating, drinking, and going places.

Paul van Vliet, a well-known Dutch comedian, used, as one of the themes in his Christmas TV show, "We are smart but very distracted." Indeed, we know and understand what we most need, but we just don't get around to it, since we are so busy playing with our toys. There is too much to play with! No real time to grow up and do the necessary thing: "Love God and each other."

The Dutch have become a distracted people—very good, kind, and good-natured but caught in too much of everything.

ASKING TO BE SENT
(Monday, December 30)

At 10 A.M. I met with my bishop, Cardinal Simonis of Utrecht. I explained to him the call from the Daybreak community and asked if he would be willing to send me there.

I has become increasingly important for me to go where I am not only called, but also sent. Being called to live and work in Canada seems to be a good thing, but if it is not supported by a mission from the Church, I don't think it will bear much fruit.

Knowing that the place where you live and the work you do is not simply your own choice but part of a mission makes all the difference. When difficulties arise, the knowledge of being sent will give me the strength not to run away, but to be faithful. When the work proves tiring, the facilities poor, and the relationships frustrating, I can say, "These hardships are not a reason to leave, but an occasion to purify my heart."

Cardinal Simonis asked me if I felt that being called there was a response to my own prayers. I could honestly say "yes" to that. Often I have prayed, "Lord, show me the way and I will follow you." Jean Vanier's invitation to introduce me to L'Arche and the call from Daybreak that grew from that first invitation were a clear response to that prayer. Yet because I am a priest ordained to serve my bishop, the affirmation of the Church is of crucial importance. To feel called is not enough. It is necessary to be sent.

At the end of our conversation the bishop said, "My first response is that I think you should go there, but give me a few days and call me Saturday at noon. That will give me a chance to read the letter you received from Daybreak and to think a little more about it."

It was a good conversation. Compared to my conversations with Jean Vanier, Père Thomas, and Père André, it was more distant and pragmatic—questions about financial responsibility, pension, and insurance came up quite soon—but I am not in France, but in Holland, asking not for spiritual guidance or emotional support, but for a new mandate. Cardinal Simonis is my bishop, who for me represents the authority of the Church. If he affirms my call, I hope that he will not only give me permission, but truly send me to this new ministry.

A LONELY NEW YEAR'S EVE
(Tuesday, December 31)

Somehow this has been a hard day for me. Early this morning I walked around Utrecht trying to find a church where I could go to pray. But the two churches I came upon were closed, and when I rang the rectory doorbell, there was no response. As I walked through the streets saying the rosary, I felt like a stranger among my own people.

Later I took a train to Amsterdam to visit a friend, and from there I went to Rotterdam to celebrate New Year's Eve with my brother and his family At 7 P.M. I celebrated the Eucharist in the nearby parish church. My little six-year-old niece was willing to go with me, but everyone else preferred to stay home. Except for the sacristan, little Sarah, and myself, there was nobody in the big old church. I felt lonely, especially because I couldn't share God's gifts with those who are closest to me. My deepest thoughts and feelings have become foreign to them.

The event that followed was pleasant and friendly, with a splendid dinner, good easy conversation, and champagne to welcome the New Year. No prayers or scripture readings as in the past. I keep wondering how, in one generation, such a pious family could lose so completely its connection with God and God's church. It is hard for me to celebrate with my whole being when there is so little to celebrate. I feel lonely while being so close to those who are dear to me.

THREE GENERATIONS
(Wednesday, January 1, 1986)

It has become a sort of tradition that I celebrate the Eucharist on the first day of the year with the Van Campen family in Lieshout, near Eindhoven. The Van Campens have been friends of my parents as long as I can remember. In October 1978, the same month that my mother died, Phillip Van Campen, sixty-eight, had a severe stroke. He has been paralyzed ever since. Once a successful bank director and businessman, he has now become an invalid totally dependent on his wife and the nurses who care for him. On his birthday, the first of January, his wife invites their six children and their families to the family home for a Eucharist and a dinner.

For me it is an annual confrontation with the tragedy of Dutch Catholicism. Phillip and his wife, Puck, are both deeply believing people. Their life centers around the Eucharist. Puck, whose days are fully dedicated to the care of her invalid husband, continues to find hope and strength in Jesus through his presence in her life. But for the children the words "God" and "Church" have become much more ambiguous and often evoke very critical and sometimes even hostile thoughts. The two older sons and their families still visit the church regularly. They see the life in Christ as important but often wonder if the services they attend really nurture their spiritual life. The younger children, however, have become much more alienated. For them, the Church has become irrelevant. For most of them the Bible is no longer used, the sacraments have become unknown, prayer is nonexistent, and thoughts about a greater life than the present are rather utopian.

The grandchildren seem most ill at ease with religious ceremonies. Six of them have not been baptized and look at me, vested in alb and stole, as at some performer who is not very entertaining.

It was quite an experience to pray and celebrate the Eucharist surrounded by a large family in which the parents are deeply committed Christians, the children find themselves less and less at home in the Church, and most of the grandchildren have become unfamiliar with the story of God's love.

All of these men and women are very good, caring, and responsible people. Their friendship means a lot to me and gives me joy. Still, I experience a real sadness that the faith that gives so much life to the parents no longer shapes the lives of all the children and grandchildren.

Who is to blame? I often wonder where I would be today if I had been part of the great turmoil of the Dutch Church during the last decades. Blaming is not the issue. What is important is to find the anger-free parts in people's hearts where God's love can be heard and received.

After the Gospel reading I spoke about God's "first love," which allows us to forgive each other for not being able to give one another all the love we desire. I realized that those who had struggled with relationships (and who among us had not?) were listening and making connections. They said "yes" to the pain I described, but not everyone seemed ready yet to say "yes" to the one who came to heal that pain. I wonder if those who are between thirty and fifty and who no longer find the Church a source of strength will ever be able to let Jesus heal their wounds. But maybe one day their children will ask them the old question again: "Is Jesus the Messiah, or do we have to wait for another?"

IN SEARCH OF MEANING
(Thursday, January 2)

I spent most of the afternoon with one of my best Dutch friends and his family. We first met in the early sixties, when we were working as clinical psychologists in the Dutch army. He now teaches medical psychology at the University of Utrecht and has become a well-known authority on mental health issues. We have stayed in touch, and over the years our friendship has deepened, though we see each other only once a year.

Our discussion soon became quite intimate. We spoke about the existential loneliness we are both experiencing at this time in our lives. This loneliness stems not from a lack of friends, problems with spouse or children, or absence of professional recognition. Neither of us has any major complaints in these areas. Still . . . the question "What am I doing, and for what reason?" lurks underneath all of our good feelings about friends, family, and work. Wim spoke about experiences of "de-realization" which are "beyond psychological explanation." As we have both passed fifty, we have discovered that at times we look at our world with a strange inner question: "What am I doing here? Is this really our world, our people, our existence? What is everybody so busy with?"

This question comes from a place deeper than emotions, feelings, or passions. It is the question about the meaning of existence, raised not just by the mind, but also by a searching heart, a question which makes us feel like strangers in our own milieu. People take on a robotlike quality. They do many things but don't seem to have an interior life. Some outside power seems to "wind them up" and make them do whatever they are doing. This "de-realization" experience is extremely painful, but it can also be the way to a deeper connection.

Wim and I spoke about this deeper connection. Without a deep-rooted sense of belonging, all of life can easily become cold, distant, and painfully repetitive. This deeper connection is the connection with the one whose name is love, leading to a new discovery that we are born out of love and are always called back to that love. It leads to a new realization that God is the God of life who continues to offer us life wherever and whenever death threatens. It ultimately leads to prayer. And from our being human, being child, brother or sister, father or mother, grandfather or grandmother comes a new experience of being held within the hand of a loving God.

WORDS HEARD BUT NOT RECEIVED
(Saturday, January 4)

Today my father celebrated his eighty-third birthday. He had invited all his children and his brothers and sisters, with their spouses, to be with him. We came from all over the country, twenty-one people altogether. At 12:30 P.M. we all went to the village church for the Eucharist.

I had put chairs in the sanctuary so that we could all gather around the altar. Although most of the family were still "practicing Catholics," I felt some distance. I spoke about Jesus, who accompanies us on our lifelong road and explains to us that our struggles and pain can become ways to break through depression and bitterness and discover a deep healing presence. My words were heard, but not received. After the service the only remarks were about cold feet and a slippery road home. One of my uncles said, "Well, you are obviously convinced of what you said. But I do not think that way."

I had hoped to offer a hopeful, life-giving message, but somehow I had not found the words. My brother gave a very funny and sympathetic toast before dinner, using an astrology book to describe my father's character. His words were eagerly received and much applauded. He knew his audience much better than I did.

The feeling of having become something of a stranger in my own family was strong throughout the whole day. I had not seen many of the people at the party for more than a decade. Our reunion made me realize how much had happened to them and to me, and made me sadly aware that I no longer know the soil on which we both stand.

My father, meanwhile, was strong, happy, and exuberant. For him the main question is how to stay young, while for me it is how to grow old. My concern about being prepared for the great encounter with the Lord was not shared.

In the midst of it all, I called Cardinal Simonis to ask his final word about going to Daybreak. He said, "Do it." He had talked about it with his staff and come to the conclusion that it was a good idea. But he also said, "Do it for three years, and maybe then you might be interested in returning to your motherland. It seems good to keep that option open."

I was very glad to have the Cardinal's blessing on my future. I mentioned it excitedly to my father and the rest of the family. But their minds were elsewhere. What for me was a major turning point in my life was for them another item of news among people trying to catch up with each other. It may be small news, but it is good news for me.

13

THE STRUGGLE OF PRAYER

∎

THE WAY TO PRAY
(Trosly, France; Friday, January 10)

PRAYER CONTINUES to be very difficult. Still, every morning when I walk in the garden of La Ferme saying the rosary and spending an hour in the oratory simply being in God's presence, I know that I am not wasting my time. Though I am terribly distracted, I know that God's spirit is at work in me. Though I have no deeply religious insights or feelings, I am aware of the peace beyond thoughts and emotions. Though my early-morning prayer seems quite unsuccessful, I always look forward to it and guard it as a special time.

A short piece on prayer by Dom John Chapman published in the December 14th *Tablet* has given me much hope. It is taken from one of his spiritual letters. He writes:

> Prayer, in the sense of union with God, is the most crucifying thing there is. One must do it for God's sake; but one will not get any satisfaction out of it, in the sense of feeling "I am good at prayer. I have an infallible method." That would be disastrous, since what we want to learn is precisely our own weakness, powerlessness, unworthiness. Nor ought one to expect "a sense of the reality of the supernatural" of which I speak. And one should wish for no prayer, except precisely the prayer that God gives us— probably very distracted and unsatisfactory in every way.
>
> On the other hand, the only way to pray is to pray; and the way to pray well is to pray much. If one has no time for this, then one must at least pray regularly. But the less one prays, the worse it goes. And if circumstances do not permit even regularity, then one must put up with the fact that when one does try to pray, one can't pray—and our prayer will probably consist of telling this to God.

As to beginning afresh, or where you left off, I don't think you have any choice. You simply have to begin wherever you find yourself. Make any acts you want to make and feel you ought to make, but do not force yourself into *feelings* of any kind.

You say very naturally that you do not know what to do if you have a quarter of an hour alone in church. Yes, I suspect the only thing to do is to shut out the church and everything else, and just give yourself to God and beg him to have mercy on you, and offer him all your distractions.[8]

The sentence that I like most is, ". . . the only way to pray is to pray; and the way to pray well is to pray much." Chapman's sound wisdom really helps me. No-nonsense advice, and very true. It all boils down to his main point: We must pray not first of all because it feels good or helps, but because God loves us and wants our attention.

CHOOSING THE WAY OF HUMILITY
(Sunday, January 12)

Today is the feast of the baptism of the Lord. I have been thinking much about this feast, yesterday and today. Jesus, who is without sin, stands in line with sinners waiting to be baptized by John. As Jesus starts his ministry, he chooses to enter into solidarity with sinful humanity. "John tried to dissuade him with the words 'It is I who need baptism from you, and yet you come to me.' But Jesus replied, 'Leave it like this for the time being; it is fitting that we should, in this way, do all that uprightness demands'" (Matthew 3:14–15).

Here we see how Jesus clearly chooses the way of humility. He does not appear with great fanfare as a powerful savior, announcing a new order. On the contrary, he comes quietly, with the many sinners who are receiving a baptism of repentance. His choice is affirmed by the voice from heaven: "This is my Son, the Beloved; my favor rests on him" (Matthew 3:17).

How radical this choice is becomes clear in the temptations that follow. The devil suggests another option: "Be relevant, do something spectacular, accept world power." This is the way of the world. Jesus rejects this option and chooses God's way, a way of humility revealing itself gradually to be the way of the cross.

It is hard to believe that God would reveal his divine presence to us in the self-emptying, humble way of the man from Nazareth. So much in me seeks influence, power, success, and popularity. But the way of Jesus is the way of hiddenness, powerlessness, and littleness. It does not seem a very appealing way. Yet when I enter into true, deep communion with Jesus I will find that it is this small way that leads to real peace and joy.

At this feast of the Lord's baptism, I pray for the courage to choose the small way and to keep choosing it. L'Arche will certainly help me in this.

HEALING PRAYER
(Tuesday, January 14)

In the first reading of today's liturgy we heard the story of Hannah's prayer in the book of Samuel. Hannah was deeply depressed because Yahweh had made her barren. As she went to the temple she fervently prayed that Yahweh would give her a son and thus take her humiliation away. Her prayer was so intense that the priest, Eli, thought she was drunk. But she said to him, "No, my Lord, I am a woman in great trouble; I have not been drinking wine or strong drink— I am pouring out my soul before Yahweh. Do not take your servant for a worthless woman; all this time I have been speaking from the depth of my grief and resentment" (1 Samuel 1:15–16).

Eli then blessed her, and when she came home her depression left her and "she began eating and was dejected no longer" (1 Samuel 1:18). Later she conceived and gave birth to a son whom she called Samuel.

What touches me most in this story is that depression left Hannah after her prayer, but long before Yahweh responded to it by giving her a son. It was her agonizing prayer, which brought all of her feelings of humiliation, rejection, and resentment before God, that took her inner darkness away. Her husband, Elkanah, had not been able to console her, even though he had said to her, "Hannah, why are you crying? Why are you not eating anything? Why are you so sad? Am I not more to you than ten sons?" (1 Samuel 1:8). But when she had poured out all "the bitterness of her soul" (1 Samuel 1:10) to God and had allowed God to touch her, she became a new woman and knew that God would hear her prayer.

Prayer heals. Not just the answer to prayer. When we give up our competition with God and offer God every part of our heart, holding back nothing at all, we come to know God's love for us and discover how safe we are in his embrace. Once we know again that God has not rejected us, but keeps us close to his heart, we can find again the joy of living, even though God might guide our life in a different direction from our desires.

Prayer is so important. It invites us to live in ever closer communion with the one who loves us more than any human being ever can. After her prayer, Hannah knew once again that she was loved by God. In prayer she rediscovered her true self. Her happiness was no longer dependent upon having a child, but only upon the total and unlimited love of God. Thus she could wipe away her tears, eat again, and see her depression depart. When God in his love gave her a son, she was truly grateful. Because God's goodness, not her own, was the main source of her joy.

A PRAYER OF ABANDONMENT
(Wednesday, January 15)

This morning during my hour of prayer, I tried to come to some level of abandonment to my heavenly Father. It was a hard struggle since so much in me wants to do my will, realize my plans, organize my future, and make my decisions.

Still, I know that true joy comes from letting God love me the way God wants, whether it is through illness or health, failure or success, poverty or wealth, rejection or praise. It is hard for me to say, "I shall gratefully accept everything, Lord, that pleases you. Let your will be done." But I know that when I truly believe my Father is pure love, it will become increasingly possible to say these words from the heart.

Charles de Foucauld once wrote a prayer of abandonment that expresses beautifully the spiritual attitude I wish I had. Sometimes I pray it, even though the words do not yet fully come from my heart. I will write them down here:

> Father,
> I abandon myself into your hands;
> do with me what you will.
> Whatever you may do, I thank you;
> I am ready for all, I accept all.
> Let only your will be done in me,
> and in all your creatures.
>
> I wish no more than this,
> O Lord.
>
> Into your hands I commend my soul;
> I offer it to you with all the love
> of my heart,
> for I love you, Lord,
> and so need to give myself,
> to surrender myself into your hands,
> without reserve
> and with boundless confidence.
> For you are my Father.

It seems good to pray this prayer often. These are the words of a holy man, and they show the way I must go. I realize that I can never make this prayer come true by my own efforts. But the spirit of Jesus given to me can help me pray it and grow to its fulfillment. I know that my inner peace depends on my willingness to make this prayer my own.

14

DEEP ROOTS

∎

AN INVITATION
(Thursday, January 16)

ON SUNDAY, January 19, Mr. Herman Herder, president of the Herder Publishing Company, will celebrate his sixtieth birthday. I have been invited to participate in the celebration. So tomorrow I will go to Freiburg in Germany. There will be a dinner, an organ concert, a reception, and a lecture by Rudolf Schnackenburg. I look forward to being part of it all.

I have decided to use this occasion to stay for six weeks in Germany to work closely with my German editor and to finish a small book on icons.

BEAUTY AND ORDER
(Freiburg, West Germany; Friday, January 17)

Another language, another style, another "tone." I continue to be surprised by how small Europe is and how great the differences are between people who live so close to each other.

I took the train from Paris to Strasbourg. There Franz Johna, my friend and editor at Verlag Herder, met me and drove me over the border to Freiburg. A beautiful, charming, rather intimate city built around the splendid Münster Cathedral, Freiburg sits like a precious gem in the valley between the Rhine and the first hills of the Black Forest. It is a university town, with very little industry. The center is kept free from cars. People walk in the middle of the streets, which are lined by narrow gutters of running water. There are many beautiful churches, city gates, small medieval-looking alleys, and little squares with contemporary sculptures. It is a new city completely rebuilt after the Second World War. Yet it is a very old city rebuilt in the style and atmosphere of ages past. Everyone looks well-to-do. The stores are many and filled with a great variety of goods: clothes, food, books, modern appliances, artwork, and so on. There seems to be no end to the abundance.

At 11 P.M. Franz drove me to my place of residence, the mother house of the Vincentian Sisters in the Habsburger Strasse. The sisters received me with enthusiasm and warm hospitality and gave me a large room to stay in. I feel very happy to be here. I have been in this country only a few times in my life and always for a very short time. The occupation of Holland during the Second World War made it hard for us to go to Germany. Somehow all my attention was directed westward. But now I can get to know a new country, a new people, and a new way of praising God.

THE DEEPER QUESTION
(Tuesday, January 21)

My breakfast and dinner discussions with the priests who live in the mother house of the Vincentian Sisters have helped me to get some idea of the struggles of the Church in Germany. That these struggles are not minor became clear from the simple fact that my fellow priests disagreed with each other on most issues they discussed. I was often the surprised witness of fierce debates involving both body and mind.

Still, there is agreement about one thing. Questions concerning birth control, abortion, and euthanasia, as well as questions about the Pope, bishops' appointments, clerical dress, liturgical styles, and so on, are all symptoms of a much deeper question, which is "Do we truly believe in God?" The Germans, no less than the French and the Dutch, have moved into a new age. The existence of God, the divinity of Christ, and the spiritual authority of the Church are no longer foundational elements of Western European society. Whereas the society of the seventeenth, eighteenth, and nineteenth centuries could still build upon a value system deeply molded by the Christian tradition, the late twentieth century finds hardly a common value left. When it comes to legislation about central social issues such as giving life and causing death, there is no longer a common point of reference considered sacred by all. The central Christian vision, that life is a gift from God, to be nurtured, developed, and at all cost respected, no longer guides the decisions of all lawmakers. Thus laws, rules, and regulations tend to become increasingly functional and pragmatic. The question then becomes, "What seems best at present for the majority of the people?"

Meanwhile, many church leaders spend and often waste precious energy on issues which do more to distract us than to deepen our sense of mission. Progressives and conservatives fight each other within the Church, but both are in constant danger of becoming completely irrelevant to what molds our contemporary society.

Is there a God who cares? Are there any signs that history is guided by a merciful hand? Are there relationships which reach beyond the limits of the interpersonal, intercommunal, or international? Is life more than what psychologists, sociologists, biologists, and chemists can define? Is there anything to hope for after we have returned to dust? These questions are far from speculative. They touch the core of our civilization. Is the Church prepared to deal with these issues not just on an intellectual level, but on the level of daily life? Many Germans who still go to church no longer believe in a life after death. They come for very different reasons than the words they read or hear in church suggest. It is doubtful that they will stay very long.

The coming weeks will give me ample chance to think about all of this. I am happy to have fellow priests to help me articulate the questions and think about them. It forces me to go to the heart of the Christian faith, first of all my own.

PREDICTABILITY: VIRTUE AND LIABILITY
(Wednesday, January 22)

Living in a country in which little or no place remains for the unexpected or the surprising, the reading about David's election by Samuel and his victory over Goliath offers a real warning to me. I must confess that I like the predictability of life as it is lived here. When people tell me that they will pick me up at 4 P.M., they do not come a minute earlier or later. When the concert is supposed to start at 5 P.M., the first organ tones can be heard a moment after the clock has sounded its five strokes. When they tell me that the meal will be served at 6:15 P.M., it *is* served at 6:15 P.M. And the places are as proper as the times are precise. Everything has its place. Returning to my room after breakfast, I find everything back in the place where it was before I touched it.

For the time being, this great predictability offers me much peace. The absence of the unexpected allows me to work steadily on the realization of my plans. But still, David was the least expected king and his victory over Goliath the least predictable outcome of the battle with the Philistines. And what about Jesus, the "son of David"? Of him Nathanael says, "What good can come from Nazareth?" (John 1:46). And many of Jesus' followers lived lives as surprising as that of their master. There is a way of organizing life that leaves no room for the unpredictable. Maybe that explains that while many young German men and women have spent long periods of time at L'Arche in France, they have not yet been able to build L'Arche communities in Germany itself. Care for the handicapped in Germany is so well organized that the rather casual, somewhat free-floating style of L'Arche finds little acceptance. But can the spirit of God be bound? Jesus says, "The wind blows where it pleases . . . so it is with everyone who is born of the Spirit" (John 3:8). And Paul writes, "Do not stifle the Spirit" (1 Thessalonians 5:19).

If I want to get my work done, Germany is probably the best place to be. But if I want to give the spirit a real chance to work in me, I had better keep some of the French "laissez-faire" alive within me.

PROCLAIMING THE RICHES OF CHRIST
(Friday, January 24)

Today, my fifty-fourth birthday, the text of the first reading of the liturgy in honor of St. Francis de Sales summarizes my feelings succinctly. Paul writes to the Ephesians: "I, who am less than the least of all God's holy people, have been entrusted with this special grace, of proclaiming to the Gentiles the unfathomable treasure of Christ and of throwing light on the inner workings of the mystery kept hidden through all the ages in God, the Creator of everything" (Ephesians 3:8–9).

As I reflect on my life today, I feel indeed like the least of God's holy people. Looking back, I realize that I am still struggling with the same problems I had on the day of my ordination twenty-nine years ago. Notwithstanding my many prayers, my periods of retreat, and the advice from many friends, counselors, and confessors, very little, if anything, has changed with regard to my search for inner unity and peace. I am still the restless, nervous, intense, distracted, and impulse-driven person I was when I set out on this spiritual journey. At times this obvious lack of inner maturation depresses me as I enter into the "mature" years.

But I have one source of consolation. More than ever I feel the desire to proclaim "the unfathomable riches of Christ" and to throw light "on the inner working of the mystery kept hidden through all the ages in God." This desire has grown in intensity and urgency. I want to speak about the riches of Christ much more than when I was ordained in 1957. I vividly remember that the man who ordained me, Bernard Cardinal Alfrink, had written, on his coat of arms, "Evangelizare Divitias Christi" ("to proclaim the riches of Christ"). Today, when I read these same words in the liturgy, I realize that I have made these words increasingly my own. I really do want to speak loudly and clearly about the great riches of Christ. I want to do it simply, directly, plainly, and with deep personal conviction. Here I feel that something has grown in me. Here I sense that I am not the same person that I was twenty-nine years ago.

Maybe an increasing awareness of my sinfulness, as well as an increasing desire to make known the unfathomable riches of Christ, will prevent me from becoming proud, self-righteous, manipulative, and oppressive. I pray today that my sins will make me humble and my call to witness for Christ courageous. Francis de Sales is the best possible example I can have on this day to thank God for my life and to ask for faithfulness to the ministry given to me.

A MEDIEVAL LESSON IN HUMILITY
(Monday, January 27)

One of the stone reliefs of the Romanesque portal of the Münster, the splendid cathedral of Freiburg dating from about 1210, attempts to nudge the churchgoer in a playful way toward humility. A king is seated in a small basket which is hanging by a cord bound on both ends to the necks of two huge birds. The king holds in his hands two long spits on which two rabbits are impaled. By trying to reach the rabbits with their beaks, the hungry birds lift up the king into the air.

This comic relief portrays the story of Alexander the Great, who, after having conquered the whole world, also tries to make it to heaven. Although different versions of the story exist, one of them says that when Alexander saw the earth beneath him as a small hat in a large sea, he realized how tiny the world really is and how ridiculous it had been to spend his life trying to conquer it. Thus Alexander is presented to the pious churchgoer as an example of silly pride.

Konrad Kunze, the author of the beautiful book about the Münster entitled *Heaven in Stone,* summarizes a sermon of Berthold von Regensburg given around 1260: "Alexander, for whom the world was too small, becomes in the end only seven feet of dust, just like the poorest man ever born; Alexander thought that he could pull down the highest stars from heaven with his hands. And you, as he, would love to go up in the air, if you could only do it. But the story of Alexander shows the result of such high flying, and proves that the great Alexander was one of the greatest fools the world has ever seen."[9]

Well, no subtleties here! I wonder what Berthold would have thought about Boeing 747s. Still . . . the Münster itself, with its high-rising Gothic arches, might prove to be as much a sign of civic pride as of humility in the eyes of God. People always had mixed motives! God have mercy on us.

HUMAN GRIEF
(Thursday, January 30)

All the newspapers are proclaiming the tragic death of seven astronauts. The United States grieves. Millions who saw it happen on TV are still in shock, most of all the children who came to see one of their teachers participate in the great adventure of space exploration. They expected to see human greatness, and they saw human vulnerability.

Many people worry about the lasting effects of this tragedy on the children who saw it happen before their eyes. In the United States death has become almost invisible. Suddenly it becomes so visible that its significance can hardly be grasped. How can we grieve and help others to grieve? Do we grieve about a failure in our human ability to conquer space? Do we grieve about the deaths of our heroes, who risked their lives in the service of human progress? Do we grieve in order to find new energy to continue the work begun with so much self-assurance?

When I think about the fact that the United States space program is closely tied to the defense program and that this tragedy is at least in part the result of an international race for superiority and world domination, I cannot but wonder if the grief will lead to peace or to a more determined preparation for war. After all, the Strategic Defense Initiative is being prepared for in part by the space shuttle program.

Real human grief means allowing the illusion of immortality to die in us. When those whom we love with an "endless love" die, something also has to die within us. If we do not allow this to happen, we will lose touch with reality, our lives will become increasingly artificial, and we will lose our human capacity for compassion.

The national grief for the death of the seven astronauts will be fruitful if it helps us to die to our vainglory and our national desire to be the best and the most powerful at all costs, and stimulates us to search for a way of peace not dependent on military superiority. Christa McAuliffe stepped into the *Challenger* in the hope of teaching her children something new about the universe in which they live. The real challenge now will be to help these children understand and accept without fear the brokenness and mortality of their parents, their teachers, their heroes, and themselves. If this tragedy gradually helps them to love themselves and the adults who guide them as precious, extremely vulnerable, mortal human beings, they may become peacemakers for whom solidarity and compassion are greater gifts than technical genius and the ability to dominate others.

A STERN GUIDE
(Tuesday, February 4)

This afternoon I went downtown to pay another visit to the Münster. Together with a middle-aged woman, I took a guided tour. It was a wonderful experience. The guide, a retired civil servant, not only told us the history of the church, the names of the architects and artists, and the meaning of the statues, paintings, and altars, he also viewed the tour as an occasion to preach. He saw it as his task to convert us and bring us to prayer.

As he showed us the majestic portal on which both the saved and the condemned are vividly portrayed, he said, "Let us pray that we end up in the right group." As he showed us a large tapestry of Melchizedek, he recounted elaborately the Old Testament story and its eucharistic application. As he explained the New Testament scenes portrayed in stone or glass or on canvas, he quoted long passages from the Gospels by heart. In between the art treasures he demonstrated to us the ugly wooden contemporary confessionals with lights to indicate if they are free or occupied, and exhorted us to go to confession at least once every two weeks.

At times he expressed his political preferences. In the two "emperor chapels" with splendid stained glass windows portraying the powerful Habsburgers, Maximilian I, Phillip I, Charles V, and Ferdinand I, he said, "Today they don't teach schoolchildren about these great men. Now they teach them about Marx and Lenin. But we had better keep thinking about these Christians."

As we walked through the huge central nave, our guide spotted a young man with a cap on his head. The guide told him without subtlety that this was God's house and that he had to remove his cap or leave. The man left, rather perplexed about the encounter. I was shocked by this confronting, pious, nationalistic, and very moralistic guide. It struck me that the man fits the Münster perfectly. His way of guiding reveals both its greatness and its medieval, clerical, and authoritarian qualities. But what about the young man who was sent away? Would he ever be able to come back and discover the gentle all-forgiving love of God?

I bought a few booklets from the guide and promised him I would return. He brings me closer to the mentality of those who built this house of God, which took more than three centuries to finish. He also makes me ask some painful questions about ministry to those who can no longer relate to the powerful God of the Middle Ages but are searching for a tender, compassionate God, who can heal their wounded hearts.

15

CHOOSING LIFE

∎

FREIBURG IS THE CITY of Martin Heidegger (1889–1976). Shortly after I arrived here, Franz Johna drove me past 47 Rötebuckweg, where Heidegger lived and wrote many of his philosophical works.

There are few philosophers who have had as much influence on my thinking as Martin Heidegger. Though I never studied Heidegger directly, many of the philosophers, psychologists, and theologians who formed my thinking were deeply influenced by him. Walgrave, Binswanger, and Rahner cannot be fully understood apart from Heidegger's existentialism.

Today I read a short address given in 1955 in Messkirch, his birthplace, in honor of the musician Conrad Kreutzer, who was also born there. The address is entitled "Gelassenheit."

Heidegger states that the greatest danger of our time is that the calculating way of thinking that is part of the technical revolution will become the dominating and exclusive way of thinking. Why is this so dangerous? Heidegger says, "Because then we would find, together with the highest and the most successful development of our thinking on the calculating level, an indifference toward reflection and a complete thoughtlessness . . . then humanity would have renounced and thrown away what is most its own, its ability to reflect. What is at stake is to save the essence of humanity. What is at stake is to keep alive our reflective thinking *(das Nachdenken).*"[10]

Heidegger calls for an attitude in which we say "yes" to the new techniques, insofar as they serve our daily lives, and "no" when they claim our whole being. He calls for a *Gelassenheit zu Dingen* (letting reality speak) and an openness to the mystery of things. This calmness and openness, Heidegger says, will give us a new rootedness, a new groundedness, a new sense of belonging. Thus we can remain reflective human beings and prevent ourselves from becoming victims of a "calculating" existence.

It is clear how important Heidegger's thoughts remain today. We need to safeguard our reflective minds more than ever. Indirectly, Heidegger also touches on the need for a new spirituality, a new way of being in the world without being of it.

FEELING PROTECTED
(Friday, February 7)

Gradually I am becoming aware of a new dimension in my prayer life. It is hard to find words for it, but it feels like a protective presence of God, Mary, the angels, and the saints that exists in the midst of distractions, fears, temptations, and inner confusion.

While my prayers were not at all intensive or profound, I had a real desire to spend time in prayer this week. I enjoyed just sitting in the small dark side chapel of the mother house of the Vincentian Sisters. I felt surrounded by goodness, gentleness, kindness, and acceptance. I felt as if angels' wings were keeping me safe: a protective cloud covering me and keeping me there. Though it is very hard to express, this new experience is the experience of being protected against the dangers of a seductive world. But this protection is very soft, gentle, caring. Not the protection of a wall or a metal screen. It is more like a hand on my shoulder or a kiss on my forehead. But for all this protection, I am not taken away from the dangers. I am not lifted from the seductive world. I am not removed from violence, hatred, lust, and greed. In fact, I feel them in the center of my being, screaming for my full attention. They are restless and noisy. Still, this hand, these lips, these eyes are present and I know that I am safe, held in love, cared for, and protected by the good spirits of heaven.

So I am praying while not knowing how to pray. I am resting while feeling restless, at peace while tempted, safe while still anxious, surrounded by a cloud of light while still in darkness, in love while still doubting.

It is such a grace that I have the time to step out of my room any time during the day and go to the chapel just to be there and to be reassured. The angels of God are always waiting there for me and eager to stand around me and cover me with their wings and let me rest, not giving much attention to all that clamors in my inner darkness. They do not say much; they do not explain much. They are just there to let me know that God's heart is so infinitely greater than my own.

THE COMPASSIONATE EYES OF CHRIST
(Saturday, February 8)

Christ on a Donkey, in the Augustiner Museum in Freiburg, is one of the most moving Christ figures I know. I have sent many postcards of it to my friends, and I keep one in my prayer book.

This afternoon I went to the museum to spend some quiet time with this *Christus auf Palmesel* (Christ on palm-donkey). This fourteenth-century sculpture originally comes from Niederrotweil, a small town close to Breisach on the Rhine. It was made to be pulled on a cart in the Palm Sunday procession. In 1900 it was sold to the Augustiner Museum, where it now stands in the center of the first exposition hall.

Christ's long, slender face with a high forehead, inward-looking eyes, long hair, and a small forked beard expresses the mystery of his suffering in a way that holds me spellbound. As he rides into Jerusalem surrounded by people shouting "hosanna," "cutting branches from the trees and spreading them in his path" (Matthew 21:8), Jesus appears completely concentrated on something else. He does not look at the excited crowd. He does not wave. He sees beyond all the noise and movement to what is ahead of him: an agonizing journey of betrayal, torture, crucifixion, and death. His unfocused eyes see what nobody around him can see; his high forehead reflects a knowledge of things to come far beyond anyone's understanding.

There is melancholy, but also peaceful acceptance. There is insight into the fickleness of the human heart, but also immense compassion. There is a deep awareness of the unspeakable pain to be suffered, but also a strong determination to do God's will. Above all, there is love, an endless, deep, and far-reaching love born from an unbreakable intimacy with God and reaching out to all people, wherever they are, were, or will be. There is nothing that he does not fully know. There is nobody whom he does not fully love.

Every time I look at this Christ on the donkey, I am reminded again that I am seen by him with all my sins, guilt, and shame and loved with all his forgiveness, mercy, and compassion.

Just being with him in the Augustiner Museum is a prayer. I look and look and look, and I know that he sees the depths of my heart; I do not have to be afraid.

WINDOW FACES
(Monday, February 10)

Rosenmontag (Carnival's Monday) in Freiburg. At 2 P.M. I went downtown for the carnival parade and saw clowns, bands, small and large floats, an endless variety of masks, and an abundance of confetti. It was bitterly cold. People kept themselves warm with waffles and *Gluhwein* (hot spiced wine). The parade numbered 149 shows, and it took two hours to pass.

Most impressive were the huge masks. They were often pieces of art expressing a variety of emotions: anger, joy, hatred, love, goodness, and evil. Some masks were so realistic I could hardly imagine that the people wearing them had a different feeling from what the mask expressed.

Some heads were so huge that their wearers' faces could be seen only through windows in the neck. Many blew trumpets, flutes, or horns through the windows. I was struck by the contrast between the faces on the masks and the faces in the windows. The "window faces" all looked quite serious, compared to the wild faces on the heads above them. While the parade invited us to be fools for a day, it convinced me how hard it is for people to relax and truly celebrate. Also, the people on the sidewalks watching the parade took it all in with great seriousness. If there had not been so many bands, it would have been an extremely dull event. It all had a somewhat obligatory quality. Even wildly dressed people had a hard time smiling! It was a serious job for them. The children seemed the most serious of all. Whether they looked like cats, mice, polar bears, screwdrivers, Indians, Mexicans, or witches, their little faces showed that they were performing an important task!

I watched all this, ate a waffle, drank two cups of *Gluhwein*, and went home. The sister who opened the door greeted me with an open face, a big smile, and a free laugh. I suddenly realized that no mask can make people really happy. Happiness must come from within.

A LENTEN PRAYER
(Tuesday, February 11)

Dear Lord Jesus,

Tomorrow the Lenten season begins. It is a time to be with you in a special way, a time to pray, to fast, and thus to follow you on your way to Jerusalem, to Golgotha, and to the final victory over death.

I am still so divided. I truly want to follow you, but I also want to follow my own desires and lend an ear to the voices that speak about prestige, success, human respect, pleasure, power, and influence. Help me to become deaf to these voices and more attentive to your voice, which calls me to choose the narrow road to life.

I know that Lent is going to be a very hard time for me. The choice for your way has to be made every moment of my life. I have to choose thoughts that are your thoughts, words that are your words, and actions that are your actions. There are no times or places without choices. And I know how deeply I resist choosing you.

Please, Lord, be with me at every moment and in every place. Give me the strength and the courage to live this season faithfully, so that, when Easter comes, I will be able to taste with joy the new life which you have prepared for me.

Amen.

CHOOSING JOY
(Thursday, February 13)

In the first reading of the Eucharist today I heard: "I am offering you life or death . . . choose life, then, so that you and your descendents may live in the love of Yahweh your God, obeying his voice, holding fast to him" (Deuteronomy 30:19–20).

How do I choose life? I am becoming aware that there are few moments without the opportunity to choose, since death and life are always before me. One aspect of choosing life is choosing joy. Joy is life-giving, but sadness brings death. A sad heart is a heart in which something is dying. A joyful heart is a heart in which something new is being born.

I think that joy is much more than a mood. A mood invades us. We do not choose a mood. We often find ourselves in a happy or depressed mood without knowing where it comes from. The spiritual life is a life beyond moods. It is a life in which we choose joy and do not allow ourselves to become victims of passing feelings of happiness or depression.

I am convinced that we can choose joy. Every moment we can decide to respond to an event or a person with joy instead of sadness. When we truly believe that God is life and only life, then nothing need have the power to draw us into the sad realm of death. To choose joy does not mean to choose happy feelings or an artificial atmosphere of hilarity. But it does mean the determination to let whatever takes place bring us one step closer to the God of life.

Maybe this is what is so important about quiet moments of meditation and prayer. They allow me to take a critical look at my moods and to move from victimization to free choice.

This morning I woke up somewhat depressed. I could not find any reason for it. Life just felt empty, useless, fatiguing. I felt invaded by somber spirits. I realized that this mood was lying to me. Life is not meaningless. God has created life as an expression of love. It helped me to know this, even though I could not feel it. Based on this knowledge, I could again choose joy. This choice means simply to act according to the truth. The depressed mood is still there. I cannot just force it out of my heart. But at least I can unmask it as being untrue and thus prevent it from becoming the ground for my actions.

I am called to be joyful. It gives much consolation to know that I can choose joy.

ALL IS WELL AROUND THE MÜNSTER
(Saturday, February 15)

Saturday afternoon, 5 P.M. at the Münster. It is very still on the Münster square. A very light, hardly noticeable snow falls softly on the cobblestones. The houses standing around the Münster form a quiet, peaceful community, like children sitting around a bonfire listening to a story. There is hardly any noise. The stores have been closed since noon. No cars, no shouting voices, not even the noise of children playing. Here and there I see people crossing the empty snow-covered square and entering the church.

The sun has gone down, but it is not fully dark yet. The grey sky is filled with little white dots. A few lights burn outside the guesthouses, inviting people to come in and drink some wine or eat some hearty food.

I look up at the tower of the Münster. She tells her story without words, a wise old grandmother smiling at her grandchildren, who say, "Tell us that story again." Beams of light cover her full length, and through the open spire a warm inner light shines forth from her. I look and feel comforted and consoled. She seems to say, "Do not worry so much. God loves you."

In the church it is dark. But there is an island of light in front of the large statue of the Virgin and Child. The flames of hundreds of small candles make the light look like something alive and moving. A few people are standing there praying with closed eyes.

In the little side chapels surrounding the main altar priests are hearing confessions. People come and go silently. I kneel in front of one of the priests to confess my sins. He listens to me attentively and speaks gentle words about the importance of being joyful at all times. As he absolves me in the name of the Father, the Son, and the Holy Spirit, I feel some of the joy he spoke about.

I pray for a while in front of the statue of the Virgin. Then I walk home with a heart full of peace. It has become very dark now. The glowing tower still stands there and smiles at me. All is well.

A HAPPY REUNION
(Wednesday, February 19)

Tonight at 7 P.M. Jonas arrived from Boston! A few weeks ago he called and said he would like to spend the last few days of my stay in Germany with me. I was overjoyed.

Jonas was able to take a few days of vacation and had found a cheap flight to Europe. This morning he arrived in Brussels and came to Freiburg by train via Cologne. It continues to amaze me how small the world has become. Last night we were still thousands of miles away from each other. Tonight we had supper together, talked about a thousand things, and prayed together in the chapel. We are looking forward to a few peaceful days together.

LETTING GO OF DIVISIONS
(Friday, February 21)

This morning Jonas and I read in the Gospel Jesus' words: "If you are bringing your gift to the altar, and there you remember that your brother or sister has something against you, leave your gift in front of the altar; go at once and make peace with your brother, and then come back and offer your gift" (Matthew 5:23–24).

These words have stayed with us for the whole day. I realize that there are still many people with whom I am not fully at peace. When I think back on the friendships, encounters, and confrontations of the past, I realize that islands of anger, bitterness, and resentment still lie hidden in my heart. And when I bring to mind all whom I personally know or about whom I have heard or read, I know how I divide them between those who are for me and those who are against me, those whom I like and those whom I do not like, those whom I want to be with and those whom I try to avoid at all costs. My inner life is so filled with opinions, judgments, and prejudices about my "brothers and sisters" that real peace is still far away.

As I think about Jesus' words, I know that I must let go of all these divisive emotions and thoughts so that I can truly experience peace with all of God's people. This means an unrestrained willingness to forgive and let go of old fears, bitterness, resentment, anger, and lust, and thus find reconciliation.

In this way, I can be a real peacemaker. My inner peace can be a source of peace for all I meet. I can then offer gifts on the altar of God as a testimony to this peace with my brothers and sisters.

I have to start thinking about concrete ways to make peace with my brothers and sisters who have something against me. What do I have to lose? To make peace is to free myself from my easy judgments so that I can love my enemy and the God who holds me and my enemies together in the palm of his hand.

Today I experience deep gratitude for the friendship between Jonas and me. It is the visible fruit of our peacemaking in November.

GOD'S LIGHT SHINING THROUGH OUR BODIES
(Strasbourg; Sunday, February 23)

At 8 A.M. Franz and Robert Johna drove Jonas and me to Strasbourg. At 11 A.M. we participated in the eucharistic celebration in the cathedral. The dean of the cathedral invited me to concelebrate with him. A tall young Franciscan priest serving as chaplain at the University of Strasbourg was giving the sermon.

After the Gospel reading of the transfiguration, the Franciscan climbed the richly carved pulpit in the middle of the cathedral. All the worshipers turned their chairs around so that they could see him and listen attentively. He spoke about the transfiguration not only of Jesus, but of all creation. As he spoke he pointed to the brilliant yellow, white, and blue rose window above the cathedral entrance. He said, "Though this is a great piece of art, we can only see its full splendor when the sun shines through it." Then he explained how our bodies, the work of our hands, and all that exists can shine with splendor only when we let God's light shine through them. As he spoke, I kept looking at the magnificent rose window—at thirteen meters across, the largest ever made—and I had a new sense of the transfiguration that took place on Mount Tabor: God's light bursting forth from the body of Jesus. Six centuries ago a rose-window was made that today helps me to see the glory of Christ in a new way. Again I felt part of the long journey of the people of God through the centuries. There was much that was old and much that was new. There were statues of saints, kings, and queens of long ago. There were also friendly priests in dungarees and turtlenecks, women acolytes, and many cars parked around the cathedral. I could see history moving.

But again and again there recurred that same story on the second Sunday of Lent, the story of the transfiguration of Jesus.

At 12:45 P.M. the moment of departure arrived. As Jonas and I waved to Franz and Robert from the slowly moving train, I felt we had become part of something deep and lasting of which the cathedral of Strasbourg had been only one last reminder.

16

THE DESCENDING WAY

■

FRIENDS MEET FRIENDS
(Trosly; Monday, February 24)

A DAY FULL OF HELLOS and good-byes back at Trosly. Madame Vanier, Paquita, Barbara, Simone, Mirella, and many others welcomed us warmly and showed sincere joy at seeing both of us again. The most important event of the day for me was a lunch with Jonas and Nathan. Although Jonas had met Nathan during his last visit, they had not come to know each other well. Since my friendship with Nathan has grown so quickly and deeply during the past few months, I was eager to give Jonas and Nathan a chance to get to know each other better. Friendships need to be shared; I was very glad that Jonas could spend some more time with Nathan before his return to Boston. We spoke mostly about friendship and its importance in our lives. What I remember most was our discussion about the importance of confessing our struggles to each other, not just when they became unbearable, but very early on. Jonas said, "The demons love darkness and hiddenness. Inner fears and struggles which remain isolated develop great power over us. But when we talk about them in a spirit of trust, then they can be looked at and dealt with. Once brought into the light of mutual love, demons lose their power and quickly leave us."

I realized that what Jonas said was the core of the sacrament of penance. Through confession and forgiveness we can experience the healing, reconciling, and recreating power of God's love. I was glad to realize that what I had learned through the practice of the sacrament of confession had implications for a life of faithful friendship. Just as the celebration of the Eucharist calls us to gratitude at all times and places, so, too, does the celebration of the sacrament of penance call us to a way of living in which we are always willing to confess and forgive.

When I took Jonas to the railroad station tonight and waved good-bye to him, I felt deeply grateful for the bonds of friendship that had grown during the last months. These bonds make large distances seem small and heavy burdens feel light.

ON SLOWING DOWN THE SUN
(*Tuesday, March 4*)

Since returning from Freiburg I have been busy with countless tasks, yet feeling that nothing is being accomplished. From early in the morning to late at night I have been occupied with letters, phone calls, visits, meetings, and other seemingly urgent things. But I have not done much of what I think I am here for: praying and writing. I have kept up with my morning hour of meditation, I have celebrated the Eucharist every day, I have said my evening prayers, but I haven't felt any vitality. I have been somewhat wooden, hard, and dry! And I have let the days go by just keeping up with the little things. I found a suitcase filled with letters which had piled up during my six weeks in Germany. Wonderful, lovely letters. But as I start reading and answering them the hours flow by and the days melt away.

I am frustrated because in the midst of this busy life I keep having ideas, insights, and feelings which I want to pour out on paper. And the more ideas, insights, and feelings I have, the more frustrated I get: too many to hold, too much to remember, too much to save for later. I want to write now, not later.

One friend wrote in his letter, "I hope you find time to write, but don't take yourself too seriously!" Maybe I have to smile a little about my obsessions and compulsions. Maybe I have to trust that there will be time when there has to be. Meanwhile, I keep protesting to God that the days are created so short. I keep saying, "Please, Lord, slow that sun down!" But it keeps going as always, round and round and round. No faster, no slower, twenty-four hours each day!

Peter called today and said that the magazine *America* had rejected the meditation on the Pentecost icon I wrote in Freiburg. I felt it was the best of the four icon meditations I had written, but the editor of *America* wrote in a short note, "It is not up to the standard that we are used to from Henri Nouwen." Well that might slow *me* down a little instead of the sun! It was a good way to help me take myself less seriously.

Maybe this is one way of reminding myself that I cannot make myself holy. Holiness is a gift from God, not something I can ever claim as the result of my own doing.

Life is humbling, very humbling. I have to let it be that way. Someone said today, "We need a lot of humiliation for a little bit of humility."

STAYING CONNECTED WITH JESUS
(*Wednesday, March 12*)

Today in the Gospel reading of the liturgy, Jesus reveals that everything he does is done in relationship with his Father: "The Son can do nothing by himself; he can do only what he sees the Father doing; and whatever the Father does the Son does too" (John 5:19).

After the intense experience of disconnectedness I had yesterday, Jesus' words have a special meaning for me. I must live in an ongoing relationship with Jesus and through him with the Father. This relationship is the core of the spiritual life. This relationship prevents my life from being consumed by "keeping up" with things. This relationship prevents my days from becoming boring, fatiguing, draining, depressing, and frustrating.

If all that I do can become more and more an expression of my participation in God's life of total giving and receiving in love, everything else will be blessed and will lose its fragmented quality. This does not mean that everything will become easy and harmonious. There will still be much agony, but when connected with God's own agony, even my agony can lead to life.

I guess it all boils down to a call to pray unceasingly.

I LOVE JESUS, BUT . . .
(Saturday, March 15)

The Gospel today reveals that Jesus not only had good, faithful friends willing to follow him wherever he went and fierce enemies who couldn't wait to get rid of him, but also many sympathizers who were attracted, but afraid at the same time.

The rich young man loved Jesus but couldn't give up his wealth to follow him. Nicodemus admired Jesus but was afraid to lose the respect of his own colleagues. I am becoming more and more aware of the importance of looking at these fearful sympathizers because that is the group I find myself mostly gravitating toward.

I love Jesus but want to hold on to my own friends even when they do not lead me closer to Jesus. I love Jesus but want to hold on to my own independence even when that independence brings me no real freedom. I love Jesus but do not want to lose the respect of my professional colleagues, even though I know that their respect does not make me grow spiritually. I love Jesus but do not want to give up my writing plans, travel plans, and speaking plans, even when these plans are often more to my glory than to the glory of God.

So I am like Nicodemus, who came by night, said safe things about Jesus to his colleagues, and expressed his guilt by bringing to the grave more myrrh and aloes than needed or desired.

To his colleagues, the Pharisees, Nicodemus said, "our Law does not allow us to pass judgment on anyone without first giving him a hearing and discovering what he is doing" (John 7:51). These are careful words. They are spoken to people who hate Jesus. But they are spoken on their terms. They say, "Even if you hate Jesus and desire to kill him, do not lose your dignity, follow your own rules." Nicodemus said it to save Jesus, but he didn't want to lose his friends. It didn't work. He was ridiculed by his friends: "Are you a Galilean too? Go into the matter, and see for yourself: prophets do not arise from Galilee!" His personal and professional identity are attacked.

It is such a familiar scene. I have spoken like Nicodemus in episcopal committees and faculty meetings many times. Instead of speaking directly about my love for Jesus, I make a smart remark suggesting that maybe my friends should look at another side of the question. They usually respond by saying I have not studied my sources well enough, or that I seem to have some sentimental attachment that got in the way of a truly professional approach. Those who have said these things have had the power of right thinking and thus forced me to silence. But it has been fear that has prevented me from speaking from the heart and risking rejection.

Nicodemus deserves all my attention. Can I stay a Pharisee and follow Jesus too? Doesn't that condemn me to bringing costly spices to the grave when it is too late?

ON RETREAT
(Nevers; Monday, March 17)

Tonight I am in Nevers, five hours by car from Trosly. I am here to make a "covenant retreat" with Jean Vanier and forty L'Arche assistants. We will be here the whole week to pray, listen to Jean's reflections on living the Gospel at L'Arche, share ideas and experiences, and explore the bond we have with handicapped people.

THE CRY OF THE POOR
(Tuesday, March 18)

Two themes run through Jean's reflections: the descending way of God and the call to find God not just by serving the poor, but by *becoming* poor. God, who created the universe in all its splendor, decided to reveal to us the mystery of the divine life by becoming flesh in a young woman living in a humble village on one of the small planets of God's own creation. Jesus' life is marked by an always deeper choice of what is small, humble, poor, rejected, and despised. The poor are the preferred dwelling place of God. Thus they have become the way to meet God.

Handicapped people are not only poor; they also reveal to us our own poverty. Their primal call is an anguished cry: "Do you love me?" and "Why have you forsaken me?" When we are confronted with that cry, so visible in those people who have no capacity to hide behind their intellectual defenses, we are forced to look at our own terrible loneliness and our own primal cry. We hear this cry everywhere in our world. Jews, blacks, Palestinians, refugees, and many others all cry out, "Why is there no place for us, why are we rejected, why are we pushed away?" Jesus has lived this primal cry with us. "My God, my God, why have you forsaken me?" He, who came from God to lead us to God, suffered the deepest anguish a human being can suffer, the anguish of being left alone, rejected, forgotten, abandoned by the one who is the source of all life.

L'Arche is founded on this cry of the poor. L'Arche is a response to the cry of Jesus, which is the cry of all who suffer anguish and who wonder if there can be any real bond with anyone. Jesus came to reunite, to heal, to form bonds, to reconcile. He shared our anguish so that through our anguish we would be able to find the way back to God. Jesus descended to ascend. "He emptied himself

. . . he was humbler yet, even to accepting death, death on a cross . . . for this God raised him high and gave him the name which is above all other names" (Philippians 2:7–9).

L'ARCHE BUILT UPON THE BODY
(Thursday, March 20)

One of the most important things that Jean Vanier is saying to me during this retreat is that L'Arche is built upon the body and not upon the word. This helps to explain my struggle in coming to L'Arche. Until now my whole life has been centered around the word: learning, teaching, reading, writing, speaking. Without the word, my life is unthinkable. A good day is a day with a good conversation, a good lecture given or heard, a good book read, or a good article written. Most of my joys and pains are connected with words.

L'Arche, however, is built not on words, but on the body. The community of L'Arche is a community formed around the wounded bodies of handicapped people. Feeding, cleaning, touching, holding—this is what builds the community. Words are secondary. Most handicapped people have few words to speak, and many do not speak at all. It is the language of the body that counts most.

"The Word became flesh." That is the center of the Christian message. Before the Incarnation, the relationship between body and word was unclear. Often the body was seen as a hindrance to the full realization of what the word wanted to express. But Jesus confronts us with the word that can be seen, heard, and touched. The body thus becomes the way to know the word and to enter into relationship with the word. The body of Jesus becomes the way to life. "He who eats my body and drinks my blood will have eternal life."

I feel a deep resistance against this way. Somehow I have come to think about eating, drinking, washing, and dressing as so many necessary preconditions for reading, speaking, teaching, or writing. Somehow the pure word was the real thing for me. Time spent with "material" things was necessary but needed to be kept to a minimum. But at L'Arche, that is where all the attention goes. At L'Arche the body is the place where the word is met. It is in relationship to the wounded body of the handicapped person that I must learn to discover God.

This is very hard for me. I still find a long meal in the middle of the day a waste of time. I still think that I have more important things to do than to set the table, eat slowly, wash the dishes, and set the table again. I think, "Surely we must eat, but the work which comes after is what counts." But L'Arche cannot be endured with this mind set.

I wonder when and how I will learn to fully live the Incarnation. I suppose that only the handicapped people themselves will be able to show me the way. I must trust that God will send me the teachers I need.

THE COVENANT
(Friday, March 21)

This is a covenant retreat. A covenant retreat is a retreat in which those who have lived and worked at L'Arche for some years are invited to announce publicly the covenant with Jesus and the poor which has grown in them. Announcing the covenant is not a vow, nor even a promise. It is a public acknowledgement that a special bond with the poor and with Jesus, who lives in the poor, has developed over the years.

This covenant is something new in the Church. It does not make you a member of an order or religious association. It does not incorporate you into an institution. It does not give you special status or privilege. It does not bind you to stay at L'Arche and continue working with mentally handicapped people. The covenant is something much more intimate, personal, and hidden. It is a bonding that is not created, but acknowledged as having in fact taken place. It is a work of God that is announced to brothers and sisters of the same community. The announcement is a witness to what God is doing through Jesus in people who work with the poor, and is thus a sign of hope and encouragement for all who search to be faithful to the Gospel.

It is very clear that I am far from announcing the covenant myself. I have just come to know L'Arche and have not yet lived full-time in a foyer. I know something of the spirituality of L'Arche, but that knowledge has not yet become flesh in me. I am drawn to various handicapped people and assistants, but a deep bonding with them has not yet taken place. I need to "live L'Arche" much longer and more deeply, so that the covenant can grow in me; only then can I announce it to others as a gift freely given to me.

This retreat is making me aware of how fragmented my life has been so far. There has been so much individualism, competition, rivalry, privileges, favors, and exceptions in my way of living that few deep and lasting bonds could grow. But Jesus came to create bonds, and living in, with, and through Jesus means discovering these bonds in myself and revealing them to others. There are bonds between handicapped people and their assistants, between handicapped people and their families, between handicapped people and their neighbors, and most of all between handicapped people and their fellow handicapped people. There are bonds between Catholic Christians and Protestant Christians, between Christians and those who believe in God, between those who believe in God and all who share the same humanity. There are bonds between human beings and animals, between human beings and the earth, and between human beings and the whole universe. Satan divides, pulls apart, fragments, and disrupts. Jesus unites, reconciles, heals, and restores. Wherever we experience bonding, there is Jesus. He came to invite us to enter with him into that intimate covenant that exists between himself and his Father. This is the bond that is the source and goal of all bonding. All creation is called to unity with God in and through Jesus, whose whole being is being bonded in love to his divine Father.

ANNOUNCING THE COVENANT
(Saturday, March 22)

It was very moving to see the retreatants stand in front of the altar and announce their covenant with Jesus and the poor. As I looked into the faces of my brothers and sisters who had chosen the downward way of Jesus, I realized that they would give me the strength to announce the same covenant when the time for it comes.

The more I ponder what Jean Vanier has said, the more I realize how seemingly impossible is the way he calls me to go. Everything in me wants to move upward. Downward mobility with Jesus goes radically against my inclinations, against the advice of the world surrounding me, and against the culture of which I am a part. In choosing to become poor with the poor at L'Arche, I still hope to gain praise for that choice. Wherever I turn I am confronted with my deep-seated resistance against following Jesus on his way to the cross and my countless ways of avoiding poverty, whether material, intellectual, or emotional. Only Jesus, in whom the fullness of God dwells, could freely and fully choose to be completely poor.

I see clearer now that choosing to become poor is choosing to make every part of my journey with Jesus. Becoming truly poor is impossible, but "nothing is impossible to God" (Luke 1:37). In and through Jesus I believe that the way to true poverty will open itself to me. After all, it is not *my* poverty that has any value, but only God's poverty, which becomes visible through my life.

This sounds unreal, but when I saw the men and women who announced their covenant with Jesus and the poor, I saw how real this downward way of Jesus is and how, if I go this way, I go not alone, but as a member of the "body of Jesus." Seldom have I experienced so directly the difference between individual heroism and communal obedience. Whenever I think about becoming poor as something I must accomplish, I become depressed. But as soon as I realize that my brothers and sisters call me to go this way with them in obedience to Jesus, I am filled with hope and joy.

This afternoon we all returned to our different communities and foyers. It was a very hard week for me, but full of blessings.

17

PASSION, DEATH, AND RESURRECTION

■

BEING HANDED OVER
(Trosly; Tuesday, March 25)

JESUS, sitting at table with his disciples, said, "One of you will betray me" (John 13:21). I read this today in the Gospel.

As I look more closely at Jesus' words as they are written in Greek, a better translation would be "One of you will hand me over." The term *paradidomi* means "to give over, to hand over, to give into the hands of." It is an important term not only to express what Judas did, but also what God did. Paul writes, ". . . he did not spare his own Son, but 'handed him over' for the sake of all of us" (Romans 8:32).

If we translate Judas's action as "to betray," as applied to Judas, we do not fully express the mystery because Judas is described as being an instrument of God's work. That is why Jesus said, "The Son of Man is going to his fate, as the scriptures say he will, but alas for the man by whom the Son of Man is betrayed [handed over]" (Matthew 26:24).

This moment when Jesus is handed over to those who do with him as they please is a turning point in Jesus' ministry. It is turning from action to passion. After years of teaching, preaching, healing, and moving to wherever he wanted to go, Jesus is handed over to the caprices of his enemies. Things are now no longer done *by* him, but *to* him. He is flagellated, crowned with thorns, spat at, laughed at, stripped, and nailed naked to a cross. He is a passive victim, subject to other people's actions. From the moment Jesus is handed over, his passion begins, and through this passion he fulfills his vocation.

It is important for me to realize that Jesus fulfills his mission not by what he does, but by what is done to him. Just as with everyone else, most of my life is determined by what is done to me and thus is passion. And because most of my life is passion, things being done to me, only small parts of my life are determined by what I think, say, or do. I am inclined to protest against this and to want all to be action, originated by me. But the truth is that my passion is a much greater part of my life than my action. Not to recognize this is self-deception and not to embrace my passion with love is self-rejection.

It is good news to know that Jesus is handed over to passion, and through his passion accomplishes his divine task on earth. It is good news for a world passionately searching for wholeness.

Jesus' words to Peter remind me that Jesus' transition from action to passion must also be ours if we want to follow his way. He says, "When you were young you put on your own belt and walked where you liked; but when you grow old you will stretch out your hands, and somebody else will put a belt round you and take you where you would rather not go" (John 21:18).

I, too, have to let myself be "handed over" and thus fulfill my vocation.

RUNNING AWAY OR RETURNING
(Wednesday, March 26)

During this week Judas and Peter present me with the choice between running away from Jesus in despair or returning to him in hope. Judas betrayed Jesus and hanged himself. Peter denied Jesus and returned to him in tears.

Sometimes despair seems an attractive choice, solving everything in the negative. The voice of despair says, "I sin over and over again. After endless promises to myself and others to do better next time, I find myself back again in the old dark places. Forget about trying to change. I have tried for years. It didn't work and it will never work. It is better that I get out of people's way, be forgotten, no longer around, dead."

This strangely attractive voice takes all uncertainties away and puts an end to the struggle. It speaks unambiguously for the darkness and offers a clear-cut negative identity.

But Jesus came to open my ears to another voice that says, "I am your God, I have molded you with my own hands, and I love what I have made. I love you with a love that has no limits, because I love you as I am loved. Do not run away from me. Come back to me—not once, not twice, but always again. You are my child. How can you ever doubt that I will embrace you again, hold you against my breast, kiss you and let my hands run through your hair? I am your God— the God of mercy and compassion, the God of pardon and love, the God of tenderness and care. Please do not say that I have given up on you, that I cannot stand you anymore, that there is no way back. It is not true. I so much want you to be with me. I so much want you to be close to me. I know all your thoughts. I hear all your words. I see all of your actions. And I love you because you are beautiful, made in my own image, an expression of my most intimate love. Do not judge yourself. Do not condemn yourself. Do not reject yourself. Let my love touch the deepest, most hidden corners of your heart and reveal to you your own beauty, a beauty that you have lost sight of, but which will become visible to you again in the light of my mercy. Come, come, let me wipe your tears, and let my mouth come close to your ear and say to you, 'I love you, I love you, I love you.'"

This is the voice that Jesus wants us to hear. It is the voice that calls us always to return to the one who has created us in love and wants to re-create us in mercy. Peter heard that voice and trusted it. As he let that voice touch his heart, tears came—tears of sorrow and tears of joy, tears of remorse and tears of peace, tears of repentance and tears of gratitude.

It is not easy to let the voice of God's mercy speak to us because it is a voice asking for an always open relationship, one in which sins are acknowledged, forgiveness received, and love renewed. It does not offer us a solution, but a friendship. It does not take away our problems, but promises not to avoid them. It does not tell us where it all will end, but assures us that we will never be alone. A true relationship is hard work because loving is hard work, with many tears and many smiles. But it is God's work and worth every part of it.

O Lord, my Lord, help me to listen to your voice and choose your mercy.

WASHING THE FEET OF THE POOR
(Thursday, March 27)

This afternoon I took the train to Paris to celebrate the Holy Thursday liturgy with the L'Arche community, "Nomaste." It was a very moving celebration. We gathered in the community room of Nomaste. There were about forty people. In his welcome, the director of the community, Toni Paoli, expressed his vision that L'Arche should be not simply a comfortable place for handicapped people, but a Christian community in which people serve one another in the name of Jesus. After the Gospel reading, he again proclaimed his deep love for Jesus. Then he stood up and washed the feet of four members of his community.

After the Eucharist, a rice dish, bread, and wine were brought and put on the altar. In silence, deepened by three short Gospel readings about God's love, we shared this simple food.

Sitting in the basement room in Paris surrounded by forty poor people, I was struck again by the way Jesus concluded his active life. Just before entering on the road of his passion he washed the feet of his disciples and offered them his body and blood as food and drink. These two acts belong together. They are both an expression of God's determination to show us the fullness of his love. Therefore John introduces the story of the washing of the disciples' feet with the words: "Jesus . . . having loved those who were his in the world, loved them to the end" (John 13:1).

What is even more astonishing is that on both occasions Jesus commands us to do the same. After washing his disciples' feet, Jesus says, "I have given you an example so that you may copy what I have done to you" (John 13:15). After giving himself as food and drink, he says, "Do this in remembrance of me" (Luke 22:19). Jesus calls us to continue his mission of revealing the perfect love of God in this world. He calls us to total self-giving. He does not want us to keep anything for ourselves. Rather, he wants our love to be as full, as radical, and as complete as his own. He wants us to bend ourselves to the ground and touch the places in each other that most need washing. He also wants us to say to each other, "Eat of me and drink of me." By this complete mutual nurturing, he wants us to become one body and one spirit, united by the love of God.

When Toni spoke to his community about his love for Jesus, and when I saw how he washed their feet and gave them the bread and wine, it seemed as if—for the moment—I saw a glimpse of the new kingdom Jesus came to bring. Everybody in the room knew how far he or she was from being a perfect expression of God's love. But everybody was also willing to make a step in the direction to which Jesus pointed.

It was an evening in Paris I will not easily forget.

THE IMMENSE SUFFERING
OF HUMANITY
(Friday, March 28)

Good Friday: day of the cross, day of suffering, day of hope, day of abandonment, day of victory, day of mourning, day of joy, day of endings, day of beginnings.

During the liturgy at Trosly, Père Thomas and Père Gilbert, a former assistant who has become a priest for the L'Arche community in Trosly, took the huge cross that hangs behind the altar from the wall and held it so that the whole community could come and kiss the dead body of Christ.

They all came, more than four hundred people—handicapped men and women and their assistants and friends. Everybody seemed to know very well what they were doing: expressing their love and gratitude for him who gave his life for them. As they were crowding around the cross and kissing the feet and the head of Jesus, I closed my eyes and could see his sacred body stretched out and crucified upon our planet earth. I saw the immense suffering of humanity during the centuries: people killing each other; people dying from starvation and epidemics; people driven from their homes; people sleeping on the streets of large cities; people clinging to each other in desperation; people flagellated, tortured, burned, and mutilated; people alone in locked flats, in prison dungeons, in labor camps; people craving a gentle word, a friendly letter, a consoling embrace; people—children, teenagers, adults, middle-aged, and elderly—all crying out with an anguished voice: "My God, my God, why have you forsaken us?"

Imagining the naked, lacerated body of Christ stretched out over our globe, I was filled with horror. But as I opened my eyes I saw Jacques, who bears the marks of suffering in his face, kiss the body with passion and tears in his eyes. I saw Ivan carried on Michael's back. I saw Edith coming in her wheelchair. As they came—walking or limping, seeing or blind, hearing or deaf—I saw the endless procession of humanity gathering around the sacred body of Jesus, covering it with their tears and their kisses, and slowly moving away from it comforted and consoled by such great love. There were signs of relief; there were smiles breaking through tear-filled eyes; there were hands in hands and arms in arms. With my mind's eye I saw the huge crowds of isolated, agonizing individuals walking away from the cross together, bound by the love they had seen with their own eyes and touched with their own lips. The cross of horror became the cross of hope, the tortured body became the body that gives new life; the gaping wounds became the source of forgiveness, healing, and reconciliation. Père Thomas and Père Gilbert were still holding the cross. The last people came, knelt, and kissed the body, and left. It was quiet, very quiet.

Père Gilbert then gave me a large chalice with the consecrated bread and pointed to the crowd standing around the altar.

I took the chalice and moved among those whom I had seen coming to the cross; looked at their hungry eyes and said, "The body of Christ . . . the body of Christ . . . the body of Christ" countless times. The small community became all of humanity, and I knew that all I needed to say my whole life long was, "Take and eat. This is the body of Christ."

A PROMISE OF RESURRECTION
(Saturday, March 29)

Easter vigil. The Lord is risen indeed. They shouted it in French, German, English, Spanish, Portuguese, Italian, Dutch, and Arabic. There were bells, alleluias, smiles, laughter, and a deep sense that there is hope. This community of handicapped people and their assistants was loudly proclaiming that Christ's body did not remain in the tomb, but was raised to new life, and that our own bodies will join him in glory.

While all this joy was filling the chapel, I saw that Nathan stood up with Philippe in his arms and left the church. Philippe's body is severely distorted. He cannot speak, walk, dress, or feed himself and needs help every second of his waking hours. He had been lying in an assistant's lap, quietly sleeping. But when the celebration became more lively he started to howl, an anguished howl coming from deep down in his being. After a while his howls became so intense and loud that Nathan had to carry him to the car and drive him home.

When I saw Philippe in Nathan's arms I suddenly realized what we were proclaiming on this Easter vigil. Philippe's body is a body destined to a new life, a resurrected life. In his new body he will carry the signs of his suffering, just as Jesus carried the wounds of the crucifixion into his glory. And yet he will no longer be suffering, but will join the saints around the altar of the lamb.

Still, the celebration of the resurrection of the body is also the celebration of the daily care given to the bodies of these handicapped men and women. Washing and feeding, pushing wheelchairs, carrying, kissing, and caressing—these are all ways in which these broken bodies are made ready for the moment of a new life. Not only their wounds but also the care given them will remain visible in the resurrection.

It is a great and powerful mystery. Philippe's poor distorted body will one day be buried and return to dust. But he will rise again on the day of the resurrection of the dead. He will rise from the grave with a new body and will show gloriously the pain he suffered and the love he received. It will not be just *a* body. It will be *his* body, a new body, a body that can be touched but is no longer subject to torture and destruction. His passion will be over.

What a faith! What a hope! What a love! The body is not a prison to escape from, but a temple in which God already dwells, and in which God's glory will be fully manifested on the day of the resurrection.

AN INTIMATE EVENT
(Sunday, March 30)

Easter morning. A very simple, quiet Eucharist around the table in Madame Vanier's dining room. There were five of us: Madame Vanier, Sue Hall from Canada, Elizabeth Buckley from the United States, Liz Emergy from England, and myself. A small group of friends happy to be together.

After the Gospel we spoke together about the resurrection. Liz, who works with many anguished people, said, "We have to keep rolling away the large stones that prevent people from coming out of their graves." Elizabeth, who lives with four handicapped people in a L'Arche foyer, said, "After the resurrection Jesus had breakfast again with his friends and showed them the importance of the small, ordinary things of life." Sue, who is wondering if she might be called to go to Honduras and work with the L'Arche community there, said, "It is such a comfort to know that Jesus' wounds remain visible in his risen body. Our wounds are not taken away, but become sources of hope to others."

As everyone spoke, I felt very close to the Easter event. It was not a spectacular event forcing people to believe. Rather, it was an event for the friends of Jesus, for those who had known him, listened to him, and believed in him. It was a very intimate event: a word here, a gesture there, and a gradual awareness that something new was being born—small, hardly noticed, but with the potential to change the face of the earth. Mary of Magdala heard her name. John and Peter saw the empty grave. Jesus' friends felt their hearts burn in encounters that find expression in the remarkable words "He is risen." All had remained the same, while all had changed.

The five of us, sitting in a circle around the table with a little bread and a little wine, speaking softly about the way we were recognizing him in our lives, knew deep in our hearts that for us too all had changed, while all had remained the same. Our struggles are not ended. On Easter morning we can still feel the pains of the world, the pains of our family and friends, the pains of our hearts. They are still there and will be there for a long time. Still, all is different because we have met Jesus and he has spoken to us.

There was a simple, quiet joy among us and a deep sense of being loved by a love that is stronger, much stronger, than death.

KNOWING AND LOVING
(Tuesday, April 1)

Today we heard the story of the encounter between Jesus and Mary of Magdala, two people who love each other. Jesus says, "Mary." She recognizes him and says, "'Rabboni,' which means Master" (John 20:16). This simple and deeply moving story brings me in touch with my fear as well as my desire to be known. When Jesus calls Mary by her name, he is doing much more than speaking the word by which everybody knows her, for her name signifies her whole being. Jesus knows Mary of Magdala. He knows her story: her sin and her virtue, her fears and her love, her anguish and her hope. He knows every part of her heart. Nothing in her is hidden from him. He knows her even more deeply and more fully than she knows herself. Therefore, when he utters her name he brings about a profound event. Mary suddenly realizes that the one who truly knows her truly loves her.

I am always wondering if people who know every part of me, including my deepest, most hidden thoughts and feelings, really do love me. Often I am tempted to think that I am loved only as I remain partially unknown. I fear that the love I receive is conditional and then say to myself, "If they really knew me, they would not love me." But when Jesus calls Mary by name he speaks to her entire being. She realizes that the one who knows her most deeply is not moving away from her, but is coming to her offering her his unconditional love.

Her response is "Rabboni," "Master." I hear her response as her desire to have Jesus truly be her master, the master of her whole being: her thoughts and feelings, her passion and hope, even her most hidden emotions. I hear her say, "You who know me so fully, come and be my master. I do not want to keep you away from any part of myself. I want you to touch the deepest places of my heart so that I won't belong to anyone but you."

I can see what a healing moment this encounter must have been. Mary feels at once fully known and fully loved. The division between what she feels safe to show and what she does not dare to reveal no longer exists. She is fully seen and she knows that the eyes that see her are the eyes of forgiveness, mercy, love, and unconditional acceptance.

I sense that here, in this simple encounter, we can see a true religious moment. All fear is gone, and all has become love. And how better can this be expressed than by Jesus' words, "go and find my brothers, and tell them: I am ascending to my Father and your Father, to my God and your God" (John 20:17). There is no longer any difference between Jesus and those whom he loves. They are part of the intimacy that Jesus enjoys with his Father. They belong to the same family. They share the same life in God.

What a joy to be fully known and fully loved at the same time! It is the joy of belonging through Jesus to God and being there, fully safe and fully free.

18

LARGER CONNECTIONS

∎

FEELING CAUGHT
(Tuesday, April 8)

A LOT OF very dark feelings today. Hard to dispel. Most powerful are the feelings of being caught. The powers of darkness have such a grip on me that "coming into the light" seems hardly possible. People leave without saying good-bye, people write saying that I am selfish, people grow angry because I have not written them. People have farewell parties without inviting me, people tell me that the things they promised cannot be done, and so on. Suddenly I feel lost, disconnected, forgotten, left alone, misused, manipulated, confused, angry, re-sentful, spiteful, and full of self-pity. So little is needed to slip into a depression! I am amazed by the fragility of my emotional balance. The only thing I can do is look at my emotional state with a certain distance and realize how easily everything turns dark.

Happily, the Gospel today has much to tell me—it is the conversation of Jesus with Nicodemus. If there is any conversation I should take seriously, it is this one. So much of me is like Nicodemus, wanting to see the light, but coming to Jesus during the night. Jesus says to Nicodemus, "though the light has come into the world, people have preferred darkness to the light" (John 3:19). In me I can feel this strange preference for the darkness. It seems as if I resist coming into the light and enjoy staying in my self-made darkness. Jesus offers the light, the truth, the life coming from above. He makes it clear that God wants to pull me away from the darkness; he wants to offer me a solid love to dwell in, a firm ground to stand on, a faithful presence to trust in. But I have to look upward instead of inward, and embrace the gifts that are given.

Yet why all this resistance? Why this powerful attraction to the darkness? Jesus says, "Everybody who does wrong hates the light and avoids it, to prevent his actions from being shown up; but whoever does the truth comes out into the light, so that what he is doing may plainly appear as done in God" (John 3:20–21). That is an answer to my question. I do often prefer my darkness to God's light. I prefer to hang on to my sinful ways because they give me some satisfaction, some sense of self, some feeling of importance. I know quite well that moving into God's light requires me to let go of all these limited pleasures and no longer to see my life as made by me, but as given by God. Living in the light means acknowledging joyfully the truth that all that is good, beautiful, and worthy of praise belongs to God.

It is only a truly God-centered life that will pull me out of my depressions and give me hope. It is a clear path, but a very hard path as well.

TESTING THE CALL
(Wednesday, April 9)

What will going to Daybreak in Canada mean? I do not know, but the letters that I have been receiving indicate that those I most expected to be there might not be there, that the house I expected to live in might not be available, and that the way I expected to live there might not be possible. It is hard for me not to become upset by all this dashing of expectations, but I have to trust that Jesus will be with me more and more as I let go of my riches and join him on the road to poverty. My call is being tested.

The hardest aspect of poverty lies in my not being able to control my own life, but in this Jesus reveals himself to me as my Lord. When I look up at the cross, just as the sick looked up to the serpent that Moses lifted up in the desert (John 3:14), I can expect to be healed and to discover a joy and peace in my heart far beyond the changing moods of everyday living. It is the joy and peace of eternal life that already now can be tasted. I see every day more clearly how much I have to let go of in order to be poor enough to "taste and see" the goodness of the Lord.

SEXUALITY: PERSONAL AND COMMUNAL
(Thursday, April 10)

This afternoon I spent time talking with Charles Busch, a friend from Harvard who is visiting me, about chastity. It was an important discussion for me because, as we spoke, we came to see that chastity is a communal virtue.

Often we think about sexuality as a private affair. Sexual fantasies, sexual thoughts, sexual actions are mostly seen as belonging to the private life of a person. But the distinction between the private and the public sphere of life is a false distinction and has created many of the problems we are struggling with in our day. In the Christian life the distinction between a private life (just for me!) and a public life (for the others) does not exist. For the Christian, even the most hidden fantasies, thoughts, feelings, emotions, and actions are a service or a disservice to the community. I can never say, "What I think, feel or do in my private time is nobody else's business." It is everyone's business! The mental and spiritual health of a community depends largely on the way its members live their most personal lives as a service to their fellow human beings.

The complications of living a chaste life are obvious. If I keep my sexual life a hidden life (just for myself), it will gradually be split off from the rest of my life and become a dangerous force. I wonder more and more how much of the sexual compulsions and obsessions that we experience are the result of this privatization of our sexuality. What remains hidden, kept in the dark and uncommunicable, can easily become a destructive force always ready to explode in unexpected moments.

The first step toward chastity rests in knowing that my sexuality is personal *and* communal. I have to dare to realize that I can harm my neighbors not just by what I do or say, but also by what I think. Confession means sharing my inner mental struggles with a trustworthy human being who can receive that confession in the name of the community. The confession can take place in the context of the sacrament of penance, but it does not have to. What is important is that I start becoming accountable to the community for my inner life. This accountability will gradually take away the obsessive and compulsive quality of sexual thoughts and fantasies. The more I give up my private life and convert it into a personal life for which I am responsible to the community, the easier it will become to live a chaste life—because the community formed and kept together by Jesus will transform my selfish desires into a desire to serve the people of God with every part of my being. Once I have confessed my inner life, the community can let the love of Jesus unmask my false desires, expel the demons, and lead me into the light so that, as a child of light, I can witness to the risen Lord. Thus I can live a truly chaste life.

SMALL PEOPLE AND SMALL THINGS
(Friday, April 11)

Being at L'Arche helps one to understand the Gospels in a new way. Today we read the story of the multiplication of bread. "Looking up, Jesus saw the crowds approaching and said to Philip, 'Where can we buy some bread for these people to eat?' . . . Andrew said, 'Here is a boy with five barley loaves and two fish; but what is that among so many?'" (John 6:5–9). For Jesus, the small gifts of an insignificant boy were enough to feed everyone and even have twelve large baskets with scraps left over.

This again is a story about the value of the small people and the small things. The world likes things to be large, big, impressive, and elaborate. God chooses the small things which are overlooked in the big world. Andrew's remark, "five barley loaves and two fish; but what is that among so many?" captures well the mentality of a calculating mind. It sounds as if he says to Jesus, "Can't you count? Five loaves and two fish are simply not enough." But for Jesus they were enough. Jesus took them and gave thanks. That means that he received the small gifts from the small people and acknowledged them as gifts from his heavenly Father. What comes from God must be enough for all the people. Therefore, Jesus distributed the loaves and the fish "as much as they wanted." In giving away the small gifts from the small people, God's generosity is revealed. There is enough, plenty even, for everyone—there are even many leftovers. Here a great mystery becomes visible. What little we give away multiplies. This is the way of God. This is also the way we are called to live our lives. The little love we have, the little knowledge we have, the little advice we have, the little possessions we have, are given to us as gifts of God to be given away. The more we give them away, the more we discover how much there is to give away. The small gifts of God all multiply in the giving.

Something of that mystery is becoming clear to me at L'Arche. How little is L'Arche! The few hundred handicapped people who are cared for in the L'Arche foyers all over the world seem a tiny, insignificant group, considering the countless handicapped people who remain without the necessary care. Statistically, L'Arche makes little sense. And still, something of God is taking place through L'Arche. The little that L'Arche does affects people from the most different countries, religions, races, and social backgrounds. Many are fed by the little food L'Arche is giving away; not just mentally handicapped people, but also the rich, the powerful, the leaders of the church and the society, students, scholars, doctors, lawyers, magistrates, businessmen and women, and people who do not even know what a mental handicap is. They all receive something from L'Arche and are strengthened by it. Thus the miracle of the multiplication of bread continues. It is just a question of having an eye for it.

THE POOREST OF THE POOR
(Saturday, April 12)

Regina, an assistant at L'Arche community in Honduras who came to visit Trosly, had many interesting things to say about life in Honduras. She stressed the low self-esteem of the Honduran people. A small country with a withdrawn, extremely poor, and oppressed Indian population consisting mostly of Mestizos, Honduras has been completely dependent—first on Spain and later on the United States. It now feels threatened by both Nicaragua and El Salvador and greatly fears any signs of revolution. It feels "safe" under the protection of the United States, which has built large military bases there, but it can do nothing without the permission of its powerful protector. Honduras is very, very poor. In contrast to the poor of Haiti, who are liberated blacks from imperial France and often show pride and joy, the poor of Honduras have a much more self-rejecting attitude.

It is not easy for L'Arche to be there. It is hard to find Honduran assistants who can make long-term commitments. They themselves are often part of large, poor families, and most of their energy is used to survive their poverty or, if possible, to escape it. The United States is a land of promise to which they all hope to go and become rich.

Just listening to Regina made me realize how great the poverty of Honduras is. With so little national consciousness and so little pride, living there with handicapped people must be extremely difficult. It is, indeed, living with the poorest of the poor. Still . . . the L'Arche assistants in Honduras are full of peace and joy. They like to be there and hope to remain there. Cathy Judge from Daybreak has visited the community and is full of hope to go and live there. Pilar's letters from Honduras are filled with excitement. Barbara's heart is in Honduras, even though she must stay here in Trosly. Everyone who speaks of the community speaks of it as a most blessed place. Regina herself radiates joy, and it seems that all those who have chosen to live there have found a true treasure. "Happy are the poor of spirit, for the kingdom of heaven is theirs."

I very much hope to visit the Honduras community.

THE INTERRELIGIOUS STRUGGLE
(Monday, April 28)

Today I spoke for two hours with Dorothy, an Indian woman who is leader of L'Arche community in Madras, India. She is spending a few months in Trosly to stay in touch with the European communities, to take some rest after many full years of work, and to deepen her own spiritual commitment.

Her description of her life and work in Madras filled me with awe. Moslems, Hindus, and Catholics live in the same house. It is a real struggle to find a common life of worship. In the beginning, when all the assistants were Catholics from Europe, there developed a clearly Catholic liturgical life. But now that Indian assistants from different religious backgrounds have joined, things are much less simple. The Hindu assistants do not have a clear worship ritual, the Moslems do not accept any images, whether Christian or Hindu, and the Catholics do not feel at ease with Hindu or Moslem forms of worship. Moreover, not everyone, whether Catholic, Hindu, or Moslem, is interested in the spiritual life. Some see their work as a paying job that gives them a certain social status and prestige. They do not all share the vision that gave birth to L'Arche.

The development of some common forms of prayer seems impossible. Once one of the handicapped people went to his family home chanting "Oooooomm," the Hindu meditation chant he had learned at L'Arche. His father, a Moslem, was so disturbed that he immediately took his child out of the community.

And yet something very beautiful is happening in India with L'Arche. The handicapped people are bringing people together who otherwise would never meet. They are truly a uniting force. Often we focus on the problems and difficulties that are so obvious and visible. But underneath it all, God, the God of all people, is doing something very beautiful through the little ones.

Dorothy, one of the first Indian assistants, who has been at L'Arche in Madras for more than fourteen years, is herself a true sign of hope. Her vibrant personality, her deep faith in God, and her commitment to L'Arche in India gives me a glimpse of the mystery of God's unifying work through the poor.

19

THE GIFT OF FRIENDSHIP

■

PRUNING
(Wednesday, April 30)

JESUS SAID, "I am the true vine, and my Father is the vinedresser. Every branch in me that bears no fruit he cuts away, and every branch that does bear fruit he prunes, to make it bear even more" (John 15:1–2).

These words in today's Gospel open a new perspective on suffering for me. Pruning helps trees to bear more fruit. Even when I bear fruit, even when I do things for God's kingdom, even when people express gratitude for coming to know Jesus through me, I need a lot more pruning. Many unnecessary branches and twigs prevent the vine from bearing all the fruit it can. They have to be clipped off. This is a painful process, all the more so because I do not always know that they are unnecessary. They often seem beautiful, charming, and very alive. But they need to be cut away so that more fruit can grow.

It helps me to think about painful rejections, moments of loneliness, feelings of inner darkness and despair, and lack of support and human affection as God's pruning. I am aware that I might have settled too soon for the few fruits that I can recognize in my life. I might say, "Well, I am doing some good here and there, and I should be grateful for and content with the little good I do." But that might be false modesty and even a form of spiritual laziness. God calls me to more. God wants to prune me. A pruned vine does not look beautiful, but during harvest time it produces much fruit. The great challenge is to continue to recognize God's pruning hand in my life. Then I can avoid resentment and depression and become even more grateful that I am called upon to bear even more fruit than I thought I could. Suffering then becomes a way of purification and allows me to rejoice in its fruits with deep gratitude and without pride.

BROUGHT TOGETHER
(Reims; Saturday, May 3)

This afternoon Nathan and I went to Reims for a long weekend.

The plan to spend a few quiet days together away from it all came up when Nathan and I realized that our time in Trosly would soon be over. On May 12

I am leaving on a six-week trip to the United States, Canada, and England, and after that we both have only a few weeks left before we conclude our time in France.

Friendship does not grow strong and deep when you do not give it the time and attention it deserves. My friendship with Nathan has been one of the most sustaining and nurturing aspects of my stay at Trosly.

The great joy of our friendship is that we both deeply feel that it is Jesus who has brought us together so that we would be able to help each other to grow closer to him. Therefore, we want to spend time together in prayer and silence acknowledging that the love we feel for each other is a love that is not of our own making.

So here we are in Reims in the convent of the Sisters of St. Claire. It is a space filled with silence, prayer, and contemplation. Through the window of my room I see in the distance the majestic Cathedral of Notre Dame rising up in the center of the city. Tomorrow we will both see it and pray there.

Thank you, Lord, for the grace of your love, for the grace of friendship, and for the grace of beauty. Amen.

THE CATHEDRAL AND THE PRAYER ROOM
(Sunday, May 4)

In the convent where we are staying there is a small prayer room. It is decorated with a simple stained glass window representing the burning bush, a wooden pillar in which a small tabernacle is carved, some prayer stools and benches, and some small lamps attached to the bamboo-covered walls.

Nathan and I prayed our psalms there and spent some time in silence. It felt very peaceful and restful. Hardly any sounds could be heard.

In the afternoon we went to downtown Reims to visit the Cathedral of Notre Dame. Coming from the small prayer chapel into the majestic nave of the cathedral felt like touching the two extremes of the presence of God in our world. God's hiddenness and God's splendor, God's smallness and God's majesty, God's silence and God's creative word, God's humility and God's triumphant glory.

Here in this sacred space, built in the thirteenth century, the Saint-King Louis was consecrated (1226), Jeanne d'Arc attended the coronation of Charles VII (1429), Charles X was crowned (1825), and Charles de Gaulle and Konrad Adenauer celebrated the reconciliation between the French and the Germans (1962). So many emotions and feelings, so many tragic and joyous events, so many ugly and beautiful memories, so much pride and so much faith, so much desire for power and so much simple faith.

During World War I, much of the cathedral was burned and destroyed. But in 1937, after twenty years of restoration, it was reopened and reconsecrated by Cardinal Suhard, and today visitors come and gaze at its splendor. After some time trying to absorb some of the cathedral's majesty, Nathan and I sat at a little terrace on the cathedral square and just looked at the three saint-filled entrance portals, at the rosette, at the statues of kings and bishops, and at the two massive towers. Cars and buses came and went, people walked in and out of the entrance doors, some took pictures, others just looked and talked, few prayed. I had a slight headache and wanted to go back to the little prayer room of the convent with the one window of the burning bush, and be there with Jesus and pray. And so we did.

FROM OPAQUENESS TO TRANSPARENCY
(Monday, May 5)

As Nathan and I talked together, sharing our struggles and our hopes, it became increasingly clear to me that I know quite well the difference between darkness and light but often do not have the courage to name them by their true names. A strong temptation exists to deal with the darkness as if it were light, and with the light as if it were darkness. The more we talked about our lives, the more I became aware of the inner ambiguities that lead me away from the light and make me hide in dark places.

Knowing Jesus, reading his words, and praying create an increasing clarity about evil and good, sin and grace, Satan and God. This clarity calls me to choose the way to the light fearlessly and straightforwardly. The more I come to know Jesus, the more I also realize how many such choices have to be made and how often. They involve so much more than my public acts. They touch the deepest recesses of the heart, where my most private thoughts and fantasies are hidden.

Reflecting on my life, I saw how opaque it has been. I often did one thing while saying another, said one thing while thinking another, thought one thing while feeling another. I found many examples in which I had even lied to myself. Not seldom have I told myself that I had gone somewhere to help someone but did not allow the truth to enter my mind that I had been driven by much less elevated motivations. I have not acknowledged the subtle desire for power and honor and for emotional and physical satisfaction and have kept playing little games with myself.

How to go from this opaqueness to transparency? A transparent life is a life without moral ambiguities in which heart, mind, and gut are united in choosing for the light. I am discovering the importance of naming the darkness in me. By no longer calling the darkness anything else but darkness, the temptation to keep using it for my own selfish purposes gradually becomes less. As long as I continue to tell lies in the service of the truth, to play death games in the service of life, and to satisfy my impulses in the service of love, I remain hopelessly opaque and become like a preacher fishing for compliments for a sermon on humility.

A hard task is given to me—to call the darkness darkness, evil evil, and the demon demon. By remaining vague I can avoid commitment and drift along in the mainstream of our society. But Jesus does not allow me to stay there. He requires a clear choice for truth, light, and life. When I recognize my countless inner compromises, I may feel guilty and ashamed at first. But when this leads to repentance and a contrite heart, I will soon discover the immense love of God, who came to lead me out of the darkness into the light and who wants to make me into a transparent witness of his love.

I feel grateful for these insights, which emerged from our discussions. Thinking alone is so different from thinking together. As we return to Trosly tomorrow, there will be much good to remember.

SIX WAYS OF PEACEMAKING
(Trosly; Thursday, May 8)

Today is Ascension Day, a holiday in France and open house at L'Arche in Trosly. Hundreds of friends came to pray and play, to buy L'Arche products, to listen to the local band, and to hear speeches by the director of the community, Alain St. Macary, and Jean Vanier.

The theme of the day was peacemaking. While dozens of little children were running around and making joyful noises, and while many of the handicapped and their assistants were walking around in clown costumes, Jean Vanier offered six ways of being a peacemaker. The loudspeakers were loud enough to let him be heard by those who wanted to hear him. A group of fourteen girls who had heard Jean speak in Lourdes last week had come from Paris for the occasion and welcomed his speech with cheers.

Here are the six points Jean Vanier offered for peacemakers: (1) Respect every individual human being; (2) create space for people to grow and become mature; (3) always stay in dialogue; (4) keep adapting mutual expectations; (5) enjoy the differences among people; (6) always direct your attentions to those who suffer most.

Jean offered these points to help us deal with the many conflicts that keep arising among us. They are the way to peace—whether it be in the family, in the community, or in the world.

After Jean's talk, the band played a few more tunes and people gathered here and there in small groups, exchanging greetings, dancing, singing, or just talking. Then we all walked to the chapel to attend Mass. Against all expectations, the sun kept shining and the heavy clouds drifting by threw only a few drops of rain on us while Jean gave his talk. It was a good Ascension Day!

A SPIRITUAL STRATEGY
(Saturday, May 10)

More than ever I am aware of the great temptations facing me as I prepare for my journey. On the one hand, I am excited about returning to the United States and Canada, seeing friends, giving talks, counseling people in pain, and being involved again with the "great issues" of the day. On the other hand, I realize how easy it will be to lose touch with Jesus, to become submerged in the countless stimuli coming upon me, and to lose my spiritual balance.

It has helped me to express my fears openly and directly and to ask for spiritual support. Being in the world without being of it involves very hard work. It requires a clear vision of what I want to do and how to do it. It requires a discipline of the eyes, the mind, and the heart. It requires a deep desire, as well as a strong commitment to live without interruptions in the name of Jesus.

I made two concrete promises: to stay close to Jesus by daily prayer and to stay close to my friends by letter and phone. In this way I will be able to remain home even when I travel and to remain in community even when I am alone. Thus I will be able to think, speak, and act not in my own name, but in the name of Jesus and those who sent me.

THE GIFT OF UNITY
(Sunday, May 11)

Jesus prays for unity among his disciples and among those who through the teaching of his disciples will come to believe in him. He says: "May they all be one, just as, Father, you are in me and I in you . . . " (John 17:21).

These words of Jesus reveal the mystery that unity among people is not first of all the result of human effort, but rather a divine gift. Unity among people is a reflection of the unity of God. The desire for unity is deep and strong among people. It is a desire between friends, between married people, between communities, and between countries. Wherever there is a true experience of unity, there is a sense of giftedness. While unity satisfies our deepest need, it cannot be explained by what we say or do. There exists no formula for unity.

When Jesus prays for unity, he asks his Father that those who believe in him, that is in his full communion with the Father, will become part of that unity. I continue to see in myself and others how often we try to make unity among ourselves by focusing all our attention on each other and trying to find the place where we can feel united. But often we become disillusioned, realizing that no human being is capable of offering us what we most want. Such disillusionment can easily make us become bitter, cynical, demanding, even violent.

Jesus calls us to seek our unity in and through him. When we direct our inner attention not first of all to each other, but to God to whom we belong, then we will discover that in God we also belong to each other. The deepest friendship is a friendship mediated by God; the strongest marriage bonds are bonds mediated by God.

This truth requires the discipline to keep returning to the source of all unity. If, in the midst of conflict, division, and discord, we would always try to enter together in the presence of God to find our unity there, much human suffering could be relieved.

20

ONE AMONG MANY

•

(Cambridge, Mass.; Monday, May 12)

TRAVELING FROM Paris to Boston made me sharply aware of the contrast between the great advancements in technology and the primitive quality of human relationships. While the most sophisticated machinery took me from Paris to London in one hour and from London to Boston in six hours, the entire trip was clouded by security concerns. More than an hour before the departure of the flight I had to say good-bye to Nathan and Brad, who were with me at Charles de Gaulle Airport in Paris. They were not allowed to be with me while I was checking in my luggage. In London I had to go through countless security checks and a body search and had to identify the luggage that I had asked to be sent directly to Boston. The delays were connected not with technical concerns, but with security problems.

It is obviously a good thing that so many precautions are being taken to prevent terrorist attacks, but the fact that every step of the way you are made aware that someone might try to kill you gives you a sense that the world is a precarious place to live in. The more advanced the method of transportation, the less safe it seems to be transported! Quite a few of my friends have canceled their vacation plans because of fear of being hijacked, bombed, or attacked on airplanes or in airports.

Technology is so far ahead of human relations! There is such a need for new ways for people to be together, to solve conflicts, to work for peace. On the level of human relations, we are still in the Stone Age, thinking that power games and fear tactics will settle our problems. Suicide attacks and military reprisals are such primitive ways to respond to threatening situations. With the technology now at hand, these primitive responses may cause the end of all human life.

More than ever it is necessary for people, who can fly to each other from faraway distances within a few hours, to speak to each other about living together in peace. Now it seems that the smaller the physical distance, the larger the moral and spiritual distance. Why do we human beings learn so much, so soon, about technology, and so little, so late, about loving one another?

Peter and Jonas welcomed me at Logan International Airport. We were very grateful to be safely together again. Given the violent state of our world, we shouldn't take such reunions for granted.

THE BATTLE FOR SPIRITUAL SURVIVAL
(Tuesday, May 13)

A day filled with joyful reunions. Peter and Kate, Jonas, Marta and Michael, Jutta, David, Jim, and Charles . . . they all came and we talked and prayed together again.

What most strikes me, being back in the United States, is the full force of the restlessness, the loneliness, and the tension that holds so many people. The conversations I had today were about spiritual survival. So many of my friends feel overwhelmed by the many demands made on them; few feel the inner peace and joy they so much desire.

To celebrate life together, to be together in community, to simply enjoy the beauty of creation, the love of people and the goodness of God—those seem faraway ideals. There seems to be a mountain of obstacles preventing people from being where their hearts want to be. It is so painful to watch and experience. The astonishing thing is that the battle for survival has become so "normal" that few people really believe that it can be different. I now understand better why my friends who came to Trosly were so deeply touched. A world they didn't know existed had opened up for them.

The people I saw today are all such good people. They are generous, loving, caring, and filled with a desire for a community of faith; but they all suffer immensely, without always knowing it. Having been away from here for ten months, I can see what I couldn't see when I was in it myself. After having experienced so much spiritual freedom at L'Arche, I am better able to see how much my friends miss. I want so much to bring them to new places, show them new perspectives, and point out to them new ways. But in this hectic, pressured, competitive, exhausting context, who can really hear me? I even wonder how long I myself can stay in touch with the voice of the spirit when the demons of this world make so much noise.

Oh, how important is discipline, community, prayer, silence, caring presence, simple listening, adoration, and deep, lasting, faithful friendship. We all want it so much, and still the powers suggesting that all of that is fantasy are enormous. But we have to replace the battle for power with the battle to create space for the spirit.

FRIENDS OF JESUS
(Wednesday, May 14)

The heart of this day was a eucharistic celebration in which about twenty of my Cambridge friends participated. Jesus' words "I shall no longer call you servants, because a servant does not know his master's business; I call you friends, because I have made known to you everything I have learned from my Father" (John 15:15) expressed powerfully the meaning of my reunion with them. We are friends of Jesus not in a sentimental fashion, but as participants in the divine life. If we dare to claim boldly that friendship, then we can also trust in the lasting bond among each other. This mutual friendship is the splendid fruit of our kinship with Jesus. It is much more than an idea. Rather, this friendship is a tangible reality.

Many friends had asked my associate, Peter, if they could come for a short visit; Peter suggested that they all come for a eucharistic celebration, and then lunch. I am convinced that everyone received more than I would have ever been able to give in individual encounters. What I was able to give was the friendship of Jesus expressed in the gifts of bread and wine. At the same time, people from the most different age groups, educational backgrounds, lifestyles, and characters could be together in harmony and peace and discover that their differences actually reveal their deep unity in Christ.

I have been increasingly struck by the fact that the main source of suffering of the people in a city such as Cambridge seems to lie in a sense of disconnectedness, separation, and alienation. Why should I talk with each of them individually about their pain if together they can become a healing community around the table of Christ? It was a truly joyful time in which prayer, songs, and sharing stories revealed the faithful presence of Jesus.

THE POVERTY OF THE RICH
(New York: Thursday, May 15)

This morning Peter and I flew to New York City to visit Murray McDonnell. I had never met Murray, but during my time in France, Murray and Peter had come to know each other and had developed a good friendship.

Murray is a New York banker who personally knows countless people I have only heard about on TV or read about in the newspapers. He has read many of my books and feels that his world needs the word of God as much as my world does. It was a very humbling experience to hear a man who knows "the best and the brightest" say, "Give us a word from God, speak to us about Jesus . . . do not stay away from the rich, who are so poor."

Jesus loves the poor—but poverty takes many forms. How easily I forget that fact, leaving the powerful, the famous, and the successful without the spiritual food they crave. But to offer that food, I have to be very poor myself—not curious, not ambitious, not pretentious, not proud. It is so easy to be swept off one's own feet by the glitter of the world, seduced by its apparent splendor. And yet the only place I can really be is the place of poverty, the place where there is loneliness, anger, confusion, depression, and pain. I have to go there in the name of Jesus, staying close to his name and offering his love.

O Lord, help me not to be distracted by power and wealth; help me not to be impressed by knowing the stars and heroes of this world. Open my eyes to the suffering heart of your people, whoever they are, and give me the word that can bring healing and consolation. Amen.

POLITICIANS AND MINISTRY
(Washington, D.C.; Friday, May 16)

Yesterday Peter returned to Boston and I flew on to Washington to visit my friends there. It was a very joyful day, mostly because I was able to stay very close to Jesus during all my conversations and speak simply and directly about him. This was not always easy because of the distraction of so many people and things. Having lunch with Senator Mark Hatfield in the stately quarters of the Senate Appropriations Committee, hearing about the struggle against the fabrication of nerve gas and the attempts to get some solid information about human rights violations in Guatemala, meeting Henry Kissinger in the corridor, and sensing the general atmosphere of busyness and urgency—all of this gave me ample occasion to leave the house of the Lord and roam around curiously searching for power, influence, and success. Yet all day Jesus remained in the center, and the hours were filled with a sense of God's presence.

What most impressed me was the eagerness of all the people I met today to hear about God's presence in this world. It seemed as if I couldn't say enough about it. During my two-hour luncheon with Senator Hatfield and his aides, not a minute was spent talking about politics. All our attention went to questions about the message of the New Testament, living a fruitful life, developing meaningful relationships, prayer, obedience, and faithfulness. As we were talking, I realized that, in fact, we were coming closer to the real problems of the world than a debate on current political issues would have brought us.

At one point in our conversation I asked Senator Hatfield, "How can I be of any help to the U.S. Senate?" He said, "Come and speak to us about forgiveness, reconciliation, and ways to live in peace with each other. So much bitterness and resentment, jealousy and anger exist in the lives of politicians, at work as well as at home, that any healing word will be received with open hands."

Later, Doug Coe asked me to give a retreat to twenty members of the young presidents' organization. I asked him, "Who are the young presidents?" He said, "They are people, mostly men, who have made more than a million dollars before they were thirty years old, who head a company with at least fifty employees, and who have significant influence." I asked, "Why do they want a retreat?" He answered, "They have a great desire to come to know Jesus. They will come to any place in the world, on any day you want, to hear you speak about Jesus."

How much more do I have to know? Why should I want anything but Jesus, where everyone I meet asks me to proclaim him? My only task is to stay in God's house and stop roaming around in the world.

In the midst of all of this, I kept in close touch with Nathan and Jonas. Their prayers and support gave me a sense of safety and protection. I am sent into this world; my friends have to help me not to become part of it.

BEING SILENT WITH FRIENDS
(Cambridge, Mass.; Monday, May 19)

Back in Cambridge, the thought keeps coming to me that it is as important to be silent with friends as to speak with them. Seeing so many people and talking with them about all that has happened and is happening to them often leaves me with a sense of not really being together. The exchange of countless details about people's lives can often create more distance than closeness. Words are important in order to come close, but too many words create distance.

I feel an increasing desire to be silent with friends. Not every event has to be told, not every idea has to be exchanged. Once an atmosphere of mutual trust is present, we can be silent together and let the Lord be the one who speaks, gently and softly. Listening together to Jesus is a very powerful way to grow closer to each other and reach a level of intimacy that no interpersonal exchange of words can bring about. A silence lived together in the presence of Jesus will also continue to bear many fruits in the future. It seems as if a caring silence can enter deeper into our memory than many caring words. Maybe not always, but certainly often. But to create this silence requires much spiritual work. It is not the most obvious style for a reunion! And still, it may be the most blessed.

I will try to put this conviction into practice in the days to come.

WELCOMING THE CHILD
(Tuesday, May 20)

"Anyone who welcomes a little child such as this in my name, welcomes me; and anyone who welcomes me, welcomes not me but the one who sent me" (Mark 9:37).

What does welcoming a little child mean? It means giving loving attention to those who are often overlooked. I imagine myself standing in line to meet a very important person and noticing a little child passing by. Would I leave the line and pay all my attention to this child? I imagine myself going to a grand party where I will meet very interesting and powerful people. Could I forget about the party to sit on the street for a few hours with a man who stretches out his hands and asks me for some money? I imagine myself being invited to receive an award. Could I let the honor go to spend the time with a depressed, elderly woman who is forgotten by her friends and feels isolated in her apartment?

Yesterday I was stopped on the street by a beggar. He asked me for some change to buy a bite to eat. He didn't expect any response, but when I gave him ten dollars he jumped up and said, "Thank you, thank you very, very much." He was extremely surprised by this large gift, but I suddenly felt a deep sadness. I was on my way to a meeting I did not want to miss. My gift was an excuse for walking on. I had not welcomed the beggar—I had just tried to feel generous. My "generosity" had revealed my deep resistance toward welcoming the "little child."

To welcome the "little child" I have to become little myself. But I continue to wonder how great I am. Even my generosity can help me to feel great. But Jesus said, "If anyone wants to be first, he must make himself last of all and servant of all" (Mark 9:35). Am I willing to become the servant of this beggar? By giving him ten dollars I became his master, who could make him say, "Thank you, thank you very much."

It is becoming clear to me that I still have not understood that Jesus revealed his love to us by becoming our servant, and calls us to follow him in this way.

21

A HARD BUT
BLESSED VOCATION

■

EARLY THIS MORNING I flew to Toronto, where Sue Mosteller welcomed me and drove me to Daybreak in Richmond Hill.

I have been looking forward to my days at Daybreak because it is going to be my home for at least three years. I now feel that my year at Trosly is coming to an end and that I am getting ready to accept a new responsibility. During the past few months so many different things have been happening in my life that I have hardly had the time or energy to think about my future life and work at Daybreak; but now that seems the only important thing.

At 2:30 P.M. the Daybreak council invited me to tell them about my own spiritual journey and reasons for accepting their call to come to Canada and be their pastor. After having tried to express to them as best I could my own sense of being called away from Harvard and being called to a life with handicapped people and their assistants, they told me about the way they had been thinking about my future presence at Daybreak.

Five aspects arose: (1) I have a lot to learn. I have never really lived in community or close to handicapped people. It will not be easy to enter into this small world after having moved around so much in the big world. Therefore, I will need a good period to become a true part of the life here. (2) Together we need to develop a rich spiritual life that allows us to celebrate the liturgical year, broaden our knowledge of the scriptures, and deepen our prayer life. (3) One of my main tasks will be to help start "The Dayspring," a small spiritual center that can be a source of renewal for English-speaking L'Arche members and their friends. (4) I should continue writing. This will not be easy, since there are so many things that will compete for my attention. But the community will not only honor, but also protect and support my vocation to write. (5) Then there will be the letters, the phone calls, the speaking engagements, and so on. It is a blessing to know that Connie Ellis is available to assist me in this work.

As we talked, I had the distinct feeling that it will not be easy to be here, but also that I will not be alone in my struggle. I thought, "It is going to be hard but blessed. I am called to his place of weak and broken people. It is a call coming from God and God's people. Do not worry, just move into it and trust that you will find what your heart most desires." Daybreak is not a place of power. It is not a smooth operation in which efficiency and control are priorities. On the contrary, it is a fellowship of the weak, in which nothing is fully together and everything has a somewhat tentative quality. I can see how frustrating this can be for me, considering my desire to get things done, and done quickly. But I trust that the slow and inefficient way of life at Daybreak will teach me something new about God's love that has remained unknown to me so far.

THE WAY TO A SECOND CHILDHOOD
(Saturday, May 24)

This morning I wondered what the Gospel reading would be. Often I have the feeling that the Gospel of the day will tell me all I have to know.

I read, "Let the little children come to me; do not stop them; for it is to such as these that the kingdom of God belongs. In truth I tell you, anyone who does not welcome the kingdom of God like a little child will never enter it" (Mark 10:14–15).

What is so special about a little child? The little child has nothing to prove, nothing to show, nothing to be proud of. All the child needs to do is to receive the love that is offered. Jesus wants us to receive the love he offers. He wants nothing more than that we allow him to love us and enjoy that love. This is so hard since we always feel that we have to deserve the love offered to us. But Jesus wants to offer that love to us not because we have earned it, but because he has decided to love us independently of any effort on our side. Our own love for each other should flow from that "first love" that is given to us undeserved.

As I was reflecting on Jesus' words, I started to see more clearly how Daybreak could help me not only to receive the little children, but also to become like one of them. The handicapped may be able to show me the way to a second childhood. Indeed, they can reveal to me God's first love. Handicapped people have little, if anything, to show to the world. They have no degrees, no reputation, no influence, no connections with influential people; they do not create much, produce much, or earn much. They have to trust that they can receive and give pure love. I have already received so many hugs and kisses here from people who have never heard of me and are not the least impressed by me that I have to start believing that the love they offer is freely given, to be freely received.

My dream is that Daybreak can increasingly become a place where the first love of God is revealed to people anxious to prove they deserve love. A house of prayer and welcome, in which handicapped people could receive guests searching for God, might be a concrete way to exercise the ministry of that first love.

During the meeting of the Daybreak board today, I expressed some of these thoughts. The members—lawyers, doctors, and businessmen—were very open and very receptive. They themselves had come to know within their busy lives that they, too, need to hear that still small voice saying, "I love you whether you are important or not, whether you are a failure or not, whether you have money or not, whether you are handsome or not." They had joined the board of this unpretentious community because they wanted to stay in touch with that voice.

A NEW FAMILY
(Sunday, May 25)

A new family! I have been invited to make the "New House" my home. It is the home of Raymond, John, Bill, Trevor, Adam, Rose, and their three assistants, D.J., Heather, and Regina. I am staying with them for this short visit, but it appears as if I will live here when I return in August and make this my permanent home. It is a remarkable family. Rose and Adam are deeply handicapped and need constant attention and care. They cannot speak or walk, feed or dress themselves; they live in a world seemingly impenetrable. They need to be dressed, washed, fed, and carried. Only when they sleep can they be alone.

Raymond, John, Bill, and Trevor are quite independent compared with Rose and Adam. They speak a lot, go to workshops during the day, and can help with small tasks in the house.

It was a special joy to see Raymond again. He was completely recovered from his October accident and looked better than before. He didn't remember me at all, but his parents had told him so much about me that he received me with special kindness. We soon became friends and spent quite a bit of time together.

D.J., the house leader, is a very caring twenty-four-year-old Canadian who gives all his time and energy to his Daybreak family. Heather, from Omaha, Nebraska, is finishing her year in the house and will return to her family within a few months. Regina came from Brazil and will soon be joined by her sister.

Living in community is not going to be easy for me. But after two days with this family, I already feel a desire to come back and get to know them all more intimately. That is all that counts for the moment.

22

CONTRASTS AND CHOICES

■

(Berkeley, Calif.; Tuesday, May 27)

AFTER A MEETING with the assistants of Daybreak, we celebrated a quiet and prayerful Eucharist together. Soon after the conclusion of the Eucharist, Sue Mosteller drove me to the Toronto airport, where I caught a plane to San Francisco to visit my friend Don McNeill.

Don is a Holy Cross priest and director of the Center for Social Concerns at the University of Notre Dame. We have been close friends since 1966, when I went to Notre Dame as a visiting professor. Last year Don was suddenly hit by brachial plexus neuropathy, a muscular disease that has seriously affected his physical movements. Doctors expect that he will need at least two years before he will regain his full strength. Don himself has some real doubts about whether he will ever again be the agile, fast-moving man he was before the disease hit him. Presently he is spending a year at one of the Holy Cross houses in Berkeley to have the rest and space needed for his recovery. I decided to spend a few days with him, to offer him some courage and confidence in this trying time in his life and to celebrate the twentieth anniversary of our friendship.

We are now sitting on the balcony of the Holy Cross house in Berkeley. It must be one of the most beautiful spots in the world. I am looking out over San Francisco Bay. In the far distance I recognize the lighthouse of Alcatraz Island, and behind it the outline of the Golden Gate Bridge. As the darkness slowly covers the bay area, the view is gradually transformed by a myriad of lights telling me of all the different people living around the water. It is very quiet on the balcony—the city is too far away to hear its sounds. The air is gentle and warm, full of scents coming from the blooming trees.

After the busy day at Daybreak and the long, tiring flight, sitting quietly with my friend on this balcony overlooking the wide waters and the city aglow with lights, I marvel at being alive and being able to be part of it all.

THE SENSES AND THE SPIRIT
(Wednesday, May 28)

Being in California is exciting as well as disturbing to me. It is very hard for me to describe the emotions this world calls forth in me. The pleasant climate, the lush gardens, the splendid trees and flowerbeds, the beautiful view over the bay, the city, the island, and the bridges call forth in me words of praise, gratitude, and joy. But the countless car lots, the intense traffic, the huge advertisements, the new buildings going up all over the place, the smog, the noises, the fastness of living—all of this makes me feel unconnected, lonely, and a little lost.

Maybe the word that summarizes it all is "sensual." All my senses are being stimulated, but with very little grounding, very little history, very little spirit. I keep wondering how my heart can be fed in this world. It seems as if everyone is moving quickly to meet some person or go to some place or some event. But nobody has much of a home. The houses look very temporary. They will probably last a few decades, maybe a century, but then something else will take their place.

The people we meet are very friendly, easygoing, casual, and entertaining; but I keep wondering how to be with them, how to speak with them, how to pray with them. Everything is very open, expressive, and new; but I find myself looking for a space that is hidden, silent, and old. This is a land to which people go in order to be free from tradition, constraints, and an oppressive history. But the price for this freedom is high: individualism, competition, rootlessness, and frequently loneliness and a sense of being lost. When anything goes, everything is allowed, everything is worth a try, then nothing is sacred, nothing venerable, nothing worth much respect. Being young, daring, original, and mobile seems to be the ideal. Old things need to be replaced by new things, and old people are to be pitied.

The body is central. The sun, the beaches, the water, and the lushness of nature open up all the senses. But it is hard to experience the body as the temple of the spirit. That requires a very special discipline. To reach that inner sanctum where God's voice can be heard and obeyed is not easy if you are always called outward. It is not surprising that California has become a place where many spiritual disciplines are being discovered, studied, and practiced. There are many meditation centers—Buddhist, Christian, and nonreligious. More and more people feel a need to discover an inner anchor to keep themselves whole in the midst of the sensual world.

So here I am, somewhat overwhelmed by it all and somewhat confused. How am I to be faithful to Jesus in a world in which having a body is celebrated in so many ways? Jesus is the God who became flesh with us so that we could live with his spirit. How do I live out this truth in this sun-covered, sensual, nontraditional place? Maybe I wouldn't even have raised this question had L'Arche not opened my eyes to a completely different way of thinking about the body. At L'Arche, too, the body is central, but what a difference!

I am glad to be with Don, who is suffering so much in his body, and to share with him Jean's vision that the community of L'Arche is formed around the wounded bodies of handicapped people. I realize that Don and I are bound together by twenty years of friendship, a friendship that seems so very long and solid when set against this transitory milieu.

DEATH IN THE CASTRO DISTRICT
(San Francisco; Saturday, May 31)

Don dropped me off in the Castro district of San Francisco to visit a friend who had recently moved there. It is hard to find words to describe this glittering gay district of San Francisco.

If ever the word "gay" seemed a euphemism, it is in today's Castro, where many young men die of AIDS every day and thousands more worry that they are carrying the virus that causes the disease. As my friend and I walked through the busy streets to find a restaurant, I thought of John. A few years ago he showed me the district and told me all about the life there. Then the word "AIDS" was hardly known. Now John is dead after a long, devastating illness, and many have shared his agony. Behind a facade of opulent wealth, a great variety of entertainment, large stores with posters, printed T-shirts, greeting cards, and all sorts of playful knickknacks lies an immense fear. And not only fear but also guilt, feelings of rejection, anger, fatalism, careless hedonism, and, in the midst of it all, trust, hope, love, and the rediscovery of God in the face of death.

As I walked with my friend on the streets of the Castro district, we saw countless men walking up and down the sidewalks just looking at each other, gazing into store windows, standing on corners in small groups, and going in and out of bars, theaters, video shops, drugstores, and restaurants. It seemed as if everyone was waiting for something that would bring them a sense of being deeply loved, fully accepted, and truly at home. But evident in the eyes of many was deep suffering, anguish, and loneliness, because what they most seek and most desire seems most elusive. Many have not been able to find a lasting home or a safe relationship, and now, with the AIDS threat, fear has become all-pervasive.

And yet AIDS has unleashed not only fear, but also an enormous generosity. Many people are showing great care for each other, great courage in helping each other, great faithfulness, and often unwavering love. I sensed an enormous need for God's love to be made known to these fearful and often generous people. More than ever the Church has to live out Christ's love for the poor, the sinners, the publicans, the rejected, the possessed, and all who desperately need to be loved. As I saw the countless gay men on the streets, I kept thinking about the great consolation that Jesus came to offer. He revealed the total and unlimited love of God for humanity. This is the love that the Church is called to make visible not by judging, condemning, or segregating, but by serving everyone in need. I often wonder if the many heated debates about the morality of homosexuality do not prevent the Christian community from reaching out fearlessly to its suffering fellow humans.

Happily, many encouraging new initiatives are being taken. On February 2, Archbishop Roger Mahony published a pastoral letter in which he took concrete steps to assist the victims of AIDS and offered important guidelines for the overall pastoral care of gay Catholic men and women. He called for the establishment of a hospice for AIDS victims and for the formation of gay Catholic groups that would help their members to live chaste lives "according to the will of the Father as manifested in the Scriptures and the official teachings of the Roman Catholic Church."

My friend and I talked much about Jesus, and as I left he said, "I am glad you came. There are too few people who mention his name in the district. There are so many negative associations with his name, and still he is the greatest source of hope."

THE BODY OF CHRIST
(Sunday, June 1)

Today is the feast of Corpus Christi, the body of Christ. As Edward Malloy, a visiting Holy Cross priest, Don, and I celebrated the Eucharist in the little Chapel of the Holy Cross house in Berkeley, the importance of this feast touched me more than ever. The illness that has severely impaired Don's movements made him, and also me, very conscious of the beauty, intricacy, and fragility of the human body. My visit yesterday to the Castro district, where physical pleasure is so visibly sought and bodily pain so dramatically suffered, reminded me powerfully that I not only *have* a body, but also *am* a body. The way one lives in the body, the way one relates to, cares for, exercises, and uses one's own and other people's bodies, is of crucial importance for one's spiritual life.

The greatest mystery of the Christian faith is that God came to us in the body, suffered with us in the body, rose in the body, and gave us his body as food. No religion takes the body as seriously as the Christian religion. The body is not seen as the enemy or as a prison of the spirit, but celebrated as the spirit's temple. Through Jesus' birth, life, death, and resurrection, the human body has become part of the life of God. By eating the body of Christ, our own fragile bodies are becoming intimately connected with the risen Christ and thus prepared to be lifted up with him into the divine life. Jesus says, "I am the living bread which has come down from heaven. Anyone who eats this bread will live forever; and the bread that I shall give is my flesh, for the life of the world" (John 6:51).

It is in union with the body of Christ that I come to know the full significance of my own body. My body is much more than a mortal instrument of pleasure and pain. It is a home where God wants to manifest the fullness of the divine glory. The truth is the most profound basis for the moral life. The abuse of the body—whether it be psychological (e.g., instilling fear), physical (e.g., torture), economic (e.g., exploitation), or sexual (e.g., hedonistic pleasure seeking)—is a distortion of true human destiny: to live in the body eternally with God. The loving care given to our bodies and the bodies of others is therefore a truly spiritual act, since it leads the body closer toward its glorious existence.

I wonder how I can bring this good news to the many people for whom their body is little more than an unlimited source of pleasure or an unceasing source of pain. The feast of the body of Christ is given to us to fully recognize the mystery of the body and to help us find ways to live reverently and joyfully in the body in expectation of the risen life with God.

EXPENSIVE SANDBOX GAMES
(Los Angeles; Monday, June 2)

Yesterday, Don and I said our good-byes and I flew to Los Angeles to spend a day with my friends Chris Glaser and Richard White before moving back eastward.

My friendship with Chris dates from the years that I taught at Yale Divinity School. For several years he worked as a lay minister at the West Hollywood Presbyterian Church, and presently he dedicates all of his time to writing. It was good to see Chris at the airport and to hear him speak with enthusiasm about the last phases of his book *Uncommon Calling: A Gay Man's Struggle to Serve the Church*, a book full of pain, full of struggle, but also full of hope. Chris is a man of great faith who has never allowed bitterness to conquer gratitude. During his many years in the ministry, Chris has shared many of his struggles with me, and his current book is a public testimony of his faithful search to integrate his sexuality with his faith.

Together with Chris's friend George Lynch, we had a very nice dinner in a quiet West Hollywood restaurant and ample opportunity to share what we had been living during the past few years.

This morning Chris drove me to the house where Richard White is staying. Richard and I have been friends since 1966, when we met in Cuernavaca, Mexico. Our common interest in Latin America brought us together and was the beginning of a friendship that—though stormy at times—has always grown deeper and stronger. This time, unexpectedly, Richard gave me a fascinating glimpse into the filmmaking industry.

I stayed in the house of Richard's friend Jack, a Los Angeles film producer. For four months he had been out of work, and his financial situation had become so critical that he was thinking about subletting parts of his house to get enough money to pay his bills. But last week everything changed. He was hired to become the producer of an NBC situation comedy called "Amen," which will be broadcast this coming fall. Suddenly Jack has a splendid office with a large staff and a salary of $2,700 a week! If the series proves to be successful, his salary will substantially increase, and if he establishes himself as a sought-after producer, he will be a millionaire within a few years. If things fail, he will be subletting his house soon because he likes to spend money as much as to earn it.

The "Amen" series revolves around the shenanegans of an outrageous deacon who manipulates his all-black church and its congregation. Although its scripts include some social and ethical issues, it is still very much the standard formula TV network sitcom.

My friend Richard White, who has been staying with Jack for the past few months, called Jack's work "sandbox games." Jack totally agreed—he was playing with a two-million-dollar project, the purpose of which was to make a lot of money by giving a couple of million viewers some good laughs.

As Jack was talking to me, full of excitement about his new job and all the money he was going to make, I was struck by the blatant superficiality of it all. Jack himself is a paradox of our culture. He reads Jean-Paul Sartre, is trying to find funding for an excellent movie script he wrote on one man's courageous stand against the Nazis, and is working on another script about apartheid in South Africa. At the same time he calls himself a "hired gun," eager to sell his talents to the Hollywood production companies. Like many cinemagraphic artists, he sees the world through the eyes of the camera and is enthralled with the visual effects his art can create almost without regard for the subject matter.

As Richard and I had dinner, Richard asked me, "Why do the people who want to stop war, prevent torture, make people aware of injustice, and care for the sick and the handicapped never have enough money, while those who play these sandbox games earn more than they know what to do with?"

It is the question that haunted the Old Testament prophets and psalmists and is still haunting us today. I could only say, "Let us not be jealous. God loves the poor and the humble of heart. That knowledge should be enough." But the fact that I was not wholly without jealousy and resentment showed that maybe God was not as real for me as the sandbox games are for Jack.

A VISION AND A TASK
(London; Wednesday, June 11)

On my way from California to Paris I am spending a few days in London. This afternoon I visited Donald Reeves, the pastor of St. James's Anglican Church in Piccadilly.

Donald Reeves is a man of many gifts: He is an activist, a contemplative, a social worker, an artist, a caring pastor, a restless mover, a visionary, and a pragmatist. In five years he converted a practically lifeless downtown Anglican parish into a vibrant center of prayer and action. When I arrived at the rectory I could sense the vibrancy of the place: Within a few minutes I had met a bishop, a Jew, an ex-convict, an artist, and an administrator. Donald introduced them all to me with words of praise and encouragement. You could sense that people were doing new things here, things they believed in. The parish is a place for meditation, counseling, art events, concerts, peacemaking, book publishing, and hospitality. It is a place that welcomes traditional Christians as well as people who feel alienated from the Church. It is an incredibly diverse place, embracing charismatics as well as activists, Christians as well as non-Christians.

Listening to Donald, I realized how much he had been influenced by new communities in the United States, especially the Sojourners' Fellowship and the Church of the Savior in Washington, D.C. I felt invigorated just being with him and walking around the place with him. I was ready to promise all sorts of things: lectures, retreats, writing, conversations, and discussions. But I controlled my impulse to help and asked for simple fellowship instead. Being connected with this church as a friend, a supporter, and a fellow traveler seems most important of all.

As I left, Donald gave me some of his writings. On the cover of his "ten-year plan" for the Church he wrote:

A vision without a task is a dream;
A task without a vision is drudgery;
A vision and a task is the hope of the world.

Nothing better can sum up the spirit of St. James's of Piccadilly than these words.

FILMMAKING FOR PEACE
(Thursday, June 12)

I spent the whole day with Bart Gavigan and Patricia Beall. They first came to see me in Cambridge in May 1985, while they were preparing a film about George Zabelka, the Air Force chaplain turned pacifist. Although we had met for only a few hours, we had experienced a deep bond among us and a sense that Jesus had brought us together to support each other in our spiritual journeys. Seldom have I felt so strongly that friendship is a gift of God, not the result of long hours of conversation, shared activities, and deep knowledge of each other's lives. It was simply there—suddenly, directly, unprepared-for. We stayed in touch by letter, and when we saw each other again last night it felt as if we had known each other for a long time and were part of a God-given union.

During the morning we spoke about our lives, not so much to get to know each other as to be witnesses to each other of the marvelous ways in which God has touched our hearts.

After celebrating the Eucharist together in the parish church and having a meal in a London restaurant, we went to the Soho district, where Bart had rented a studio to cut *The Reluctant Prophet*, the film about George Zabelka that is now in its final stage of editing. It was quite an experience for me. We walked through the crowded district full of market stalls, porno shops, and shouting people. In the middle of all this craziness, we found Bart's little cutting room. Then we sat watching the beginning of a gripping documentary about the priest who after having blessed those who dropped the atomic bomb on Hiroshima, was converted to a committed peacemaker. It struck me that we were sitting in a dark upstairs studio watching a film about peacemaking while voices of lust and violence surrounded us on all sides.

Bart is a very unusual filmmaker. When he discovered that in most filmmaking the communication of ideas and ideals is completely subservient to the making of profits, he joined a Christian community to test his priorities. Now, many years later, he is ready to make films not for money, but to follow Jesus' way. In this lustful and violent world he has to risk his money and reputation to do what he feels called to do, but he is determined to do what is just and right, and he trusts that the rest will be given to him. For Bart, filmmaking is ministry.

I never dreamed that I would meet within a few days a filmmaker so different from the one I met in Los Angeles. What Jack is doing in the splendid offices of Johnny Carson Productions and what Bart is doing in his upstairs cutting room in Soho is the same work of filmmaking. But they reveal two completely different worlds. I keep being struck by the importance of making choices.

EVALUATING A JOURNEY
(Paris; Monday, June 23)

When I arrived in Paris, Brad Wolcott was waiting for me. Together we went to the Foyer Sacerdotal, a hostel for priests in Paris where Brad had reserved a room for me.

So here I am back in Paris. The bright evening sun made the city look festive and welcoming. Brad called it the "New Jerusalem." During supper I tried to express my feelings about the journey that had started on May 12. As I spoke, I became more and more conscious of the ups and downs of my inner journey that had gone on while I traveled the world. It had become possible for me to identify clearly when I had been faithful and when not. There were days in which I felt very much connected with Jesus—thinking, speaking, and acting in communion with him. But there were also days when I felt so needy, distant, anxious, or restless that Jesus seemed far away. There were days during which I could speak loudly and clearly about the love of God and was listened to with great attention. But there were other days when I seemed to have lost even my inner spiritual life and looked with jealous eyes at those who enjoyed the good life without even the slightest thought of God.

It is important that I know the difference between these two states of mind and can identify when and how I move from one to the other. The most important criterion is prayer. As long as I pray daily, intimately and long, I stay in the right place and continue to walk on the road to faithfulness. But when I let my prayer go because of fatigue, distraction, or laziness, I know that I will soon be on the other side of the fence. The second criterion is a deep, confessing friendship. I now realize that I need regular contact with a friend who keeps me close to Jesus and continues to call me to faithfulness.

As I talked to Brad, I realized that I had come to know my limits better and to realize more clearly how to deal with them.

TRUE BELONGING

(Tuesday, June 24)

Being back in France makes me think much about countries and cultures. During the past few months I have been in Holland, Germany, Canada, the United States, and England, and in all these countries I have had intense contact with people and their ways of living, praying, and playing.

There is a great temptation to want to know which culture is the best and where I am most happy and at home. But this way of thinking leads to endless frustrations because the Dutch, the Germans, the French, the Americans, and the Canadians are all people who have unique ways of feeling, thinking, and behaving, none of which totally fits my needs, but all of which have gifts for me.

I know people who complain about the Germans while in Germany and about the Americans while in America, moving themselves and their families back and forth, always wondering what the best place is to live without ever being truly content. Some people, then, are always disappointed with someone or something. They complain about the rigidity of the German Church and the sloppiness of the American Church. Or they may complain about the critical attitude of the Dutch, the mystical attitude of the French, the pragmatic attitude of the Americans, and the formalistic attitude of the English, while never really worshiping deeply at any one place.

I am increasingly aware of how important it is to enjoy what is given and to fully live where one is. If I could just fully appreciate the need for independence of the Dutch, the spiritual visions of the French, the concreteness of the Americans, the theological concepts of the Germans, and the sense of ceremony of the English, I could come to learn much about life everywhere and truly become present to where I am, always growing deeper in the spirit of gratitude.

Do we really need to belong to one country or one culture? In our world, where distances are becoming less each day, it seems important to become less and less dependent on one place, one language, one culture, or one style of life, but to experience oneself as a member of the human family, belonging to God and free to be wherever we are called to be. I even wonder if the ability to be in so many places so quickly and so often is not an invitation to grow deeper in the spirit and let our identity be more rooted in God and less in the place in which we happen to be.

23

ENDINGS AND BEGINNINGS

·

QUESTIONS ABOUT FAITHFULNESS
(Trosly; Wednesday, June 25)

LAST NIGHT I returned to Trosly; it was a mixed experience to be back. On the one hand, it felt like coming home after six weeks of traveling. On the other hand, it made me aware that Trosly had not become a true home for me. I had remained too much on the periphery of the life here. People said "Hello" and "Welcome back," but it was clear that I had remained a stranger who lives his own life and does his own things.

Nathan was so busy in his foyer that we had to wait until this afternoon to see each other. I was so eager to reconnect with him and feel welcomed back by him that the delay was painful and frustrating. But when he could finally leave his work and come to my room, we had a blessed time together. It was like a spiritual debriefing.

The question "How was the trip?" was not a question about events and people, but a question about faithfulness to God amidst all the events and people, faithfulness in thoughts, words, and deeds. It was good for me to "confess" to Nathan my many ups and downs in the struggle to remain anchored in Jesus. As I looked at my journey in the perspective of this struggle, I found much to confess, much to be grateful for, but also much to feel repentant about. It is so important to be specific and concrete and to identify accurately the moments of faithfulness and unfaithfulness, as generalities do not help much in the spiritual life. Specifics are crucial—they tell the real story. They reveal the real sin and the real grace; they point the real way to renewal.

After this "confession" to Nathan, I felt more at home again and more connected. I will only be here for two more weeks. I hope I can live these weeks in a faithful and prayerful way.

SPIRITUAL FATIGUE
(Friday, June 27)

My long journey has harmed my prayer life. I have discovered how hard it has become for me to spend one hour in the morning simply being present to Jesus.

I experience a certain nausea or apathy that I did not have before I left. It is a sort of spiritual fatigue, a state of lukewarmness in which I find it hard to know exactly what I feel, what I think, or what I want. It is like being a piece of driftwood on still water. Nothing seems to move, and there seems to be no way to get things moving again. I am tired, but I do not sleep well. I am talking to people, but I do not feel well connected. I do many things, but not much is happening. I do not feel depressed, just empty and somewhat indifferent. Maybe it is a temporary "burnout." Well, I am not panicky about it and try to stay in touch with Jesus. What helps me most is praying with others. I very much enjoy saying my morning and evening prayers with friends, and I am very grateful when Nathan prays with me. Friends keep me close to Jesus. I just have to drink in their love and let them pray with and for me.

PETER AND PAUL
(Sunday, June 29)

Today is the feast of Sts. Peter and Paul. I have often wondered why these two great apostles are celebrated on the same day. Is not each of them worth a special day?

In his sermon, Père Thomas responded to this question. He explained how there is always a danger of playing out one against the other: Peter, the simple, uneducated fisherman who had hardly any knowledge of the theological debates of his time and who responded to Jesus in a direct, impulsive way without much distance or criticism; and Paul, the well-educated disciple of Gamaliel, a Pharisee, sharp, intelligent, deeply concerned about the truth, and willing to persecute those whom he considered in grave error. The Church is built on the foundations laid by both Peter and Paul. There are not two churches, one for the simple people who trust their emotions more than their brains and the other for the intellectuals who are willing to debate the current issues. There is only one church, in which Peter and Paul each has his own role and importance. Uncritical Christianity is as dangerous as "pure brain" Christianity. And indeed Paul had deep emotions and Peter engaged in fierce debates. Within the Church there will always be people who romanticize Peter or intellectualize Paul. It is important that both stay together, not only on their feast day, but also in our own way of living a faithful life.

TRUSTING THE FIRST LOVE
(Tuesday, July 1)

Tonight I celebrated my last Tuesday Mass for the English-speaking people in the community. Quite a few visitors came, and there was a spirit of quiet, joyful celebration.

Coming "home" to Trosly has not been easy for me. After the long trip, I felt a need to be truly welcomed back. But with so many people coming and going, the permanent members of the community often cannot pay attention to everyone's needs. What I have learned is that God's unlimited love often expresses itself through the limited love of God's people. This means concretely that we broken, sinful people need to confess and forgive day in and day out, and thus continue to reveal a love that we ourselves cannot make true. Over and over again we experience moments of disappointment and disillusionment which can lead to resentment and feelings of anger unless we keep confessing our unfulfilled needs and forgiving each other for not being God for each other. Thus, a community in which confession and forgiveness is a way of life keeps us close to Jesus, who calls us together to make his divine love known.

Today's celebration became an occasion for me to express my own struggles and help others recognize their own. As I looked around the circle, I realized that this small congregation contained representatives from at least six different countries. We knew each other only superficially, but around the word of Christ and his body and blood we became an intimate community of people able to express to each other the unlimited and unconditional love, the "first love" of God. I marveled at this mystery, and I started to feel its healing effect in my heart.

IN A PRISON WITHOUT WALLS
(Thursday, July 3)

A very intense day. Many people came by for the Sacrament of Reconciliation or just to talk about their pains and fears. As I listened to their feelings of loneliness, rejection, guilt, and shame, I became overwhelmed by the sense of isolation we human beings can feel. While our sufferings are so similar and our struggles so much a part of our shared humanity, we often live as if we are the only ones who experience the pain that paralyzes us! At one point during the day I felt a desire to bring together all those who had spoken to me this day. I wanted to ask them to share their stories with one another so that they could discover how much they had in common and in this way become a source of consolation and comfort to each other.

Why do we keep hiding our deepest feelings from each other? We suffer much, but we also have great gifts of healing for each other. The mystery is that by hiding our pain we also hide our ability to heal. Even in such a loving and caring community as this, there is more loneliness than necessary. We are called to confess to each other and forgive each other, and thus to discover the abundant mercy of God. But at the same time, we are so terribly afraid of being hurt more than we already are. This fear keeps us prisoners, even when the prison has no walls! I see better every day how radical Jesus' message of love really is.

A YEAR FULL OF GRACES
(Sunday, July 6)

A day of farewell. My year in Trosly is coming to an end. On Tuesday I am going to Belgium to visit Cardinal Daneels, on Wednesday and Thursday I will be in Holland to say good-bye to my father, brothers, and sister, and on Friday I will be on my way back to Boston.

During the past few days I have been trying to evaluate my time at L'Arche. Was it worth it? I didn't write as much as I had planned; I didn't pray as much as I had hoped; I didn't learn French as well as I had desired; and I didn't come to know the handicapped people as intimately as I had wanted. And still the year has been full of graces.

The first grace was getting back in touch with Europe. Spending time in France, Germany, Belgium, Holland, and England has helped me to feel strongly connected with my roots and to understand in more depth the spiritual tradition of which I am a part. I feel as if I have come into closer touch with the great movement of the spirit of God that has shaped the hearts and minds of many of my European contemporaries, and I have come to trust their spiritual institutions as the main source of my own ministry.

The second grace is friends. If there is any name I would like to give this year, it is "the year of friendships." Much of my time has been dedicated to making new friends and deepening old friendships. Sometimes I felt guilty about spending so little time doing things and so much time "just talking." But now I know that many of the bonds that have been formed have created a mysterious network of affection that will allow me not only to speak with new vigor about God's first love, but also to act more simply, directly, and unambiguously in the service of Jesus, whose mission was to reveal that first love to us. The many old friends who came here from the United States and discovered L'Arche with me, and the many new friends who were given to me, have truly showed me that God became flesh and that the divine love becomes tangible in the affection of God's people.

I will never think about this year without a deep gratitude for my friendship with Nathan and our long hours of sharing our joys and pains. Often it seems to me that the main reason for my being in Trosly was to be given this friendship as the safe context for a new vocation. Whatever happens at Daybreak, I am not going to be alone in my struggle, and Nathan will be there with me to keep me faithful to my promises.

I will also never think about the year without thinking about the friendship of Jean Vanier, Madame Vanier, Simone, Barbara, Thérèse-Monique, Jean-Louis, and the Peeters family. This afternoon Jean-Louis invited all of us to his foyer, La Vigne, where I celebrated the Eucharist. A reception followed with kind words and a joyful dinner. As I felt overwhelmed by the affection shown to me, I tried to receive it as an expression of God's generous love and an affirmation of being called to L'Arche.

The third grace is the beginning of a deeper contact with handicapped people. When I saw Gérard and Michelle of Le Surgeon and all the men of La Vigne at the Eucharist and sensed their presence, a deep gratitude welled up in me and I knew that a new knowledge had been given to me, the knowledge of God that comes from the poor. Gérard's silent smile and the simple way he reached out from his wheelchair to touch my cheek told me things that no words can say. Gérard will never be able to express his inner life in words and will never be able to say, "I love you," and yet he still says something about God's unconditional love that only he can say. Michelle, as always, pointed with her spastic fingers to her own cheeks to be sure that I give her at least two kisses, and the men of La Vigne had their own—often funny—ways of making me feel welcome.

I know that the world of handicapped people is still rather unknown to me. During this past year I did not live in a foyer and remained somewhat an outsider. Still, the year has helped me to make my first steps into this new world, and it has opened in me the hope of a more committed life at Daybreak. I am grateful for all that this year has given to me, and I pray that I can remember it all as a source of hope during difficult times.

WHERE SADNESS AND JOY BECOME ONE
(Tuesday, July 8)

At 7 P.M. I celebrated the Eucharist in Madame Vanier's living room. Madame Vanier sat in her great chair. Around her were Barbara, Simone, Nathan, Christine, Jean-Louis, Jeff, and Micha.

After the Eucharist Jean-Louis embraced me for a long time and let his tears flow freely. I felt immensely grateful. His abundant tears were the greatest gift he could have given me. Except for my mother, I had never seen anyone cry for me. Jean-Louis simply cried for me. He wore the cap and scarf I had given him on Sunday. As I looked into his eyes and held him in my arms, I felt a communion that cut to the heart. I felt both sadness and joy; two friends were deeply feeling the pain and joy of friendship.

I gave Madame Vanier my chalice and communion plate with the lectionary and the sacramentary. I wanted her to feel that while something was coming to an end, something would also endure.

I was first welcomed to Les Marronniers by Madame Vanier only eleven months ago. We have celebrated the Eucharist together in her living room many times since then. A bond has grown, a bond that will last, a bond, too, that makes this farewell very hard. But the fact that I was going to Canada, her home country, and was joining the Daybreak community, where she has so many friends, eased the pain a little. "It won't be easy there. It won't be easy," she kept saying, "but you will do all right." I was glad that leaving was, in fact, going to the place she most wanted me to go to. As we embraced, I felt deep gratitude for the home she made for me and great joy that in that home I had heard so clearly the call of Jesus to follow him to a new place.

EPILOGUE

■

MORE THAN A year has passed since I wrote the last entry in this journal. Much has happened since, and I feel that the observations and reflections in these pages will remain somewhat ambiguous unless I tell the story of what followed.

At the end of August I came to Daybreak, the L'Arche community in Canada, and moved into the New House, where six handicapped people—Rose, Adam, Bill, John, Trevor, and Raymond—and their four assistants welcomed me warmly. One of the first things I was asked to do was to help Adam in the mornings. Adam is a twenty-five-year-old man. He does not speak. He cannot let you know whether he likes his food or not, whether you are hurting him or not, whether he wants something or not. He seldom smiles. You are never sure if he recognizes you. For all the basic things of life—dressing and undressing, walking, eating, going to the bathroom—he needs careful attention. Every day he suffers from epileptic seizures which often exhaust him so much that he needs hours of extra sleep to recuperate. In the beginning I was afraid to be with Adam. He is so fragile that I was always worried I would do something wrong. But gradually I came to know and love this stranger. As I gave him his bath, brushed his teeth, combed his hair, gave him his breakfast, and talked to him as if he could fully understand me, my fears were gradually cast out by emerging feelings of tenderness and care. I even began to miss him when I was away for a few days, and when home I came to enjoy just sitting with him, rubbing noses, caressing his face, or playing with his fingers. Thus a stranger became a friend. Friendships also developed with the other handicapped members of the house. Bill started to give me hugs and John to take me out for a beer. Trevor began to give me flowers and Raymond to show me the new ways he had decorated his room. And even Rose, who is profoundly handicapped like Adam, volunteered some really beautiful smiles. It was not always easy to feel at home with these wounded people because there is so much pain and rejection hiding underneath the hugs, the beers, the flowers, and the smiles, but what they give is so freely given that it creates deep affective bonds.

But these bonds did not develop without great cost. It was the cost of facing my own handicaps! I had always known they were there, but I had always been able to keep them out of sight. But those who cannot hide their handicaps do not allow the assistants to hide theirs either. The director of the community and some of the long-term members, as well as the assistants in the house, offered me much support and guidance during my first months. They knew from their own experience that a life with handicapped people involves a radical self-confrontation, and they showed remarkable patience and care as I lived through my own fears and insecurities. Once I said to them, "I first thought I came to help you care for handicapped people, but now I feel as if you had accepted one more handicapped person among you." Indeed, the facing of my own handicaps was the hardest battle of all.

First of all, I had to come to terms with the fact that I had not lived a family life since I was eighteen years old, and here I was faced with a large house to be cleaned, big meals to be cooked, countless dishes to be washed, and stacks of laundry to be done, not to mention shopping, doctors' appointments, bookkeeping, transportation, and the never-ending need for repairs. After thirty-seven years of living in schools where all these things were taken care of, family life made me aware of my lack of the most ordinary skills. Making a dinner for eleven people filled me with great fear and, except for sunny-side-up eggs, every request at breakfast, whether for pancakes, omelettes, French toast, or waffles, threw me into utter confusion. Writing books and giving lectures seemed like easy hills to climb compared to the mountainous complexities of daily living. No wonder that I soon gave up on the idea that some of us are handicapped and others not. My handicaps were so blatantly visible in the face of what normal life is all about that I felt deeply grateful for every sign of sympathy, every smile of understanding, and, most of all, every helping hand. Maybe it was around these very down-to-earth kitchen type of things that I first started to experience the possibility of real friendship with handicapped people and their assistants. My own handicap became the way to it.

But this was obviously only the outer side of a much deeper struggle. As I entered more fully into the Daybreak community and tried to develop new and lasting relationships, I was faced with all the stresses of intimacy. My need for friendship and a deep sense of belonging had brought me to L'Arche. But the handicapped people who form the core of the community are often most wounded in places of intimacy. They easily feel rejected, disliked, put aside, or ignored and are very sensitive toward those who offer friendship, care, support, and affection. The questions are always there: Is it real? Is it lasting? Can I trust it? It is no wonder that in such a context my own anguish concerning intimate relationships was brought into the open.

I vividly remember how one of the handicapped men did not want to say "hello" to me after I had been absent for two weeks. While I felt a need to be welcomed back, he wasn't sure if I really was willing to become part of his life.

And so our dark fears were rubbing up against each other and triggered off deep anguish in both of us. As he kept saying, "I don't care that you are back, I don't need your gift. I have enough things already, don't bother me. I am busy. . . ," my own deep fear of not being loved was brought to the surface, and to my own embarrassment I found myself crying uncontrollably, like a little child who feels rejected.

It was the affective wounds of the handicapped people in my own home that opened the door to my own wounded affectivity. Very soon I was asking myself, "Do I really care for these people? Am I really willing to make them the center of my life? What do I really mean when I say to them, 'I love you'? How faithful am I really? Am I capable of a lasting relationship? Or . . . is my attention for these broken people little more than my way of feeling better about myself?" Very few stones remain unturned. Care, compassion, love for neighbor, promise, commitment, and faithfulness . . . I turned and turned these concepts in my mind and heart, and sometimes it felt as though the spiritual house I had built up over the years was now proving to be made of cardboard and ready to go up in flames. The handicapped men and women and their assistants forced me to look at myself in ways that were very humbling. Often I doubted whether there was any solid ground under my feet. I am still in the midst of this struggle, and I feel quite poor in the face of it. It is hard to discover that I am very awkward in the ordinary tasks of life. But it is much more painful for me to be brought to the realization that I am very weak and fragile precisely where I had thought I had the most to give.

But even this struggle proved not the most excruciating. Where I really was brought to my knees was at a place beyond questions about housekeeping skills, even beyond the questions about true commitment. The most radical challenge came out of the question, "Is Jesus truly enough for you, or do you keep looking for others to give you your sense of worth?" If anyone had asked me in the past, "Who is the center of your life?" I would have answered without much hesitation, "Jesus, who called me to follow him." But now I do not dare say that so easily. The struggle to become a full member of a community of faith has proved to be a struggle to let go of many idols along the way and to choose again and again to follow Jesus and him alone. Choosing life in community and choosing Jesus are increasingly appearing to me as two aspects of the same choice. And here my deepest handicap appeared.

When I came to Daybreak, I didn't come alone. Nathan, with whom I had developed a deep and nurturing friendship in Trosly, came with me. I came to Daybreak to become its pastor. He came to live as a part-time assistant while studying theology in Toronto. As I approached the new life in community, I came to think about my friendship with Nathan as the safe place in the midst of all the transitions and changes. I said to myself, "Well, whatever happens, at least I have a friend to rely on, to go to for support, to be consoled by in hard moments." Somehow I made Nathan the center of my emotional stability and related to the life in community as something I would be able to cope with. In this way my dependence on Nathan prevented me from making the community the true center of my life. Unconsciously, I said to myself, "I already have a home. I do not really need another one." As I entered community life more deeply, however, I became gradually aware that the call to follow Jesus unreservedly required me to look for God's guidance more in the common life with handicapped people than in a unique and nurturing friendship.

This discovery created such an excruciating inner pain that it brought me to the edge of despair. I had to change my ways of coming to a sense of being accepted so radically that it seemed as if I needed to have another personality to make this come true. When I had said "yes" to the call of Daybreak to join the community as their priest, I hadn't realized how many painful "nos" were included in that "yes": "no" to choosing the people you want to live with, "no" to spending quality time with people you feel very close to, "no" to a self-defined form of solitude, "no" to centering my life in the beautiful and supportive friendship with Nathan. My many years of the independent and individualized life of a university professor had certainly not prepared me for this side of following Jesus. It led me to the second loneliness, a loneliness with Jesus in community. I discovered that this second loneliness was much, much harder to live than the loneliness resulting from physical or emotional isolation—because it is a loneliness not to be removed as a stumbling block to full human maturity, but to be embraced as the way to follow Jesus to the end.

At the end of my trip to Canada, the United States, and England, about which I wrote in this journal, I met a young man who told me about his own spiritual journey in a way that helped me to think about this second loneliness. He said, "First, I was traveling on a highway with many other people. I felt lonely in my car, but at least I was not alone. Then Jesus told me to take an exit and follow a winding country road which was pleasant and beautiful. People who passed by greeted me, smiled, and waved to me; I felt loved. But then, quite unexpectedly, Jesus asked me to take a dirt road, leave the car, and walk with him. As we were walking we did not see anyone anymore; although I knew that I was walking with Jesus, I felt very lonely and often in despair. I was tired and felt forgotten by my friends. Now it looked as if I was getting more lonely as I was getting closer to Jesus. And nobody seemed to understand."

My life at Daybreak became increasingly an invitation to enter into this second loneliness. It is such a painful experience that I hesitate to write about it. It is a loneliness of which I know no special friend can free me, even though I keep clinging desperately to such a friend. It is a loneliness that asks of me to throw myself completely into the arms of a God whose presence can no longer be felt and to risk every part of my being to what seems like nothingness. It is the loneliness of Jesus, who cries out, "My God, my God, why have you forsaken me?"

In her novel *Henry and Cato*, Iris Murdoch writes:

> It's the greatest pain and the greatest paradox of all that personal love has
> to break at some point, the ego has to break, something absolutely natural

and seemingly good, seemingly perhaps the only good, has to be given up. After that there's darkness and silence and space. And God is there. Remember St. John of the Cross. Where the images end you fall into the abyss, but it is the abyss of faith. When you have nothing left you have nothing left but hope.[11]

The last thing I ever expected from going to the Daybreak community was this truly abysmal experience of being ripped apart from the inside out. I expected to live with and care for mentally handicapped people, supported by a deep friendship and surrounded by a beautiful network of Christian love. I was not prepared to have to deal with a second loneliness.

But . . . hesitantly and even reluctantly, I am coming to see the mystery that the community of Daybreak was given to me precisely to offer me a "safe" context in which to enter into the second loneliness with Jesus. There is nothing charming or romantic about it. It is dark agony. It is following Jesus to a completely unknown place. It is being emptied out on the cross and having to wait for new life in naked faith.

But the same cross that calls for dying from what seems so good and beautiful is also the place where a new spiritual community is being born. The death of Jesus was the dying of the grain destined to bear much fruit. My life will never be fruitful if I am not willing to go that same painful but hopeful route.

I express this with fear and trembling because I am just starting to see the light of a new day and I still do not know if I will have the courage to walk the long road ahead of me. But by writing this down I am able to look directly at my own words and that in itself is a step forward.

On July 21, 1987, I celebrated the thirtieth anniversary of my ordination to the priesthood. Considering all that I had experienced during the first year at Daybreak, I didn't feel like having a party. Instead, I asked a few of the permanent members of the community to pray with me, reflect with me on my vocation, and offer me some critical guidance. It was a very painful experience. I had to face all my handicaps directly, share them with my friends and reach out to God and the community for help. But it was also a very life-giving experience. Seeing my handicaps so clearly, those surrounding me offered all their support, guidance, and love. This helped me make them not just stumbling blocks, but gateways to solidarity with those who cannot hide their handicaps and who form the core of our community.

During this anniversary celebration, I made three promises for the years to come and asked the community to help me to be faithful to them. I want to conclude this journal by writing down these promises, to give a first articulation of the way I have begun to see the road ahead of me.

First of all, I promised to pray more. If, indeed, Jesus is the center of my life, I have to give him much time and attention. I especially want to pray the prayer of adoration in which I focus on his love, his compassion, and his mercy and not on my needs, my problems, and my desires. Much of my prayer in the past has been very introspective. The time has come to look up to him who comes to me and says, "You did not choose me, I chose you" (John 15:16). I want my life to be based on the reality of Jesus, and not on the unreality of my own fantasies, self-complaints, daydreams, and sand castles. I know that by moving from self-centered reflections to simple adoration I will come increasingly in touch with reality, the reality of God and the reality of the people of God with whom I live.

It will be very hard to be faithful to this promise. There are countless pressures to do more important things than pray. But I know that only through long and persistent prayer will I be able to follow the one who asks me to walk the lonely road with him.

Second, I promised to do everything possible to come to know my own community better. Many of the handicapped people and their assistants have remained strangers for me during this first year. The many invitations to do things outside of the community and my tendency to look for support in one or two friendships have prevented me from making the whole of the community my true home. Having meals in the different houses, "wasting time" with my own people, talking, playing, and praying with them, and allowing them to really know me, that requires a special discipline. It asks for a new way of scheduling my hours, for more "nos" to outside requests and for the strong conviction that those with whom I live are my true neighbors.

Thus I will come to know Jesus not only in the solitude of prayer, but also in the community of love. Thus the same Lord who reveals himself in the most intimate place of my heart will also reveal himself in the fellowship of the weak. It will not be easy to be faithful in this, since the temptation to search for consolation and comfort in the intimacy of a unique friendship is so great, especially during periods of depression and spiritual fatigue. My response to stress so far has been to talk it out with a spiritual director, a counselor, or a friend. It has always been in the one-to-one relationship that I have sought healing. But now I feel a strong invitation to let the community be my primary spiritual resource and to trust that there I will find the spirit of God, the true consoler I have always been looking for.

Finally, I promised to keep writing. In the generally over-scheduled life of a community such as Daybreak, it is very hard to find the quiet hours necessary to write. During the past year, writing has seemed practically impossible. And still the call to come to Daybreak included the call to keep writing. Without writing I am not truly faithful to the ministry of the word that has been given to me. It is through writing that my hidden life with God and the handicapped people can become a gift to the Church and the world. Keynote addresses, commencement speeches, and even retreats no longer seem part of my primary task. But writing still is. Many people whose judgment I trust have assured me of this. So it is up to me to discipline myself and withdraw from the urgencies and emergencies of every day and write words that emerge from my prayer and my life with the handicapped people and their assistants. Even though following Jesus might well become a more and more hidden journey for me, I do not think it should ever become a private journey. "Laying down your life for your friend" is what Jesus asks of me. For me that includes communicating as honestly as possible the pains and the joys, the darkness and the light, the fatigue and the vitality, the despair and the hope of going with Jesus to places where I would rather not go. By giving words to these intimate experiences I can make my own life available to others and thus become a witness to the word of life whom "I have heard, seen with my own eyes, watched and touched with my own hands" (1 John 1:1).

I am glad to be at Daybreak surrounded by people who want to keep me faithful to my promises. It is good to be here, even though it is hard. I feel that I have been called to be here, that I have been sent here, that I belong here. But after a year I have come to realize that I have just started on a long and arduous journey in which there will be not only many daybreaks, but also many nights. When Abraham followed God's call, he had no idea how much would be asked of him. His faith would be tested every step of the way. This is true for everyone God calls with a "jealous" love. Even though I keep daydreaming about an easy and conflict-free tomorrow, I know that *my* faith too will be tested. God's love is indeed "a harsh and dreadful thing" (Dorothy Day) but worth giving one's whole life for.

This brings me to the end of this journal. I have tried to describe carefully the road that led me to Daybreak, to express honestly my first experiences here, and to lay out frankly the promises I have made for the future. It is becoming increasingly clear to me that Jesus led me to where I never wanted to go, sustained me when I felt lost in the darkness of the night, and will guide me toward the day no longer followed by night. As I travel with Jesus, he continues to remind me that God's heart is, indeed, infinitely greater than my own.

NOTES

.

1. Sheila Cassidy, "Precious Spikenard," *Catholic New Times of Toronto,* 1985.
2. Xavier Léon-Dufour, *Saint Françoise Xavier: Itinéraire Mystique de l'Apôtre* (Paris: Edition du Vieux Colombier, 1953), pp. 34–35.
3. *Messages des Sécours Catholique,* no. 376, November 1984, p. 7.
4. Ibid.
5. Rainer Maria Rilke, *Letters on Cézanne* (New York: International Publishing Corporation, 1985).
6. Ibid., p. xv.
7. Ibid., p. 10.
8. *The Spiritual Letters of Dom John Chapman, O.S.B.* (London: Sheed and Ward, 1938), pp. 52–53; quoted in *The Tablet,* December 14, 1985.
9. Konrad Kunze, *Himmel in Stein: Das Freiburger Münster* (Freiburg: Herder, 1980), pp. 84–85.
10. Martin Heidegger, *Gelassenheit* (Pfüllingen: Verlag Günther Neske, 1959), p. 25.
11. Iris Murdoch, *Henry and Cato* (London: Triad Grafton Books, 1987), p. 348.